Contemporary British History 1931–1961

Politics and the limits of policy

Edited by Anthony Gorst, Lewis Johnman and W. Scott Lucas

Published in Association with
The Institute of Contemporary British History

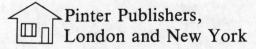

Pinter Publishers,
London and New York

© The Institute of Contemporary British History, 1991

First published in Great Britain in 1991 by
Pinter Publishers Limited
25 Floral Street, London WC2E 9DS

British Library Cataloguing in Publication Data

A CIP catalogue record for this book is available from the
British Library
ISBN 0-86187-177-4

For enquiries in North America please contact PO Box 197,
Irvington, NY 10533

Library of Congress Cataloging-in-Publication Data

Contemporary British History, 1931–1961: politics and the limits of
    policy/edited by Anthony Gorst, Lewis Johnman, and W. Scott Lucas.
        p.   cm.
    "Published in association with the Institute of Contemporary
British History."
    "Selection of papers presented at the second Conference on
Contemporary History, organised by the Institute of Contemporary
British History and the London School of Economics, in July 1989"—
Pref.
    Includes bibliographical references and index.
    ISBN 0-86187-177 -4
    1. Great Britain—Politics and government—1945–1964—Congresses.
2. Great Britain—Politics and government—1936–1945—Congresses.
3. Great Britain—Politics and government—1910–1936—Congresses.
I. Gorst, Anthony.   II. Johnman, Lewis.   III Lucas, W. Scott.
IV. Conference on Contemporary History (2nd : 1989 : London,
England)   V. Institute of Contemporary British History.   VI. London
School of Economics and Political Science.
DA566.7.C597   1990
941.082—dc20

90-48872
CIP

Typeset by GCS, Leighton Buzzard, Bedfordshire
Printed and bound in Great Britain by Biddles Ltd of Guildford and Kings Lynn

Contents

List of contributors

Richard Aldrich is a Lecturer in the Department of Politics and Contemporary History at the University of Salford.

Malcolm Baines received his D.Phil. from Exeter College, Oxford in 1990.

Stephen Brooke is Assistant Professor of History, Dalhousie University, Canada.

Larry Butler is an Assistant Keeper of the Public Records at the Public Record Office, Kew and teaches history at the Polytechnic of Central London.

Frank Furedi is a Lecturer in the Department of Sociology and Social Anthropology and Chair of Development Studies at the University of Kent, Canterbury.

Till Geiger is a Lecturer in Economic History at the University of Aberdeen.

Anthony Gorst is a Lecturer in History at the Polytechnic of Central London.

Susan Howson is Professor of Economics at the University of Toronto, Canada.

Lewis Johnman is Senior Lecturer and Head of the Economics Division at Thames Polytechnic and a visiting researcher at the Business History Unit, London School of Economics.

Harriet Jones teaches twentieth-century history at the University of London.

W. Scott Lucas is a Lecturer in the School of History at the University of Birmingham.

Callum MacDonald is a Lecturer in History at the University of Warwick.

C.J. Morris is a research student in the Institute of Communications Studies, University of Leeds.

Scott Newton is a Lecturer in History at the University of Wales, Cardiff.

Richard Roberts is Lecturer in Economic History in the School of Social Sciences at the University of Sussex. He is currently writing a history of the merchant bank, Schroders.

Tracy Lee Steele is a research student at the London School of Economics.

Nick Tiratsoo is a Lecturer in Social History at the University of Warwick and a researcher at the Business History Unit, London School of Economics.

List of figures

List of tables

Preface

This book is a selection of the papers presented at the second Conference on Contemporary History, organized by the Institute of Contemporary British History and the London School of Economics, in July 1989. As with the essays in the previous volume, *Postwar Britain, 1945–1964: Themes and Perspectives*, these papers aim to re-evaluate both issues in and approaches to the study of twentieth-century British history.

Although each of these papers was presented on a specific thematic day of the conference, they reflect the aim of the conference which is to broaden the scope of historical research by bringing together younger historians from different disciplines and encouraging the use of differing methodologies and techniques from a variety of specializations. Thus Till Geiger, in examining the question of British 'decline' after 1945, uses the tools of the economic historian to shed light on British economic *and* defence policy. Nick Tiratsoo blends neglected material from business, retailing and advertising surveys with little-used political sources to reappraise critically the issues of affluence and politics in the 1950s.

This recognition of the interdependence of the historical specializations has become increasingly important in recent years. The researcher in contemporary British history, however, is confronted with a vast range of sources and it is tempting to react by specializing in ever narrower fields. As such the tendency is for the study of history to produce a series of disparate fragments rather than provide an understanding of the interrelationship between different events and processes.

Whilst this collection does not claim to be interdisciplinary in any full sense it does strive towards this end. Hopefully, these papers will encourage further discussion and examination of the British experience since 1945. In the light of the recent debate on the teaching of history in secondary education, the editors wish to reiterate their belief in the value of the study of contemporary history and their conviction that the dangers of political indoctrination are higher when the young are *not* informed of the recent past.

The editors wish to thank Stephanie Maggin of the ICBH and Sara Wilbourne of Pinter publishers.

1 The Labour Party and the Second World War

Stephen Brooke

It has become a well-worn truism that the years between 1945 and 1979 represent a period of consensus in British politics. This framework of political agreement embraced the acceptance of a mixed economy, the management of that economy towards the end of full employment, and the creation and protection of a comprehensive welfare state. Consensus formed 'parameters which bounded the set of policy options regarded by senior politicians and civil servants as administratively practicable, economically affordable and politically acceptable', according to two recent commentators; ideological differences were merely the stuff of electioneering, 'nuance or rhetoric' (Kavanagh and Morris, 1989: 13–14). It was this landscape that the ghost of Mr Butskell stalked, until vanquished by Mrs Thatcher.

The work of Paul Addison and Keith Middlemas has lent academic credence to the notion of 'consensus'. In 1975 Addison published an accomplished study of the politics of the Second World War. *The road to 1945* portrayed the Churchill Coalition as the crucible of the post-war consensus, an élite consensus shared by civil servants and politicians alike and buttressed by a leftward movement in public opinion. In the realm of high politics, the war saw the 'convergence' of the Labour and Conservative parties and the acceptance by both of a centrist, progressive course, whose principal architects were William Beveridge and John Maynard Keynes. The road to 1945 was thus paved with the 1941 Budget, the Beveridge Report, the Education Act of 1944 and the White Paper on Full Employment. With Labour's election victory of July 1945, the consensus of the people and the politicians 'fell like a branch of ripe plums into the lap of Mr Attlee'. Though proposing to 'extend the wartime consensus in a socialist direction', the Labour governments simply 'completed and consolidated the work of the Coalition' (Addison, 1975: 271–8). According to Addison, Attlee's consensus thus had very little to do with socialism. Middlemas's work has further explored the 'corporate bias' of state, capital and labour during the war, which also marginalized ideological differences in British politics (Middlemas, 1979, 1986).

'Consensus' or similar arguments for a binding post-war settlement are clearly of crucial importance to the history of the Labour Party. Because it plays down the importance of ideology, the 'consensus' thesis undermines the claims Labour makes for 1945 as a decisive break in British politics. The inheritance the party left in 1951 was fraught with ambiguity: were its reforms merely the coping-stones to wartime consensus or signposts toward the Socialist Commonwealth?

The shadow of consensus soon fell over the achievements of the Attlee governments. By the end of the 1940s, G.D.H. Cole and other critics were noting with concern the apparent continuity between the Coalition government and the post-war socialist government (see, for instance, Cole, 1949). Since 1945, it has become a common observation that Labour's reforms 'did not add up to socialism' (Addison, 1984: 960). Marxist historians of the party, such as Ralph Miliband, David Coates and James Hinton, have formed a sympathetic audience to such arguments, declaring that the path of consensus further illustrates Labour's fatal proclivity for gradualism and the preservation of capitalism. From this perspective, one man's consensus becomes another's conspiracy.

Recently, the idea of 'consensus' has come under more critical scrutiny. For the most part, the road from 1945 has been the focus of attention. In his history of the Attlee governments, Kenneth O. Morgan was careful to point out where Labour departed from the initiatives of the Coalition (Morgan, 1984). In 1988, Ben Pimlott attacked the 'myth of consensus' in a more broad-ranging fashion (Pimlott, 1988). But there has been only one detailed corrective to the argument that the war itself was the crucible of a binding post-war settlement. Concentrating on the Conservative party, Kevin Jeffreys has set out the very different approaches toward social reform taken by the Coalition partners (Jeffreys, 1987).

The present chapter is a further contribution to the debate on 'consensus' by focusing on the experience of the Labour party during the Second World War. It will argue that from this perspective, the question of wartime 'consensus' is far more complicated than has been suggested by the work of Addison and Middlemas.

An examination of Labour's involvement in wartime government and its approach to reconstruction reveals that the common ground between the political parties during the war in fact had very limited borders. We can first of all observe that expediency tempered Labour's perception of coalition. The party's leaders certainly saw joining government in May 1940 as an essential contribution to national unity, but this contribution was not without strings; Attlee, Dalton, Morrison and Bevin were also determined, in different ways, to wrest some measure of socialist reform from partnership in government. Generally, this aim was frustrated with regard to the actual direction of the war economy, but another chance came when the Coalition began to discuss seriously post-war policy after 1943. In this period, Labour ministers found that agreement on general and often vaguely defined aims was indeed possible; full employment and social security were good examples. But beyond this, differences of perception and disagreement over means and ends remained so deep as to frustrate Labour's aspirations. Whether in the civil service or in the realms of high politics, wartime 'consensus' could not accommodate the distinctive concerns Labour continued to pursue up to 1945. A brief examination of health policy and economic reconstruction will illustrate this point. Instead of accepting the notion of a pervasive political 'consensus' which left ideological differences irrelevant, we should, therefore, pay closer attention to the persistence of ideology in 1945.

Of course, it is still important to ask why, by the end of the 1940s, Labour's distinctive socialism seemed lost in the tide of Keynes and Beveridge, with demand management replacing socialist planning and the 'socialist advance' of public ownership faltering with iron and steel.[1] The answer lies less in the party's appropriation of a centrist course during the war than in its failure to resolve long-standing tensions in its own socialist tradition. Kenneth Morgan has written that the Attlee governments 'brought the British labour movement to the zenith of its achievement as a political instrument for humanitarian purposes' by 'evading, rather than resolving, those dilemmas inherent in the potent, beguiling vision of socialism in our time' (Morgan, 1984: 503). The party's development during the Second World War illustrates this observation acutely.

We must first examine the position taken by Labour before the formation of the Churchill Coalition in May 1940. This will underline the strength of Labour's ideological concerns throughout the rest of the war.

Between September 1939 and May 1940, Labour concentrated its energies on what Hugh Dalton called 'influence from without': the articulation of an alternative, socialist view of the war effort and peace aims, rooted in the socialism the party had developed during the 1930s.[2] This rested on the assumption that the war should serve as a vehicle for the realization of the socialist programme of central economic planning, public ownership, and social reform. 'If you want to win this war you will have to have a great deal of practical socialism', Clement Attlee told the Commons in November 1939, '[and] while planning for war we have to plan for peace'.[3] The peace would be best shaped by socialism. This was the ethos guiding Labour's interests throughout the war, whether in government or outside.

When Attlee went before his party's annual conference in May 1940 to plead the case for joining a government under Winston Churchill, it was not only with arguments for national unity but also with the understanding that coalition offered the possibility of achieving these partisan ends. After nine years out of power, Labour had a chance to put the socialist argument within Whitehall. Labour could ensure, Attlee said, that 'the world that must emerge from this war must be a world attuned to our ideals' (Labour, 1940: 125).

However, the journey Labour set out upon in May 1940 was a difficult one, which required balancing the demands of party with those of coalition. The discomforts were clear; shaping the post-war world from within the government had to be set against the compromise implicit in coalition. At first, the determination to wring the Coalition dry of socialist reform was shared by the Labour Left. Harold Laski, for instance, saw the Coalition as an opportunity to 'renew the foundations of the State' through socialist planning and reform (Labour, 1940: 144–5). The Left might well have paraphrased Disraeli to call their account of the war years, 'Labour does not love coalitions', but the subtitle would still have been 'Great expectations'. By the end of 1940, however, the Left had despaired of coalition, convinced that Attlee and the other leaders were too weak to fight against the Conservatives for socialist measures. This pressure, kept up throughout the war, itself made any binding political co-operation at the level of high politics ultimately untenable (see Brooke, 1988: 44–85). It did, however, force the Labour leadership to make a defence of coalition to its increasingly unruly supporters. Arthur Greenwood, the Deputy Leader, spoke of a 'common ground' in the government that could be tilled with some success' (Labour, 1941: 165). In public and private, Attlee maintained that 'much has been done by this Government which is right along the line of policy which we have always advocated'.[4] In fact, such statements masked deep divisions within the government, knowledge of which would undoubtedly have made the leadership's position within the party more uncomfortable than it already was. Far from being indications of a pervasive consensus with the Conservatives, remarks of this kind are best seen in the context of an often bitter dialogue within the party.

What is striking when one looks at the efforts of the Labour ministers within the government is, first of all, how infused these efforts were with clearly ideological concerns, and, second, how much disagreement and frustration they produced. These concerns could not be accommodated within the Cabinet or by the civil service. Two areas of policy—health reform and economic reconstruction—illustrate just how narrow the scope of wartime consensus was in practice. Labour could find agreement on general aims—the establishment of a national health service and the maintenance of high levels of employment—but the differences of perception remaining between the coalition partners jars with the prevailing impression of an essentially harmonious reconstruction initiative tipped in Labour's favour.

When the nettle of reconstruction was grasped in 1943—only after much dissension between Labour and the Conservatives over the Beveridge Report—debate on particular issues often fell into clear party lines within the War Cabinet and its reconstruction committees. Labour pressed for radical advance against rearguard actions fought by Conservatives like Kingsley Wood and Andrew Duncan. It is hard to see how the situation could have been otherwise, particularly over economic policy when Conservative ministers naturally opposed the collectivism just as naturally espoused by their Labour counterparts. Consensus, as the Minister of Reconstruction, Lord Woolton, stated, was the result of considerable effort: 'agreement . . . will involve much sacrifice both by the Conservatives and the Labour Party'.[5] For reasons of expediency both parties were willing to make some sacrifices; in 1944, for instance, Hugh Dalton remarked, 'unless we get Social Insurance through, the Tories will use it as bait for the electors' (Pimlott, 1986: 800). But there were rarely sacrifices of principle. Nor were such compromises regarded as binding by the Labour leadership or the party's rank and file. However important a reforming administration, the Churchill Coalition was ultimately of limited use to the Labour party. Coalition could not accommodate all that Labour hoped to achieve; what Dalton called its 'internal division' was far too great.[6] Differences more substantial than mere nuance or rhetoric persisted.

The commitment to a national health service, assumption 'B' of the Beveridge Report, provides one particularly useful illustration. Before the war, Labour's health policy had been distinctively radical. Shaped by planners drawn largely from the Socialist Medical Association, the party's programme rejected the mere extension of the panel system or health insurance. Instead, a socialist health service would be set up on an entirely new basis. Central to this vision was the proposal that a co-operative medical profession subject to local democratic control would replace the existing competitive and unrepresentative system. Towards this end, Labour and the SMA were determined to establish a salaried medical service working through a network of local health centres.

War heightened general interest in health reform. The medical profession set up bodies such as Medical Planning Research and the Medical Planning Commission to contribute reconstruction blueprints to any initiative emanating from Whitehall. Though the government believed that such bodies indicated that 'the minds of the profession have moved rapidly in recent years', they had not moved far enough to accept proposals for salaried payment or local control.[7] By contrast, the various health policy groups within the Labour movement, such as the party's Public Health Sub-committee, the SMA, and the Medical Practitioners' Union (which advised the Trades Union Congress), all continued to expound a more radical message. Labour's health service would include free and universal provision, a salaried, full-time medical profession, a comprehensive system of health centres and a unified hospital service run under local control (see Labour Party, 1943; MPU, 1942; SMA, 1944). This was clearly at variance with the consensus accepted by Whitehall and the British Medical Association (see Webster, 1988a and 1988b).

When the Cabinet and its reconstruction committees began to consider health reform in 1943 and 1944, Attlee, Ernest Bevin and Herbert Morrison resolutely pursued the party's distinctive concerns in health policy. In October 1943, for instance, Attlee strongly attacked proposals for the remuneration of doctors by capitation payment rather than by salary.[8] He used a memorandum by the late Stephen Taylor, then a temporary civil servant at the Ministry of Information and a Labour party member (he was a candidate in 1945), to cajole the new Minister of Health, the Conservative Henry Willink.[9]

But Willink's appointment deepened Labour's apprehensions about the shape of Coalition health reform. When the Reconstruction Committee turned to Willink's draft White Paper in February 1944, Attlee, Bevin and Morrison voiced sharp criticisms of it. All three fought to include proposals in line with a socialist health policy. In particular, they pressed the Reconstruction Committee to ensure that any White Paper would clearly set out that the development of whole-time salaried group practices in health centres would be a 'primary aim' of any national health service.[10]

These efforts and divisions demonstrated the fragility of 'consensus' and its limited use to Labour. The three Labour Cabinet ministers clearly saw health reform in a very different light from Willink. They were reluctant to accept any compromise that departed from Labour policy. If compromise was conceded, it was not regarded as ultimately binding. Regarding the future of the voluntary hospitals, for example, Attlee told Woolton, 'I am prepared to acquiesce in the continuation of voluntary hospitals as a matter of practical policy, but I cannot be expected to express a wish as to the future which runs directly counter to my Party's policy'.[11] Realizing more radical partisan ends obviously remained paramount for the Labour minsters. It was undoubtedly for this reason that Woolton told Anthony Eden that it had been a struggle to 'get the Labour Party to "the middle of the road"' over health policy; he was not confident it would stay there for long and advised Churchill that he could not expect Labour to accept any further compromises in health reform.[12]

There was considerable dissatisfaction in the party with the result, both in government and outside (see Brooke, 1988: 182–9). But Attlee, Bevin and Morrison could comfort themselves with the knowledge that the White Paper on *A national health service* (February 1944) did offer a wedge in the door for socialist health reform with its proposal that the establishment of a network of health centres would introduce a full-time salaried medical profession.

The reception accorded the White Paper outside Whitehall again underlines the difference of perception between Labour and the Conservatives. Labour opinion was not overwhelmingly favourable. The general view was best caught by the Fabian Society's Medical Services policy committee: an 'irreducible minimum capable of great improvement'.[13] The Parliamentary Labour Party's praise for the White Paper was economical; it was welcomed simply as 'a great contribution towards the kind of plan which we, in the fullness of time, would like to see established in this country'. The emphasis was firmly on future improvements.[14] The Medical Practitioners' Union pulled fewer punches; the White Paper was a 'mass of unhappy compromises' (MPU, 1944). Both the SMA and Labour's Public Health Advisory Committee (dominated by members of the SMA) saw it as an interim measure only. 'Amendments to improve the scheme will have to be introduced', the PHAC agreed in March 1944.[15] In the meantime, it was thought that Labour should concentrate on the White Paper's most radical aspect—the proposal for health centres—and protect this against the British Medical Association and other vested interests. The strength of such opposition was soon clear and its focus was the very aspect that made the White Paper acceptable to Labour—the proposal for a salaried service working in health centres. The *British Medical Jounal* commented that this was indicative of 'political drift ... in the direction of socialization of medicine' and all the concomitant ruin that a 'whole-time salaried medical service' implied.[16] In the Commons, Conservative back-benchers took up this refrain, attacking that proposal most loudly applauded by their parliamentary colleagues across the floor.

In response to pressure from the doctors, Willink made significant concessions to the medical profession, including an agreement that health centres would be merely experimental rather than the cornerstones of a new service. These concessions turned the face of Labour opinion further against coalition reform in health. Willink's proposals, the SMA argued in 1945, would 'destroy all hope of a comprehensive health service'.[17] Just before the break-up of the Coalition, Labour's annual conference decided to wash its hands of coalition reform (Labour, 1945: 154). Once again, this underlines the deep differences of perception over social policy during the war years.

Although agreement on the general aim of a national health service was possible within the Coalition, there was considerable disagreement on the essential aspects of that health service at the level of high politics. Labour opinion outside the corridors of power tended to emphasize the radical elements of health policy which were, apparently, beyond the ambit of wartime consensus. The proposals for a salaried medical profession working in health centres under local control set Labour a significant distance from the Conservatives and the medical profession. One can see similar patterns in other spheres of social policy: the importance to Labour of multilateral secondary schools in education and of the national minimum in social insurance, for instance. All suggest the persistence of ideological differences, rather than a prevailing 'consensus'.

An important strand of the arguments of Addison and Middlemas concerns economic policy. Both claim that Labour's economic strategy after 1945 consisted largely of the appropriation of the administrative structure of wartime controls, upon which was imposed a superstructure of corporation-style public ownership. The last seemed superficially controversial but was, in fact, largely beyond ideological debate. At the same time, the thesis continues, Labour had been imbibing Keynesian demand management; to this end, the White Paper of June 1944 on *Employment policy* is seen as a point of *nexus* for consensus between Labour and the Conservatives and between socialists and capitalists. As a consequence, a truly socialist economy was never established (see, for instance, Middlemas, 1986).

A better appreciation of Labour policy reveals several difficulties with this analysis. First of all, it shows little understanding of Labour's socialism. It is hardly surprising that Labour's planners and intellectuals viewed wartime controls as useful tools towards a socialist economy, given that they had spent most of the 1930s proposing to establish the same kinds of controls. There is as well the suggestion that the permanent retention of economic controls was acceptable to the Conservatives and to the civil service. It was not. While Labour continued to see the permanent retention and transformation of controls as essential to the construction of a planned, rather than free market economy, the Conservatives and the civil service accepted controls only on a temporary basis, before an eventual return to the free market. Finally, some attempt must be made to correct the misconception that Labour had been completely converted to Keynesianism before 1945. This was not at all clear. On all three points, we can, instead, see the persistence of ideological concerns on Labour's part.

When Labour set about clarifying its economic strategy in 1931, central economic planning became the lingua franca of socialist intellectuals. But socialist economic planning was different in significant respects from the planning of non-socialists of the centre, particularly with the emphasis socialists gave to a large, publicly-owned sector through which economic decisions could be made without recourse to the market. Labour's policy-makers, such as Hugh Dalton, Evan Durbin, Hugh Gaitskell, and Douglas Jay, proposed to erect a lattice-work of public sector institutions to control a planned economy physically. These included a Central Credit Control Office to regulate the movement of capital, a National Investment Board to plan and direct investment, and a Foreign Exchange Control Board to control capital export and foreign exchange.

With the outbreak of war, many of these same policy-makers moved into the wartime civil service. They were able to watch and participate at close quarters as the economy was 'laid bare', in the words of Evan Durbin (Pimlott, 1986: 96) and as life was breathed into many of the controls they themselves had proposed in the 1930s. The wartime Capital Issues Committee fulfilled many of the same functions as had been planned for Labour's Central Credit Control Office. The Emergency Powers Acts of 1939 and 1940 subjected foreign exchange to the kind of control and regulation that Labour had hoped to invest in its Foreign Exchange Control Board. The Bank of England came under the control of the Treasury. Given these developments, is it then particularly surprising that one of Labour's economic policy-makers wrote, undoubtedly with a sense of vindication, that almost 'every one' of their pre-war ' "ideas" had become a reality' during the war?[18] Wartime controls were understandably perceived, as Evan Durbin told Attlee in 1944, as 'embryo[s]' for the kind of institutions envisaged by Labour in the 1930s (see Brooke, 1989).[19] The wartime experience with controls was really one of confirmation, rather than instruction.

Full employment and financial policy (1944), the party's major wartime statement on economic reconstruction, consequently declared that reconstruction would be accomplished by 'following the same principles in peacetime that have served us well in war'. This rested on the retention and expansion of the network of 'principal wartime financial controls' (Labour Party, 1944). It was a belief that broke significantly with the external consensus on controls. As Keith Middlemas has shown, the administrative consensus of Whitehall accepted controls only as a temporary expedient (Middlemas, 1986: 52). In March 1944 an official subcommittee pointed out that the objectives of the projected two-year transition between the fall of Germany and the defeat of Japan demanded the retention of economic controls, but it still maintained that a return to 'free' economic activity was desirable as soon as possible.[20] This was obviously at considerable variance with Labour's views.

This difference of opinion was also reflected at the highest levels of the Coalition. In September 1944, for instance, the ministerial subcommittee on Industrial Problems was in 'general agreement' that 'the maintenance of the general fabric of the present economic controls would be required in the transition period', but the Conservatives and Liberals on the subcommittee wanted emphasis placed on the relaxation of controls at the earliest possible moment, a position Ernest Bevin opposed forcefully. Because of this difference, the subcommittee decided that it was not politic to produce a White Paper on the question; a simple parliamentary statement would be more appropriate and less controversial.[21] A memorandum on the future of economic controls was submitted to the War Cabinet by Lord Woolton in October 1944. This raised much dissension between the Coalition partners. The Conservatives objected to the suggestion that controls might be retained indefinitely or taken as a 'step towards the nationalization of industry'. Labour thought it unacceptable because it tied the use of controls to the state of trade; they 'could not accept the proposition ... that the ultimate aim was a return to the pre-war condition of *laissez-faire*'. The compromise worked out by the War Cabinet served only to underline the serious differences between the Conservatives and Labour: controls would be retained in the transition period, 'whether that transition was to a more socialised state or to the system of private enterprise which prevailed before the war'.[22] Far from being a litmus test of consensus, therefore, Labour's affection for wartime economic controls was actually evidence of the persistence of its distinctive ideological concerns.

The same persistence of ideology accompanied Labour's approach to Keynesian economics. To a certain extent, the 1941 Budget and the 1944 White Paper on *Employment policy* reflected a fuller acceptance of Keynesian prescription by Whitehall. It is often suggested that Labour also embraced demand management at this time. This is, however, something of a misconception. There were certainly influential Keynesians within the Labour party; Douglas Jay is an important example. But we cannot state with confidence that this was a majority view. If one looks at the 'Post-war finance' policy subcommittee, which shaped Labour's economic policy during the war, we can see that important figures in this group resisted the allure of Keynes. Hugh Gaitskell and Evan Durbin are interesting examples. Both were academic economists who took up positions in the wartime civil service, Durbin at the Ministry of Supply, the Cabinet's Economic Section, and the Office of the Deputy Prime Minister, and Gaitskell under Hugh Dalton at the Board of Trade. Before 1939 Durbin and Gaitskell had been sceptical of Keynesian proposals on both theoretical and political grounds (see Durbin, 1985). The war served to leaven this scepticism somewhat. Both saw that demand management could be used to control inflation, a major concern of socialist planners before and during the war. This made them confident when they turned to Labour policy that an expansionary post-war programme would not necessarily be threatened by inflation. As Durbin remarked to Attlee in 1944, 'we have been remarkably successful in controlling far stronger impulses to inflation during the war and there is no reason why we should fail after it'.[23] *Full employment and financial policy*, which they helped write, reflected a new ease with the use of expansionist techniques on the Keynesian model. It is important to understand, however, that these techniques were perceived simply as adjuncts to physical planning. Neither Durbin nor Gaitskell fully embraced Keynesianism during the war. In 1943, for instance, Gaitskell remarked that such measures were 'less satisfactory in the long run' than physical controls.[24] Durbin expressed to G.D.H. Cole serious reservations about the theoretical basis of Keynes's work and its political implications.[25] After 1945, when both were serving as junior ministers, both Durbin and Gaitskell appeared to favour more clearly socialist avenues of policy, in contrast with other left-inclined economists such as James Meade and Arthur Lewis. There were others on the 'Post-war finance' subcommittee who had similar doubts about fiscal policy. The Member of Parliament George Benson and the Cambridge economist Joan Robinson, for instance, preferred more radical measures of physical planning; Hugh Dalton himself cannot be simply categorized as a Keynesian (see Pimlott, 1985).

A resistance to techniques of demand management is also clear if one looks at wider Labour opinion. This was brought out particularly by reactions to the White Paper on *Employment Policy*. Aneurin Bevan made a spirited attack on its proposals, arguing that they were irreconcilable with socialism (see, for instance, 'Celticus', 1944). His doubts about financial methods which, in the words of the *New Statesman*, would be 'compatible with a complete retention of the profit-making system in every part of the nation's economic life', were shared across Labour's spectrum of opinion (*New Statesman*, 1944). Other groups within the Labour movement were willing to accept the general aim of full employment but not the means outlined by the Keynesianism of the White Paper. For its part, the Trades Union Congress had serious reservations. Similarly, the Parliamentary Labour Party welcomed the White Paper only with the proviso that 'it did not pledge the party to support the particular proposals contained in the White paper but only the general question of the acceptance by the Government of responsibility for the maintenance of full employment after the war.'[26]

To suggest that the White Paper somehow represents the point of *nexus* for consensus on economic issues, or a compact between the major political actors on a particular course of post-war policy, or Labour's espousal of demand management is therefore seriously misleading. Ideological consider-ations continued to dominate Labour's economic outlook during the war, concerns which broke with any formative Keynesian 'consensus'. In 1949 Barbara Wootton remarked that it was a matter of dispute whether 'what may be called the Beveridge Acts were, in fact, agreed measures'; we can also question how 'agreed' were the questions of wartime controls and the means to full employment (Wootton, 1949: 101).

This was reflected in the Coalition's failure to resolve important questions of economic reconstruction. In November 1944 Lord Woolton complained that when he reviewed 'the progress made in [their] consideration of post-war problems, [he was] impressed by the contrast between what [had] been achieved on the side of social reconstruction and the small progress made in the field of industry and commerce.'[27] The Distribution of Industry Act of 1945 might be considered an exception, but Ben Pimlott has shown that it was the result of a long, hard fight on the part of Hugh Dalton and Douglas Jay (Pimlott, 1985).

The persistence of ideology is confirmed by the way in which Labour ministers pursued what Lord Beaverbrook called the 'terrible issue' of nationalization.[28] In 1941, for instance, Bevin and Attlee argued strenuously, but unsuccessfully for public ownership of the railways. Attlee suggested that unification and nationalization of the railways followed from Labour's partnership in the Coalition. 'Railway nationalization has for many years been a plank in the Labour platform', he told the Lord President's committee in July 1941, 'it is not unreasonable that Labour, as a partner in the Government, should desire that some part of its programme should be implemented.'[29] But Labour found that these concerns could not always be accommodated within the Coalition, whether over the railways, coal or economic reconstruction. In September 1944, for instance, Hugh Dalton pressed in vain for a substantial reorganization of the steel and cotton industries. Herbert Morrison tried a similar tack over iron and steel, transport and electricity. Both met stiff opposition from Conservative ministers such as Andrew Duncan and Oliver Lytellton, whose free market views provided no ground for agreement with collectivists (see Brooke, 1988: 193–204). The example of electricity is particularly surprising. The McGowan report had recommended reorganization as had the Coalition's Electricity sub-committee, despite the dissent of Conservative members Ralph Assheton and Allan Chapman. However, by the end of the coalition, Woolton was forced to tell Churchill that 'there was no basis of agreement within the Government' over the question.[30]

Coalition was thus of limited value to Labour's ministers. They were happy to wring whatever reforms they could out of government and (on the assumption that Churchill would win any post-war general election) hoped to stay within the corridors of power as long as was tenable, though the Labour rank and file was making this increasingly difficult. But Labour's ideological concerns, particularly in the economic sphere, meant that the limited borders of 'consensus' and coalition were a source of continuing frustration. As Dalton told Morrison in October 1944: I doubt whether there is any real chance in the course of the next few months, of getting out of this Government composed as it is... any serious constructive contribution to the increased efficiency of this central group of industries.[31] At the same time, Bevin told Attlee that this task would have to wait upon a general election and a change in government (Bullock, 1968: 338–40).

As a concluding observation, one can suggest that, though Labour maintained a distinctive outlook during the war which made a binding political 'consensus' unlikely, it failed to reconcile long-standing difficulties within this ideology. A particular example is the scope of socialist planning. In the 1930s Labour's planners had proposed that all economic resources should be planned. This included manpower. During the war, the government directed manpower through the Emergency Powers Act and the Essential Work Order. The permanent institution of labour direction was not only completely unacceptable to the unions, it also profoundly violated the concern for 'liberty and consent' that socialist intellectuals thought should temper central planning.[32] But manpower still had to be planned. In an often circumspect way, socialist intellectuals talked of changing the traditional attitudes and practices of Labour's union partners by adopting a wages policy which would steer the movement of labour and control wage inflation under conditions of full employment (see Durbin, 1935; and Wootton, 1945). This would also, of course, undermine the very foundation of union power, that of free collective bargaining, and, by implication, the unions' *raison d'être*.

Labour's official policy committees remained oddly silent on the question. Trade union opposition undoubtedly encouraged such silence. The aim of a socialist economy was irrelevant; a wages policy was anathema to the unions. In 1944, for instance, Walter Citrine told William Beveridge that the TUC was 'resolutely opposed to any method of wage fixation by decree'.[33]

Exit a wages policy. With it went the future of socialist planning as perceived before 1945. The point is central to the sea-change in Labour's economic policy after the crises of 1947. These highlighted the problem of manpower in a planned economy under conditions of full employment. Samuel Beer has argued effectively that the unions' failure to accept a wages policy within the ambit of a planned economy shifted the direction of Labour policy from socialist planning to demand management, a more acceptable course, but also an 'approach to planning... quite compatible with private ownership, competition and profit-making' (Beer, 1965: 199). From the physical planning favoured during the war, the attention of the Labour government moved to demand management. '[T]he Budget itself', Stafford Cripps told the Commons in April 1950, 'can be described as the most important control and the most powerful instrument for influencing economic policy which is available to the Government.[34] Thus socialist planning became the unlikeliest casualty of the Attlee government. Well into the 1950s and 1960s, the problem of a planned wages or incomes policy troubled discussions of a distinctive socialist economic policy. As Richard Crossman complained in 1956, such discussions were likely to be condemned by the unions as 'dangerous heresy' (Crossman, 1956: 8). The failure to resolve this difficulty during the war, when faith in physical planning was at its height, perhaps made inevitable an impasse on the road to a socialist economy (see Brooke, forthcoming).

This leads one to suggest, however, that it is within the tensions of Labour's own ideological tradition that we can best understand the nature of political and economic change in the immediate post-war period. For whatever the ambiguities plaguing it, this distinctive socialist direction was alive and well in 1945. It made any pervasive 'consensus' far from certain. In a letter written to Attlee in November 1944, but left unsent, Churchill lamented the persistence of Labour's distinctive ideological concerns, noting that the party's ministers had 'a theme, which is Socialism, on which everything is directed'.[35]

Notes

1. *Parliamentary Debates* (Commons), 5th Ser. Vol. 422, 21 May 1946, c. 201.
2. British Library of Political and Economic Science, London [BLPES], Hugh Dalton Diary, 6 September 1939.
3. *Parliamentary Debates* (Commons), 5th Ser. Vol. 355, 28 November 1939, cs. 21–29.
4. Bodleian Library, Oxford, Attlee Papers, 9/51, speech, Alloa, 10 July 1943.
5. Bodleian Library, Woolton Papers, 15/82, Woolton to W.S. Morrison, 3 January 1944.
6. BLPES, Hugh Dalton Papers, 7/7/19, Dalton to Attlee, 6 February 1945.
7. Public Record Office, Kew [PRO], CAB 87/13, PR (43) 3, 'A comprehensive medical service: memorandum by the Minister of Health and the Secretary of State for Scotland', 2 February 1943.
8. PRO, CAB 87/12, PR (43) 24, Reconstruction Priorities Committee minutes, 15 October 1943.
9. PRO, MH 77/42, Attlee to Willink, 11 December 1943.
10. PRO, CAB 87/5, R (44) 4, Reconstruction Committee minutes, 11 January 1944 and PRO, CAB 87/5, R (44) 13, Reconstruction Committee minutes, 4 February 1944.

11. PRO, CAB 124/244, Attlee to Woolton, 1 February 1944.
12. PRO, CAB 124/244, Woolton to Eden, 10 February 1944 and Woolton to Churchill, 10 February 1944.
13. Nuffield College, Oxford, Fabian Papers, K10/5, Medical Services Research Group, 'A National Health Service', 15 March 1944.
14. *Parliamentary Debates* (Commons), 5th Ser., Vol. 398, 17 March 1944, cs. 557–8.
15. Labour Party Archives, London, Public Health Advisory Committee minutes (16), 13 March 1944.
16. *British Medical Journal*, 25 March 1944 and 26 February 1944; see also ibid., 22 April 1944.
17. Brynmor Jones Library, Hull, Socialist Medical Association Papers, DSM 4/2, 'B.M.A. and Ministry of Health: "New Proposals"', 10 April 1945.
18. BLPES, William Piercy Papers, 8/12, 'Notes on the machinery of control', no date [1943].
19. BLPES, William Piercy Papers, 8/12, Durbin to Attlee, 25 April 1944.
20. PRO, CAB 124/678, R(I.O.) (44) 3, 'Economic control during the transition period', 2 March 1944.
21. PRO, CAB 87/14, R (I) (44) 4, Ministerial sub-committee on industrial problems minutes, 29 September 1944.
22. PRO, CAB 65/44, WM (44) 145, War Cabinet minutes, 2 November 1944.
23. BLPES, William Piercy Papers, 8/24, Durbin to Attlee, 20 January 1944.
24. Labour party archives, RDR 222, Hugh Gaitskell, 'Notes on post-war taxation policy', January 1943.
25. BLPES, Evan Durbin Papers, 6/1, Durbin to G.D.H. Cole, 25 January 1943.
26. House of Commons, Westminster, Parliamentary Labour Party minutes, 14 June 1944.
27. PRO, CAB 124/606, Woolton to Leathers, 11 November 1944.
28. PRO, PREM, 4/65/61, Beaverbrook to Churchill, 4 February 1944.
29. PRO, CAB 71/3, LP (41) 104, 'The railways and the war: memorandum by the Lord Privy Seal', 1 July 1941.
30. PRO, PREM 4/88/4, Woolton to Churchill, 9 April 1945.
31. BLPES, Hugh Dalton Papers, 7/6/67, Dalton to Morrison, 24 October 1944.
32. BLPES, Evan Durbin Papers, 4/7, 'Nationalisation', no date [1945–8].
33. Congress House, London, TUC Archives, Economic committee minutes (8), 9 February 1944.
34. *Parliamentary Debates* (Commons), 5th Ser. Vol. 474, 18 April 1950, c. 40.
35. PRO, PREM 4/88/1, Churchill to Attlee, 20 November 1944 [unsent].

References

Addison, Paul (1975), *The Road to 1945*, London, Jonathan Cape.
Addison, Paul (1984), 'Attlee's new order', *Times Literary Supplement*, 4248: 960.
Beer, Samuel (1965), *Modern British Politics*, London, Faber and Faber.
Brooke, Stephen (1988), 'Labour's war: party, coalition, and domestic reconstruction, 1939–45', Oxford, D.Phil. (forthcoming).

Brooke, Stephen (1989), 'Revisionists and fundamentalists: the Labour party and economic policy during the Second World War', *Historical Journal*, 32: 157–75.

Brooke, Stephen (forthcoming), 'Problems of "socialist planning": Evan Durbin and the Labour government of 1945', *Historical Journal*, 34.

Bullock, Alan (1968), *The Life and Times of Ernest Bevin*, Volume II: *Minister of Labour*, London, Heinemann.

'Celticus' [Aneurin Bevan] (1944), *Why not trust the Tories?*, London, Gollancz.

Cole, G.D.H. (1949), 'The dream and the business', *Political Quarterly*, 20: 201–10.

Crossman, Richard (1956), *Socialism and the new despotism*, London, Fabian Society.

Durbin, Elizabeth (1985), *New Jerusalems*, London: Routledge and Kegan Paul.

Durbin, Evan (1935), 'The importance of planning', *New trends in socialism*, ed. G.E.C. Catlin, London: Routledge.

Jeffreys, Kevin (1987), 'British politics and social policy during the Second World War', *Historical Journal*, 30: 123–44.

Kavanagh, Dennis and Morris, Peter (1989), *Consensus Politics from Attlee to Thatcher*, Oxford, Blackwell.

Labour Party (1940), *Annual conference report*, London, Labour Party.

Labour Party (1941), *Annual conference report*, London, Labour Party.

Labour Party (1943), *A national service for health*, London, Labour Party.

Labour Party (1944), *Full employment and financial policy*, London, Labour Party.

Labour Party (1945), *Annual conference report*, London, Labour Party.

Medical Practitioners Union (MPU) (1942), *The transition to a state medical service*, London, MPU.

Medical Practitioners Union (MPU) (1944), *Mr Willink's lost opportunity*, London, MPU.

Middlemas, Keith (1979), *Politics in Industrial Society*, London, Deutsch.

Middlemas, Keith (1986), *Power, Competition and the State*, Stanford, Hoover Institution Press.

Morgan, Kenneth O. (1984), *Labour in power 1945–51* Oxford, Oxford University Press.

New Statesman and Nation (1944), 'Full employment', 27, No. 693: 363.

Pimlott, Ben (1985), *Hugh Dalton*, London, Jonathan Cape.

Pimlott, Ben (1986), *The Second World War Diaries of Hugh Dalton*, London, Jonathan Cape.

Pimlott, Ben (1988), 'The myth of consensus', *Echoes of Greatness*, ed. L.M. Smith, London, Channel Four.

Socialist Medical Association (SMA) (1944), *A Socialised Medical Service*, London, SMA.

Webster, Charles (1988a), *The Health Services since the War*, London, HMSO.
Webster, Charles (1988b), 'Labour and the origins of the national health service', *Science, Politics, and the Public Good*, ed. N. Rupke, London, MacMillan.
Wootton, Barbara (1945), *Freedom under planning*, London, Gollancz.
Wootton, Barbara (1949), 'Record of the Labour Government in the Social Services', *Political Quarterly*, 20: 101–12.

2 The survival of the British Liberal Party, 1933–59

Malcolm Baines

In March 1942, Mass Observation produced a report for the Liberal leadership. It surveyed the attitude of the wartime public towards the party. The conclusions held little joy. Few electors thought the Liberals worth voting for; most saw them as too weak to count. The report commented that, 'over and over again we come back to the widespread feeling, among pro Liberals, anti Liberals and apathetics, that the Liberals are essentially *something of the past* rather than *of the future.*' Virtually nothing was known by those interviewed of Liberal policy. Of those sampled, 85 per cent had no idea what it was. Free trade was the only distinct issue associated with the party and that by a mere 4 to 5 per cent. Liberal politicians were only a little less obscure. Twice as many recognized Lloyd George's name as that of Sinclair, the current Liberal leader, but incredibly five Luton Liberals still believed Asquith to be alive.[1]

Academic assessment of Liberal prospects at the time held out as little hope of the party's survival as did the opinion pollsters. In the 1950s Maurice Duverger, the distinguished French political scientist, sketched out an unwholesome end for any party which was not rooted in any particular class or section of the electorate. 'The fate of the Centre is to be torn asunder, buffeted and annihilated: torn asunder when one of its halves votes Right and then Left, annihilated when it abstains from voting' (Duverger, 1954: 215). Such a fate was seen as inevitable for the British Liberals throughout the period reviewed in this chapter. A pamphlet published by the French Ministry of Information after the 1945 General Election, considered that only two options were now left to the British Liberal Party: merge with the Conservatives or die (Duverger, 1954: 210). Abroad that choice had often already been made. In Australia, conservatives and liberals fused to fight socialism in 1909; in New Zealand in 1935. On the European continent many Liberal parties were struggling from the turn of the century as the apparently inexorable rise of trade union based political movements gathered force. In Britain the Liberals had been in constant electoral decline since 1929; returning 21 Members of

Parliament in 1935, 12 in 1945 and as few as 6 in 1951. Throughout the 1930s, 1940s and 1950s the independent Liberals were in continual battle with their Simonite rivals, who advocated co-operation with the Conservatives, for the mantle of the Liberal tradition.

Against this background of constant struggle and defeat it was not surprising that many Liberals greeted the by-election gain at Torrington in March 1958 with rapturous hyperbole. It was, after all, the first tangible sign of the party's revival. *Liberal News* confessed: 'Never before in our history has a political party appeared so finished (we can say that now) and then—fighting on—won its place in the life of the nation as the Liberal Party is now doing' (Wallace, 1983: 43). Roger Fulford began his presentation in 1959 of *The Liberal Case* with the stirring words: 'In politics of recent times there has been only one miracle—that is the survival of the Liberal party' (Fulford, 1959: 10). To some extent their interpretation was right. No other Liberal party in either Europe or the Commonwealth has survived for several decades as a small third party within a simple majority electoral system. Political scientists have tended to focus on less central aspects of the British Liberals. Rasmussen, Lemieux and Brier, for example, examined the role of third parties within the political system, the character of their activists and supporters or the social environment in which they continued to exist (Rasmussen, 1964; Lemieux, 1977; Brier, 1967). Only Rose and Mackie in their general survey, *Do Parties Persist of Disappear?*, tackled the fundamental question of party survival. After studying 369 parties across 13 Western nations, they concluded that proportional representation, initial electoral success, participation in government and a stable social base correlated most closely to a party's survival (Rose and Mackie, 1984). Some of these are applicable to Liberal survival in Britain, where the party did have the asset of its record as a major force before 1914, together with a lingering appeal to rural Wales and Cornwall. This chapter, however, will seek to place the mid-twentieth-century Liberals within the less familiar historical perspective: laying more stress on Westminster, the outcome of the party's internal strategic debates and relations with its Conservative and Labour rivals.

The aftermath of the fiscal and political crisis of August 1931 set the context of Liberal survival for the next two decades. The demand for a balanced budget not only brought down MacDonald's second Labour government, it also ended Lloyd George's strategy of using his balance of power position to force political concessions, including electoral reform, which would entrench the Liberals within the British political system. However, the Liberals as a whole supported the NationalGovernment until the Conservative protectionists within it persuaded the Cabinet to call an election for October 1931. The Liberal Party then split into three sections: Lloyd George and his family declared the election a Tory ramp; Samuel decided to work within the National Government against the protectionists and for free trade; while Simon, whose faith in traditional liberal economics had been badly shaken by the severity of the depression, aimed to co-operate with the Conservatives to liberalise them from within. Thereafter Liberal politicians of all complexions were preoccupied with the question of the best means to exercise Liberal influence in an unfriendly political system. The strategic debate was not resolved until the later 1950s. By then, the National Liberals had lost all credibility; Labour's disarray raised hopes of new opportunities, and the Liberals had found a new role as the vehicle for protest votes against a tired Tory government.

The future survival of the Liberals was dependent upon their disengagement from the National Government. In February 1932 they ceased to abide by collective ministerial responsibility over trade matters; in September of the same year, they left office in protest at the Ottawa Agreements, which entrenched tariffs within the British economic system. By November 1933 the independent Liberals had moved from the government's back-benches into outright opposition. The Samuelites, as they became known, were characterized by the conviction that the most powerful advocate for Liberal values and policies was the preservation of a separate parliamentary group. The wider party's enthusiastic reaction in June 1936 to the Meston Report, which restructured its organization and constitution, reassured many parliamentary Liberals that continuing independence might have some future. Apart from a brief period between 1950 and 1951, the Liberal leadership supported this 'party in being' strategy. They undertook a constant struggle in Parliament and the wider establishment to maintain the privileges of a major party in their reduced electoral circumstances. Immediately after the 1935 Election, the Liberals had to fight off a threat from their Simonite rivals to take over the third largest set of whips' rooms in the Commons (Harris, 1946: 125), while Sinclair endeavoured to obtain the same confidential information from the government about foreign affairs as was accorded to the Labour opposition.[2]

The Liberals laboured under three major problems in the 1930s: they had to fend off the challenge of the Liberal Nationals under Sir John Simon; counterbalance their lack of a distinct programme compared to the moderate Conservatism of Baldwin; and find a compensating income for the withdrawal of funds by Lloyd George. None of these problems had been successfully tackled by the end of the decade. Not surprisingly, the 'party in being' strategy did not remain unchallenged. Under the pressure of continued electoral decline individual Liberals lobbied for a wide range of alternative courses, which they trusted would ensure the survival of liberalism, if not of the party itself. Some argued for arrangements with other parties, some for a return to Gladstonian values, still others for a closer identification with the greater state regulation supported by bodies like the 'Next Five Years' group. Faced with these divisions, Liberal leaders took refuge in inertia. Sinclair wrote in 1936 to Harcourt Johnstone, a former chief whip, that 'To throw all our weight on one side or the other would create another split.' The new Liberal leader argued instead that the party should stress those slogans which united it: peace, support for the League of Nations, freedom and social reform, while waiting for the voters to tire of the National Government.[3]

Throughout the mid-twentieth century the Liberal leadership felt similarly constrained by fear of provoking division. Clement Davies wrote to Gilbert Murray, the Oxford classicist and a distinguished, if elderly, Liberal, in May 1950 that if he could see meetings of either the parliamentary party or the party committee, he 'would come to the conclusion that there is no party today but a number of individuals who because of their adherence to the Party, come together only to express completely divergent views'. Although the MPs agreed strongly that the party should remain independent, they disagreed equally over the means. Davies's position was one of supine weakness, always seeking to minimise any danger of a recurrence of those splits, which he blamed for the party's past decline.[4] All three Liberal leaders, Samuel, Sinclair and Davies, pursued a strategy of attempting to keep as wide a range of opinion as possible within the party. By 1956, however, the defection of Dingle Foot to Labour removed the last prominent spokesman for a rival strategy to that of the leader. Grimond's charismatic appeal to both left and right-leaning Liberals allowed him to unify the party in his own person, while the gathering momentum of electoral success after the Torquay by-election in December 1955 did much to defuse potential opposition.[5]

Despite their limited success in retaining the trappings of an establishment party, the Liberals were not an effective force at Westminster. Much speaking responsibility devolved upon the party's leaders. Sinclair filled many columns of Hansard in the 1930s, while Clement Davies ten years later had constantly to persuade the Speaker to grant the LPP the privileges of a separate group.[6] Both leaders were plagued by frequent absenteeism by their back-benchers. Out of the 21 Liberal MPs elected in 1935, only 12 attended a parliamentary meeting in March 1937 to discuss the Defence White Paper. Sinclair's description of this as the largest gathering they had yet held in this Parliament was scant praise for the group's commitment.[7] At the 1936 budget debate, the parliamentary party's bench was so deserted that the Tories occupied it.[8] Similar problems occurred after 1945. Emrys Roberts, the MP for Merioneth, complained that without the remunerative directorships that the party's whips had promised him, he could devote little time to the Commons.[9] Davies confessed his difficulties to Sinclair:

> My greatest difficulty is to get a regular attendance. I cannot blame them, we all need to earn our own living and every now and then the Bench is empty. The moment that it is empty the other Parties call attention to it. In a way this is a compliment. A hundred can be absent on either side and no one misses them, but if our little band is absent we are missed.[10]

The party's continued acceptance of the Westminster system both helped and hindered its survival. While it gave the Liberals access to the media, honours and confidential information, it constrained their freedom to manœuvre. At times of crisis, their leaders invariably felt constrained to rally round the establishment to the diminution of the Liberal Party's independent identity. While Sinclair patriotically buried himself at the Air Ministry during Churchill's Coalition government, his party was unable to find an alternative role as either a defender of civil liberties against wartime abuse or as a focus for the growing tide of opinion against the administration's Conservative supporters. Nor did the Liberals help fashion the post-war consensus despite its indebtedness to the ideas of Keynes and Beveridge. The LLP's small size meant that it was excluded from not only the War Cabinet itself, but also from important Cabinet committees, including the one which considered post-war reconstruction and the Beveridge Report (Addison, 1975: 221).

Liberal survival was not helped either by the party's inability to project an attractive image of itself. In the 1930s, unemployment at home and high tariffs abroad had reduced the faith of many Liberals in their traditional creed of free trade, balanced budgets and the Gold Standard. Liberal economics and the party associated with it seemed to the electorate like the fossilized relics of a bygone era. Among their rivals, the Conservatives appeared to be in firm occupation of the middle ground of retaliatory tariffs and collective security. Sir William Sutherland, a former Coalition Liberal MP for Argyllshire, articulated the Liberals' political problem to Lloyd George just after the Samuelites crossed the floor. He wrote: 'so long as Baldwin presses so far to the middle and is at war with his Diehards it is not clear where Samuel is going to crash in with a separate identity and policy.'[11] The National Government had, in fact, seized the traditional Liberal rhetoric of fiscal probity and retrenchment, while many electors now equated free trade with the dole queues of the immediate post-war era. Liberal leaders, however, did not wish the party to appeal only to the declining constituency of free traders. They refused to pledge the party to its immediate restoration. While many rank-and-file Liberals looked back with nostalgia to late nineteenth-century Britain, its leading MPs and policy-makers supported instead compromise low-tariff unions as a first step towards the gradual reduction of tariffs. The Scotsman was provoked to comment in April 1935 that a Liberal party that did not stand for free trade had nothing left to distinguish it from the other two parties. It no longer had any reason to exist.[12]

The Liberals were able to establish even less distinctive positions on many other issues. Despite Sinclair's support for collective security to resist German aggression in the later 1930s, his position often appeared difficult in practice to distinguish from Labour's advocacy of an anti-fascist alliance. The party's standpoint was clouded as well by the parliamentary party's divisions over the Munich settlement and conscription. While Sinclair argued passionately for the rights of small nations, the party's former leader, Herbert Samuel, briefly considered joining the Cabinet to support Chamberlain's sacrifice of

Czechoslovakia for peace.[13] Proportional representation was still too new a theme to enthuse most active Liberals. It merited only a sentence in the 1935 manifesto compared with an entire section devoted to reducing tariffs (Craig, 1975: 109–111). The most successful Liberal campaign in the 1930s was a monster petition against the rising cost of living; an adaption of traditional Liberal protests in favour of a free breakfast table and against the imposition of tariffs. Outside agriculture and trade, where the administration attempted to intervene and regulate activity, the Liberals found it difficult to muster more than lukewarm opposition to the National Government.

While before the Second World War the Liberals were seen as the peddlers of outdated, impractical shibboleths—an essentially reactive party against the onset of collectivism—by 1950 the same kinds of ideas were viewed as exciting and new. *The Times* commented in 1955 that the Liberal approach was refreshing and original. It wrote: 'the domestic scene would stand to be affected more profoundly by the Liberal Party's policy, right or wrong, than by that of either of the other two great contestants for power.'[14] Free trade was at the centre of the Liberal programme well into the 1950s. Many Liberals argued that its application to home-produced foodstuffs would mark out the party from its rivals. With its representation concentrated in rural areas, Liberal parliamentarians and some candidates felt such distinctiveness would be bought at too high an electoral cost. The 1953 Assembly's decision to abandon fixed prices for agricultural produce and guaranteed markets for the industry's production of foodstuffs brought Jeremy Thorpe to the microphone to refuse to stand on such a platform.[15] Although Clement Davies had told Sinclair in April 1950: 'I want something said so distinctly that any ordinary man can then understand and be able to say that is our distinguishing mark', he did not want it said so distinctly that it cost the Liberals some of their few remaining seats.[16] However, unlike its monopolization of free trade the Liberal Party never succeeded in capturing the cause of free enterprise. Here, as elsewhere, the Liberal agenda proved vulnerable to the depredations of the other parties. Arthur Holt, Liberal MP for Bolton West from 1951 to 1964, wrote in the *Political Quarterly* for Summer 1953:

> In matters of trade, industry, finance and economics where there are the greatest differences between Socialists and Liberals, the Conservative Party has appeared to the people as the most effective champion of a freer economy.... They have associated themselves in the public mind with 'Setting the People Free'. (Wallace, 1968: 103)

Most Liberals, however, were preoccupied with issues remote from the Conservative/Labour agenda such as internationalism, home rule, the status of women and electoral reform. These concerns handicapped one strand of strategic thinking which ran throughout the period. This sought to substitute questionnaires addressed to Labour and Conservative candidates for a

Liberal electoral challenge. The responses garnered would advise the Liberal vote, still believed to be considerable, where its decisive influence should be thrown. This strategy was seen by Liberals at all levels as a possible alternative to maintaining a full-scale party organization. It rapidly ran into difficulties. Many Liberals knew whom they wished to support before any questions were sent out. In July 1936 Brock, the party's chief agent, reported that the questionnaire submitted at the Derby by-election had been deliberately framed to enable Noel-Baker, the Labour candidate, to give the more favourable answers. In fact, the responses were hopeless. Both contenders were about equally equivocal on the League of Nations and the reduction of tariffs, while Church, the National Government candidate was far better on proportional representation.[17] Sinclair wryly commented after a later by-election that questionnaires covering several subjects did not seem to work as a tactic and the party might do better to stick to the single topic of electoral reform.[18] The strategy had no more success in the 1950s. Central Office drafted standard answers to the Liberal Party's questionnaires and did its best to limit the latitude of individual MPs and candidates to go beyond them.[19] Not only were the Liberals unable to drive many wedges into the coherence of their opponents, but the entire basis of the approach was flawed. There is little evidence that a sizeable core Liberal vote existed, certainly after 1945, or that the party's potential electorate paid much attention to the findings.

Despite the ineffectiveness of Liberal efforts to influence their rivals from the outside, relations with the two larger parties proved vital to the party's survival. Between 1933 and 1959, its parliamentary representation was very fragile. In 1935 one-third of the MPs had majorities of less than a thousand and only six had been elected in three-way fights. In 1945 only in Eye, Merioneth and Anglesey were Liberals elected against both Labour and Conservative opposition. At the General Elections of 1951 and 1955, Jo Grimond alone faced a Tory opponent. The existence of the Liberal Parliamentary Party rested on the goodwill of its rivals. Numerous attempts were made at both national and local level to shape arrangements with either the Conservative or Labour Parties, which would allow the Liberals to survive at Westminster. For a party committed through its heritage to upholding the parliamentary system, the return of only one or two members from its few safe seats would probably have destroyed it, or at the very least radically altered its perceptions of the Liberal role in the British political system.

Labour on the whole had little sympathy for the Liberals. Its lack of candidates in 1935 and 1945 was due as much to organizational weakness on the fringes of rural England as to local bargaining. Liberal attitudes to Labour were very divided. Among parliamentarians and intellectuals the language of progressivism was still common. Even the staunchly capitalist Lothian, formerly a Samuelite Minister in the National Government, explained to the 1934 Liberal Summer School that 'Liberalism had to convince Labour that Socialism was incompatible with Labour and that the way forward was to control Capitalism scientifically and not to destroy it.'[20] Agitation, however, for a 'Popular Front' before 1939 was confined to the parliamentary fringes of both parties. Among many rank-and-file Liberals the prevailing mood was anti-socialist. Atholl Robertson, the Liberal candidate at a by-election in Mid-Buckinghamshire in 1938, commented that there would never be a straight fight again, for the Liberals were Labour's worst enemies. Those socialists who had broken away from Labour to help Robertson in the by-election had done more harm than good.[21] Sinclair himself felt the Liberal Party was too weak to approach Labour and any rebuff would only damage the party still further.[22] Sporadic approaches to Labour politicians by Liberals were treated with limited interest. Dalton greeted with incredulity claims from Lord Rea, a former Liberal whip, that the party would stand two hundred candidates in a 1940 election. There might be some possibility of a few quiet withdrawals, but none of a more far-reaching arrangement (Pimlott, 1986: 249–50). Joe Toole, MP for Salford South from 1923 to 1924 and 1929 to 1931, expressed the most common Labour doubt. He told Sir Henry Fildes, then an adviser to Lloyd George, that Labour could see little point in allying itself with a party with no electoral clout—like a Mile End tie and collar shop proposing to amalgamate on equal terms with Austin Reed.[23] After the Second World War, individual Liberals such as Dingle Foot and Megan Lloyd George met outwardly sympathetic Labour MPs like Morrison, but to no effect. These, however, were preludes to defection, rather than genuine attempts to negotiate some arrangement which might keep the Liberal Party alive.

More common were those Liberals who feared the danger to civilization posed by the rise of socialism. In 1934 Harcourt Johnstone reported that Reading, then Liberal leader in the Lords, was 'nervous lest the Liberal Party fighting independently at the next election should succeed in returning the Labour party to office'.[24] Once Labour gained power in 1945, these fears multiplied. The extent of Churchill's defeat encouraged the party leadership that the Liberals might be able to take advantage of Conservative weakness; others concluded that simple electoral arithmetic showed that if both anti-socialist parties had co-operated, then Labour's majorty of 138 would have been toppled without any further swing against them. Many Liberals justified this course by pointing to the new, modern, middle-of-the-road, Conservative Party shaped by Butler and Macmillan as the logical heir to Edwardian Liberalism.[25] However, even after thirty years of almost continual electoral decline, the Liberal Party remained too much of a broad church to exercise any such decisive electoral influence. Its members were united only around a passive acceptance of the status quo of an independent party. Any attempt to mobilize them to achieve a specific strategic goal would be bound to destroy through division what little bargaining power they possessed.

The party's losses in the 1945 Election were blamed on lack of preparation. Its leaders convinced themselves that revival could be achieved through a combination of a credible number of candidates and an organizational overhaul. In 1950 450 Liberals stood for election—the party's broadest front since 1929. The number of MPs declined still further to only nine. This seemed a meagre reward for its effort and raised for the first time widespread doubts among the Liberal leadership that the 'party in being' strategy was in itself adequate as a means of keeping the party alive. Equally significantly, Labour crept back into office after the election with a majority of eighteen. Those in the party like the peers Reading and Rennell, who had advocated co-operation with the Conservatives, had had their worst fears realized. Lord Milverton, a former colonial administrator, wrote to the Liberal whip in the House of Lords just before he defected to the National Liberals, that anti-socialist co-operation was essential if the liberal way of life was to be preserved:

> If you cut out purely personal and party interests and indications, if you turn your eyes from wistful contemplation of a glorious but buried past to the facts of an unhappy present and a grim future, what is your inevitable conclusion?[26]

Two years before, Violet Bonham-Carter, daughter of Asquith, the former Liberal Prime Minister, had already expressed her doubts about the effectiveness of the limited Liberal organizational improvement since 1945. By 1947 it had become clear to her that the party might well lose even more seats at the next election. An extra 750,000 votes would win the Liberals only another half-dozen seats, while of their current seats only one or two were safe. She wrote to Megan Lloyd George: 'One must face the *possibility* of Parliamentary extinction—*Or do you think this an exaggerated fear*?' Bonham-Carter argued that only through an electoral pact with the Conservatives could the proportional representation needed if the Liberals were to survive be achieved.[27] Unlike Reading, Rennell and Milverton, she saw a deal with the Conservative opposition as a means to save the party, not as the keystone of an united anti-socialist block. One development at the 1950 General Election reinforced Bonham-Carter's case. The Liberal gain of Huddersfield West from Labour seemed to provide a possible blueprint for the party's survival along the lines she wanted. In exchange for an informal pledge to vote against socialist measures and a reciprocal withdrawal in Huddersfield East, Donald Wade, the Liberal candidate, had had no Conservative opponent. Many Liberals believed the Huddersfield arrangement could be extended to other seats throughout the country. Sinclair, for example, informed Davies that he would support local arrangements on that model in exchange for a firm pledge from the Conservatives to introduce electoral reform.[28]

With the tacit approval of Samuel and Davies, leaders in the Lords and Commons respectively, Violet Bonham-Carter entered into negotiations with Rab Butler. The lack of any wide measure of agreement within each party regarding the desirability of a deal encouraged a considerable amount of indiscipline. Within the Conservatives, Churchill, who had always seen an alliance between Liberals and Tories as the rule rather than the exception, was positively enthusiastic for some form of arrangement (Coote, 1965: 267), while Eden favoured a more negative anti-socialist pact (Rhodes James, 1986: 326). However, Central Office which explored the practicalities, was much less optimistic. Its strategists had a diametrically opposed vision of any pact to that of the Liberals. Most Tories favoured assimilation into one anti-socialist force dominated by themselves as had occurred to the National Liberals. The Liberals, however, wanted to use Conservative doubts about their capacity to defeat Labour unaided to win their implicit help to rebuild a Liberal presence. As early as November 1945 the Central Office area agent in Wales reported: 'As Liberalism even in Wales is slowly fading, I think we could win these seats [Anglesey and Montgomery] if our organization was improved and the Conservatives could be persuaded to give up their "defeatist" attitude.'[29] Like Labour, the Conservatives regarded the Liberals as a party too weak to count. In their analysis the so-called 'Liberal' vote was in fact a half-way house not amenable to national direction by the Liberal leadership. The party's diffuse structure and weak or non-existent local organization meant that as had happened at the South Bradford by-election of December 1949, 'rogue' Liberal candidates would poll as well as official ones and would not be stopped by any national deal.[30]

Not only did Central Office and many back-benchers believe there was little reward for the Conservatives in any arrangement, but rumours of negotiations began to disturb the party's internal unity. By September 1950 the 1922 Committee had become very hostile and Butler feared that Churchill's pursuit of the Liberal chimera was losing him the respect of his back-benchers.[31] Bonham-Carter's shame at Liberal divisions in the Commons over the party's attitude to the Labour government's wafer-thin majority caused her to break off negotiations for several months. When they were renewed in February 1951, the Conservatives were able to tell Bonham-Carter there were no seats left for Liberals to fill and blame her for the breakdown of the negotiations.[32]

The significance of Violet Bonham-Carter's campaign was that it was successful in so far as it won the support of a majority of leading Liberal politicians for a profound change in the party's hitherto independent status. Of the party's central committee, only one member dissented from her course of action. It is certainly arguable that if the party had been able to conclude an alliance with the Conservatives along the lines she suggested, it would not have been able to preserve any independence. It can also be maintained that if such a deal had achieved a measure of proportional representation, then the Liberals could have had a more substantial impact on later British politics.

Paradoxically, although the incompatibility of Liberal and Conservative views on any national arrangement helped the Liberals to survive as an independent party, so too did the successful conclusion of a few pacts at local level. During the 1950s, only Cardiganshire and Orkney and Shetland of the

Liberal seats could have been defended with certainty against both major parties. Deals were concluded in Huddersfield and Bolton because both towns retained a lingering Liberal tradition represented in either local government or the local newspaper and the Tories had failed to establish themselves as the dominant anti-socialist party, able to beat Labour unaided. Even more crucial was the division in 1948 of what had formerly been two double-member boroughs, which enabled each party to feel it had a stake in the town's representation. Periodically, however, some local Conservatives would seek to overturn the pact and nominate candidates in both seats. Central Office's endorsement for the deal was necessary to head off their challenge. National support for the local Tory establishment against the rebels revealed the crucial impact of Churchill's election victory in 1951 on the relationship of the two parties.[33] While the narrowness of his majority led Central Office regretfully to put the short-term consideration of socialist defeat before the longer perspective of eliminating the Liberals, its inauguration of 13 years of Tory rule ultimately allowed a more promising Liberal realignment as an anti-Conservative, rather than an anti-socialist force. The period of Churchill and Eden's administrations in the 1950s also dispelled the illusion that the Conservative party had in fact become a liberal party as progressive sensitivities were inflamed by the Lord Chancellor's shelving of Samuel's Liberties of the Subject Bill, the continuation of the Seretse Khama affair and disillusionment with Tory foreign policy after Suez.

Almost by default the 'party in being' strategy was readopted, while Conservative fears of Labour provided the insurance of the local pacts against continuing Liberal electoral weakness. The accession of Grimond renewed Liberal enthusiasm, while the defection of those who had favoured closer relations with Labour enabled him to articulate a more clearly defined strategy as the Labour Party itself began to stumble. However, Grimond rebuilt the party's self-confidence rather than its electoral base. In the later 1950s the Liberals found a role as a protest party on behalf of the 'little man' against the political and economic establishment encouraged by increasing votes at by-elections. Even though its 1959 Election performance was no better in terms of seats then the party's 1951 nadir, it was clear that like its two larger rivals, the Liberals would try to campaign for their ideas and values through a political party which would aim for power at Westminster.

Most of the other options which were examined by members of the party between 1933 and 1956 were flawed. The illusion of an all-powerful centre party, able to dispense votes to eager suitors in return for policy concessions, was dashed on the rock of class-based politics. Neither Labour nor the Conservatives believed by 1951 that either properly completed questionnaires or the entreaties of Liberal leaders could make the myth of the Liberal vote a reality for them. The Liberal Party at a national level was too weak, even in 1935, for either major party to consider making a permanent alliance on terms the Liberals would accept. In New Zealand, similarly, the original negotiations between Reform and the Liberals broke down. It was not until the latter's revival in the 1928 Election three years later had made the Liberal alliance valuable to them that Reform found it worthwhile to make previously elusive concessions (Milne 1966: 44–5). It was the Liberals' lack of substance within the worlds of Westminster and Whitehall, which enabled them to survive as an independent party. Yet 'high politics' alone is clearly inadequate as an explanation of Liberal survival. Under the British electoral system, national weakness often implies national extinction. An analysis of Liberal survival must, therefore, go some way towards accounting for the successes of individual MPs. Apart from the crucial electoral pacts already glanced at, the other important aspect of the party's survival was Liberal retention of a fairly secure base in mid-Wales and some credibility throughout much of remote rural Britain.

Politics on the Celtic fringe was certainly different from that practised elsewhere in the United Kingdom. Liberal strength between 1933 and 1959 was almost exclusively confined to Wales. The split between the Liberal Nationals and the Samuelites had far-reaching effects in Scotland, where many Liberals aligned themselves with Simon. Not until the late 1950s were the independent Liberals able to re-establish themselves as their derisory votes in the East Fife and Ross and Cromarty by-elections showed. Liberal organization at all levels was poor, but on the Celtic fringe, connections, contacts and small village meetings were more important than canvassing. Sinclair's own predominance in Caithness and Sutherland, for example, did not rest on any formal organization. His factor was his agent when necessary. He gauged the strength of popular feeling through correspondents placed throughout the two counties and tried to influence it through articles and speeches placed in a still sympathetic local press. It was Sinclair's disappearance from the constituency as Air Minister between 1939 and 1945 which cost him the seat. Likewise Liberal strength elsewhere remained only as strong as the MP.

R.T. Evans's neglect of Carmarthen was blamed for his defeat in 1935. Granville took most of the Liberal vote with him in Eye when he defected to Labour. The Liberal share was reduced from 36.1 per cent in 1951 to only 11.8 per cent in 1955. Even in densely populated Bethnal Green, the Liberal vote seemed a personal vote. Commenting to Sinclair on the London County Council Elections in 1934, Sir Percy Harris, South West Bethnal Green's MP, wrote:

> We had neither candidates nor money & even when we did put up a couple there was no effective organisation behind them. I am afraid even in B.[ethnal] G.[reen] those who did vote for us, did so far more on personal grounds than because of a consciousness of Liberalism.[34]

Certainly Liberal survival owed nothing to the party's structure. The party remained rooted in the Edwardian era, dependent on a small number of large subscribers. Like Liberal parties around the world it was a cadre party organized from the top down. Throughout the 1930s, for example, two-thirds of the Western Counties Federation's income came in grants from the Whips' Office.[35] Attempts to move over to a membership card system or to increase the party's reliance on smaller donations came to naught. Equally unsuccessful was the establishment of the Independent Traders' Alliance during the war years, which it was hoped might provide a conveyor organisation to parallel the trade unions and big business. Local parties were in structural decline for most of the period, sometimes punctuated by short-lived revivals. In January 1939, for example, Lord Davies of Llandinam contrasted the £232 raised to liquidate the Montgomery Association's debt with the £400 raised in 1929.[36] Another symptom of Liberal debilitation was the willingness in the 1930s of the party to abandon the struggle against the Conservatives, even in areas of great Labour weakness. Arnold Jones, for example, who had fought Wells in the past, thought seriously of abandoning the candidature to Labour, even though the Liberals had been second in 1935.[37]

The Liberal vote has been assessed from both sociological and geographical perspectives. Although the party, especially in the United Kingdom as a whole after 1945, represented a rootless, anti-establishment section of the electorate, it relied on the traditions of the static, egalitarian communities of rural Wales for its representation. Unlike the simple social structures of Australia and New Zealand, Britain shared the cultural and social diversity of other older societies, which were difficult to contain entirely within two class-based parties. These rural Celtic communities were themselves isolated from the mainstream of British political life and less susceptible to the definition of British political issues by London-based media, which increasingly set in after the First World War. In this they resembled other localized, inward-looking areas around the globe like the Canadian Maritimes and Southern Norway, districts which have continued to give disproportionate support to Liberal parties. Even on the Celtic fringe, however, Liberals were squeezed by the situation at Westminster as they were in England. One Highland Liberal identified the party's lack of credibility as a serious handicap to its electoral prospects:

> The great factor against the Liberals is that many electors (especially in Kinross and West Perthshire) firmly believe that the Liberal Party is *fast* dying out, that it has no truly progressive policy, and that it will have practically little representation as a result of the impending General Election.[38]

Explanations of party survival are invariably complex. After 1933, British Liberals were confronted with three choices of how they should seek to inject their ideology into the British political system: from inside one of the rival party groupings with Sir John Simon; from outside the party system with Lloyd George and his Councils of Action; or as an aspirant to majority power with Samuel and Sinclair. Until 1950 the last group were able to hold out a prospect of Liberal revival, which was at least credible to its own supporters. The importance of Grimond was that he re-established belief in the party's structural future. Despite its internal divisions, the Liberal Party survived the middle years of this century. The Liberal vote did not. Within a context of national decline, it lost its social and geographic distinctiveness. By 1945, areas where the Liberals had polled 4 per cent in 1935 were recording 10 per cent. As their electoral base widened, so the Liberal Party's influence over the so-called Liberal vote diminished. The other parties increasingly realized that the 'floating vote' was the real king of British politics; and that the Liberal Party was not its kingmaker. The acceptance of that analysis based on post-war developments in opinion polling removed the rationale for the continued existence of the National Liberals, and destroyed the politics of influence based on the questionnaire for the independent Liberals. Inside the rigid party system of British politics there was no obvious alternative to the 'party in being' strategy. Only in a few particular areas did the Liberal Party remain strong enough to obtain those vital local deals with Conservative associations, fearful of socialism. Those pacts were enough to keep a parliamentary party alive at Westminster; while the party's national weakness made its formal absorption into the orbit of either major party undesirable and unnecessary for both its rivals.

Notes

1. Graham White Papers, House of Lords Record Office, G/2/1/3, Mass Observation report commissioned by the Education and Propaganda Committee on 'The British Public's Feelings about Liberalism', 4 March 1942.
2. Thurso Papers II, Box 29, File 1, Mander to Sinclair, 26 August 1936.
3. Thurso Papers II, Box 60, File 5, Sinclair to Harcourt Johnstone, 17 February 1936.
4. Clement Davies Papers, J/3/26i, Davies to Gilbert Murray, 11 May 1950.
5. Interview with Sir Leonard Smith, 25 July 1988. See also Roger Levy, 'Third Party Decline in the U.K.: The S.D.P. and S.N.P. in Comparative Perspective', *West European Politics*, II, no. 3 (July 1988) for the importance of electoral success to the internal cohesion of small cadre prties.
6. Thurso Papers II, Box 60, File 1, Sinclair to Harcourt Johnstone, 21 September 1936; and Clement Davies Papers, T/5/32, 'A few notes by Sir Henry Morris-Jones for use by or by the direction only of Mrs. Clement Davies, if desired'.
7. Thurso Papers II, Box 58, File 1, Sinclair to Sir Francis Acland, 6 March 1936.
8. Thurso Papers II, Box 60, File 1, Sinclair to Harris, 24 April 1936.
9. Interview with Emrys Roberts, 11 August 1987.
10. Thurso Papers IV, Box 1, File 10, Davies to Sinclair, 12 April 1946.

11. Lloyd George Papers, House of Lords Record Office, G/19/7/6, 'Notes on the Political Situation', 26 November 1933, by Sir William Sutherland.
12. Lloyd George Papers, House of Lords Record Office, H/127, *Scotsman*, 17 April 1935.
13. Crewe Papers, Box C/44, Samuel to Crewe, 25 and 27 October 1938.
14. Samuel Papers, A/142/6, *The Times*, 12 May 1955.
15. Cardiganshire LiberalAssociation, Item 53, General Correspondence 1953-6, Correspondence with Liberal Headquarters, 1953-9, *Manchester Guardian*, 11 April 1953.
16. Clement Davies Papers, J/3/22, Davies to Sinclair, 28 April 1950.
17. Thurso Papers II, Box 60, File 5, Brock to Sinclair, 22 July 1936.
18. Thurso Papers II, Box 62, File 1, Sinclair to Brock, 19 October 1937.
19. Conservative Party Archives, CC03/4/74, 'Liberal Party Questionnaire'; and CC03/3/92, Marjorie Maxse to A.E. Holdsworth, 9 October 1951.
20. N.L.W. Ms. 20487E, Lloyd George Mss. 3425, Volume of Press Cuttings relating to Megan Lloyd George 1932-5, *The Times*, 3 August 1934.
21. Thurso Papers II, Box 64, File 2, Atholl Robertson to W.R. Davies, n.d.
22. Thurso Papers II, Box 30, File 3, Sinclair to Harold Macmillan, 19 August 1936.
23. Lloyd George Papers, House of Lords Record Office, G/6/15/2, Fildes to Sylvester, 13 August 1934.
24. Samuel Papers, House of Lords Record Office, A/155/VIII/85, Harcourt Johnstone to Samuel, 26 July 1934.
25. Conservative Party Archives, CC03/3/103, *Why National Liberal?* by Lord Milverton and eight former Independent Liberal parliamentary candidates.
26. Samuel Papers, House of Lords Record Office, A/129/17, Milverton to Willingdon, 16 April 1950.
27. N.L.W. Ms. 20475C, Lloyd George Mss. 3127-3182, letters to Megan Lloyd George, Violet Bonham-Carter to Megan Lloyd George, 17 November 1947.
28. Clement Davies Papers, J/3/23, Sinclair to Davies, 3 May 1950.
29. Conservative Party Archives, CC03/1/63, Piersenné to Blair, 20 June 1949.
30. Conservative Party Archives, CC04/3/44, Piersenné to Hay, 30 March 1950.
31. Conservative Party Archives, CC01/8/541, J.P.L. Thomas, 'Negotiations with the Liberals'. Sent to Woolton, Piersenné and Maxse, 15 September 1950.
32. Butler Papers, H16, Thomas to Butler, 14 February 1951; and Butler to Thomas, 16 Feburary 1951.
33. Conservative Party Archives, CC01/9/100-101, 'Note of Interview between G. Rawsthorne, Chairman Bolton W. and the G.[eneral] D.[irector]', 8 June 1953.
34. Thurso Papers II, Box 18, File 2, Harris to Sinclair, 15 March 1934.
35. Western Counties Liberal Federation, Minute Book 1927-1963, Finance and General Purposes Committee, 18 February 1939.
36. Lord Davies of Llandinam Papers, A/13/5, 'Lord Davies's Address at Liberal Gathering, Plas Dinam, 14 January 1939'.
37. Thurso Papers II, Box 58, File 2, W.R. Davies to Sinclair, 29 May 1936.
38. Thurso Papers II, Box 25, File 2, Charles Sutherland to Sinclair, 1 November 1935.

References

Addison, P. (1975), *The Road to 1945: British politics and the Second World War*, London, Jonathan Cape.

Brier, A.P. (1967), 'A study of Liberal Party constituency activity in the mid 1960s', Exeter University, Ph.D. thesis.

Coote, C. (1965), *Editorial*, London, Eyre & Spottiswoode.

Craig, F.W. (1975), *British General Election Manifestos 1900–1974*, London, Macmillan

Duverger, M. (1954), *Political Parties: Their organisation and activity in the modern state*, London, Methuen.

Fulford, R. (1959), *The Liberal Case*, Harmondsworth, Penguin.

Harris, Rt. Hon. Sir P. (1946), *Forty Years in and out of Parliament*.

Lemieux, P. (1977), 'The Liberal Party and British political change: 1955–1974', Massachusetts Institute of Technology, Ph.D. thesis.

Levy, R. (1988), 'Third party decline in the U.K.: the S.D.P. and S.N.P. in comparative perspective', *West European Politics*, 2, no. 3.

Milne, R.S. (1966), *Political Parties in New Zealand*, Oxford University Press.

Pimlott, B. (ed.) (1986), *The Political Diary of Hugh Dalton. 1918–40 and 1945–60*, London, Jonathan Cape.

Rasmussen, J.S. (1964), *The Liberal Party: a study of retrenchment and revival*, London, Constable.

Rhodes James, R. (1986), *Anthony Eden*, London, Weidenfeld & Nicholson.

Rose, R. and Mackie, T. (1984), *Do Parties Persist or Disappear? The big tradeoff facing organisations: Studies in Public Policy 134*, Glasgow, Centre for the Study of Public Policy.

Wallace, W. (1968), 'The Liberal Revival: The Liberal Party in Britain, 1955–1966', Cornell University, Ph.D. thesis.

Wallace, W. (1983), 'Survival and Revival' in V. Bogdanor (ed.), *Liberal Party Politics*, Oxford University Press.

3 New tricks for an old dog?: The Conservatives and social policy, 1951–5

Harriet Jones

The General Election of October 1951 resulted in a slim majority for the Conservative Party; in fact, the Party polled fewer votes than Labour, although it won more seats. The central issues of the campaign were the war in Korea and the state of the economy; social policy was of concern primarily as it affected the latter. In general, there was little public debate on social policy and the party manifestos differed little in their proposals. The Conservatives were still pledged not to tamper with the basic structure of the welfare state, and had also burdened themselves with the promise of producing 300,000 houses a year. At the same time, however there was much talk of 'setting the people free' and of the 'property-owning democracy'. The economy was in a grave condition, worse even than the party had suspected; and it was difficult to see how all of these conflicting and vague commitments could be carried through in any cohesive fashion. But it did appear that a trend towards moderate, consensual politics in post-war Britain was emerging. Gaitskell, from the Right of the Labour Party, was succeeded as Chancellor by Butler, and the 'Butskellist' era which followed was indeed marked by its lack of *sudden* change.[1]

However, at least in the field of social policy, underneath this veneer of consensual politics there lay deep differences between party attitudes towards the state provision of social benefits. Indeed, it is fair to say that the differences between Labour and Conservative social policy from 1950 were actually growing more pronounced, if rank-and-file opinion is anything to go on. Thus, for example, on the basis of party conference motions, Labour was calling for comprehensive secondary schools, and in 1953 called for bringing selected public schools into the state system, while the Conservatives from 1950 were vehemently opposed to any change in the grammar school system.

33

In *Challenge to Britain* Labour declared as housing policy the aim of bringing all privately rented accommodation under the control of the local authorities, and a conference motion carried in 1954 reaffirmed that 'housing must be made a social service operated for the benefit of the people and not for private profit'.[2] Meanwhile Conservative manifestos and statements were stressing greater private ownership through the jargon of the 'property-owning democracy,' and conference motions urged the reduction of public housing subsidies with greater confidence throughout the decade. Similarly, with regard to the National Health Service, Labour policy called for the reduction of charges, put stress on the development of health centres, and hinted at the abolition of private beds in NHS hospitals; while Conservative policy began to stress the development of private medicine and the expansion of means-tested benefits in the health service.[3]

The fact was that consensus in British domestic policy had less to do with agreement than with the limited choices which faced the governments of those years. The Labour administration had been forced to impose charges on NHS patients, and to cut back other social services as a result of slow economic recovery from the war. The new Conservative ministers found that their freedom to change policies was limited, not only by the economy but in other ways as well. So even if radical ministers had come into office with the intention of carrying out sweeping changes to the new welfare state, their ability to change the system would nevertheless have been hampered by a combination of factors: the economy, local authority power, civil service bureaucracy, a prime minister whose main domestic objective was to play it safe, a strong and confident trade union movement, demographic changes, and above all, the climate of public opinion. The enormity of these considerations was such that one is struck when going through the records by the few choices available to ministers in the social services sector. In short, the social policy record of the 1951–5 government reveals a consensus born of constraint.

It would be a mistake, though, to conclude that there were no differences between the social policies of the Labour and Conservative eras. Social policy did change markedly under the Conservatives, albeit slowly. The pace of change was hindered to a large extent, for example, by the logistics of social administration. Until 1953, in fact, the Conservatives were essentially overseeing the plans approved under Labour ministers. It simply takes several years for policy changes to filter through the system; the schools opened in 1952, for example, were approved in the previous decade. This 'bathtub curve' exacerbates the apparent consensus in social policy administration, and helps smooth the transition of political power. Already by 1955, a Conservative style of welfare administration was emerging in Britain, and this difference should not be underestimated when assessing the extent to which the 'consensus' argument is still a valid one.

The smooth transition from Labour to Conservative in the social services ministries also owed a great deal to Churchill's choice of ministers. Butler, Macmillan, and later Iain Macleod and David Eccles, were all pragmatic and moderate men with no burning wish to overturn the new welfare system. The emphasis was put rather on efficiency and good administration; decisions were made more often than not on the basis of economic capacity rather than the necessity for change.

As far as the Prime Minister's personal opinions were concerned, Churchill had only vague and general ideas on social policy and was, of course, preoccupied with international diplomacy. The position of the 'common man' could capture his emotions in a romantic sort of way from time to time, but his record since the war, when his support for the Beveridge Plan had been lukewarm, was based on hot and cold war politics. He rarely waded into the domestic side of things in these last years of his leadership, and when he did it was generally on a flight of fancy which betrayed his distance from and ignorance of modern life.

For example, in the early autumn of 1954 Churchill took the Ministry of Pensions and National Insurance to task over the cost of living for pensioners. Apparently at Chartwell he had come across the announcement that the price of tea was to be raised by 8d in the pound. In a sudden flash of sympathy he requested an investigation into the possibility of a programme of cheap milk and tea for pensioners. Cabinet Secretary and close friend Sir Norman Brook patiently wrote back explaining that it would really be much easier simply to raise pensions; and an attached memorandum from the Minister, Osbert Peake, estimated in some detail that, while certainly a kind gesture, such a plan would cost an extra £30 million a year to the Exchequer. Rather touchingly, the Prime Minister marked the memorandum 'Lady Churchill to see'.[4]

All this is not to say, however, that apart from such outbursts Churchill ignored or had no feeling for social policy. Indeed, he gave unwavering support to the housing programme from the outset, and refused to reconsider his position when it became apparent that Macmillan's efforts were placing the economy under considerable strain.[5] But he was interested in the grand ideas rather than the mechanics of social policy.

Churchill's acceptance of the welfare state was tied up with the government's general attitude towards labour problems. Just as Walter Monckton was directed to avoid industrial conflict at all cost, so too were the social services ministers warned off controversial proposals. The Prime Minister sharply rebuked ministers responsible for any hint of press disapproval, and in Cabinet favoured the path least likely to stir up trouble.[6] It is worth noting as well that when TUC General Secretary Vincent Tewson voiced his criticism of specific social policy proposals, his correspondence was always taken most seriously with every effort made to smooth his ruffled feathers.[7] Such was the strength of the trade unions in these years, that TUC co-operation with social policy proposals was vital to ensure success.

It is also clear that the Prime Minister did not always personally approve of the policies which he went along with. His own views reveal a much less modern outlook than the impression often given by his government's policies. This is true especially in education, where he held rather Victorian opinions on what one should do with idle boys.[8] There is also evidence that he took Lord Moran's advice, on the best ways to cut back the NHS, quite seriously.[9] In public, however, Churchill was careful to nurture an impression of fatherly approval of modern social policy. He was deeply wounded in 1953 when, in his autobiography, Lord Beveridge charged that Churchill had frozen him out of official discussion surrounding his report during the war (Beveridge, 1953: 319). The left-wing press took up the story, and the *Mirror*'s Cassandra wrote an especially virulent piece with the headline 'Did Churchill try to Scotch the Beveridge Plan.'[10] Of course Beveridge was largely correct; the PM's distaste for the 'father' of the welfare state was no secret. But Churchill was beside himself. 'To read this scribbler Cassandra you would imagine that there was some elaborate, complicated intrigue or boycott,' he noted irritably.[11]

One is left with the impression that here was a great statesman who was forced to watch the emerging tensions of Cold War politics from the sidelines, because his party suffered disastrous defeat in 1945 largely on domestic issues. He had no particular allegiance to Conservative dogma on social policy; indeed his personal record in the area dated largely from his Liberal early years in politics. When re-elected in 1951, it was with a slim majority in the House. Churchill was well aware at the time of the nervy state of public opinion on what his government would attempt to do (or undo) on the domestic front. Anxious above all to secure international negotiations on the reduction of East–West tensions, he had good reason to ensure that domestic conflict would not hamper his diplomatic efforts. Thus, in industrial relations he directed that there should be no confrontation with the unions, and in social policy that the public must be reassured that Conservative intentions were not reactionary. This explains his choice of moderate leaders for ministerial posts, and should provide the context in which to assess the government's record on the welfare state.

The first few months of Butler's Chancellorship were dominated by a balance of payments crisis. A new drain on the country's gold reserves had been exacerbated by the rearmament programme, which had caused so much controversy in the last years of the Labour government. On the advice of Treasury officials and with the full support of the Prime Minister, Butler undertook a series of remedial measures to cut public spending. In the social services sector this hit education and the health service the hardest. Opposition protest was muted, however, because the Labour government from 1949 had also been forced to take harsh measures, approving NHS charges, and developing strict building regulations for the schools and for the design of smaller council houses.

Butler's biggest headache was the housing programme. It was indeed foolhardy to try to carry out the pledge of building 300,000 houses in light of the country's precarious economic situation. But in the first of a long series of clashes with Macmillan, Butler found it difficult to challenge the authority of a strong, determined and ambitious minister; and it was exasperating when Macmillan would agree amiably in Cabinet to make vague cuts, but would completely ignore Cabinet instructions in issuing orders to his civil servants. And, at least at the beginning, Macmillan's relationship with Churchill was such that he got away with it.[12] So the housing drive continued, hampered only by the materials shortage which affected steel and softwood supplies.

Butler himself was no economist. Churchill, moreover, still did not fully trust him, and appointed a series of people in strategic positions in an attempt to check his actions.[13] Thus he proved at first to be a cautious Chancellor. He also very early on formed an alliance with his powerful civil servants, heavily reliant on them for advice and support. This partly explains the 'Butskellist' temperament of his economic policy, as it soon came to be known. Butler personally believed in Keynesian economics and in the role of the state in regulating the economy, although there were certainly significant differences of outlook between himself and Gaitskell.[14] He was deeply troubled by the implications of heavy expenditure on the welfare state, and this discomfort continued well after the economic situation had eased. In a Cabinet memorandum of May 1952 he wrote:

> [The] task of winning national solvency through production and export must not be subordinated to other objectives—defence, social services, etc.—which, however desirable in themselves, do not contribute directly to our paramount aim and which would in any event be impossible to achieve if we failed in our first task.
>
> Apart from defence...the main fields of Government expenditure are social services, education, and subsidies. We must face the fact that no major changes are possible in any of these without changes in basic policy, and that such a change involves major political difficulties and will require very careful consideration. Nevertheless it is vital that we should prevent the very large claims which the Government makes on the economy from rising any further and that we should make all possible economies, however small they may be individually, so as to reduce them as far as we may.[15]

Butler's dilemma was clearly expressed. He perceived a need to change social services policy in order to curb rapidly rising expenditure, but was hampered by the force of public opinion which desired freedom from rationing and other controls, but was still firmly behind the ideals of the welfare state. Raising the standard of living is rarely compatible with comprehensive social services provisions, however, and in that sense the public was expecting the impossible from the Conservatives, who had promised to 'set the people free', without reversing Labour social policy.

The political dilemma facing any Chancellor wanting to slow the growth of spending on the welfare state was such that even colleagues well to the Right of

Butler on the issue were still cautious where social policy was concerned. Lord Woolton, one of his most vehement adversaries in the government, advised Churchill, 'I have no doubt about the wisdom of making severe cuts in Government expenditure, but . . . we shall find ourselves in politically difficult waters if we begin by making serious cuts in the social services.'[16]

In his first budget of March 1952, Butler skirted the problem by cutting food subsidies by £160 million, thus enabling him to distribute rewards elsewhere in the budget, raising pensions and other benefits for example, as had been promised in the manifesto. His good fortune continued as well, as external economic conditions ran in his favour. With the easing of the terms of trade, the balance of payments problem righted itself, and Butler did not have much cause for serious worry again until 1955. But the basic conflict in Conservative policy continued, however well disguised by the slow healing of the economy. The party's road to prosperity fundamentally involved a freedom from controls and a decreasing state role in the working of the economy, goals which were basically incompatible with a large welfare state. The decision not to change or reverse social policy was taken primarily because of the fear of political reprisal, and as discussed earlier, because of the Prime Minister's particular desire not to rock the boat over domestic issues. This meant that the political transfer of power from Labour to Conservative did not seem to have much effect on social policy.

Meanwhile, other party colleagues were far from satisfied that Butler was moving fast enough along the road to a 'property-owning democracy'. As the new government settled into office, pressure steadily increased to make more drastic changes in the structure of the post-war economy. Woolton, in particular, championed this cause, and in 1952 began to press his case in earnest. 'I think you may like to know,' he confided to Churchill,

> that I told the Home Affairs Committee last Friday that I thought we were making small progress with our professed desire to set the people free, and that we had done little to reduce the cost of Government. I said that I thought it was important, both for the economic life of the nation and for its pleasure, that we should reduce the amount of taxation, but we could not do this until we had reduced the cost of Government.[17]

Woolton urged the high-spending Ministers to press forward with cuts in public services. In particular, he targeted housing, which represented one of the major long-term drains on the Exchequer, and submitted a Cabinet memorandum on the subject of a property-owning democracy to argue his case. In it, he reasoned that housing policy was concentrating too much on council housing, and that private sector housing should be increased far more rapidly than had been previously contemplated. He proposed to subsidize the private sector, and argued that private building subsidies 'would remove in some measure the herding of more people into these huge County Council housing areas, which become predominantly Socialist in political outlook'.[18]

However, Woolton did not make much progress. In 1952 domestic economic production was still limited strictly by materials shortages, and that as much as anything else dictated the continuing need for close controls on investment. Macmillan fought against the reduction of council house building for several years, and the Ministry of Housing and the Treasury could not agree on terms for private housing subsidies. In the other big domestic spending ministries there was simply no fat left to trim. 'Setting the people free' proved to be a very difficult principle to put into practice.

Butler could not take the political risk of the more drastic changes which Woolton and his supporters wanted to see, and the task of trying to control social services expenditure therefore fell back on the budget. Long after the immediate economic crisis had eased, Butler still continued to enforce extremely strict expenditure levels on the high-spending ministries. This affected the day-to-day financing problems of the NHS and education programme as well as the other social services ministries—staffing levels, the availability of supplies, the level of benefits, etc.—but the most serious casualty was undoubtedly long-term investment.

Labour had had the time to pass the new legislation, but had not been in any position after the war to put much towards a social services investment programme. By 1953 the Conservatives were in such a position and failed to take advantage of it. By 1955 there were new investment programmes for action on the schools and hospitals, but strictly limited in scope. Housing, for one thing, had been allowed to drain any excess financing away from the other service sectors, again because Butler proved unable to curb Macmillan's fanatical determination. In addition to that, the whole structure of investment financing was altered in 1953, as a part of the larger effort to free the economy.[19] Because the materials shortage had eased, the Treasury saw no need to continue to vet building investment programmes across the whole economy. Henceforth only public sector investment was strictly controlled. This meant that cinemas, shops, office blocks and so on were free to be built as private resources allowed, and on one level this drained building resources away from social projects like schools, health centres and hospitals. But more importantly, a conscious decision was made to limit social services investment, no matter what resources were available to proceed. From 1954 the public housing programme began to fall, while at the same time investment resources were rising at an annual rate of about £100mn.[20] This opportunity was even more dramatic than the numbers show, as housing investment had wide implications over the whole social sector. Especially in the new towns and on the larger housing estates, new schools, hospitals and other public facilities had to be built to accommodate the shift of population. The money which was saved as the number of new housing subsidies declined could have been reinvested in the long-term development of the social services. But this the government failed to do, preferring instead to initiate a more modest investment programme. The failure of the government to reinvest available funds in the future of the social services is indeed one of the principle criticisms to be made of its social services record. This is where the chant of 'thirteen wasted years' takes on some validity.

Another basic problem facing the Conservatives was the nature of the role of local government in determining how resources were to be spent. While central government ministries played a strategic role in defining policy objectives, it was still the local housing authorities which decided how many and what sort of houses to build, the local education authorities which decided when and where to build the schools and how many teachers to employ, and the local health authorities which decided how to allocate NHS resources. While Whitehall retained considerable financial authority over many of these programmes, its punitive power was largely indirect and difficult to exercise stringently without incurring widespread political debate, which was exactly what Churchill was directing his ministers to avoid.

One obstacle was that the local authorities with the largest social programmes naturally tended to be those with a tradition of social deprivation, and in the general scheme of things, such areas tend to be Labour strongholds. This meant that the authorities which were really crucial to win over to a policy of stringency and economy were often the most obstructive politically. For example, the authorities with the largest council housing programmes were generally Labour controlled, and had quite a large rent pool to reinvest in continued building. Thus central government under the Conservatives at this time was generally flexible in negotiations with local government, in part to avoid political controversy with popular local Labour leaders, and in part because local governments wielded a great deal of power.

There were also other factors at work in the 1950s which complicated the task of rolling back the welfare state. Demographic changes in British society put increasing pressure on the social services. To give just one example, long-term decline in mortality rates combined with general worry over a long-term decline in the birth rate meant that Britain was faced with an 'ageing' population. The proportion of the population over the age of 65 has been rising throughout this century: in 1921, for example, the proportion was 6 per cent, but by 1951 the figure had risen to nearly 11 per cent. This meant that there would be continuing pressure on the cost of pensions, and indeed pensions policy proved to be a continuing headache for the government.[21] Less obviously, an ageing population also places increasing strain on health expenditure, as more money has to be set aside for geriatric care. Similarly, the housing needs of the elderly imply expenditure on sheltered accommodation. These were the sorts of problems which many Conservatives had not anticipated and about which they could do absolutely nothing.

When the Conservatives entered office in 1951, they were determined to limit the growth of the welfare state. To their dismay, however, chasing the carrot of reduced state spending on the social services turned out to be like a hurdling event with no finishing-line. Even factors within the control of the government were not managed as well as they could have been. Churchill's own lack of interest in domestic matters was part of this problem; the vacuum at the top meant that management of domestic policy lacked the co-ordination necessary to implement a balanced programme. This was not helped either by the friction between Butler and Macmillan.

Nevertheless, despite the obstacles militating against change, between 1951 and 1955 there was a gradual shift of emphasis in social policy. Instead of expanding services provided by the public sector, the government exercised financial controls to reduce the scale of the programmes initiated under the Labour administration, although the cost of the welfare state continued to rise. At the Ministry of Housing, Macmillan did indeed reach and even exceed the target of 300,000 houses; in the short term this meant that council house building was expanded. But at the same time the standards of council housing were cut right back to the minimum acceptable level, and a long-term policy decision was taken to allow the housing market to be run with minimal intervention from the state. By 1955 local authorites were no longer permitted to build for 'general needs' but were directed instead to concentrate on targeting slum clearance projects. This was the housing equivalent of a means test; in many ways the housing sector had turned back to the model of the 1930s.

Education policy under the Churchill government did not enjoy such a high profile as housing. The Butler Act of 1944 had been generally welcomed by both parties, and Labour policy had been broadly concerned with its implementation, so that there was little contentious policy for the Conservatives to challenge in power. The problems in education in those years stemmed more from underinvestment. The schools had suffered considerably in the war years, both through direct war damage and through a lack of maintenance. In the 1950s there were increasing numbers of children entering the primary schools as a result of a mini baby boom which ended in 1948, and the Ministry was still coping with the new pressures brought about by universal secondary education. Thus the Ministry had a good case for a large investment programme, but the government neglected to remedy these problems. What is more relevant to this discussion, however, is the growth of controversy in the 1950s over the nature of secondary education. The Butler Act represented a brittle consensus; it was agreed that all children were entitled to some form of secondary schooling, but the debate over the structure of secondary education was left to simmer. By 1955 the question of comprehensive versus tripartite schools was becoming one of the most important issues facing British society, and the argument was divided along ideological lines. Education had become a party issue again, so that here too the existence of a basic consensus is questionable.[22]

The party entered office determined to curb health expenditure, but found it very difficult to do so without dismantling much of the NHS, and this would have been virtually impossible to do without sparking off an explosion of protest. So while in the short term the government continued to support the health service, an independent inquiry was set up to consider ways in which the growth of health expenditure could be contained in the future. The government originally hoped that politically independent advice would enable them to carry out long-term policy changes to the service which would curb expenditure and avoid the provision of free universal health care with a minimum of public controversy. However, the Guillebaud Report of 1956 which resulted was rather a disaster from this point of view, in that it was highly complimentary of the present structure of the NHS, and the party found itself forced into a long-term acceptance of its recommendations. Consequently, while Conservative health policy continued to support the NHS, this had less to do with support for a universal health service, than with a political inability to turn away from this highly popular programme.[23]

So to conclude, there are two basic points to bear in mind when considering the social policy of the Churchill government. First, the party continued to administer Labour's welfare state, and indeed expenditure on the social services expanded in the 1950s. But consensus here was not the product of what has been called the 'new Conservatism'. Instead, there were a bewildering number of obstacles to overcome in those years. It had proved to be far more difficult in practice to curb social services expenditure than the party had anticipated. The government was simply unwilling to risk the political controversy involved in making basic social policy changes: for one thing they had pledged in the manifesto not to do so, and for another, with a small majority in the House, they were in no position to make major changes even if the will had been there.

Clearly, the Conservatives were never comfortable with such a large role for the state in the provision of social benefits, and there continued to be considerable pressure from within the party to take a faster road away from the welfare state. This brings us to the second point: while there were no dramatic reversals of social policy under Churchill, it is nevertheless true that by 1955 the Conservatives had put their own stamp on the social services. As far as it was possible in that era to turn away from Labour's 'fair shares' model and toward a 'property-owning democracy', the government did so. Conservative objectives in social policy in the 1950s were no different from what they had ever been.

Notes

1. The term originates from an article on economic policy in *The Economist*, 13 February 1954, pp. 439–41.
2. For a record of party conference decisions, see Craig, 1975.
3. The Labour position on private medicine emanated from the NEC; see Seldon, 1981, p. 579. The 1955 Conservative Manifesto states that 'private practice and

contributory schemes have a part to play'.

4. PRO, PREM11/710, 20 September 1954.
5. He was unswayed, overriding the advice of Lord Cherwell in support of Butler's opinion (PRO, PREM11/688). See also PRO, T229/476, Churchill to Butler, 25 October 1952.
6. One thinks, for example, of Churchill's reaction to a press leak on proposed education cuts (PRO, PREM11/88, December 1951). See also his reaction to planned cuts in further education (PRO, PREM11/385).
7. See, for example, PRO, PREM11/86 on proposals to lower the school-leaving age; PRO, CAB128/25, C.C. (52)59 on the scrapping of a proposed inquiry into the future of the pensions scheme; PRO, CAB128/26, part I, C.C. (53)18 on cuts to adult education; and Churchill's reply to the latter, PRO, PREM11/385, March 1953.
8. PRO, PREM11/84.
9. PRO, PREM11/495.
10. *Mirror*, 19 November 1953.
11. PRO, PREM11/730.
12. See, for example, PRO, HLG68/76, Macmillan note, 7 November 1951.
13. See Howard, 1987, pp. 180-2. Many of the leading powers in the Party continued to mistrust Rab Butler, and although his relationship with Churchill improved enormously during the life of the government, he had at first a weak relationship with Number 10.
14. Lord Butler, 1982, p. 160. 'I shared neither his convictions, which were unquenchably Socialist, nor his temperament, which allowed his emotion to run away with him rather too often, nor his training which was that of an academic economist. Both of us, it is true, spoke the language of Keynesianism, but we spoke it with different accents and with a differing emphasis.'
15. PRO, CAB129/52, C. (52)166, 17 May 1952.
16. PRO, PREM11/132, 28 December 1951.
17. PRO, CAB124/1164, Woolton to Churchill, 28 June 1952.
18. PRO, CAB129/53, C. (52)207, 20 June 1952.
19. See PRO, T229/484. The Investment Programmes Committee was replaced with the Treasury Investment Committee.
20. PRO, T229/668, TIC memorandum, 8 December 1953.
21. See, for example, PRO, CAB128/24, C.C. (52)27, 7 March 1952.
22. PRO, ED34/192.
23. PRO, T227/333.

References

Craig, F.S. (1975), *Conservative and Labour Party Conference Decisions 1945-1981*, London, Macmillan.

Lord Beveridge (1953), *Power and Influence*, London, Hodder and Stoughton.

Lord Butler (1952), *The Art of the Possible*, London, Macmillan.

Howard, A. (1987), *RAB: The life of R.A. Butler*, London, Jonathon Cape.

Seldon, A. (1981), *Churchill's Indian Summer*, London, Hodder and Stoughton.

4 Popular politics, affluence and the Labour party in the 1950s

Nick Tiratsoo

Right now the basic insecurity the workers feel is this: they are haunted by the spectre of the van driving to the door to take away the T.V. set.

(Elizabeth Braddock, Labour MP)

And most of all—most, most of all—what do we know about 'uneducated' people, their daily lives, their vast pop culture? The answer is nothing much.

(Colin MacInness, *Encounter*, April 1959[1])

In looking at some of the literature which deals with popular politics in the period from the end of the Second World War to the early 1960s, it is difficult not to be struck by a sense of contrast.[2] Descriptions of the later 1940s, in particular, often carry a strong radical flavour and emphasize the degree of class antagonism. Raphael Samuel, for example, has remembered that period in the following terms:

The polarization of opinion between Left and Right, already overwhelming in 1945, grew even more dominant in the subsequent years, with regional differences succumbing to national opinion. Two great parties with huge memberships rising to an all-time peak in the early 1950s, confronted each other in two class blocs ... The vertical division between 'us' and 'them', however these might be defined, was the dominant idiom in the perception of social life, informing not only politics and culture but also personal comportment.

(Samuel, 1985: 9)

Yet, against this, the late 1950s and early 1960s seem to have a rather different character. Working-class interest in politics, especially radical politics, now appears as the preserve of the minority, with the majority either apathetic or subscribing unenthusiastically to a loose Conservatism. The focus of popular concern has shifted, becoming most closely associated, perhaps, with a new kind of consumerism. Viv Nicholson's priorities on winning the pools in 1961—hair dyed champagne blonde, a new Chevrolet Impala, a holiday in Las Vegas and a Spanish-style bungalow in Garforth called 'The Ponderosa' (Nicholson and Smith, 1977)—seem to convey the essence of the now typical approach to life.

The aim of the following paragraphs is to look in a little more detail at this apparent change in the make-up of popular politics, by first analysing its dimensions and then going on to look at various propositions that have been advanced in explanation. Particular attention will be given to the ways in which affluence might have modified working-class attitudes, since it has often been argued, quite bluntly, that the popularity of shopping and the unpopularity of politics which observers noted of the late 1950s were not unrelated. Put in its most dramatic form, can it be concluded, as Blackwell and Seabrook suggest, that this was a time when the working-class finally began succumbing to the embrace of capitalist materialism? (Blackwell and Seabrook, 1985: 82 and 111).

The first thing to settle in this enquiry is the size of the phenomenon to be explained. From the vantage point of late 1959, and the Conservatives' third successive General Election victory, working-class disillusionment with Labour looked massive, big enough even to threaten the future of the party, and subsequent interpretations, as has been indicated, have sometimes suggested that this judgement was somewhere near the truth. Does the evidence support this view of a major re-orientation of popular attitudes occurring over the decade, or was change perhaps more measured and uneven?

The case for a sharp decline in working-class involvement in politics, especially radical politics, during the 1950s is easily made. Data on election turn-outs, collected in Table 4.1, indicate a growing popular disinclination to vote, at least in England and Wales. Antipathy towards Labour, too, became considerably more developed as the decade wore on. Women were consistently less inclined to support the party than men, but there were now pronounced antagonistic swings amongst the young, and in certain geographic areas, notably the Midlands and the South East.[3] Given these trends, Labour's electoral performance could only be unimpressive. Local government results were variable,[4] but in national contests the position was bleak, with three straight defeats in 1951, 1955 and 1959, and a vote declining from 13.9 million (48.8 per cent of the total) at the first date to 12.2 million (43.8 per cent of the total) at the last (Butler and Sloman, 1980: 208–9). The party's predicament was summed up by its inability to gain new recruits except through union affiliation, so that individual membership fell by 13 per cent (117,969) between 1950 and 1960 (Labour Party, 1951 and 1961).

Such evidence seems clear-cut, but in fact a degree of caution is necessary in its interpretation. The first point to make is about perspective. For the data just quoted has sometimes been made to appear more dramatic by evaluating

Table 4.1 Turn-outs in national and local elections 1950–9, England and Wales
(all figures per cent)

Year	Elections for: Parliament	Admin. counties	County boroughs	Municipal boroughs and urban districts	Rural districts
1950	84		46	48	46
1951	83		44	46	45
1952		43	50	51	52
1953			45	47	47
1954			43	46	47
1955	77	37	44	45	48
1956			38	39	41
1957			40	44	45
1958		33	40	43	46
1959	79		41	42	42

Source: The Registrar General's *Annual Reports* 1951–61; and Butler and Sloman, 1980: 209–9.

it, more or less explicitly, against the proposition that class and party had just recently been very much in step. Yet it is as well to remember that even during Labour's parliamentary ascendancy between 1945 and 1951, working-class support was by no means all-pervasive. Zweig records that the popularity of socialist ideas amongst ordinary people varied considerably 'according to the industrial group, age, status, education and upbringing' (Zweig, 1952: 87). Doris Lessing's *In Pursuit of the English*, recording her impressions on arriving in London during 1949, reinforces this view, since the world she found was almost totally unconnected to any form of party politics (Lessing, 1960).

Conversely, it may equally be argued that the degree of support for Labour in the working class across the 1950s was perhaps more stable than at first sight seems likely. Part of the explanation for the party's poor electoral performance had, of course, to do anyway with shifting middle-class loyalties (Abrams, 1961: 342–3). Moreover, though the elections from 1951 to 1959 gave the Conservatives significant parliamentary majorities, as contests they were far from being overwhelmingly one-sided. The 1959 election was Labour's supposed nadir, yet in the months preceding polling day the party was certainly not considered an outsider (e.g. *The Economist*, 12 September 1959). In the event, Labour's campaign went well, until Gaitskell, as admitted by his biographer, made a major political blunder (promising the bribe, as his opponents were quick to interpret it, of stable tax rates if his party won) and turned things very much the Conservatives' way (Williams, 1982: 310–11). In the end, Labour lost, but only narrowly in terms of votes. Indeed, it has been calculated that, at any of the elections from 1951 to 1959, a net swing of three votes in a hundred from the Conservatives would have given victory to

Labour (Pinto-Duschinsky, 1970: 71). It may be concluded, therefore, that what needs to be explained about popular politics in the 1950s is not so much a rupture in working-class support for Labour, but rather a measured and uneven drift away from the party—but a drift which was nevertheless powerful enough to produce three General Election defeats.

What explains this change? Without doubt, some of Labour's problems stemmed from narrowly political factors, like the leadership blunder in 1959. But it has also been generally agreed that the party's predicament was too serious and too sustained to be explained only in these terms, and that reference must be made also to developments that were simultaneously occurring in the social and economic background of politics. Specifically, many have argued, this means giving due attention to the growing popular affluence of the 1950s, since it was this factor, more than any other, that corroded left-wing loyalties. If, as the social historian Harry Hopkins put it, 'Semi-detachment on the Open Plan sapped solidarity' (Hopkins, 1964: 372), how was this process supposed to be working?

For most commentators of the late 1950s and early 1960s, the answer to this question could not be conceived without reference to the social revolution that they felt had been in progress since around 1955—a revolution, to quote Hopkins again, 'according to Marks not Marx' (Hopkins, 1964: 315). In detail, what was being proposed here depended upon a number of interlinked assertions.[5] First, reference was made to the recent and severe period of austerity enforced by the impact of the war. Next, it was argued that with the lifting of rationing, there had been a transformation in the scale and character of popular consumption. Adults were spending more than ever before on luxuries and on items, like durables, which had previously been either unavailable or the general preserve only of the middle class. Teenagers, too, were playing an increasingly important role in many markets. Moreover, there had been significant developments in the infrastructure of selling— refurbished shops and greatly expanded advertising budgets. Finally came the social and political consequences. The new pattern of spending, so it seemed, was tending to make people more inward-looking, more concerned with their own particular problems and possibilities. One example of this was the growth of a teenage culture emphasizing individualism or group rather than class loyalty. Another was the emergence of a novel kind of companionate marriage, reflecting men's greater commitment to their homes and their dependants and women's growing status in the restyled and partly automated domestic world. The result, it was concluded, must inevitably be a more conservative approach to politics. At the very least, the argument ran, previous class loyalties, with their emphasis on the collective, would now be increasingly revealed as inappropriate. At the same time, it seemed logical to believe that contentment with the current government's approach, with its stress on the possibilities for individual achievement, must be becoming more widespread. Put in a stronger form, the whole package of changes could be seen as amounting to a process of de-proletarianisation, in which working-class people were actually coming to see themselves as middle-class and thus 'naturally' Conservative. Politics, in this version, was being transformed by the rise of 'a new type of bourgeois worker' (Zweig, 1960: 400).

How seriously should these various claims be taken? The initial point to establish is whether or not there had been some kind of major change in relation to consumption over the 1950s, and here the contemporary view seems to hold good, as a brief review of the evidence on spending and the sales infrastructure indicates.

The upward trend in working-class consumption during the decade certainly cannot be doubted. Rationing continued in the early 1950s, limiting the choice and availability of goods (Hall, 1962). However, from around 1956 things changed very rapidly, with the upper-half of the working-class, especially enjoying something of a 'breakthrough' in standards (*The Economist* 26/12/1959; and Abrams, 1960: 57). Moreover, commentators of the time were clearly right in seeing this as a qualitative development. Data on the make-up of the new popular consumption patterns are not abundant, but they do point to increased expenditure on luxuries that had previously been well out of reach (for example, smart clothes and foreign holidays) (Abrams, 1964: 32–3); growing investment in a range of newly obtainable durables, like washing-machines and televisions; and a jump in home-ownership (Table 4.2). Finally, the perception that new sections of the population were being drawn into the consumption process also seems to be accurate. The much discussed arrival of the teenage consumer is a case in point. Youngsters had always been involved in the purchase of toys and novelties, but in the 1950s, the scope of their ambitions became almost totally transformed:

Table 4.2 Working-class home-ownership and possession of durable goods, 1957 and 1960 samples

Per cent of households:	*1957*	*1960*
Living in own house	24	29
In possession of		
TV set	53	78
Lawn mower	33	34
Washing-machine	21	37
Car	17	22
Refrigerator	5	13

Source: Abrams in *The Observer* 23 October 1960.

Before the war many young workers handed over their earnings to 'Mum' and received back an austere allowance of a few shillings to cover fares, snacks, and pocket money. In the post-war world the roles tend to be reversed. 'Mum' is given £1 or £2 as a contribution to the family's household expenditure and the young earner holds onto the rest. Compared with the younger workers of [the pre-war years] the working boy or girl of today are magnificently well off, and their spending is one of the mainstays of many flourishing markets.

(Abrams, 1956: 39)

As for the contemporary comment on innovations in the sales infrastructure, this, too, seems broadly correct. Millions were spent on shops and shopping centres during the 1950s, so that by 1960 many high streets had taken on an almost entirely new look (Hopkins, 1964: 314–5). Integral to this restyling was the spread of the multiple and the large self-service grocery outlet. In 1948 there had been only ten self-service shops in the whole of Britain. Twelve years later, the number was probably well in excess of 7,000, including 360 big new supermarkets.[6]

Accompanying this redevelopment had been a considerable increase, as Table 4.3 shows, in the scale of advertising, which was fuelled in part by the launch of commercial television during 1955. Finally, mention should also be made of some developments that were occurring in the popular medium that probably dealt most comprehensively with consuming, the women's magazines. Women's titles had, of course, always covered a range of topics to do with shopping and the home, but in the 1950s they were becoming decidedly more 'functional',[7] as, to quote their historian, 'the balance of power between editorial and advertising departments began to swing in favour of the latter' (White, 1970: 157). The end result was that women were offered publications where advertisements made up between 40 and 50 per cent of the total space, and in which much of the editorial content was of questionable independence (White, 1970: 197; and Rix, 1958: 84).

However, were these changes necessarily producing the social effects that contemporaries thought they detected? A definitive answer to this question is difficult, since much of the evidence is circumstantial, but three points seem

Table 4.3 Advertising expenditure 1950–60

Advertising expenditure:

	total (£m)	as proportion of nat. income	amount spent on TV adverts (£m)	per cent of total spent on TV adverts
1950	162	1.5	–	–
1956	309	1.8	11	3.4
1960	454	2.2	72	15.8

Source: The Advertising Association *Advertising Expenditure 1960* (1962) pp. 27 and 32.

worthy of note. First, it may readily be agreed that some reordering of popular attitudes and aspirations was certainly occurring because of the consumer boom. This was most visible amongst teenagers, with the emergence of pop culture. But it was also detectable in the wider adult environment. Consumption for ordinary people in the 1950s, it has been pointed out, was no longer simply about eking out scarce resources, but had come to involve a growing measure of choice and, because of the wider availability of luxuries, pleasure. Consequently, many were willing to invest time and money preparing for, and enjoying, consuming as never before. Thus, to return to an example already discussed, though the changes in women's magazines over the decade were generally regretted by 'high brow' critics, their effect on the ordinary reader was wholly different, and circulations boomed (Rix, 1958: 84–5). But the reverse side of this coin was that other aspects of life inevitably attracted less interest. The relative priorities of a sample of 1500, interviewed at the beginning of 1960, illustrate the general mood:

> The...survey provided abundant evidence that rather than discuss politics the average citizen greatly prefers to discuss a new car model or clothes styles. When neighbours and workmates turned to him (or her) for an opinion, it was rarely about politics. Although the survey was carried out only a few months after the General Election of 1959 only one-third of the respondents could recall any recent occasion on which anyone had asked their advice on either national or local politics. On the other hand, three-quarters had been consulted about television programmes; a good deal more than three-quarters of the men had been asked to give their judgement on football teams and racing horses, and almost as many women had been asked for their views on clothes, washing machines and synthetic detergents. Apparently, it is mainly in the area of consumption and leisure that conversation and argument acquire a lively and widespread reality.
>
> (Abrams, 1964: 41)

Nevertheless, accepting this, it must also be emphasized that the case for a more fundamental transformation in working-class attitudes at this time is remarkably thin. Some researchers, it is true, met workers who claimed that they had become middle-class because of their new possessions (Turner, 1963: 97–8). However, a much larger body of evidence points to a continuity of values and behaviour, with change, if it was occurring at all, merely involving different ways of being working-class. The new pop culture appeared to be a significant departure, but a close examination of its characteristics reveals strong class patterning (Clarke *et al.*, 1975: 9–74). Elsewhere, even surface variation was absent. Firm data on the sexual division of labour in the home during the 1950s are scarce, but some survey results from 1962, summarized in Table 4.4, suggest that relations between men and women remained unaltered, with the companionate marriage hoped for rather than real. Again, looking at more general popular values, the striking thing is not their propensity to alter or even their fluidity, but rather their adherence to long-standing customs.

Table 4.4 Average time spent on various tasks in the home by men and women, from a sample of 1,250 adults interviewed in early 1962

	Men:	hours	minutes	Women:	hours	minutes
Preparing and eating meals		1	54		3	17
Housework			22		2	28
Knitting, sewing, child care, laundry			4		1	17
(Total time at home		7	30		11	24)

Source: Abrams, 1964: 46.

This was particularly true of older industrial communities, as John Summerfield found on a trip to Bolton in 1960, 22 years after he had worked there as a Mass Observer:

> Go into almost any pub and you would never deduce that this is the era of nuclear fission, computer thinking, sputniks, the cold war and all the rest of it. The winds of change *have hardly ruffled the surface of a single gill of best mild.*
> (Harrisson, 1961: 194)

It was also often the case on post-war housing estates in developing areas, environments which might have been thought to be most conducive to the spread of new norms. Peter Willmott could therefore end his 1958–9 study of one recently-built London overspill area at Dagenham by emphasizing this very point about persistence: the people of the inner-city slums who had settled in the new houses were clinging to their established values, so that, in his striking phrase, Dagenham could be seen as 'the East End reborn' (Willmott, 1963: 109).

Given this situation, it is unsurprising to find much middle-class opinion of the period not celebrating its growing influence but rather regretting the 'mediocrity' and 'intransigence' of the ordinary mind.[8] Indeed, seen from the Home Counties residence or the City boardroom, 'old fashioned' proletarian antipathies remained depressingly commonplace, as the editor of *The Director*, citing an Economic League study on class attitudes, ruefully remarked:

> Feelings against 'the rich' can crop up anywhere. It is often caused by newspaper reports of "expensive parties . . . young people 'at college' misbehaving, or deals in millions in the world of finance." Conspicuous wealth rather than wealth as such is resented. The attitude towards finance is basically that it is all a fiddle.[9]

The third point to make is about advertisers and advertising. Many argued at the time that the advertising agencies were playing a key role in promoting new values. There was much talk, then, of 'a commercialized society', of 'conditioning', and even of the 'hidden persuaders' having become the Fourth Estate. On the Left, at least, the self-interest which advertising was supposed to encourage could be directly correlated with the decline of radicalism (Samuel, 1960: 48–53). Nevertheless once again, a close examination of the evidence reveals the contemporary view to be somewhat exaggerated.

It can be conceded, of course, that as has been mentioned, the amount spent on advertising did increase very sharply over the decade. Against this, it must also be pointed out that expenditure tended to be concentrated on a relatively narrow range of products, so that many areas of consumption were not framed by advertising.[10] Moreover, the tone of advertising at this time tended to be fairly muted: advertisements that explicitly used the promise of status enhancement, for example, were virtually unknown (Pearson and Turner, 1965: 30).

Second, there is a considerably amount of data which suggest that the efficacy of advertising was not as great as many claimed. Some campaigns, for example, floundered on popular prejudice or had to be substantially redrawn to take account of popular attitudes. Thus, frozen foods were extensively promoted from the mid-1950s, but did not take off until the middle of the next decade. On the other hand, the promotional effort to push Limmits, an early slimming product, had to be rethought when research found that working-class women did not particularly mind being overweight, and indeed associated stoutness with a range of positive characteristics (Millar, 1963: 12; and Pearson and Turner, 1965: 126–31).

Consumer resistance of this kind was especially marked in relation to television advertising. The independent channel did, at first, seem like a golden opportunity to advertisers, and there were big increases in expenditure. However, the honeymoon period between the agencies and the television companies soon ended, as comprehensive results on viewers' attitudes began to emerge. Many people, it was found, did not like commercial breaks at all, and were actively irritated by the disruption of their favourite programmes (Tracey, 1957: 95; and *Advertiser's Weekly* 13 March 1959). A bigger problem for the agencies was the pattern of viewing that seemed to be prevalent in most households, since the television was revealed as rarely holding the full attention of all its audience. Thompson's survey of 1961, for example, involving interviews with 11,500 housewives, found that between 20 and 25 per cent of the women were actually out of the room while the television set was switched on during peak periods, while another 40 per cent were either combining viewing with some other activity or else 'not viewing' for other reasons. That left only 35 to 40 per cent paying full attention (Pearson and Turner, 1965: 207).

In the light of these points, it might be predicted that the structure of popular taste in the 1950s would be at least as remarkable for its conservatism as for its susceptibility to innovation, and this is in fact what the evidence reveals. Gallup surveys on the perfect meal illustrate the point well. In 1947 a sample of the public was asked what they would like on a special occasion, with no expense spared. Their answer was sherry; tomato soup; sole; roast chicken with roast potatoes, peas and sprouts; trifle and cream; cheese and biscuits; and coffee. In 1962, a repeat survey was given exactly the same answers, except that fruit salad was now favoured over trifle.[11]

All in all, then, the idea of a commercialized society filled with 'bourgeois workers' to explain Labour's difficulties in the 1950s is rather unsatisfactory. Many ordinary people were becoming more and more involved in consumption and related activities during the decade, but there is little evidence to indicate that this was in some way either convincing them of middle-class values or making them excessively prone to manipulation by vested interests. Can the new consumerism and the Left's demise be linked in any other way?

One potentially fruitful alternative approach is to look at the problem in a more interactive framework, and see Labour in the 1950s not as a helpless victim of economic and social change, but rather as, at least in part, the architect of its own failures. For one of the things that is noticeable about politics at this time is the way in which the two main parties differed in their approach to popular affluence, with the Conservatives welcoming developments, and Labour behaving much more ambiguously. How sharp was this contrast, and what evidence is there that it may have helped shape electoral choices?

Conservative reactions to developments in the late 1950s were in most cases very positive.[12] The party had decided after the 1955 election that it needed to monitor public opinion more closely, and consequently use was made over the following years of formal market research techniques to find out what was, and what was not, in the minds of the electorate (Hennessy, 1961: 238–56). The upshot of this was a recognition that prosperity had come to be a key issue, and a campaign, started well before the 1959 election, aimed at convincing the electorate that new interests and aspirations were very much in harmony with Conservatism. What was significant, here, was not only the basic premise, but also the way it was translated into propaganda. The Tory advertisements and leaflets featured a much wider and more imaginatively drawn set of stereotypes than had previously been usual—not just the 'young scientist' and the 'cloth-capped lumber-yard hand', but also the housewife, 'diverse young people', and 'a family washing its new small car'. The ambience was 'the classless world of the affluent suburbia', and the message was that the 'new people' with their new values were very much part of the Conservative dream (Hennessy, 1961: 238–256; and Sampson, 1968: 163–4).

By contrast with this, Labour's response to change was very much less straightforward. Opinions concerning consumerism, first, remained quite sharply polarized. Crosland welcomed developments and saw them as producing a greater equality of standards (Crosland, 1960b; 15–16; Crosland,

1981). In addition, there were occasional bursts of enthusiasm from the membership about just how different and exciting things were becoming, as when Mabel Crout reported on her 'Impressions of America' for readers of *Labour Woman*:

> The outstanding thing is Shopping, with a capital S... The most fascinating shops to me were the huge Food Markets.... They are really super. The variety and quantity (and, I must add, the quality) of foods is beyond anything we English ever see.... Meat is pre-weighed and wrapped in Cellophane with the weight and price clearly marked. For anyone preferring something specially cut and weighed there is no difficulty.... The purchasing of fruit and vegetables is a veritable joy.... All look so fresh by having ice placed between them. Some are pre-packed.... They can also.... be purchased loose, and for this you pick up a paper bag, select individually your apples... or whatever it might be, have them weighed and the price put on....
>
> I wonder what some of the retail greengrocers here would say if their customers suggested this kind of self-service. 'You're taking all the best,' I can imagine some of them saying. And why not? The method of putting the best in front and being served from behind would not be tolerated by the American housewife.[13]

A more common reaction, however, was one of suspicion. In part, this was fuelled by a nostalgia for the apparently disappearing world of the corner shop. The 'man behind the counter' was best, Mrs. Jean Mann MP of the National Labour Women's Advisory Committee told assembled Labour women, and anyway 'What man eating cornflakes wanted to be in danger of swallowing a toy submarine?' (Labour Party, 1958: 16). More usually, however, it stemmed from a deep mistrust not so much of the new methods and products, but more of the framework within which they were being introduced. The villains here were normally the 'smooth salesman' and the 'unscrupulous advertisers' who were daily employing 'immense resources' to mislead the public (Darling, 1955: 182–3; Socialist Union, 1956: 43–4; and Noel-Baker, 1959: 98–9). In this situation, argued the Socialist Union, if the consumer was 'not actually a dupe', he or she was 'likely to be an innocent abroad' (Socialist Union, 1956: 44).

Opinion on developments in other areas tended to be equally unfavourable. Home-ownership was widely regarded as a middle-class aspiration, which at the very least would damage the policy that was really needed to solve Britain's housing crisis (the production of more and better municipal units for rent) but might also actively corrupt (Pawley, 1978: 71). A delegate from Yorkshire put the latter point in the following way to the 1959 Conference:

> I was without a house, and I have a wife and child. I looked over, and by God! When I bought my little rural hovel for which I borrowed the money, I loved it and I was very proud, and would have fought anybody for its possession. This is the evil of capitalism, that makes people demand things so much that when at last they get hold of something they go rotten inside.
>
> (Labour Party, 1959c: 148)

Teenagers and teenage culture fared little better. Labour opinion was not resolutely against mass entertainment, but it was often based on the belief that the arts could be rated hierarchically, with 'serious' drama, painting and music at the apex. In this perspective, much of the burgeoning pop culture appeared unworthy of comment. Thus, *Leisure for Living*, a policy document of 1959, admitted jazz into the magic circle of worthwhile entertainment (it was allegedly the 'colloquial musical idiom of the twentieth century'), was lukewarm about skiffle ('though it has produced little of intrinsic artistic merit, [it] has at least provided hundreds of thousands of young people with a "do-it-yourself" musical outlet') and ignored rock and roll and pop altogether (Labour Party, 1959a: 28 and 9). Nevertheless, if this was the official line, unofficial comment could often be far more censorious, and in fact indistinguishable from the prejudice which existed in society at large. Critics on the Left, for example, shared the prevailing middle-class attitudes to Teddy Boys and Girls, either patronizing them or else characterizing them, as in this piece from T.R. Fyvel in *Socialist Commentary*, in terms normally reserved for the most dissolute of the bourgeoisie:

> Analyse the Teddy Boy outlook and it becomes a confused amalgam of all the sordid aspects of their actual environment—an environment where, as they choose to see it, nothing counts except money and the ruthless satisfaction of one's desires, where newspapers deal with crime, sensation and gambling, where the chosen film is the gangster film, and the smart thing is always to get what you can for as little as you can give.
>
> (Fyvel, 1958: 15)

The consequence of all this was that Labour's actual politics in relation to groups at the centre of change remained fairly threadbare. Some parts of the party were keen on consumer protection and a number of pamphlets and articles appeared on the subject, though with only limited impact on official policy (Burton, 1955; Davies, 1957: 181–2; and Labour Party, 1959b: 8–9). A clause promising to 'assist *all* house purchasers by keeping down rates of interests on repayments' appeared in the 1959 election manifesto, but, again, this commitment was somewhat peripheral, and certainly not at the heart of the party's housing policy (Labour Party, 1959b: 2–4). Policy on youth questions, finally, was hardly more innovative. The major issues here were seen, as they had been traditionally, in terms of freeing access—removing blockages which prevented working-class students from climbing the academic ladder, for example. The 'future of the Arts' was admitted to be a special matter of concern for young people, but the panacea prescribed— 'Labour will make more money available'—could not be called imaginative (Labour Party, 1959b: 11).

Did any of this matter? In other words, is there evidence to suggest that these Labour positions and pronouncements acted to put people off supporting the party? Definitive answers to these questions are impossible, since a wide variety of factors shaped voting intentions. But a strong impression, at the very least, remains that Labour's standing with groups at the centre of the kinds of social change described was rarely actually improved by the politics it proposed (Rowland, 1960; Crane, 1960). The problem was as much about 'speaking another language' as anything else, a point underlined by MacInnes in his perceptive description of the party's relationship with young adults:

> When I read Labour propaganda addressed to youth, and then think of the kind of teenagers I've met in coffee bars, in jazz clubs, at the palais, buying separates or Italian shoes, or holidaying together on Lambrettas in England or abroad, I have the feeling of a total failure of communication.
>
> (MacInnes, 1959: 20).

What made this more significant was the fact that equivalent Tory campaigns were generally thought to have gained a satisfactory degree of influence: as their chronicler records, 'a gratifying large number of the right sort of people' were reached, and comment about the central propositions being advanced was often favourable (Hennessy, 1961: 250).

It may be reasonably concluded, then, that Labour's problems in the 1950s *were* partly self-inflicted, in that the party was not nearly as responsive to social change as its main rival. This, of course, begs one final question: why was Labour so incapable of understanding what was going on around it?

This is not an easy question to answer, but it seems that there were two broad kinds of impediment discouraging a sharper focus.[14] One problem stemmed from the way in which many of the party's rank-and-file understood socialism and their role in its creation.[15] Socialism was most generally defined in terms of a total system of ethics, an overarching set of moral imperatives which were seen as being very different from those found in other ideologies. Activists had the responsibility of delivering enough votes to allow this specific vision to be put into practice. Obviously, the conditions of success here were several, and included perfecting the party's electoral machinery. However, it was also usually held that real progress could only, in the end, be guaranteed by 'making socialists'—winning over or converting people to the socialist panoply—for the simple reason that if this were not achieved, any electoral gain would be vulnerable, and perhaps easily eroded by the temptations of more materialist creeds.

This approach had its advantages, not least because it encouraged internal party coherence and clarity of purpose. But it also caused problems, the most serious of which was the promotion of an 'us' and 'them' mentality in relation to the broader electorate. Thus, party members tended to see themselves as 'saved', almost 'otherly' because they had rejected 'the evils' of the world at hand in favour of a morality which prefigured the one expected to govern the coming socialist millenium.[16] On the other hand, those not won to the cause could all too easily appear to be swimming in a sea of irrationality, totally ignorant of the simple truths which could make life better for all.[17] In such a scenario, it was hardly surprising that, for example, pop culture and the new consumerism would not be judged the stuff of politics. Indeed such manifestations of social change could only appear either as largely irrelevant to the fundamental questions of moral choice or else as further proof of the frivolity and irresponsibility of a world without socialism.

What made this situation all the more serious was that further up the party, among its leaders and intelligentsia, myopia about the real pattern of developments in 1950s Britain was just as bad, though for rather different reasons. Here the problem was caused by a bias in the pervasive modes of analytical thinking—a bias which made it look as if serious engagement in social or cultural developments was simply unnecessary in plotting a Labour advance.

The most obvious manifestation of this was on the Left of the party, where a long flirtation with the cant of neo-Marxism had encouraged a belief in the primacy of economic contradictions. The 'present veneer of prosperity' (Maynard, 1959: 538) might have produced all kinds of aberrations and confusions in proletarian behaviour, but underneath this the weight of capitalist exploitation guaranteed that working people still formed the party's most natural constituency. Labour had a duty, therefore, not to be diverted by, say, the strange manifestations of youth culture, but to reach beyond the superficial to a more fundamental area, where 'traditional' socialist values still remained very relevant. Lena Jeger made this point very clearly to the 1959 Conference:

> The young people of our country are not asking to be given coffee bars and jazz and fun. They are waiting for us to make demands on them . . . The most important thing in attracting our young people is to put the issues with clarity, with no compromise . . . Then they can understand . . . .
>
> (Labour Party, 1959c: 149)

Of course, the Right in the party felt that it had long since moved beyond this kind of approach, and, free from dogma and 'ideology', prided itself on 'being in touch'. Yet on closer inspection, over-materialist assumptions were at play here too, with equally damaging results; all that was different was the base-line characterization of capitalism. Thus, Crosland began from the assertion that capitalism had changed, partly because of self-reform, partly because of Labour's previous success. However, he then went on to presume an economic determinism which any neo-Marxist would have been proud of: reformed capitalism allowed workers 'a middle-class standard of life' which in turn produced in them 'distinct symptoms of a middle-class psychology' (Crosland, 1981: 216). Labour's political role was, therefore, to change its orientation, to 'fit' this situation better (Crosland, 1960a: 5). Again, key assumptions can be seen short-circuiting the analysis; again, the real nature of what was going on in the 1950s remained hidden, with the characterization of social and cultural developments owing most to an extrapolation from a presumed set of economic determinants.

In his *Chicken Soup with Barley*, Arnold Wesker has one of his characters look back from the vantage point of the mid-1950s over the political changes she has seen during her life. In the 1930s, she remembers, with unemployment, 'the world was a communist'. A decade and a half later, things were much changed:

> its different now. Now the people have forgotten ... You give them a few shillings in the bank and they can buy a television so they think it's all over, there's nothing more to be got, they don't have to think any more! Is that what you want? A world where people don't think any more? Is that what you want me to be satisfied with—a television set?
>
> (Wesker, 1964: 73)

Such a view was quite common on the Left at the time, and continues to have its adherents today. The 1950s, then, are the apathetic years, a decade when the people, fascinated by the baubles of capitalism, forgot.

The aim of this chapter has been to reassess this view and suggest it is somewhat misleading. Working-class living standards were, certainly, rising in the 1950s, and this did encourage a range of new popular interests and identities. But affluence did not produce 'bourgeoisification' any more than poverty had produced the proletariat. Labour's problems at this time, therefore, were as much a consequence of its own idiosyncratic traditions as anything else. In this sense, Michael Foot's verdict on the 1959 election defeat—'The Tories caught the mood of the public. Their votes prove it. But that mood was blind, smug, somnolent and, in some respects, evil'[18] explains more about where the problem lay than the author can ever have intended.

Notes

1. The Braddock quote, unfortunately undated, appears in Hopkins, 1964: 307. Colin MacInness's strictures on 'A Taste of Reality' appear in *Encounter*, vol. XII, no. 4 (April 1959), pp. 70–1.
2. I should like to thank Jim Obelkevitch, Terry Gourvish, Tony Mason and Steve Fielding for useful comments on earlier versions of this chapter, and the latter two for discussing the issues it raises with me on occasions too numerous to mention. They will all, no doubt, feel that I should have listened more and spoken less.
3. Butler and Rose, 1960: esp. p. 193, and the *Gallup Political Index Report* No. 2, (February 1960), esp. pp. 19–21.

4. See the chart in *The Economist* 17 May 1958 for a useful summary of Labour's local electoral performance.
5. Elements of the argument summarized in the following paragraph can be found, in greater or lesser combination, in Crosland (1981); M. Abrams. 'The Home-centred Society', *The Listener* 26 November 1959; Zweig (1960); F. Zweig, *The Worker in an Affluent Society*, London, Heineman, 1961; Hopkins (1964); and N. Macrea, *Sunshade in October*, London, George Allen and Unwin, 1963.
6. Millar, 1963: 108; and The Economist Intelligence Unit *Retail Business Survey*, no. 2 (August 1961), pp. 6–7.
7. This phrase is used by Abrams in his *Listener* article cited in note 5, above.
8. See e.g. the editorial in *Encounter*, vol. VI, no. 6 (June 1956), pp. 2–3 and comments in R. Lewis and R. Stewart, *The Boss*, London, J.M. Dent and Sons, 1958.
9. *The Director* September 1958, p. 410.
10. According to *The Statistical Review of Advertising*, vol. XXVII, no. 3, April 1959, press advertising in 1958 cost £72.6 million. Breaking this total down reveals that 40 per cent of it was spent on 19 of the 204 product categories listed.
11. Millar, (1963: 29). On the conservatism of working-class buying habits, see also D. Elliston Allen, *British Tastes*, London, Hutchinson, 1968.
12. Though this was not exclusively so, since some were very uneasy about materialism in general, and the party's encouragement of it in particular: see e.g. Anon, '"Never Had it so Good"', *The Conservative Agent's Journal*, no. 457 (December 1956), p. 210; and J. Baker White, 'What of Our Future', *The Conservative Agent's Journal*, no. 462 (May 1960), pp. 4–5.
13. *Labour Woman*, vol. XLV, no. 3 (March 1957), pp. 40–1.
14. The argument that follows owes much to insights presented in S. Macintyre, *A Proletarian Science*, Cambridge, Cambridge University Press, 1980.
15. See, particularly, on this subject, discussion in *Labour Organiser*, especially the 'Quair's Page', vol. 32, no. 373 (May 1953), p. 84; vol. 32 no. 374 (June 1953), p. 104; and vol. 32, no. 376 (August 1953), p. 159.
16. Hence the somewhat austere, 'unstylish' style of many activities. Of course, this rather priggish position was not universally respected, and particularly irritated some Labour women, who resented the hypocrisy which could easily accompany it ('Their husbands, even Socialists, are very conservative and discourage their wives from dressing too glamorously. Yet how often does that "conservative" husband admire the crazy hat or ridiculous dress on someone else?'—Alma Birk, 'Let's Talk It Over', *Labour Woman*, vol. XLV, no. 5 (May 1957), p. 74).
17. Thus, for example, Rene Short's claim to the 1959 Conference that 'Women in this country...are by and large, except those in the Labour Party, politically illiterate' (Labour Party, 1959c: 142) or Barbara Castle's alleged comment in the wake of the 1959 election that Labour's '"ethical reach was beyond the mental grasp of the average person"' (repeated in A. Hartley, *A State of England*, London, Hutchinson, 1963, p. 152).
18. Foot, quoted from *The Daily Herald* 16 October 1959, in the Conservative Research Department's *Notes on Current Politics*, 2 November 1959.

References

Abrams, M. (1956), 'The facts of young life', *Encounter*, vol. VI, no. 5, 35–42.
Abrams, M. (1960), ' "The future of the Left" ', *Encounter*, vol. XIV, no. 5, 57–9.
Abrams, M. (1961), 'Social class and British politics', *The Public Opinion Quarterly*, vol. XXV, no. 3, 342–50.
Abrams, M. (1964), *The newspaper reading public of tomorrow*, London, Odhams Press.
Blackwell, T. and Seabrook, J. (1985), *A World Still to Win*, London, Faber and Faber.
Burton, E. (1955), *The Battle of the Consumer*, (Viewpoint Pamphlet No. 1).
Butler, D.E. and Sloman, A. (1980), *British Political Facts 1900–1979*, 5th Edn., London, Macmillan.
Clarke, J. *et al.* (1975), 'Subcultures, cultures and class', *Cultural Studies*, 7/8, 9–74.
Crane, P. (1960), 'Labour its own worst enemy', *The Political Quarterly*, vol. 31, no. 3, 374–84.
Crosland, A. (1960a), 'The Future of the Left', *Encounter*, vol. XIV, no. 3, 3–12.
Crosland, A. (1960b), *Can Labour Win?* (Fabian Tract No. 324).
Crosland, A. (1981), *The future of socialism*, rev. edn. London, Jonathan Cape.
Darling, G. (1955), 'Shopping without tears'. *Socialist Commentary*, vol. XIX, 182–3.
Davies, M. (1957), 'Protection for the housewife', *The Labour Woman*, vol. XLVI, no. 2, 20–2.
Fyvel, T.R. (1958), 'The long view', *Socialist Commentary*, February 1958, 15.
Hall, M. (1962), 'The consumer sector 1950–60', in Worswick, G.D.N. and Ady, P.H. (eds) (1962), *The British Economy in the Nineteen-Fifties*, Oxford, Clarendon Press. 429–60.
Harrisson, T. (1961), *Britain Revisited*, London, Victor Gollancz.
Hennessy, D. (1961), 'The communication of Conservative policy 1957–59', *The Political Quarterly*, vol. 32 no. 3, 238–56.
Hopkins, H. (1964), *The New Look*, London, Secker and Warburg for the Readers Union.
Labour Party (1951), *Report of the Fiftieth Annual Conference of the Labour Party*, London, The Labour Party.
Labour Party (1958), *Report of the Thirty-Fifth National Conference of Labour Women*, London, The Labour Party.
Labour Party (1959a), *Leisure for Living*, London, The Labour Party.
Labour Party (1959b), *The Britain We Want*, London, The Labour Party.
Labour Party (1959c), *Report of the Fifty-Eighth Annual Conference of the Labour Party*, London, The Labour Party.

Labour Party (1961), *Report of the Sixtieth Annual Conference of the Labour Party*, London, The Labour Party.

Lessing, D. (1960), *In Pursuit of the English*, London, MacGibbon and Kee.

MacInness, C. (1959), 'Labour and youth', *Socialist Commentary*, December 1959, 20.

Maynard, J. (1959), 'Why we lost: and what now?', *Labour Monthly*, vol. XLI, 538–40.

Millar, R. (1963), *The Affluent Sheep*, London, Longmans.

Nicholson, V. and Smith, S. (1977), *Spend, Spend, Spend*, London, Jonathan Cape.

Noel-Baker, F. (1959), 'We need more light on advertising', *Labour Woman*, vol. XLVII, no. 7, 98–9.

Pawley, M. (1978), *Home Ownership*, London, Architectural Press.

Pearson, J. and Turner, G. (1965), *The Persuasion Industry*, London, Eyre and Spottiswoode.

Pinto-Duschinsky, M. (1970), 'Bread and circuses? The Conservatives in office, 1951–1964', in Bogdanov, V. and Skidelsky, R. (eds) (1970), *The Age of Affluence 1951–1964*, London, Macmillan. 55–77.

Rix, M. (1958), 'The magic of the woman's magazine', *The Director*, October 1958, 83–5.

Rowland, C. (1960), 'Labour publicity', *The Political Quarterly*, vol. 31, no. 3, 348–60.

Sampson, A. (1968), *Macmillan*, Harmondsworth, Pelican Books.

Samuel, R. (1960), ' "Bastard" Capitalism', in Thompson, E. P. (ed) (1960), *Out of Apathy*, London, New Left Books.

Samuel, R. (1985), 'The lost world of British communism', *New Left Review*, no. 154, 3–53.

Socialist Union (1956), *Twentieth Century Socialism*, Harmondsworth, Penguin Books.

Tracey, M.B. (1957), 'British retail institutions', *The Journal of Retailing*, vol. XXXIII, no. 2, 93–8 and 105.

Turner, G. (1963), *The Car Makers*, London, Eyre and Spottiswoode.

Wesker, A. (1964), *The Wesker Trilogy*, Harmondsworth, Penguin Books.

White, C.L. (1970), *Women's Magazines 1693–1968*, London, Michael Joseph.

Williams, P. (1982), *Hugh Gaitskell*, Oxford, O.U.P.

Willmott, P. (1963), *The Evolution of a Community*, London, Routledge and Kegan Paul.

Zweig, F. (1952), *The British Worker*, Harmondsworth, Pelican Books.

Zweig, F. (1960), 'The new factory worker', *The Twentieth Century*, vol. 167, no. 999, 397–404.

5 The City of London as a financial centre in the era of the depression, the Second World War and post-war official controls

Richard Roberts

I

The crisis summer of 1931 was an important turning-point in the history of the City of London as a financial centre. July witnessed the suspension of payments on the external debts of the countries of Central Europe, a development which caused problems in the City on account of the outstanding credits of London firms. It also saw the publication of the report of the Macmillan Committee on Finance and Industry, which identified short-comings in the provision of finance for domestic manufacturing industry and marked the beginning of the long-running debate about the relationship between the City and Britain's industrial performance. In August the City became embroiled in political controversy as never before with the disintegration of the Labour administration which the left wing of the party blamed on a bankers' conspiracy. September saw the demise of the City's most cherished article of faith—sterling's adherence to the gold standard. 'The end of an epoch', was the *Economist*'s instantaneous verdict.[1]

The closing years of the 1950s were also a watershed for the City. In 1958 the operation of financial services for domestic clients was facilitated by the removal of restrictions on bank lending, capital issues and hire purchase. The relationship between the City and industry was back in the public eye at the end of the year during the fiercely contested takeover bid for the British Aluminium Company. The behaviour of the City was once again a subject of political controversy following allegations of a leak of information about an increase in interest rates in September 1957 and the publication of the report of the inquiry into the episode early in 1958. Issues arising from this affair were amongst the matters considered by the Radcliffe Committee on the Working of the Monetary System, whose report was published in 1959, again casting a spotlight on the City. Finally, there was the restoration of the convertibility of sterling into other currencies in two stages in 1958 and 1961, which marked, in the words of a London merchant banker, 'the dawn of a new era' (Fry, 1970: 30).

The tumultuous closing and opening of epochs and eras at the beginning of the 1930s and the end of the 1950s suggest that there was something different about the City in the intervening decades. The face and the fortunes of the Square Mile in the intervening years, the years of the international economic depression, the Second World War, and the post-war panoply of restrictive official controls over economic activity are the subject of this chapter.

II

In 1914 on the eve of the First World War the City of London was indisputably the world's leading international financial centre. At the opening of the 1930s the City remained the home of the world's leading insurance, shipping, bullion and commodity markets. The sterling bill of exchange was still the most important instrument for the finance of international trade, and the London discount market, in which bills of exchange were traded, was a uniquely large and liquid money market. In the spring of 1931 the City was still the financial capital of the world, though the development of international financial services in New York, and also Paris, had diminished the extent of its pre-eminence.

The enormous volume of foreign loans raised in the United States during the war and after led to the emergence of the US dollar as an international medium of exchange and an important reserve currency. In the early 1920s New York eclipsed London as the leading market for the issue of securities for overseas borrowers, because of both the abundance of loanable dollar funds and the restrictions on overseas issues imposed by the British authorities (Atkin, 1970: 324–35). Moreover, the 1920s saw the vigorous development of a discount market on Wall Street and the increasing use of dollar bills of exchange to finance international trade. Nevertheless, thanks to the restoration of sterling to the gold standard in 1925, which placed the pound on an equal footing with the dollar for international transactions, the City was able to meet the challenge to its trade finance and international capital-raising activities from across the Atlantic in the second half of the decade.

The events of the summer of 1931 diminished the standing of the City as a financial centre. The first blow was the news that the Creditanstalt of Vienna, one of the most important banks of Central Europe, was insolvent. This development was damaging to a number of London firms which had provided credits to the Creditanstalt, and three of the City's leading merchant banks organized a committee to safeguard the interests of international creditors.

From Austria the crisis spread to Germany and on 13 July 1931, with the Reichsbank's reserves exhausted and banks and businesses having difficulty in paying their bills for want of credit, the German government issued emergency decrees which halted the withdrawal of foreign loans.

The suspension of external payments by Germany was a grave matter for the City. German debts to British lenders were estimated to total about £155 million, of which some 35 per cent were long-term bonds, 40 per cent short-term advances, principally by the large clearing-banks, and 25 per cent bills of exchange.[2] It was the last which posed an immediate problem for the City, for when these bills fell due for payment within the following 90 days the merchant banks and clearing-banks which had endorsed them would be obliged to honour them without having been paid by the German parties which had received the credits. For about half a dozen amongst the score or so of the leading merchant banks this would be impossible since the amount of their German obligations exceeded available funds (Sayers, 1976: 510). The failure of these merchant banks to honour their bills endangered the position of the discount houses, the firms which specialized in dealing in bills, which in turn threatened to weaken the commercial banks which provided the funds which the discount houses used to conduct their business. Thus the German suspension of payments posed a menace of major magnitude to the City.

The City bankers formed a committee to deal with the crisis which, in conjunction with a body representing American commercial creditors, and keeping closely in contact with the Bank of England, conducted negotiations with the German debtors which resulted in the conclusion of the Standstill Agreement in September 1931. This agreement, and its successors, regularized the status of the outstanding German bills, which were renewed repeatedly upon expiry. The bills remained in the discount market, supported by a Bank of England rediscount guarantee which made them acceptable to holders, thus relieving the pressure on the exposed merchant banks. Upon the approach of war the Standstill bills were removed from the discount market on the instruction of the Bank of England by the houses which had endorsed them using funds which were made available by the commercial banks and the Bank of England. These measures successfully managed the crisis which ensued from the German suspension of payments in July 1931, but until the recovery of the money owed by German creditors in the early 1950s there was a group of important City firms whose finances were in a fragile condition.

In mid-July the financial crisis spread to London. The revelation of high levels of short-term indebtedness in London in the report of the Macmillan Committee, published on 13 July 1931, the same day as the suspension of German payments, undermined confidence in sterling on the part of foreign holders. The run on sterling which developed proved unstoppable. On 21 September 1931 Britain suspended the gold standard, which meant that the paper currency could no longer be exchanged at the Bank of England for gold or other reserves, and the pound was left to find its own exchange level. It promptly plummeted from $4.86 to $3.50. The departure from the gold standard came as a shock to the City but City firms were not immediately threatened by the event. Nor was the move followed by economic collapse as City men had predicted. Sir Lawrence Jones, a partner in the issuing house Helbert, Wagg & Co, recalled his passionate and sincere advocacy in the press and on public platforms during the crisis of the City view that

> 'if this country was driven off the Gold Standard it would starve.... The country promptly went off gold, did not starve and has remained off gold ever since. The sole monetary principle for which...I had been ready to speak out publicly and with utter conviction was now shown to be a delusion'.

> (Jones, 1958: 129)

'Considerable and legitimate complaints' were received by the British authorities from the central banks of other countries which suffered heavy losses on their sterling balances because of the fall in the value of the pound (Leith-Ross, 1968: 140). Although sterling recovered in value in the later 1930s, it no longer had the reputation of being as 'good as gold' and the standing of London as a repository for funds and of the City as an international financial centre was diminished.

The background to the financial crises in Germany and in London in the summer of 1931 was the worsening world-wide economic depression. Between 1929 and 1934 the value of world exports declined by two-thirds (League of Nations, 1939: 60). The impact on the City was severe. Ship chartering, the principal activity of the Baltic Exchange, was depressed and in 1935 membership reached an all-time low (Barty-King, 1977: 355). The marine insurance business conducted by British insurance companies suffered too. In 1922 they earned £21 million in marine premiums, but over the years 1931–7 the average was only £11 million (Supple, 1970: 437). Lloyd's, the market for marine underwriting, saw a decline in the number of underwriting members in 1932, the first for 20 years. The City's various commodity markets were also adversely affected, though the extent of their difficulties varied considerably (Economist Intelligence Unit, 1958: 133–5).

The slump caused a drastic fall in the volume of the sterling bills of exchange which were issued to finance international trade. Estimates published in *The Economist* indicate a reduction in the volume of such bills from £540 million at the peak in 1928–9 to £134 million in 1933–4.[3] This was a faster rate of decline than that of world trade itself, which suggests that the end of the fixed parity of sterling may have discouraged its use in international transactions as was feared at the time (Drummond, 1981: 20). The business of the merchant banks which specialized in the finance of international trade was depressed, as was that of the discount houses which bemoaned 'the chronic dearth of foreign-drawn bills on which the greatness of the London discount market was formerly built'.[4] International trade made some recovery in the second half of the 1930s, though the universal presence of tariffs, including a British tariff from 1932, one of the new set of economic measures adopted after the departure from the gold standard, prevented a vigorous resurgence, and by 1938 the value of world trade was only 40 per cent of the value in 1929. The recovery in the volume of bills of exchange issued in connection with foreign trade was minimal and at its peak in 1937–8 was only £147 million.

The international economic depression led to a fall in the issue of long-term loans in London for overseas borrowers. Between 1929 and 1930 such new issues declined from £150 million to £103 million (Bank of England, 1966: 154). The imposition of an informal embargo upon capital issues in London for non-Empire borrowers in 1931, another of the new economic measures, reinforced this trend (Sayers, 1976: 491–2). That year new issues for overseas borrowers fell to £50 million. By 1935 they were a mere £21 million and in the second half of the decade averaged around £30 million. The principal City casualties of this development were the merchant banks which for decades had specialized in bringing out loans on behalf of foreign clients. Even without the embargo, however, further falls in the issue of foreign loans were inevitable following the debt defaults in the early 1930s by most of the nations of Central Europe and Latin America, the most avid borrowers of the 1920s. These developments cast a blight on the business of those members of the Stock Exchange who dealt in the still substantial volumes of foreign securities.

'Cheap money'—low interest rates—became the principal policy of the British government to promote economic recovery by reducing the cost of borrowing and investment. From 1932 until 1951 interest rates were held almost continually at 2 per cent. Cheap money also held the key to the reduction of public expenditure by the reduction of interest payments to bondholders through the conversion of the National Debt to a lower rate of interest. This was effected in 1932 and was generally welcomed in the City as a positive step towards the achievement of a balanced budget.[5] The implementation of the cheap money policy coincided with the beginning of Britain's economic recovery, though there has been considerable controversy about its importance in bringing about the upturn (Collins, 1988: 298–306). In 1931 new capital issues by British industrial and commercial firms totalled a mere £38 million, a fifth of the volume in the boom year of 1928 (Bank of England, 1966: 154). The recovery in domestic corporate issues began in 1932 when they reached £78 million and by 1936 the business was worth £171 million. There was an important change in the identity of the City sponsors of domestic corporate issues in the 1930s. Hitherto the merchant banks had only handled issues by long-established firms of impeccable creditworthiness. Other firms used stockbrokers or the notorious 'company promoters'. In the 1930s, with the loss of their foreign loan-issuing business and the low level of foreign bill business, the merchant banks shifted their attentions to domestic new issues and soon came to dominate this activity. They also began to take some tentative steps in the provision of venture capital for small enterprises, whose problems in finding long-term finance had been highlighted by the Macmillan Committee's report.

The early and mid-1930s saw a 'life and death' struggle against the prevailing market conditions on the part of the discount houses (Scammell, 1968: 210). The abundance of funds pushed the rate of interest which they received from their investments in Treasury bills, which had become the principal securities in which they traded, as low as 0.27 per cent in 1935. However, the minimum rate at which the clearing-banks would lend to them was 1 per cent, which meant that they incurred a loss on every transaction. At the instigation of the Bank of England, which wished to preserve the independent discount houses as a feature of the City, an agreement was reached between the discount houses and the clearing-banks in 1934 which allowed the former to conduct bill-dealing business without making a loss, but without making much in the way of profits either. In response to the dismal conditions in their traditional business the discount houses developed dealing activities in short-dated government bonds, though this brought them into competition with Stock Exchange jobbers. The difficulties experienced by the discount houses in the 1930s resulted in a contraction of their number from 24 firms at the beginning of the decade to 18 at the end.

In London the great bull market of the 1920s reached a peak in 1928. By mid-1932 equity prices had fallen by three-fifths, a precipitous descent hastened by the Hatry scandal and the Wall Street Crash of 1929, but really reflecting the deteriorating business prospects facing firms. There were many City casualties of the bear market since the practice of dealing on margin—that is using borrowed funds with the securities purchased acting as security for the loan—was widespread. From 1932 until 1937 the prices of both gilts and equities advanced and turnover reached record levels (Victor Morgan and Thomas, 1969: 224). Securities prices fell back in the final years of the decade and the increasing likelihood of war cast a pall over Stock Exchange business. The total number of Stock Exchange members was virtually identical at both the beginning and end of the decade, but this was because a decline in the number of jobbers, perhaps under pressure from the activities of the discount houses, was fortuitously matched by the expansion in the number of brokers.

The 1930s saw a rise in the liquid asset holdings of individuals and firms on account of the uncertainty of the times and the prospect of capital losses on fixed-interest securities, should interest rates rise above the prevailing low levels. As a result the deposits of the London clearing-banks, whose headquarters were in the City and whose chairmen were regarded as leading City figures, rose more rapidly than in the 1920s (Sheppard, 1971: 2). However, savings with the Trustee Savings Banks, the Post Office Savings Bank, building societies and life insurance companies grew even faster, since they paid higher rates of interest than the clearers. The result was that non-City headquartered domestic savings institutions grew faster in these years than their rivals in the Square Mile. In domestic activity the brightest businesses in the City were insurance, notably motor insurance, and hire purchase finance (Supple, 1970: 426–38). The finance houses which provided this service expanded rapidly but they constituted a tiny element amongst British financial institutions in these years (Sheppard, 1971: 184–5).

Prior to 1931 the Bank of England, still a private company, was the determinant of the nation's monetary policy, which is almost to say its economic policy. The policy of returning to the gold standard was closely associated with the Bank, and in particular with Montagu Norman, the Governor from 1920 to 1944 (Clay, 1957: 134–71). The abandonment of the gold standard was a defeat for the Bank and marked the end of its independent authority over monetary policy. Henceforth the government, advised by the Treasury, assumed control over economic policy, of which monetary policy became but one aspect, and the Bank assumed the more modest role of the agent of public policy in the City (Howson, 1975: 80–6). Yet another consequence of the crisis of the summer of 1931 was that the City emerged as the *bête noire* of the Labour Party, whose activists were convinced that their administration had been laid low by a 'bankers' ramp' (Williamson, 1985: 770–806). Leading members came to the conclusion that a future Labour government could have little chance of success so long as the banks were in private hands, and the nationalization of the Bank of England became a priority of the party.[6]

Overall, the 1930s were little short of calamitous for most aspects of the City's international activities. Their decline is summarized by the decrease in Britain's invisible earnings from shipping, insurance and financial services, which it has been estimated fell from an annual average of £200 million in 1926–30 to £110 million in 1931–3 and to £51 million in 1934–8 (Report of the Committee on Invisible Exports, 1968: 22–3). Though the domestic business record was not so bleak, the City suffered losses of other sorts. Its champion, the Bank of England, was now its policeman and it had incurred the unrelenting enmity of the alternative political party of government.

III

The outbreak of the Second World War saw no repetition of the financial crisis in the City which had accompanied the hostilities in 1914. This time the approach of war was more gradual and precautionary measures were taken. The remaining Standstill bills were purchased by the firms which had endorsed them, so the discount market was not disturbed by the presence of paper payable by enemy firms. The operation of the London clearing-system for inter-bank payments was safeguarded against air attack on London by moving it to Staffordshire in August 1939. The Stock Exchange made contingency plans for evacuation to Buckinghamshire and many City firms arranged accommodation around the Home Counties, though few actually moved out of the Square Mile even during the Blitz. A comprehensive set of controls was introduced by the authorities at the start of the war to enable the state to meet its vast funding requirements at the lowest possible cost and to direct financial resources to the war effort. Private holdings of gold and foreign currencies were compulsorily purchased, dollar-denominated securities had to be registered with the Bank of England and many were sold to pay for overseas purchases of war materials or pledged as collateral for American loans. Altogether British holdings of overseas securities fell by £1,100 million between 1939 and 1946 (Victor Morgan and Thomas, 1962: 231). Sterling was made inconvertible into other currencies and the Treasury took control of all foreign exchange and bullion transactions, with designated banks serving as its agents. Capital issues were controlled by the new Capital Issues Committee, whose brief was to provide priority in the capital market to government funding and to reserve access to firms undertaking war work (Sayers, 1976: 582).

The City's international activities declined yet further as a result of the war. The Baltic Exchange and the commodity markets were closed for the duration, and in most cases for much longer. Shipping brokers and commodity traders continued to do business, which preserved a core of expertise, but in the guise of government agents (Barty King, 1977: 362–85; Economist Intelligence Unit, 1958: 140–5). In 1941 Mincing Lane, the focal point of the commodity trades and the site of the Commercial Sale Rooms, was razed by bombing in the air-raid of 10 May, the heaviest of the war when 244 tons of high explosive and 267 incendiary devices were dropped on the City of London. Overall, German bombing destroyed a third of the City's buildings. The devastation was most severe at the eastern end of the Square Mile, in the vicinity of St Paul's and the Barbican, and along the Thames. These neighbourhoods housed many warehouses of the City's merchant and commodity firms and an inadvertent effect of the Luftwaffe's activities was to accelerate the decline in the importance of physical commodity trading in the Square Mile.

During the war the finance of international trade by the sterling bill of exchange fell to negligible amounts and the foreign bill almost disappeared from the discount market. Likewise, capital issues for overseas borrowers virtually ceased and totalled only £9.5 million for the years 1940–5 (Bank of England, 1966: 154). Foreign exchange transactions dwindled in volume and the terms on which they were conducted made the activity barely profitable. The merchant banks were hit hard by these developments and in July 1941 the *Financial News* commented that 'the pre-war problems of the merchant banks were mild indeed compared with the almost catastrophic loss of business with which they have had to contend during the past two years.'[7]

The outbreak of war had been long anticipated by the insurance industry and measures had been taken to cope with the problems of war risks both at sea and on land (Gibb, 1957: 227–42; Supple, 1970: 513–19). Essentially the risks were assumed by the government while Lloyds brokers and the insurance companies acted as government agents. The insurance industry's under-writing and reinsurance business in the United States was regarded as an important source of dollar earnings and steps were taken to retain the confidence of American clients in the ability of the British parties to meet claims whatever the outcome of the war. British insurers were thus able to benefit from the war boom in the United States and the American premium income of British insurers grew from $244 million in 1939 to $345 in 1945, a remarkable contrast to the decline of the City's other international financial services (Clarke, 1965: 73).

The Stock Exchange closed briefly at the onset of war but soon reopened, though under more stringent settlement rules. Its activities were mostly concerned with dealings in British government securities which increased in nominal value from £6.5 billion to £12.5 billion between 1939 and 1945 (Sheppard, 1971: 188). By 1946 government debt constituted 56 per cent of total quotations, a level not seen since the 1860s (Reader, 1979: 163). The stock market experienced a sharp reduction in turnover in the opening years of the war and in 1941 only half the number of bargains were struck as in 1939 (Victor Morgan and Thomas, 1969: 284). By 1945 the volume of transactions had recovered to the pre-war level but it is unlikely that there was widespread prosperity amongst the members.

The discount market became completely dominated by the Treasury bill, which increased in volume from £892 million in 1939 to £3,680 million in 1945 (Pember and Boyle, 1950: 325). However, the discount houses still found it impossible to make a profit from dealing in Treasury bills because the rates were so fine: for instance, one firm increased its Treasury bill business sixfold between 1938 and 1947, but in the last year the earnings from it covered only a third of operating expenses. Their salvation was the further development of dealing in short-dated gilts, an activity whose expansion was encouraged by the authorities to match the enormous growth of government bonds during the war. In 1942, and again at the end of the war, the discount houses were able to persuade the Capital Issues Committee that they required additional capital to conduct their activities, which were essential for the functioning of the market in government bonds. Nevertheless, the war years saw a further contraction in the number of discount houses which fell from 18 to 11.

The war led to a marked increase in personal saving, both on account of the uncertainty and because of the shortage of consumer goods. Before the war individuals saved some 5 per cent of income after tax, whereas at its wartime peak personal saving reached 25 per cent. However, most of the increase bypassed the City-based deposit-taking banks. Much was absorbed by the National Savings Movement through the sale of savings certificates and defence bonds, which was undertaken on the government's behalf by the Post Office Savings Bank and the Trustee Savings Banks. Small savers were also encouraged to accumulate balances at those institutions and both saw rises in deposits which outstripped the rate of increase of the London clearing-banks (Sheppard, 1971: 3).

The Labour victory in the election of July 1945 'certainly came as a shock to banking circles in the City', commented *The Economist*, 'some have hardly yet emerged from the phase of stunned surprise.'[8] The new government's first major measure was the nationalization of the Bank of England, which took effect on 14 February 1946, a priority which was seen in the City as the revenge for 1931. In subsequent years the fuel and power, steel and transport industries were also nationalized. The impact on the City, besides arousing fears that the programme might be extended to the banks and insurance companies, was the disappearance of several large sectors of securities from the Stock Exchange. The conjunction of the nationalizations and falling securities prices led to a decline in the volume of Stock Exchange transactions from 1946 to 1950, which suggests that the member firms made little headway in the recovery of their prosperity in the immediate post-war years (Victor Morgan and Thomas, 1962: 284).

For the City the most notable features of the years of Labour administration from 1945 to 1951 were the continuity of wartime policies and controls; cheap money; foreign exchange regulations; restrictions on capital issues and bank advances; and import restrictions, rationing and licensing. This scheme of things allowed little scope for business innovation or the resumption of international activities on the part of the discount houses or the merchant banks. The discount houses continued to conduct their curious combination of unremunerative Treasury bill transactions and gilt-dealing. The scale of their activities expanded rapidly in the immediate post-war years because of the large volume of Treasury bills, but the profits were meagre. The merchant banks benefited from the increase in capital issues of industrial and commercial companies from £18.5 million in 1945 to £308 million in 1950, and there was a modest revival in bill of exchange business for domestic firms, though by no means could it be said that they thrived.

The immediate post-war years saw a rapid expansion in the scale of international trade. In 1938 world exports totalled $21 billion, but by 1948 they were $53 billion and $75 billion in 1951 (UNCTAD, 1955: 13). This was a much more promising environment than the 1930s for City markets and firms which provided services for international trade. The ship-chartering market at the Baltic Exchange reopened in 1945 and soon resumed a leading position. Lloyd's benefited too and the net premium incomes from marine policies increased from £24.9 million in 1945 to £61.7 million in 1951. A number of commodities markets resumed trading in these years: furs, raw wool, coffee, rubber, tin, cocoa and tea. The insurance companies' American business continued to expand vigorously, as during the war, and between 1945 and 1951 premiums increased from $346 million to $586 million (Clarke 1965: 73). The outcome was that the City's invisible earnings reversed the trend of the 1930s and began once more to expand (Clarke, 1958: 94–6).

IV

The two decades of cheap money came to an end in November 1951 when the new Conservative Chancellor revived the use of interest rates as an instrument of economic control. This development had both symbolic and practical significance for the City. It indicated the intention of the government to revive market mechanisms which raised expectations of the further removal of controls. It also necessitated that firms learned how to operate in a new and unfamiliar environment. The discount houses were beneficiaries of the change since dealing in bills again became profitable and they prospered once more. However, there were pitfalls as well as profits under the new regime as they discovered to their cost in 1955 when sharp rises in interest rates inflicted considerable losses on their bond portfolios (Clarke, 1959: 10).

The 1950s saw the return of favourable operating conditions for members of the Stock Exchange and the merchant banks. The prices of equities followed an upward trend from 1952 and the volume of Stock Exchange transactions increased from 1.6 million bargains in 1949 to 4.3 million in 1959. The revival of the use of bills of exchange by British firms which had begun in the late 1940s continued and by the end of the 1950s constituted a sizeable business. This revived the banking side of the business of the merchant banks. Their issuing activities also expanded in the 1950s, which saw much larger fund-raising in the capital market by domestic firms than ever before, though the amount varied considerably from year to year. The 1950s also witnessed much merger and acquisition activity amongst British firms in which the merchant banks acted as advisers to the parties. The much publicized bid battle for the British Aluminium Company which raged at the end of 1958 and the beginning of 1959 marked a new departure in takeover tactics which made the role of City financial advisers more important than ever.

International developments presented further opportunities for the revival of City business. World exports increased from $82 billion in 1951 to $134 billion in 1961 (UNCTAD, 1964: 2). Despite strong competition from other international financial centres, notably New York, the City's shipbroking and marine insurance sectors continued to prosper. Lloyd's net premium income from marine policies rose from £62 million to £83 million between 1951 and 1961, and its total net premium income increased from £149 million to £255 million. The early and mid-1950s saw the reopening of the rest of London's commodity markets, of which the most important were the lead, coffee, wool tops, copper and grain markets (Clarke, 1965: 82). As a result the City's invisible earnings grew rapidly and it has been estimated that they increased threefold between 1946 and 1956 from £50 million to £150 million (Clarke, 1958: 94-6).

The reopening of the London gold market in March 1954 was hailed as a particularly important milestone in the revival of the City, and the official announcement commented that it marked 'a stage in the strengthening of

London as an international financial centre and of sterling as an international currency'.[9] London soon reclaimed the position of the world's leading bullion market.

A development of even greater significance was the commencement of the Euro-dollar market in London. Euro-dollars are US dollars held outside the United States. By the second half of the 1950s there was a large volume of such dollars, principally as a result of US balance of payments deficits (Fry, 1970: 30–4). In 1957, with the enthusiastic encouragement of the Bank of England, an active market in Euro-dollar lending developed in the City. The Euro-dollar market grew with astonishing rapidity in the closing years of the 1950s and the early 1960s and every internationally oriented bank around the world rushed to open an office in London to establish a position in this new market (Bank of England, 1961: 18–23). By the mid-1960s London was once again host to a larger number of overseas banks than any other international financial centre. The restoration of sterling convertibility for non-residents in 1958 removed a significant impediment to this development. The result was the re-establishment of the City as, in the words of a submission to the Radcliffe Committee, 'the Financial centre of the world'.[10]

Notes

1. *The Economist*, 26 September 1931.
2. *The Economist*, 23 January 1932.
3. *The Economist*, 26 March 1938.
4. *The Economist*, 26 March 1938.
5. *The Economist*, 5 November 1932.
6. See Fabian Society (1938), *The City Today*, London, New Fabian Research Bureau.
7. *Financial News*, 28 July 1941.
8. *The Economist*, 4 August 1945.
9. *The Economist*, 27 March 1954.
10. Memorandum of Evidence Submitted by the London Discount Market Association. Committee on the Working of the Monetary System Memoranda of Evidence. London, HMSO (1960) p. 25.

References

Atkin, J. (1970), 'Official Regulation of British Overseas Investment, 1914–1931', *Economic History Review*, 23: 324–35.

Bank of England (1961), 'The Overseas and Foreign Banks in London', *Bank of England Quarterly Bulletin*, 1: 18–23.

Bank of England (1966), 'Capital Issues in the United Kingdom', *Bank of England Quarterly Bulletin*, 6: 151–6.

Barty-King, H. (1977), *The Baltic Exchange: The history of a unique market*, London, Hutchinson.

Clarke, W.M. (1958), *The City's Invisible Earnings*, London, Institute of Economic Affairs.

Clarke, W.M. (1959), 'Freedom of the City', *National Provincial Bank Review*, 45: 9–14.

Clarke, W.M. (1965), *The City in the World Economy*, London, Institute of Economic Affairs.

Clay, Sir H. (1957), *Lord Norman*, London, Macmillan.

Collins, M. (1988), *Money and Banking in the UK: A history*, London, Croom Helm.

Drummond, I (1981), *The Floating Pound and the Sterling Area, 1931–1939*, Cambridge, Cambridge University Press.

Economist Intelligence Unit (1958), *The London Metal Exchange*, Tonbridge, Whitefriars Press.

Fry, R. (ed.) (1970), *A Banker's World: The revival of the City 1957–1970*, London, Hutchinson.

Gibb, D.E.W. (1957), *Lloyd's of London*, London, Macmillan.

Howson, S. (1975), *Domestic Monetary Management in Britain 1919–38*, Cambridge, Cambridge University Press.

Jones, L.E. (1958), *Georgian Afternoon*, London, Rupert Hart-Davis.

League of Nations (1939), *Review of World Trade 1938*, Geneva, League of Nations.

Leith-Ross, Sir F. (1968), *Money Talks*, London, Hutchinson.

Pember and Boyle (1950), *British Government Securities in the Twentieth Century: The first 50 years*, London, Pember and Boyle.

Reader, W.J. (1979), *A House in the City*, London, Batsford.

Report of the Committee on Invisible Exports (1968), *Britain's Invisible Earnings*, London, British National Export Council.

Sayers, R.S. (1976), *The Bank of England 1891–1944*, Cambridge, Cambridge University Press.

Scammell, W.M. (1968), *The London Discount Market*, London, Elek Books.

Sheppard, D.K. (1971), *The Growth and Role of UK Financial Institutions 1880–1962*, London, Methuen.

Supple, B. (1970), *The Royal Exchange Assurance: A history of British insurance 1720–1970*, Cambridge, Cambridge University Press.

UNCTAD (1955), *Yearbook of International Trade Statistics 1954*, New York, United Nations.

UNCTAD (1964), *Yearbook of International Trade Statistics 1962*, New York, United Nations.

Victor Morgan, E. and Thomas, W.A. (1962), *The Stock Exchange: Its history and functions*, London, Elek Books.

Williamson, P. (1985), 'A "Bankers' Ramp"? Financiers and the British political crisis of August 1931', *English Historical Review*, 99:770–806.

6 The Keynesian revolution debate: time for a new approach?

Scott Newton

The debate about the extent and duration of the Keynesian revolution has generated enough contributions to create a sizeable clearing in the Amazonian rain forest (see, for example, Booth, 1984; Rollings, 1988; Tomlinson, 1984; Clarke, 1988). Environmental considerations apart, another note on the subject runs the risk of falling victim to the law of diminishing returns. It is therefore with some trepidation that I should like to suggest that there is more to be said.

Why? The basic problem is that so far the debate itself has been constructed in such a way as to make the achievement of any consensus impossible. Historians continue to argue the toss both about the meaning of Keynesian economics and about attitudes towards it inside the Treasury and find evidence to justify whatever viewpoint they hold. Thus Booth, starting from a definition which identifies Keynesian policies with the control of aggregate demand, can point to the presence of disinflationary budgets after 1947 as a sign of demand management (Booth, 1984: 123). Tomlinson, by contrast, maintaining that a successful revolution would amount 'to the subordination of fiscal policy to the needs of employment creation' has been able to argue that the post-war unwillingness of the Treasury to embrace budget deficits for expansionary purposes shows that the revolution never in fact took place (Tomlinson, 1984: 259). Rollings, in an attempt to produce a feasible synthesis, has accepted Booth's definition. He has, however, suggested that this should incorporate at least some of Tomlinson's observations because the evidence of Treasury files in the Public Record Office (PRO) reveals a good deal of resistance to the *implementation* of Keynesian policies during the 1950s, although their acceptance *in principle* can be traced back at least to 1945 (Rollings, 1988: 283–93). However, this argument does not square with the one advanced by P.F. Clarke, namely that the Treasury's interpretation of Keynes was influenced by the monetary economist Hawtrey, with the result that post-war demand management increasingly centred on manipulation of the interest rate (Clarke, 1988: 319).

So after nearly a decade of argument we still are not clear whether there really was a Keynesian revolution, or, if there was, what it meant. In an attempt at clarification Middleton has suggested that Keynes's message was merely that 'capitalist economies are not self-stabilising, thereby giving a role to government, and ...external equilibrium need not be at the expense of internal equilibrium' (Middleton, 1989: 547). However, this has been challenged by Booth, who has with some justification questioned the specifically Keynesian nature of such a definition, pointing out that 'A Marxist, a Hobsonian social democrat, a radical conservative...or a Treasury official with a price–profits analysis of the slump' would find no difficulty in sharing such a view of capitalist economies (Booth, 1989: 555).

Three steps are needed if we are to escape from this morass of inconclusive claims, arguments and counter-arguments. First, we need a definition. In the end Keynes may have been saying something very simple. Yet surely it was not that 'capitalist economies are not self-stabilising.' Keynes believed that capitalist economies could stabilize themselves—*but not necessarily at full employment* (Clarke, 1988: 281). The point of any revolution must therefore have been to manage demand so that a full employment level could be secured (accepting that for Keynes this implied that about 5 per cent of the work-force would be without jobs at any given time (Clarke, 1988: 317). To this end, it would indeed be necessary for the government to ensure that internal expansion was not sacrificed in the interests of attaining external equilibrium. If we accept such a definition it becomes necessary to say something about the conduct of external economic policy during the war and post-war years—a subject almost completely ignored by all the commentators.

This is surprising because the conduct of foreign economic policy, at least between 1940 and 1951–2, was revolutionary indeed. During the 1930s, Imperial Preference notwithstanding, Britain had been perhaps the most liberal of the capitalist powers. Sterling had remained internationally convertible, and Chamberlain's government had even been prepared to consider both cuts in the defence programme and an export drive in early 1940 to avoid any deterioration of the balance of trade and its corollary, the introduction of stringent controls on the international use and availability of the pound (Newton and Porter, 1988: 91–2). However, this attempt to tailor the war effort to the demands of managing an internationally convertible reserve currency was abandoned after Churchill became Premier. Churchill, unlike his predecessor, was committed to total war. It followed that all the economy's resources of capital and labour should be mobilized so that Britain could outproduce its enemy. In consequence, from May 1940 domestic expansion was sustained by the transformation of the sterling area into a discriminatory economic bloc. The automatic convertibility of sterling was suspended for the first time since the Napoleonic wars.

There was no return to the old order in 1945. The political settlement produced by the general election guaranteed that the Labour government would maintain the controls rather than use deflationary policies to cut the level of imports at a time of massive external economic difficulties. A more liberal foreign trade policy was never repudiated but regarded as an objective which could only be achieved without prohibitive domestic consequences once the problem of the foreign balance ceased to exist.

For all the attention devoted to Wilson's 'bonfire of controls', deregulation of the external sector did not seriously begin until after the return of the Conservatives in October 1951. Progress was erratic, but by 1958 sterling convertibility had been restored. During the 1950s, for the first time since 1940, the achievement of external balance was given priority over internal expansion. In the absence of physical controls the government was driven to use fiscal and monetary measures when the balance of payments lurched into the red, so that imports would fall in response to lower domestic demand. Full employment remained, but largely because of an international boom: there can be little doubt that in these years the government was prepared to go for external equilibrium at the expense of internal equilibrium (Newton, 1986; Newton and Porter, 1988: 120–32).

This brief survey brings us to the second step needed to revive the debate about the Keynesian revolution. It is not enough to assess the extent of the revolution by confining research to the Treasury archives, invaluable though this may be. A study of the interrelation between domestic and foreign economic policy reveals a correlation between macroeconomics and political choices. These choices were themselves the outcome of shifting popular alliances. It appears, for example, that the Labour victory of 1945 was the result of support from a coalition of voters, embracing trade unionists, returning servicemen and women, middle-class technocrats, the liberal professions and even some manufacturers wanting an economic order which would guarantee growth and profits through expansion. All these groups shared a commitment to a society characterized by full employment, social justice and industrial efficiency. The electoral vehicle best equipped to fulfil these hopes in 1945 was the Labour Party, which had itself undergone at the very least a partial conversion to Keynesian ideas since 1931 (Addison, 1975: 44–52; Newton and Porter, 1988: 101–8).

By the same token, the narrow Conservative victory of 1951 seems to have been a result of a middle-class desertion from the Labour Party. The evidence suggests growing anxiety about 'red tape' and high taxes, about 'socialist regimentation' through open-ended commitments to nationalization, and about inflationary pressures which if not controlled would erode the value of personal savings. This complex of fears was accompanied by a more general, status-driven neurosis that the balance of power in Britain was swinging irrevocably in the direction of organized labour. It therefore seems possible to maintain that the Conservatives were voted in by their own coalition, founded perhaps on middle-class consumers, small businessmen and rentiers, but extending to include technocratic and manufacturing interests (Bonham,

1954; Newton and Porter, 1988: 120–32). The last now believed that the interwar problems of overcapacity and stagnation had been exchanged for new issues threatening their independence, such as state intervention and the power of the trade union movement. In these circumstances it was logical to support a political party committed to a smaller role for the state, deregulation and tax cuts *and the maintenance of economic growth and full employment*. It was when the inability of the Conservatives to deliver sustained growth became obvious that the electoral groups which had swung to the Right in 1951 deserted it for Harold Wilson's Labour Party in 1963–4. It seems, therefore, that the grip of the Keynesian revolution varied in accordance with the shifting balance of social forces. It follows that it might be profitable for economic historians writing about this subject to pay much closer attention to the work of political scientists, psephologists and sociologists, all of whom might be better placed to offer explanations of voting behaviour and political choices during the post-war era.

The third step needed for the development of this debate takes us back to the Treasury. The influence of the Treasury on economic policy makes it worthwhile attempting to see if there was a 'Treasury view' on the Keynesian revolution. Treasury archives have already been the subject of extensive research, but increasingly this has been on the level of 'what one clerk said to another'. It has in fact told us very little beyond the unsurprising fact that some Treasury officials were Keynesian while others may not have been. Perhaps the most interesting findings come from Rollings, who has noted the discrepancy between an acceptance of Keynesian theory and an apparent reluctance to implement Keynesian policy (Rollings, 1988: 283–98). So were the civil servants there intellectual cowards? Were they schizophrenic? Or was it perhaps that the implications of Keynesian political economy flew in the face of the long-term mission of the Treasury to control the level of public expenditure. Clearly, there is no necessary incompatibility between efficient control of the public purse and the pursuit of full employment. However, there may have been real difficulties for the British Treasury, whose commitment to the balanced budget had historically reinforced that of the City of London and the Bank of England to free trade and the gold standard (Ingham, 1984). Given that the return to gold was not on the agenda in 1951, it is arguable that the mid-century manifestation of this orthodoxy involved at least the restoration of sterling to convertibility (Newton, 1986).

Perhaps, then, the economic historian should study the Treasury as a political sociologist, finding out about the recruitment of staff, social and educational backgrounds, the connections with the Bank of England and the City. Did the long-standing ties and years of daily co-operation in pursuit of agreed policy objectives generate an ideology, a world view which identified the maintenance of external balance with the national economic interest? Is this perhaps the explanation for the contradictory attitudes noted by Rollings? Was there perhaps a plurality of discourses within the Treasury, rendering impossible an unambiguous commitment to the Keynesian revolution?

Bibliography

Addison, P. (1975), *The Road to 1945*, London, Quartet Books.
Bonham, J. (1954), *The Middle Class Vote*, London, Faber.
Booth, A. (1984) '"The Keynesian revolution" in economic policy-making', *Economic History Review*, 2nd ser., XXXVII: 263–7.
Booth, A. (1989) 'Britain in the 1930s: a managed economy? A reply to Peden and Middleton', *Economic History Review*, 2nd ser., XLII: 548–56.
Clarke, P. (1988), *The Keynesian Revolution in the Making*, Oxford, Clarendon Press.
Ingham, G. (1984), *Capitalism Divided? The City and industry in British social development*, London, Macmillan.
Middleton, R. (1989), 'Britain in the 1930s: a managed economy? A comment', *Economic History Review*, 2nd ser., XLII: 544–7.
Newton, S. (1986), 'Operation ROBOT and the political economy of sterling convertibility, 1951–2', Florence, European University Institute.
Newton, S. and Porter, D. (1988), *Modernization Frustrated: The politics of industrial decline in Britain since 1900*, London, Unwin Hyman.
Rollings, N. (1988), 'British budgetary policy, 1945–1954: a "Keynesian revolution"?' *Economic History Review*, 2nd ser., XLI: 283–97.
Tomlinson, J. (1984), 'A Keynesian revolution in economic policy-making', *Economic History Review*, 2nd ser., XXXVII: 258–62.

7 The monetary policies of the 1945–51 Labour governments

Susan Howson

To an economist in the 1980s the monetary policies of the first post-war Labour governments seem odd—at best misguided, at worst completely inappropriate. The UK monetary authorities (the Treasury and the Bank of England) faced a persistent problem of inflation in 1945–51. Yet the first post-war Labour Chancellor of the Exchequer (and the first professional economist to become Chancellor), Hugh Dalton, tried to *lower interest rates* in his two years in office, and his successors as Chancellor, Stafford Cripps and Hugh Gaitskell (the latter also a professional economist) failed to use monetary policy when it might have been expected to be accorded a role in helping to combat inflation. In much of my work on the monetary policy of the Attlee governments I have, therefore, concentrated on finding out the reasons for the policies adopted under the three Chancellors. In this chapter I summarize my findings so far: I describe briefly these policies and why they were carried out, and indicate *some* of their effects, also briefly.[1] First, however, some background information on the economy.

Britain had an alarmingly severe current account balance of payments problem in 1945. The dimensions of that problem were such a low level of visible exports (cut back deliberately and drastically during the war to less than half their prewar volume), together with a reduced income from invisibles (because of shipping losses and the sale of overseas assets), that although imports had also been severely reduced (to 60 per cent of prewar volume) there was no prospect of paying for them out of current earnings for several years. In 1945 imports of goods including munitions of war amounted to £1,900 million, exports including wartime reciprocal aid were only £900 million and net invisibles (including here overseas government expenditure) were in a negative balance of around £600 million. Half of the £1,600 million current account deficit for 1945 was covered by lend-lease, the other half by accumulating debts, especially in sterling (the notorious 'sterling balances'), and selling off overseas assets (Sayers, 1956: Appendix 1, Table 10).[2] Until

80

visible exports could be raised to 50–75 per cent above the prewar volume, the current account deficit would have to be financed by overseas aid of some kind. The abrupt end of the war against Japan only two weeks after the Attlee government took office meant that this aid could not be wartime lend-lease.

There was apparently nothing for it but to ask the Americans (and the Canadians) for further financial assistance. The Labour government in August sent Lord Keynes to Washington to negotiate. After three months of bitter and protracted negotiations the US administration agreed to lend $3.75 billion—at 2 per cent interest, to be repaid over 50 years from 1951—on conditions which included the commitments to make sterling convertible for current transactions within one year of the effective date of the agreement and to give up discrimination in trade at the same time. The Canadian government lent a further $1.25 billion in March 1946. (For the full story of the loan agreements see Pressnell, 1987: chapter 10.) Although this $5 billion was supposed to take care of the balance of payments problem during the transition to peace, it did not do so for long, and as Alec Cairncross has emphasized in his *Years of Recovery* (1985: 20–1), the post-war Labour governments faced a balance of payments crisis every other year (1945, 1947, 1949, 1951). In the 1947 crisis the convertibility and non-discrimination obligations were fulfilled (on 15 July), and almost immediately abandoned (on 20 August) in face of a rapid loss of official international reserves. In the 1949 crisis the pound sterling was devalued from the wartime $4.03 to $2.80 on 18 September. The 1951 crisis followed the Korean war and British rearmament. It was still in progress when the Labour government, which had been re-elected the previous year, was voted out of office in the October general election.

The Attlee government of 1945 was the first Labour government in Britain to have a majority in the House of Commons. As Elizabeth Durbin has well described in her book, *New Jerusalems* (1985), it came to office with plenty of ideas on economic and financial policy for a 'socialist' government in a mixed economy. The ideas I want to mention here were included in the Labour Party's counterpart to the wartime Coalition government's White Paper on *Employment Policy* (Cmd. 6527, May 1944): the party's *Full Employment and Financial Policy*, published in April 1944, was written by Hugh Dalton (the final version) and Evan Durbin, Hugh Gaitskell, and Douglas Jay (the earlier drafts). The presumptions and hopes behind this document can be summed up in two quotations from it:

Blame for unemployment [especially in the years between the two world wars] lies much more with finance than with industry.

Finance must be the servant, and the intelligent servant, of the community and productive industry; not their stupid master.

(Labour Party, 1944:2–3)

This meant that a Labour government would have to continue wartime financial controls for the post-war transitional period at least, as well as taking control of the Bank of England by nationalizing it (which had been Party policy since 1928). The commercial banks for their part would be obliged, as they had been during the war, to lend directly at low interest rates to the government whenever required. Wartime control over new issues of capital should be maintained and so should exchange control, which was 'vital' in order to prevent interest rates from rising immediately after the war (as they had done after the First World War). Indeed, the economists in the Labour Party, aware of the constraints on domestic monetary policy imposed by international mobility of capital, wanted to insulate the domestic capital market from external influences so as to provide policy independence. They believed—incorrectly as it turned out—that a continuation of wartime exchange control would provide this. There should also be no rigidly fixed exchange rates (certainly not the gold standard after the financial crisis of 1931 which had destroyed the second Labour government), but this did not mean a Labour government could not co-operate in international arrangements to provide stable managed exchange rates consistent with the maintenance of full employment and to reduce trade barriers. Although import controls and some state trading, introduced during the war, would continue it was essential to boost British exports by at least 50 per cent in order to be able to buy essential imports. As for the use to be made of macroeconomic policy independence, in the immediate post-war transitional period inflation could be kept at bay by the maintenance of the price controls, rationing, cost-of-living subsidies, and building and raw material controls that had been used in wartime, while money was kept cheap to finance reconstruction. After the transitional period, when a depression was feared, expansionary budgetary policy should be used to boost both consumption and investment expenditure.[3]

As I have already mentioned, the author of the final version of this report was Hugh Dalton. When he became Chancellor of the Exchequer in 1945 some of his financial policy followed the recommendations of the report. For instance, he nationalized the Bank of England, which came into public ownership on 1 March 1946, and introduced legislation to make exchange control permanent (the Exchange Control Act, 1947). However, as I have argued at length elsewhere (Howson, 1987 and 1989), his monetary policy, his 'cheaper money policy', did not follow from the published proposals of the Labour Party and it did not reflect the views or advice of most of the younger Labour Party economists who had advised him, for instance, Evan Durbin, Hugh Gaitskell, Douglas Jay, and James Meade. It reflected, I have claimed, the more Keynesian advice of Joan Robinson and of Keynes himself. (Joan Robinson was a member of the Party's wartime Post-war Finance Subcommittee of the National Executive Committee in 1943–4; Keynes was in the Treasury during the war and remained in the Treasury as Dalton's personal economic adviser until his death in April 1946.) They both argued that the authorities could and should fix long-term as well as short-term interest rates on government debt at levels which fitted in with wider economic and social objectives (wider than the objectives the Treasury and the Bank of England usually had in mind), and that in the immediate post-war period at least monetary policy need not be used to fight inflation, because physical controls would be needed to restrain investment anyway. Keynes proposed lowering short-term interest rates in 1945 and keeping long-term rates on government bonds around 3 per cent (their wartime level) to encourage saving. Robinson advocated progressively lowering long-term rates below 3 per cent in order to reduce the rewards to investors. Both saw permanently low long-term interest rates as a means to increase the rate of growth of the capital stock in the medium to long run. In other words, monetary policy could be used in the 'comprehensive socialization of investment' and for the 'euthanasia of the rentier' advocated in Keynes's *General Theory* (1936: 220-1, 375-8).[4] Dalton later claimed that he had tried to reduce long-term interest rates from the wartime 3 per cent in order 'to save public expenditure on interest, to improve the distribution of income, to encourage investment [though he did not think that this was very important when there were physical controls on investment] and to make sure of full employment . . . to keep down the cost of [public] housing programmes' and to reduce the cost of the nationalization programme (which involved the coal industry, the railways, the gas, electricity, and iron and steel industries, as well as the Bank of England). He also did not think that inflation was a serious problem in 1946 (Dalton, 1954: 233, 235 and 241).

What Dalton actually did was, first, in the autumn of 1945, to reduce short-term interest rates on Treasury bills and other floating debt held mainly by the banks. These had been fixed during the war around 1 per cent and were now cut to ½ per cent. At the same time he loudly announced he was considering whether to lower longer-term interest rates, in order to encourage expectations of lower rates. Having managed to flatten the yield curve somewhat, he tried to take advantage of it in 1946 to issue two very long-term government bonds at 2½ per cent.

The first bond issue was quite successful but by the time of the second, at the end of the year, expectations were changing, at least partly because it could be seen in the behaviour of bank deposits that the money supply was increasing rapidly to maintain the 2½ per cent yield on existing government stocks. (For the growth of the money supply—bank deposits plus currency—see Figure 7.1.) Widely read financial commentators were warning investors that the authorities might get cold feet, and that interest rates would sooner or later rise. Investors did not rush to buy the new government stock and the authorities bought most of it themselves. After the issue was closed in January 1947, the authorities reduced the extent of their intervention in the gilt-edged market, and did indeed get cold feet about the monetary and inflationary consequences of Dalton's low interest rate policy (see pp. 85-6 below).

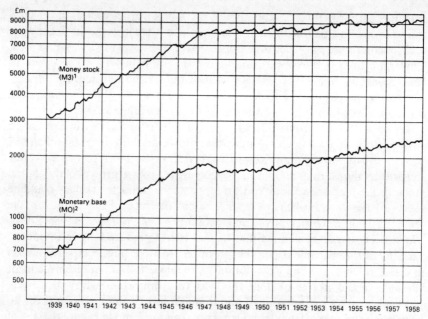

Notes:

1. M3 = Currency in circulation plus net deposits of UK banks
2. MO = Currency in circulation plus cash reserves of UK commercial banks.

Sources:

M3:   F. Capie and A. Webber, *A Monetary History of the United Kingdom 1870–1982*, vol. I, Table I(3), column I

MO: Calculated from data on currency circulation and the Bank of England's balance sheet in *Bank of England Statistical Summary* (various issues) for 1939–45 and in *Monthly Digest of Statistics* (various issues) for 1945–58; figures for banks' cash and till money in F. Capie and A. Webber, *A Monetary History of the United Kingdom 1870–1982*, vol. I, Table II(2), columns V and VI.

Figure 7.1   Money stock and monetary base, 1939–58.

What was the role of the permanent Treasury officials and the Bank of England in these developments? Briefly, the senior Treasury officials went along with Keynes's initial recommendations (for cutting short-term interest rates and keeping long-term rates at 3 per cent) and then with Dalton's desire to go down to $2\frac{1}{2}$ per cent. They did so both because low nominal interest rates reduced government expenditure on interest payments and because they shared the widespread fears of a post-war depression on the 1920s scale and hence accepted the Keynesian argument that interest rates could and should be kept down during the transition. The Bank of England, on the other hand, were not enthusiastic about Keynes's or Dalton's ideas. They thought the Treasury was being over-optimistic; but they were prepared to try to issue low interest bonds because any success would ease their problems of managing the

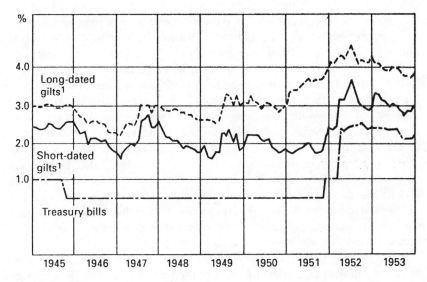

Notes:

1. Gross redemption yields for the following selected stocks:
   Short-dated: 1945-9: 2½% National War Bonds 1952/4
                  1950-2: 2¼% Exchequer Stock 1955
                  1953: 2½% Funding Loan 1956/61
   Long-dated: 1945-7: 3% Savings Bonds 1960/70
                  1948-50: 2½% Savings Bonds 1964/67
                  1951-3: 3% Savings Bonds 1965/75

Sources:

Securities yields: *Bank of England Statistical Abstract*, No. 1, 1970, Table 30.
Treasury bill discount rate: F. Capie and A. Webber, *A Monetary History of the United Kingdom 1870-1982*, vol. I, Table III(10), column III.

Figure 7.2 Yields on British government securities and discount rate on Treasury bills, 1945-53.

huge government debt (which amounted to some £22.5 billion compared with a national income of £9.9 billion in 1945 (Pember and Boyle, 1950; Feinstein, 1972: Table 3)). They also—which became apparent a couple of years later (see p. 88 below)—did not believe in controlling the money supply. The Bank therefore assisted the drive for cheaper money in 1946 by buying up government stocks from the market when market demand for them threatened to fall off, but once the second 2½ per cent long-term bond issue had been made, they ceased such intervention. Although Dalton continued to talk about continuing to provide cheaper money during 1947, nothing was being done actively to support it. His cheaper money policy can now be seen to have ended at the beginning of 1947, well before the crises of that year.

During 1947 nominal yields on government securities rose again, returning to 3 per cent for long-term securities during the balance of payments crisis in the summer (see Figure 7.2). Although Dalton's cheaper money policy was not ended by the balance of payments crisis, it is unlikely that it could have survived it. The signs of changing expectations about future rates towards the end of 1946 and the reluctance of the Bank of England to intervene to support the gilt-edged market in the first quarter of 1947, suggest that the amount of intervention that would have been necessary to hold interest rates down to Dalton's desired levels would have exceeded the intervention the authorities would have been prepared to undertake. Although the final decision to abandon $2\frac{1}{2}$ per cent was not taken until the end of 1947, after Dalton had resigned as Chancellor of the Exchequer, when the terms of the first large issue of nationalization compensation (in the form of government-guaranteed stocks) had to be settled, Dalton later recorded that he 'had been too tired that summer and autumn to fight the Bank in favour of intervention [and] had, in fact, given up that ghost, for the time being at any rate'.[5]

The balance of payments crisis of the summer of 1947 had been building up from early in the year. In the first half of the year, the six months before the date for making sterling convertible into dollars for current transactions under the terms of the 1945 loan agreement, the current account deficit, which had fallen during 1946 from £870 million to £320 million (Feinstein's estimates), was increasing again. Aggravated by an adverse shift in the terms of trade, the deficits of the overseas sterling area were also increasing. On top of this convertibility was gradually introduced in advance of 15 July 1947 by means of monetary agreements with European and other countries negotiated by the Bank of England. These did not always distinguish clearly between current and capital transactions and there were significant switches of externally held sterling into dollars before 15 July (Cairncross, 1985: chapter 6). A rapid drain of foreign exchange reserves brought home to the Labour government and its advisers that the British economy was not insulated from external factors by exchange and other controls, as well as precipitating the suspension of convertibility on 20 August 1947.

It is well established in the literature that by the time Dalton resigned after a budget leak in November 1947, there had been a major reorientation of the government's domestic financial policy. Import controls may have been tightened, convertibility and non-discrimination given up, and Marshall Aid from the Americans might be forthcoming, but none of this would cure Britain's balance of payments problem unless domestic absorption was cut to reduce excess demand and prevent inflation. Hence Dalton's two 'disinflationary' surplus budgets in April and November 1947, and the series of similar budgets of the new Chancellor, Stafford Cripps. But what about monetary policy?

Here there are two major questions: (1) Did Dalton's monetary policy contribute to the severity of the balance of payments problem and the 'convertibility crisis'? (2) What should the role of monetary policy have been from 1947 onwards? I shall save consideration of the first question until the end of this chapter.

There was little apparent change in UK monetary policy after 1947. The authorities gave up attempting to sell long-term bonds with nominal yields of less than 3 per cent—and paid nationalization compensation in government-guaranteed stocks with 3 per cent coupons in 1948 and 1949—while keeping Bank rate at 2 per cent and short-term rates on government debt at the ½ per cent introduced by Dalton in October 1945. The money supply stopped rising at the rates in excess of 10 per cent a year experienced in 1946 and during the war, and long-term nominal interest rates drifted upwards towards 4 per cent by 1951 (Figures 7.1 and 7.2). There was no change in monetary stance to accompany the devaluation of the pound in 1949, nor were there any deliberate changes in interest rates until the new Conservative government raised Bank rate in November 1951 to 2½ per cent and then to 4 per cent in March 1952.

The conventional view of this period has been that the authorities were pursuing a 'neutral money' policy, as Christopher Dow (1964: 49) put it. Dow also (ibid.: 228–9) described the period of Cripps' and Gaitskell's Chancellorships as the 'St. Lucy's day of monetary policy' because there was scarcely any mention of monetary policy or monetary conditions in government statements on economic policy. More recently the Treasury files and Economic Section papers in the Public Record Office have made it clear that despite outward appearances there was a good deal of discussion on the role of monetary policy going on behind the scenes. One individual particularly concerned was Robert Hall, who had succeeded James Meade as Director of the Economic Section of the Cabinet Offices in the summer of 1947. His participation has, therefore, been described by Alec Cairncross in his work on the history of the Economic Section, and of course by Hall himself in his recently published diary (Cairncross, 1987: 2–10; Cairncross and Watts, 1989: 213–15; and Hall, 1989). Discussions in the Treasury over the appropriate role of monetary weapons in an anti-inflationary policy in fact began in the autumn of 1947 and continued for the rest of the Labour governments' period of office (and beyond). I shall briefly indicate here the issues involved and how the Labour economists and ministers perceived them.

Although most of the plans drawn up by Labour Party economists in the 1930s dealt with unemployment in a depression, the younger Labour economists had also been concerned with avoiding inflation in boom conditions and had assumed that countercyclical monetary and fiscal policy would be used to reduce excess demand (Howson, 1988: 547–50). Several were critical of Dalton's monetary policy in 1946 and by 1947 were to be found, in and out of government, proposing a tighter monetary stance to accompany the anti-inflationary budgetary measures taken in 1947. (To cite only one example, it was at this time that James Meade, on resigning from government service, wrote his *Planning and the Price Mechanism* (1948).) When Douglas

Jay became a junior Treasury minister in October (first Dalton's Parliamentary Private Secretary and then Economic Secretary), his first attempt to influence Treasury policy was to argue for tighter monetary control. Although he weakened his case by being confused about how it could be done (he said he wanted to reduce bank deposits without raising interest rates) his agitation did lead to a Treasury–Bank working party on the possibilities of limiting the growth of bank deposits and advances.[6]

During the working party's discussions the Bank of England made it clear that they did not, and did not want to, control the money supply directly. During the war their policy with respect to the monetary base (currency in circulation plus the reserves of the commercial banks) had been accommodating, supplying currency and bank reserves whenever the banks wanted them so as to keep their reserves in line with (i.e. a more or less constant proportion of) their rapidly growing deposits. The Bank continued the practice throughout the 1940s, so the money supply was endogenously determined by the demand for money. The Bank were, however, in favour of devoting some of the budget surplus to redeeming floating debt and also of converting short-term government debt to longer-term debt whenever market conditions allowed. At this time (1948) they had no desire to raise Bank rate (which had only been above 2 per cent for one six-week period since 1932). In the Treasury the officials' concern was also with debt management. This made them reluctant to raise interest rates, especially short-term rates on floating debt, because this would immediately increase the interest burden of the debt on the budget. The reluctance to raise short-term interest rates was shared by senior ministers, including Cripps, because it would increase the interest paid by the government to the banks and boost the banks' profits.

The authorities had thus boxed themselves in, having ruled out both control of bank reserves and the use of interest rates for monetary control. Not surprisingly, the Treasury, including Douglas Jay and Robert Hall, tried to find a way out in direct controls on the assets or liabilities of the clearing banks. The Bank of England's initial line on quantitative controls was that they were impossible or at least impracticable. All that could be done was to ask the banks to be 'selective' and 'cautious' in their lending. Such requests were made to the banks by the Chancellor of the Exchequer through the Governor of the Bank of England on several occasions in 1948–51 but without conspicuous success. They did not satisfy the more concerned people in the Treasury (Jay and Hall in particular). However, by the end of 1948, the Bank—in the person of the Deputy Governor, C.F. Cobbold, who became Governor in March 1949—had decided that what they really wanted was a rise in (short-term) interest rates. Cobbold campaigned for the next three years to obtain this rise. It might be thought that since he succeeded only when a Conservative government replaced the Labour administration, the reason it took him so long was the Labour government's reluctance to increase the cost of the debt. But Cobbold's tactics were not well chosen: during the 1949 balance of payments crisis he campaigned for government expenditure cuts, first as a substitute for devaluation, and then to accompany it, and thus lost a possible chance to tighten monetary stance which the Treasury people then favoured. When he did ask to raise interest rates, after the devaluation decision and then again in December 1950 and June 1951, he failed to explain how the small interest rate rise he was asking for would significantly reduce the growth of the money supply. As the Treasury warned the Bank, 'if the Chancellor [Cripps] were to be persuaded the Bank would have to make out a very clear and detailed case', which they did not. When Cripps consulted Hugh Gaitskell, Douglas Jay and Harold Wilson on the Governor's request in September 1949, they were, in reaching a negative decision, 'influenced ... partly by their inability to agree that the very moderate increase in short-term rates which the Bank advocates would have any real disinflationary effect'.[7]

Gaitskell's attitude to monetary policy in his year as Chancellor of the Exchequer is particularly interesting. Although he was in many respects an enthusiastic supporter of 'planning' during the Attlee governments' period of office (for instance, in being reluctant to give up physical controls entirely and to rely on financial controls instead),[8] he surprised his officials on becoming Chancellor by admitting he wanted to see at least long-term interest rates rise in 1950. He had while Minister of State for Economic Affairs at the Treasury (since the February 1950 general election) asked for a review of the weapons of monetary and credit control used in other countries, in order to find out what alternative methods of monetary control might be available. When the Governor of the Bank of England asked him to permit a rise in short-term interest rates, he took some time and considerable thought to make up his mind. As he put it to his officials, 'leaving on one side the question of the additional cost to the Exchequer, he felt that the other arguments [for and against a rise in short-term interest rates] were nicely balanced.' His officials at that time (January 1951) were divided, with some strongly in favour of the Governor's proposals and others doubtful. Douglas Jay (now Financial Secretary at the Treasury since February 1950) was against, partly because it might raise the cost of the next nationalization (the iron and steel industry in 1951) and partly because the Bank had still not explained exactly how a small rise in short-term interest rates would have a major impact on bank lending and hence the money supply. Gaitskell was irritated by the Governor's refusal to produce good arguments, turning down his request in January 1951 and then delaying a decision on his next request in the summer until the autumn.[9]

I have speculated elsewhere (Howson, 1988: 562–3) that Gaitskell would have allowed a rise in short-term interest rates if he had remained Chancellor after the general election in October 1951. There were discussions at that time among economists in the Labour Party, which concluded that it would not be inappropriate (or 'unsocialist') to pursue an anti-inflationary policy involving higher short and long-term interest rates. Tony Crosland even managed to persuade Hugh Dalton that a rise in interest rates was not wicked, and would not necessarily have undesirable redistributive consequences. It was also in 1951 that the government, and economists in and out of the Party, stopped worrying about the imminence of a post-war slump like that of the 1920s.

Let me now return to the question of the effects of Dalton's cheaper money policy, and of the 'neutral money' policy that followed it.

Dalton's attempt to drive down long-term interest rates in 1946 and the subsequent abandonment of that attempt show up clearly in the monetary aggregates as well as in the behaviour of interest rates. Figure 7.1 plots a broad measure of the money supply (M3, total bank deposits plus currency in circulation) and the monetary base (currency in circulation plus commercial bank reserves) monthly from January 1939 to December 1958.[10] It shows rapid growth in both series during the war, with annual growth rates of around 12 per cent (nearly 20 per cent in 1941). There was a slowdown in late 1945 and early 1946 but the money supply took off again in 1946 and grew by 14 per cent that year. In 1947 there was a change in the trend of monetary growth, and M3 grew at an annual average rate of around 2 per cent for the remainder of the Labour governments' period of office, and at about 3 per cent a year in the 1950s. (The behaviour of a narrower measure, M1, currency plus current account bank deposits, is similar except that it grew even more rapidly than the broader aggregate in the early years of the war.) These series are nominal aggregates. If one deflates by prices (using either the Gross Domestic Product (GDP) deflator or the consumer price index), one finds the real money supply increasing by between 3 and 10 per cent per annum during the war, and by nearly 12 per cent in 1946, then declining (except in 1950, when it was roughly constant, and in 1953–4 when it rose by 2 per cent).[11] In other words, the money stock was growing faster than the price level in 1939–46 and more slowly thereafter (except in 1950 and 1953–4).

The size of the monetary shock in 1946 is even more striking if one looks at the ratio of the money stock to money income. In the later 1930s the ratios of M1 and M3 to GNP were around 33 and 55 per cent respectively. They both fell in 1940 when there was a large rise in *real* income, and then they rose steadily through the rest of the war to reach 50 per cent and 70 per cent in 1945. Both took a large further leap upwards in 1946, to 57 and 79 per cent, at which they peaked. They steadily declined 1948–51 and were back to their 1938 levels by 1952.

It has been suggested explicitly or implicitly that neither Dalton's cheaper money policy nor the subsequent neutral monetary policy had much effect on the British economy—in the case of Dalton's policy either because it was short-lived or because the variables which it could have affected in normal circumstances, for instance investment and prices, were subject to controls (see Kennedy, 1952: 193–5; Dow 1964: 21–2). However, these arguments imply that it is difficult to isolate the effects of Dalton's monetary policy, not that it had no effect. It may be true that the lower interest rates would have little impact on real investment because of physical controls, and that observed prices in 1946–7 reflect several other factors besides an increase in the money supply (such as cost-of-living subsidies and import prices). But the abnormally high money-to-income ratios, especially in 1946, suggest that people were holding excess money balances which they would have wanted to spend. There is evidence from several sources of post-war dissaving from late 1946.[12] This would have increased domestic absorption in 1946 and 1947, and hence increased the size of the policy adjustments that had to be made to cope with the balance of payments problem in 1947—and probably for the rest of the Attlee governments' period of office.

I draw several conclusions from the story of monetary policy in 1945–51 reported here. First, the policy espoused by the Labour Party as well as by the authors of the wartime Coalition government's *Employment Policy* White Paper, of maintaining wartime controls and wartime cheap money into the post-war transitional period was understandable, given the desire not to repeat the 1919–23 experience when dear money imposed to fight uncontrolled post-war inflation had preceded a severe and prolonged slump (on that experience see Howson, 1975: chapter 2). Second, Dalton's cheaper money policy went beyond that limited objective and was inappropriate in the post-war monetary situation. It was inappropriate because it exacerbated the existing 'excess' (by normal peacetime standards) liquidity of the private sector, which in itself threatened serious inflation unless the feared slump arrived soon. Dalton was not alone in his undue pessimism about the timing of the depression, but he was also excessively optimistic about the ability of controls to prevent open inflation. He therefore took an unwarranted risk in trying to use nominal interest rates as an instrument to influence income distribution and ruling out its use as a weapon of macroeconomic policy. Third, when the inflationary consequences of Dalton's monetary policy were recognized (even if not fully understood), the authorities failed to use monetary means to undo them because of disagreement between the Treasury and the Bank of England over the role of monetary policy in the post-war world. This had at least two consequences. The adjustment to lower, more 'normal' levels of real balances during the later 1940s came about slowly and indirectly, since the supply of money was endogenously determined. Also, the Labour government was obliged to place greater reliance on other macroeconomic policy instruments (including budgetary policy, incomes policy and devaluation) in order to contain inflation and improve the balance of payments.

Acknowledgements

This chapter is based, directly and indirectly, on several unpublished sources. For permission to use them I should like to thank Dr Angela Raspin (Dalton and Piercy Papers, British Library of Political and Economic Science),

Professor James Meade (Meade Papers, British Library of Political and Economic Science), Dr Stephen Bird (Labour Party Archives), and the Controller of Her Majesty's Stationery Office (Treasury Papers, Public Record Office). I am also grateful to Professor Forrest Capie, Dr Roger Middleton and Professor Donald Moggridge for helpful critical comments on the chapter when it was presented as a paper to the second ICBH/LSE Summer School on British History 1935–70 at the London School of Economics in July 1989.

Notes

1. I have already published some of my findings on the reasons behind the policies: see Howson 1987, 1988, 1989. I also utilize here a forthcoming paper on 'The problem of monetary control, 1948–51', *Journal of European Economic History* 1991.

2. If goods acquired under lend-lease and reciprocal aid are excluded, the figures for imports of goods and services amount to £1,930 million, exports to £1,110 million (Feinstein, 1972: Table 15).

3. Labour Party, 1944: 2–7. On the preparation of the document see Howson, 1988: 550–7.

4. Keynes's and Robinson's proposals for post-war monetary policy can be found in, respectively, Keynes, 1980: 388–404, and Labour Party RDR 133, 'War-time control of the rate of interest', September 1942, and 'Note to be appended to RDR 133', Labour Party Archives.

5. Dalton's diary, 20 October 1950, British Library of Political and Economic Science.

6. This and the next three paragraphs draw heavily on my paper, 'The problem of monetary control, 1948–51'.

7. Quotations from: Note by Radice, 16 September, and Trend to Wass, 21 September 1949, T233/1400, Public Record Office.

8. Gaitskell to Cripps, and 'Controls and Economic Policy' 3 January 1950, T230/319, Public Record Office. A couple of months later Robert Hall commented on a discussion he and Edwin Plowden (head of the Central Economic Planning Staff) had had with Gaitskell: 'I think we made some progress and that if we had time we could convert him to all our ways of thought' (Hall, 1989: 109).

9. Trend, 'Note of a meeting on the 5th January', 23 January 1951, T233/1400, Public Record Office; see also Gaitskell, 1983: 227 and Hall, 1989: 143.

10. I have followed the conventional definition of the monetary base in excluding notes and coin in the Banking Department of the Bank of England, which Capie and Webber include in their series (1985: chapter 1 and Table I(1)).

11. Calculated using M1 and M3 from Capie and Webber, 1985: Tables I(2) and I(3), and price indices from Feinstein, 1972: Table 61.

12. For instance, an aggregate personal sector saving ratio of only 1 per cent of personal disposable income in 1947–51, compared with over 4 per cent before the war and after 1951 (calculated from Feinstein, 1972: Table 10), and a shift in the pattern of

consumers expenditure towards durable goods (ibid., Tables 24 and 25). There is also evidence of pressure on the controls from 1946: see Mills and Rockoff, 1987: 201.

Bibliography

Cairncross, Alec (1985), *Years of Recovery: British economic policy 1945–51*, London, Methuen.

Cairncross, Alec (1987), 'Prelude to Radcliffe: monetary policy in the United Kingdom 1948–57', *Revista di Storia Economica*, 4: 1–20.

Cairncross, Alec and Nita Watts (1989), *The Economic Section 1939–1961: A study in economic advising*, London, Routledge.

Capie, Forrest and Alan Webber (1985), *A Monetary History of the United Kingdom 1870–1982*, volume I: *Data, Sources, Methods*, London, Allen and Unwin.

Dalton, H. (1954), *Principles of Public Finance* (4th edn), London, Routledge and Kegan Paul.

Dow, J.C.R. (1964), *The Management of the British Economy 1945–60*, Cambridge, Cambridge University Press.

Durbin, Elizabeth (1985), *New Jerusalems: The Labour Party and the economics of democratic socialism*, London, Routledge and Kegan Paul.

Feinstein, C.H. (1972), *National Income, Expenditure and Output of the United Kingdom 1855–1965*, Cambridge, Cambridge University Press.

Gaitskell, Hugh (1983), *The Diary of Hugh Gaitskell 1945–1956*, ed. Philip M. Williams, London, Jonathan Cape.

Hall, Robert (1989), *The Robert Hall Diaries 1947–53*, ed. Alec Cairncross, London, Unwin Hyman.

Howson, Susan (1975), *Domestic Monetary Management in Britain, 1919–38*, Cambridge, Cambridge University Press.

Howson, Susan (1987), 'The origins of cheaper money, 1945–7', *Economic History Review*, 40: 433–52.

Howson, Susan (1988), ' "Socialist" monetary policy: monetary thought in the Labour Party in the 1940s', *History of Political Economy*, 20: 543–64.

Howson, Susan (1989), 'Cheap money versus cheaper money: a reply to Professor Wood', *Economic History Review*, 42: 401–5.

Kennedy, C.M. (1952), 'Monetary policy', in Worswick and Ady (1952, 188–206).

Keynes, J.M. (1936), *The General Theory of Employment, Interest and Money*, London, Macmillan.

Keynes, J.M. (1980), *The Collected Writings of John Maynard Keynes*, vol. XXVII, *Activities 1940–1946, Shaping the Post-war World: Employment and commodities*, ed. D.E. Moggridge, London, Macmillan.

Labour Party (1944), *Full Employment and Financial Policy*, London, Labour Party.

Meade, James Edward (1948), *Planning and the Price Mechanism: The Liberal–Socialist solution*, London, Allen and Unwin.

Mills, Geoffrey and Hugh Rockoff (1987), 'Compliance with price controls in the United States and the United Kingdom During World War II', *Journal of Economic History*, 47: 197–213.

Pember and Boyle (1950), *British Government Securities in the Twentieth Century*, London, privately printed.

Pressnell, L.S. (1987), *External Economic Policy since the War*: vol. I: *The Post-War Financial Settlement*, London, Her Majesty's Stationery Office.

Sayers, R.S. (1956), *Financial Policy 1939–45*, London, Her Majesty's Stationery Office.

Worswick, G.D.N. and P.H. Ady (1952), *The British Economy 1945–1950*, Oxford, Clarendon Press.

8 'The next war is bound to come': Defence production policy, supply departments and defence contractors in Britain, 1945–57[1]

Till Geiger

The experience of the Second World War underlined the importance of a healthy economy in the age of mechanized warfare. The revolution in warfare brought a greater reliance on large-scale mechanization of the military, and a strong armaments industry and engineering sector had become one of the pillars of military power. The ability of the Allies to outproduce their enemies was seen as instrumental in their victory over Germany and Japan (Harrison 1988: 171). Immediately after the Second World War, however, the Labour government had been determined to restrict severely the resources going to defence in order to facilitate the restoration of a balanced peace economy as soon as possible.

> Defence policy must be compatible with the national need not only because of the heavy demands made on national resources—both manpower and material—by the Armed Forces, but also because a successful defence policy must find its roots in healthy social and economic conditions.
>
> (Ministry of Defence, 1947:2)

Even though the Labour government intended to give priority to the civil economy in the immediate post-war period, British defence spending as a share of GDP exceeded the share devoted to defence in all other major industrialized countries—even that of the United States—by nearly 50 per cent.[2] By 1957—as is quite apparent from the Defence White Paper of that year—the government was concerned that the hitherto large defence effort had been detrimental to the strength of the British economy, and sought to adopt a 'cheaper' defence policy (Ministry of Defence, 1957: 1–2). This statement reflected the growing appreciation of the cost of defence and realisation that Britain was no longer a major power (Harlow, 1967: 7).

A real problem for the government is to decide between two priorities: a sound budget and an adequate national defence posture (Hitch and McKean, 1960: 48). It is hard to understate this central dilemma—whether the budget or defence needs should take priority—as a constant source of conflict within the government. The element of choice made it very hard to determine how much of the nation's output should be devoted to defence. Given the increased military commitments after the war, Bevin and most of the Labour Cabinet were determined to ensure that the services received enough money to meet these commitments. During the immediate post-war period financial and economic pressures forced the government to free itself of at least some of these commitments (Dockrill, 1988: 34–9; Kennedy, 1985: 327–8).[3] At that time financial pressure presented defence planners with the serious problem of trying to formulate a defence policy that would overcome the mismatch between British defence commitments and the available financial resources (Gorst, 1990).

Many analysts believe that the British government's inability to resolve this basic dilemma was to the detriment of Britain's post-war economic performance. For example, the failure of the British economy to achieve the investment ratio of other Western European countries is often attributed to the high level of defence expenditure and to the increased share of social investment, particularly in the housing programme. Among others, Martin Chick (1986: 31–58) has argued that the Labour government curtailed productive investment because industrialists lacked political representation within the decision-making process.[4] Britain's recurring balance of payments problems have been blamed on the relatively high overseas military expenditure (Kennedy, 1985: 319–20). Others have suggested that the poor record of British productivity growth is a direct result of the generous share of defence-related research and development expenditure and a comparatively large defence industry (Kaldor, 1980: 114–9; Freeman, 1978: 66–9). While some empirical evidence[5] does not stand up to careful scrutiny, more qualitative evidence suggests that some industries were hard hit by increased military expenditure during the Korean War defence programme from 1950 to 1954 (Mitchell, 1963: 230–45).

In contrast with most studies, this chapter tries to analyse the economic impact of British defence expenditure within a macroeconomic context. This analysis rests on the premise that defence spending influenced the economy directly through the purchase of goods and services. For example, massive expenditure on military aircraft provided a major incentive for aircraft producers to develop and build combat rather than civilian aircraft. Most of the analysis will concentrate on the defence production policy of the supply departments and the defence industry after 1945. It will look in detail at procurement of military aircraft and tanks. This study will form the basis of an assessment of the macroeconomic implications of the procurement policy of the supply departments. Such an appraisal should provide a more adequate explanation of the transmission mechanism of defence policy.

An industrial policy for the next war

The 1946 Defence White Paper outlined four principles that were to guide military procurement policy (Ministry of Defence, 1946: 7). On the one hand, the government planned to maintain design teams in the armaments sector by concentrating its production expenditure on research and development of new weapons systems; on the other hand, the production capacity of the industry was to be kept intact through limited repair and maintenance contracts. According to the White Paper the services were to rely on stocks left over from the war rather than to be allowed to place orders for new equipment or stores. The only exceptions were to be jet aircraft and a limited number of new tanks (Ministry of Defence, 1947: 5). At the same time, the defence planners hoped that the armaments industry would contribute as much as possible to the reconstruction of the British economy. Even though the Labour government intended to give priority to the civil economy, it also stated quite clearly that it intended to maintain a nucleus of capacity in the key armaments industries to be able to respond to any military threat more quickly than in the 1930s.

Post-war planning and reconstruction

In late 1943 discussions between a number of government departments started concerning the future of the aircraft industry. At the time the Treasury felt that the annual allocation of about £100 million (1943 prices) for the procurement of aircraft out of a defence budget of £500 million was realistic as long as the public would tolerate this high level of defence expenditure.[6] This meant that after the war the output in the aircraft industry had to be reduced by roughly 90 per cent of its production level in 1942. In order to achieve this reduction the Treasury suggested that some development projects should be cancelled and that most of the productive capacity be released for civilian purposes at an early stage in order to avoid large-scale scrapping of new equipment at the end of hostilities.[7] While most officials were concerned about maintaining aircraft production after the end of the war, Keynes was anxious to avoid the wholesale destruction of aircraft which seemed to him 'an extreme case of digging holes in the ground'.[8] While maintaining production was one of the major concerns, officials also worried about the structure and regional distribution of the industry. Some rationalization and concentration of development work was seen as unavoidable to meet the Treasury objective that there should be a fair measure of competition both in price and quality within the industry.[9] As early as 1946 concern grew in Whitehall about whether the dependence of the aircraft industry on government contracts was excessive and whether the industry should be rationalized even further.[10] From 1945 to 1950 the Treasury maintained, at considerable expense, 19 aircraft manufacturers through development contracts and repair work. In

1950 the size and structure of the aircraft industry was reviewed and the suggestion raised to concentrate production further by reducing the number of manufacturers eligible for government contracts to 13.[11] In approving the rationalization plans in July 1950, the Defence Committee stressed the vital importance of maintaining the war potential of the industry for the future defence of Britain.[12] In the end, the Korean war delayed restructuring of the industry until the late 1950s, when the government decided to encourage mergers within the aircraft industry (Henderson, 1962: 360–9).

In 1944 the Ministry of Supply tried to develop a post-war tank production policy. The original plans drawn up in 1944 envisaged that besides the Royal Ordnance Factory (ROF) at Leeds and Vickers-Armstrong, two further private firms should be encouraged to maintain a tank production capability. The original plans stated quite clearly that the Ministry intended to attract the interest of the potential contractors (Leyland, Vauxhall, Nuffield Mechanisation, English Electric) through sufficient orders. Vauxhall was very reluctant to take on further defence work.[13] When Leyland was offered a contract for a tank design team the directors refused, believing that the post-war reconstruction boom would offer them far more lucrative opportunities than the design contract offered to them by the Ministry.[14] Interestingly enough, English Electric at the time made several approaches to the Ministry in an attempt to obtain a tank production contract. As a tank manufacturer, English Electric was very much a second-best solution for the Ministry, which argued that this company lacked the expertise to build tanks. Despite the wishes of the Ministry of Supply to keep four independent tank design teams after the war, the War Office lacked the funds to order a large number of new tanks. As a consequence, English Electric decided in 1949 to give up its small tank production and transferred its work to Vickers.[15] Another problem arising from the limited tank production after 1945 was that both Vickers and the ROF Leeds had great difficulty in obtaining certain components, particularly large castings for tank turrets. The small scale of orders for such components made the subcontractors less interested in continuing to supply the parts in sufficient numbers and in time to allow for continuous production in the tank factories.[16]

The rather negative attitude of Leyland to the advances of the supply departments was shared by other industries. For example, the radio industry showed little or no interest in Ministry of Supply contracts for the development of a communications system for aircraft. The small volume of defence work available did little to lure firms that were hoping to exploit the potential mass market for radio and television sets. At the same time, research and development in the communications field was cut by 30 per cent and some of the scientists were transferred to other more important development programmes (e.g. atomic energy, guided weapons).[17]

In October 1945 the government decided that 23 Royal Ordnance Factories were to be kept under government control. The decision about which factories were to be kept was based on several considerations. Most importantly the Ministry of Supply wished to retain at least one production facility for each weapon type. Consideration was also given to location and the local labour situation. In order to preserve a nucleus of essential labour, employment at the ROFs was fixed at about 40,000. As the service requirements in the first post-war years were insubstantial, due to adequate weapons and ammunition stocks left over from the war, capacity utilization in the ROFs during this period remained very low. It was decided that this idle capacity should be used to meet the urgent demands of government departments or industry and to contribute either directly or indirectly to the export drive. A report of the Select Committee on Estimates (House of Commons, 1948), however, revealed that the possibilities of using the ROF's capacities economically were very limited. The disappointing capacity utilization of the ROFs led the Committee to conclude that some of the factories should be run down even further as long as there were no new orders forthcoming. This experience was shared by private ammunitions manufacturers such as Vickers. The degree of under-utilization of capacity caused so much concern among the directors of Vickers that in 1948 the board decided to hold an inquiry into its causes and implications. The inquiry found that while most factories could be used for civllian production, this could only be achieved at the cost of a loss of efficiency. As some of the Vickers factories worked at only 50 per cent of their capacity and most of the work carried out was civilian orders, the report was rather pessimistic about the future prospects of most plants unless new government contracts could be obtained.[18]

This analysis reveals the essence of the supply departments' industrial policy. The salient features of the policy were maintenance of key production and design facilities for a future large-scale war economy, ensuring the health of the defence contractors through repair contracts or spreading of research contracts across firms and sustaining a fair degree of competition among defence contractors. In the early post-war years, when there was hardly any procurement of new weapons, the maintenance of this additional capacity in an economic environment characterized by shortages and still severely restrained by controls must have exacerbated the problem of excess demand.

Matters improved after the government started to place larger defence production contracts in the summer of 1948, but the defence industry was really saved by the Korean war defence programme. The industrial policy tended to subsidize the final stage of armaments production (i.e. assembly plants) rather than to encourage the formation of integrated defence contractors which would produce most of the specific weapons systems. This policy rested on the notion that in the event of major rearmament most of the economy would have to be converted to a war footing. This approach seems to have ignored the possibility of a more capital-intensive defence posture based on the constant procurement of highly sophisticated weapons systems that was to become typical for the military-industrial complex of the nuclear age (Geyer,

1984: 173–5; Kaldor, 1983: 47–54).[19] In other words, the supply departments' industrial policy can best be described as an industrial policy for all-out war rather than for the age of economic deterrence. Thus the desire to maintain the greatest possible number of armaments producers rested on the basic assumption of the likelihood of a future global war of attrition. The idea of fostering competition among the individual armaments played only a minor role in the deliberations of the supply departments.[20] Indeed, competition and the rate of technical innovation may well have been higher had fewer larger firms competed for the limited number of defence projects for which the supply departments could invite tenders.[21]

The plans of the proponents of this industrial policy were opposed by a small group of 'Keynesian' officials who believed that in the current economic circumstances defence expenditure and particularly equipment expenditure should be reduced rather than increased.[22] They believed that defence expenditure represented a potential policy tool to combat unemployment. In the crisis of 1947 they argued that the resources devoted to defence production should be reduced even further.[23] In the discussions on the autumn budget, Bevin and Alexander were able to prevent such cuts in the size of the defence industry (Peden, 1986: 249–50). When the supply departments in 1948 asked for an increase in defence production to prepare for rearmament in the early 1950s (in order to achieve a state of defence preparedness by 1957 under the informal ten-year rule), one official of the Central Economic Planning Staff condemned such an expansion as a folly that might endanger the progress of the British economy towards a full recovery from the war.[24] Such qualms were not shared by the hawkish majority in the Defence Committee and the start of phased rearmament was approved in summer 1948.[25]

The evidence seems to suggest that while very little was actually spent on the production of new equipment and stores between 1946 and 1948/9, the contribution of the defence contractors to the reconstruction of the British economy and the export drive was very limited. At the same time, the defence sector enjoyed favourable access to labour and raw materials. Thus, there can be little doubt that the retention of a nucleus of a war economy contributed to the excess demand in the economy and should be treated as an additional opportunity cost of Britain's defence posture.[26] In other words, between 1945 and 1950 the supply departments subsidized the under-utilization of capacity in certain sectors of the economy which otherwise might have shifted away from defence work into civilian markets and contributed towards easing the general excess demand.

The defence programme

When in the wake of the North Korean invasion an increased defence programme of £3,600 million was conceived, the British government planned to repair Britain's military deficiencies as quickly as possible in order to deter the Soviets from starting a new global war. The original intention was to use existing capacity[27], but by the time Attlee made his statement on the defence programme to the House of Commons in January 1951, not only had the programme been increased to £4,700 million but several projects to enlarge capacity in some armaments industries had been approved (Cabinet Office 1951: 6–7).

The production account of the key metals, engineering and vehicles sectors reveal that defence production rose slowly through 1950, gathered momentum in 1951 and levelled off after 1953. Table 8.1 also shows that there was hardly any reduction in the value of production for export and investment despite the increase in production for defence (Cairncross, 1985: 228–32). On the other hand, it is notable that the production in these key sectors of the economy more or less stagnated from 1951 to 1953. It is hard to assess to what extent this stagnation was caused by the defence programme or whether it reflected the deterioration in Britain's terms of trade.

If the industrial policy of the supply departments was a rather mixed blessing in the immediate post-war period, this changed dramatically with the outbreak of the Korean war. In 1950 the existence of a large armaments industry should have eased the opportunity cost of converting to large-scale production for defence. The excess capacity within the defence industry provided the scope for a rapid and fairly smooth transition in the early

Table 8.1 Production account of the metals, engineering and vehicles industries, 1948–57

	in £mn 1948 factory or cif values									
	1948	1949	1950	1951	1952	1953	1954	1955	1956	1957
SUPPLY										
—Production (net)	2580	2730	2950	3150	3140	3215	3520	3875	3760	3835
—Imports										
(excl. reexport)	50	50	45	55	75	65	55	65	70	75
Total	2630	2780	2995	3205	3215	3280	3575	3940	3830	3910
DEMAND										
—Consumer										
Expend.	165	180	210	225	220	275	335	390	340	380
—Defence	160	180	200	285	415	470	465	455	430	405
—Gross D.										
Capital Form.	785	835	890	920	865	900	980	1090	1130	1210
—Exports	765	860	990	985	975	960	995	1105	1200	1240
—other use	755	725	705	790	740	675	800	900	730	675
Total	2630	2780	2995	3205	3215	3280	3575	3940	3830	3910

Source: Central Statistical Office (1958: Table 17)

Table 8.2 Defence equipment (except aircraft), 1948–52

Ministry of Supply Defence Production Index
(1948=100)

Finan-cial Year	Total	Ammu-nition	Weapons Instru-ments	Signals Radar S. lights	Eng. Stores Transp.	Arm. Vehic.	Clothing
1948/49	95	105	110	95	114	81	91
1949/50	159	198	225	56	520	100	78
1950/51	160	185	248	83	396	104	121
1950/51							
Q2	144	179	184	61	491	75	92
Q3	130	149	184	59	335	90	97
Q4	176	220	280	97	356	119	136
Q1	189	193	340	115	402	133	158
1951/52							
Q2	227	243	280	93	544	178	202
Q3	241	235	277	92	492	233	220
Q4	268	...	...	...	...	...	...
Q1	358	...	391	...	828	340	329
1952/53							
Q2	352	348	397	156	1005	214	390
Q3	421	428	459	89	995	380	394

Note: ... not available
Source: PRO CAB 134/263, CAB 134/264, CAB 134/265, CAB 134/266, CAB 134/267, CAB 134/884: Economic Steering Committee Minutes and Memoranda.

stages of the rearmament programme.[28] Indeed Table 8.2 shows that production for most defence equipment rose quickly. It reveals also the extent to which certain parts of the services had relied on stocks of ammunition and engineering stores from the war. Table 8.3 shows very clearly that the Air Ministry had kept the aircraft industry in work through large repair and maintenance contracts, which explains the relative fall in the amount of repair work done. Both tables show that the defence contractors were well able to increase production significantly during the first year of the defence programme. The electronics industry seems to have experienced great difficulty in supplying radar, radio and other communications equipment.[29] This may reflect the particular problems caused by the cut in research and development of such equipment.[30] There are other indications that the defence programme caused little industrial disruption in the first year. For example, employment in the small arms and munitions industry grew only in the second year of the defence programme, after the high excess demand for labour started to drop.[31] It is difficult to gain a clear picture of the extent to which cuts in defence expenditure by the Churchill government and the super-priority scheme[32] affected defence production, because in late 1952 the Economic Steering Committee gave way to pressure from the Ministry of Supply that for security reasons the Defence Production Index should no longer be circulated to the committee.[33]

The experience of the aircraft industry provides a good illustration of these general remarks. Aircraft production did not really expand until 1952–two years into the defence programme. The number of workers started to increase immediately after the outbreak of the war in Korea but grew faster between June 1951 and June 1952 than during the first twelve months of the defence programme, when excess demand for labour had already eased. The extent of surplus capacity in the aircraft industry is indicated by the significant rise in productivity during the period. As Table 8.4 shows, both output per worker increased and the capital-output ratio of the industry improved in the period

Table 8.3 Aircraft production, 1948–52

Ministry of Supply Defence Production Index
(1948=100)

Finan-cial Year	Total	Air-frame	Engine	Aircraft Repair	Propel-lers	Instru-ments
1948/49	111	112	107	125	121	100
1949/50	135	117	185	115	137	133
1950/51	122	105	178	49	99	154
1950/51						
Q2	104	77	176	51	94	128
Q3	119	104	168	62	76	155
Q4	134	109	182	41	119	175
Q1	131	118	184	43	108	158
1951/52						
Q2	166	158	223	55	113	164
Q3	161	145	223	48	146	190
Q4	165	...	...	...	...	...
Q1	167	166	243	45	152	291
1952/53						
Q2	199	163	273	61	153	343
Q3	171	124	247	57	108	361

Note: ... not available
Source: PRO CAB 134/263, CAB 134/264, CAB 134/265, CAB 134/266, CAB 134/267, CAB 134/884: Economic Steering Committee Minutes and Memoranda.

Table 8.4 Performance indicators for the aircraft industry, 1949–58

	Index of output at constant 1958 prices	Number of employees (June)	Output per employee in £	Capital-output ratio
1949	58	183,315	1281.4	0.355
1950	57	179,465	1286.3	0.378
1951	58	193,178	1215.9	0.364
1952	73	236,420	1530.6	0.327
1953	95	261,644	1470.3	0.311
1954	107	278,998	1553.2	0.315
1955	97	294,947	1331.9	0.401
1956	97	307,632	1277.0	0.427
1957	101	311,936	1311.3	0.472
1958	100	301,419	1343.6	0.521

Source: Ministry of Aviation (1965: Appendix C Table 1, Appendix E Table 1, Appendix H Table 1).

1951 until 1954, when output in the aircraft industry reached the peak production level envisaged in the defence programme. The cuts of the 1954 Sandys' defence review meant that expenditure for new aircraft and other new equipment was spread over a longer period, which led to a drop in labour productivity as well as a deterioration of the capital-output ratio, although this may reflect the fact that aircraft production had become increasingly capital intensive.

The slow improvement in the productivity figures at the start of the defence programme indicates that at the beginning the aircraft industry had major problems of adjusting to the new large government orders. When the Ministry of Supply and the Treasury reviewed the size of the aircraft industry in early 1950, the prospects and under-utilization of capacity varied substantially among firms. While firms producing jet fighters had full order books, the producers of transport planes and flying boats faced serious problems and depended heavily on government subsidies (e.g. Handley Page, Bristol Aeroplane Company).[34] As the production of jet fighters was expanded, it became obvious that existing capacity for the production of jet engines was insufficient to meet increased demand. It was than decided, well in advance of the adoption of an overall defence production programme, to expand the capacity for the production of jet engines.[35] At the time, the approval of the expansion of capacity was seen as an exceptional deviation from the basic principle of a defence programme on the basis of existing capacity.[36] This episode shows that the industrial policy of the supply departments had preserved the industry's capacity rather than attempted to adjust its structure to the changing technological environment.[37]

Another area where the supply departments sought an expansion of the existing capacity was in the production of tanks. This is an even more bizarre case, for it was apparent from the beginning that such an expansion would represent a clear departure from the principle underlying the original defence programme. As even the supply departments admitted, any new capacity (conversion of ROF Dalmuir, new tank factory in Leyland) created under an expansion scheme was unlikely to make any substantial contribution to filling the current deficiency of tanks as part of defence programme. In other words, under the auspices of the defence programme the supply departments tried to complete their original post-war plans to have at least three independent tank manufacturers.[38] Not only would the existing capacity have sufficed to produce most of the additional tanks the War Office needed, but the supply departments exaggerated the extent of the British deficiency in tanks.[39] When the scheme was first floated by the Ministry of Supply, Treasury opposed the project because it entailed the expansion of capacity contrary to the original intention of the defence programme. In early January 1951 the Treasury opposition started to fade despite serious misgivings about the way the whole project had been pushed through.[40] Under pressure from Shinwell, Gaitskell finally approved the construction of a new tank factory to be operated by Leyland on the understanding that the Treasury would not be asked to approve any further expansion of production capacity.[41] It soon became obvious that the War Office would not be able to buy the additional tanks it had on order, so the government started to look around for foreign buyers of the superfluous tanks rather than phasing tank production over a longer period.[42] As a consequence, foreign buyers were able to profit indirectly from the government's super-priority scheme which deprived other export industries of much needed basic materials (e.g. steel).[43] By mid-1952 it was quite clear that the expanded capacity at Vickers and the ROF Leeds was already too large to be sustained by demand, even without the addition of Leyland and Dalmuir.[44]

The expansion of capacity within the aircraft industry as well as in tank production represented large shares of the investment in aircraft and vehicle industries.[45] In the aircraft industry almost half of all investment in those years was financed by borrowing. An unusually high proportion of borrowed funds was obtained from banks in the form of bank advances. This suggests that under government pressure the banks did give preference to defence contractors while they were forced to restrict severely their lending to other industries (Ministry of Aviation, 1965: 21 and Appendix H Table 4; Geiger and Ross, 1991). The regional aspect of these investments seems even more important. Most of the new expansion took place in pockets of high excess demand for labour: Preston/Blackburn[46], Coventry[47], Bristol (Lovering, 1988: 127-9) and Greater London (Willet, 1988: 142-3). Even outside the immediate vicinity of these industrial centres, the ROFs encountered problems in attracting enough skilled craftsmen for their factories in Leeds and Woolwich.[48] Most expansion projects entailed building new factories rather than converting existing Ministry of Supply reserve shadow factories. This in turn placed extra pressure on the overloaded building sector.[49] The increased demand for steel created extra pressures within the vehicle and aircraft industries. While most of the defence contractors had serious problems in obtaining components[50], private companies had to reduce production and to some extent replace sheet and alloy steel with carbon steel or even in some cases with timber.[51]

Military procurement: incentives and negative side-effects

The preceding sections examined the effects of the industrial policy of the supply departments. This policy seems to have exacerbated the overall excess demand in the economy first by subsidizing inefficient production and then by expanding the defence sector unduly during the Korean war defence programme. This raises two important issues. On the one hand, why were defence contractors better placed than civilian firms in obtaining scarce labour and raw materials? What were the incentives for a defence contractor to maintain excess capacity at a time of almost inexhaustible demand? On the other hand, did defence production policy adversely affect overall economic performance? If so, how? And to what extent?

The analysis of the relationship between the supply departments and defence contractors revealed the high degree of continuity of procurement policy throughout the period. At the time when the post-war production plans were drawn up, war production was at its peak. The planners in the supply departments were still in virtual control of the economy. Moreover, they had access to vital information for any post-war planning. For example, using preliminary public expenditure plans, the planners had a rough idea of the likely demand for military hardware in the immediate post-war years. Within these parameters they were able to evolve a compromise between the desirable and the feasible. More importantly the policy-makers had at their disposal the power to direct resources, particularly labour and steel. This allowed them to control the scaling-down of war production and release of labour. In this process the supply departments had a tremendous advantage by virtue of their privileged access to information, their influence over the running-down of the war economy and their familiarity with the allocation process.[52]

The dominant position of the supply departments within the war economy as compared with civilian production gave them advantages both in defining strategic objectives and pushing them through. Civilian producers were curtailed by their dependence on steel allocations and their ability to obtain labour. Another factor which inhibited their freedom was the necessity of increasing British exports quickly after the war. To achieve this objective the government gave preferential treatment in the allocation of steel to exporters.

The privileged position of the defence contractors in the immediate post-war period is borne out by the fact that despite being more expensive, some Royal Ordnance Factories secured work from civilian producers because they had the manpower resources (House of Commons, 1948: vii-viii). In the environment of the post-war shortages such preferential treatment placed defence contractors in a strong position to compete for civilian contracts. This enabled them to retain inefficient capacity and created a disincentive to change.

The privileged position of the defence contractors depended on their close relationship with the supply departments. Several defence contractors loaned managers and technical experts to the Ministry of Supply and the Ministry of Aircraft Production during the war. This created strong ties that were to last into the post-war period. To cite one particular case, the post-war tank production programme was drawn up while Robert Micklem (on loan from Vickers) was chairman of the Tank Board and the Armoured Vehicle Division of the Ministry of Supply. After the war Micklem returned to Vickers to become one of the directors (*Who's Who*, 1952: 1969). It was hardly surprising that he was given responsibility for tank production at Vickers. His ties with the Ministry of Supply remained close. The evidence suggests that the personal involvement of many of these managers made them more reluctant to abandon production facilities that were part of their own post-war production plans.

Such factors should not be exaggerated, because to some extent defence contractors were caught in a trap. Originally, planners intended to maintain reserve capacity by repair contracts. At no time was it envisaged that defence production would reach a level sufficient to utilize this capacity fully. The planners' aim had been to provide for the possibility of full-scale rearmament in the future.[53] As post-war production plans had been exceedingly optimistic in their financial assumptions, actual production levels fell short of the expectations. There were several reasons for this. Less money was available for defence in the post-war budgets than had been expected during the war.[54] As a consequence of the increased British military commitments all over the world, a lower proportion of the defence budget itself went towards defence production.[55] The planners underestimated the increase in development and production cost of modern weapons systems (Kaldor, 1980: 105–12). The low level of arms production meant a significant loss of economies of scale compared with wartime.

This unplanned shortfall in demand led to an increase in excess capacity among defence contractors, and the financial problems facing the government gave rise to growing uncertainty about the future military procurement budgets. The combination of these two factors resulted in defence contractors being left in a different position. The precariousness of their financial situation precluded them from investing in new equipment to reduce their dependency on the government. While most weapons contractors were able to adapt some of their specialized machinery to civilian production, they found it increasingly hard to compete with the lower production costs of their civilian rivals (House of Commons, 1948). If defence contractors had tried to develop civilian production at the expense of their military production capacity, the government might have excluded them from tendering for future arms contracts. This was a risk a defence contractor could not afford. Even approaches to the government for a subsidy to keep the surplus capacity in being were regarded as inherently risky.[56] To escape this predicament, defence contractors would have had to invest in new products and machinery for which they lacked the financial resources and which might have destroyed their relationship with the government on which their survival depended. Even if the firms had the financial resources they found it hard to obtain the necessary machinery or skilled labour (Dow, 1965: 286–9). It seems unlikely that any new investment would have yielded immediately high returns. Such factors lowered the expectations of management and made the defence contractors even more wary (Dow, 1965: 162 and 286–9).

At the same time, their civilian counterparts were doing rather better. In almost all sectors most firms had over-full order books and were making record profits (Tomlinson, 1989: 9–10). Despite excess liquidity, firms found it difficult to expand or launch new products because shortages reduced the availability of key materials or labour. Large investment projects involving building work were held up by the government by the denial of building licences (Dow, 1965: 149–53) or by the general shortage of materials and labour (Dow, 1965: 162 and 341–3). All this is typical of supply-constrained economies (Kornai, 1982: 48–50). It is hard to estimate how much disruption these constraints caused but there can be little doubt that the surplus capacity and preferential access to raw materials and labour of the defence contractors exacerbated the supply position. A rough estimate suggests that the loss in production in the defence field from 1947 to 1950 may have been as much as 2 to 3 per cent of manufacturing output or 0.5 to 1 per cent of GDP per annum.[57] This suggests that the supply departments' industrial policy inhibited the government's effort to reduce the excess demand within the economy in the immediate post-war period.

The 1949 devaluation reveals the extent to which the economy was subject to supply constraints. Firms found it hard to expand output sufficiently quickly to profit from the increased competitiveness of British exports. Many industries including the textile industry were working overtime until late 1951.[58] As already explained above, firms were either unwilling or unable to expand their productive capacity, though this would have been the only successful way of overcoming the excess demand at home. A rough indication of the extent of excess demand for labour is provided by the unemployment rates in industry (Dow, 1965: 335–43). As a rule of thumb, the lower the unemployment rate, the higher the possibility of excess demand for labour in the specific industry. Table 8.5 shows that at the beginning of the defence

Table 8.5 Unemployment rate in selected industries, 1949–54

	May 1949	May 1950	May 1951	May 1952	May 1953	May 1954
	in per cent					
Vehicles	1.0	0.9	0.5	0.7	0.8	0.5
Aircraft Production and Repair	1.1	1.0	0.5	0.4	0.5	0.4
Engineering, Shipbuilding, Electrical Goods	1.8	1.6	1.0	1.3	1.5	1.2
Shipbuilding	5.5	5.8	3.7	3.4	4.3	3.7
Engineering	1.4	1.1	0.7	1.0	1.2	0.9
Ordnance and Small Arms	2.5	2.6	1.6	1.3	1.0	0.9
Metal Industry	1.2	1.1	0.8	1.1	2.5	1.3
Textiles	0.7	0.6	0.5	15.6	1.4	1.0

Note: The employment figures are taken from the published figures for the end of April, while the unemployment figures are taken for early May from the published figures in the same issue of the *Ministry of Labour Gazette*.
Source: Ministry of Labour, *Ministry of Labour Gazette*, various issues.

programme there was considerable unemployment both in the shipbuilding and the small arms and ordnance industries. The figures in Table 8.5 reveal an interesting pattern. In some of the defence industrial categories (i.e. aircraft, ordnance and small arms but excluding shipbuilding), the unemployment rates continue to fall until 1954, in all other industries unemployment drops until May 1951, only to rise again. As most industrial categories display this pattern, the dislocation caused by the increased manpower requirement of the forces, adverse shifts in the terms of trade and the raw material shortages probably led to more dislocation than the defence programme itself (Mitchell, 1963: 56–85 and 230–45; Cairncross, 1985: 228–32). This seems particularly true for the textile industry which suffered severely from the dramatically changed market conditions caused by the shift in raw materials prices (Singleton, 1986: 102–3). One of the consequences of the collapse of international demand in 1952 was that the textile industry could not export as much as the government had originally hoped. This shortfall increased the pressure on the balance of payments. Rearmament inhibited the continued growth of engineering exports. This forced the government to tighten import controls which prolonged the 'disequilibrium system' (Dow, 1965: 162). Through the displacement caused by the Korean war, roughly 3 per cent of output growth was lost in the period 1951 to 1955.

The preceding analysis suggests that the defence production policy of supply departments contributed significantly to the excess demand within the British economy in the period 1945 to 1955. Although it is currently impossible precisely to measure the loss of output to the British economy, it is clear that to understand the effects of this industrial policy in the period from 1945 to 1955 requires a detailed analysis of the supply and the constraints. Only then will it become clear just how far Britain's large defence effort contributed to the relatively poor performance of the British economy.

Notes

1. The author is grateful to Larry Butler, David Edgerton, Anthony Gorst, Leslie Hannah, Scott Lucas, Helen Mercer, Alan Milward, Peter Payne, Duncan Ross, Lorenza Sebesta, Jim Tomlinson and Tim Whisler for their help with invaluable comments and suggestions. All errors of fact or judgement remain the author's alone.
   The permission to cite Crown Copyright material held in the Public Record Office was granted by the Controller of Her Majesty's Stationery Office. For a complete list of references and abbreviations used, see the Bibliography.
2. In 1947 the United Kingdom still spent roughly 10 per cent of GDP on defence. This was almost twice the proportion spent on defence by the United States (5.25 per cent of GDP). In 1948 the United Kingdom (7.26 per cent of GDP) spent proportionally 1.5 times more than the United States (4.78 per cent). This ratio changed radically over the next few years. At the peak of the Korean war re-armament programme, the United States (14.83 per cent of GDP) spent proportionally 1.4 times as much as the United Kingdom (10.45 per cent of GDP) (my calculations, based on Organization for European Economic Co-operation (1957)).
3. The withdrawal from Greece is often interpreted as a clear sign that the economic strain of these additional commitments was too much for the limping British economy (Roberts, 1984: 33–6).
4. The figures for social investment given by Sidney Pollard (1969: 407) suggest that the share of social investment of total gross domestic capital formation rose from 10.7 per cent in 1937/8 to 15.3 per cent in 1947/8 and 14.8 per cent in 1950/1. This increase seems hardly that significant if one bears in mind that the share of GDP invested nearly doubled compared with pre-war years. Indeed, Alan Milward (1984: 484–5) argues that social investment may have created a more stable environment for private investment and thus 'crowded in' investment. See also the comments of Jim Tomlinson (1989: 8–9).
5. There are three comprehensive surveys of the economic impact literature: Steve Chan (1985), Gavin Kennedy (1983), and Judith Reppy (1989).
6. PRO T 160/1407/F.18576: 'Post-war expenditure', Gilbert–Brittain, 7 November 1943.
7. PRO T 225/653: Gilbert–Eady and Barlow, 17 December 1943.
8. PRO T 225/653: Keynes–Eady, 17 December 1943; Eady–Barlow, 18 December 1943; Gilbert–Eady, 23 December 1943; Keynes–Gilbert, 3 January 1944. Keynes suggested in his *General Theory of Employment, Interest, and Money* (1936: 129–30) that the Treasury could increase employment in an economy with large-scale unemployment by burying money in the ground and allowing private firms to dig it out again.

9. PRO T 225/653: Eady–Barlow, 18 December 1943.

10. PRO T 225/653: Japp–Blunt, 3 June 1946.

11. PRO T 225/369: draft 'Size and shape of the aircraft industry: need for planning to preserve war potential', Musgrave–Humphrey-Davies, 18 February 1950; Humphrey-Davies-Pitblado, 29 March 1950; Minute of a meeting to consider draft paper, 20 April 1950.

12. PRO CAB 131/8: minutes of a meeting of the Defence Committee, DO 11 (50) 2, 11 July 1950.

13. PRO WO 185/232: Gibb–Duncan, 30 October 1944; Micklem–Hancock, 14 September, 1944; 'Post-war organisation for design and production of tanks, memorandum by Hancock, 19 October 1944.

14. PRO WO 185/232: note of a meeting with Leyland directors, 5 July 1945.

15. Vickers J99: Nelson–Micklem, 5 December 1949; Micklem–Nelson, 7 December 1949.

16. Vickers J99: Micklem–Muirhead, 13 January 1950; Muirhead–Micklem, 17 January 1950; Muirhead–Micklem; 27 March 1950; Pinkworth–Micklem, 20 March 1950. See also PRO WO 185/162: minutes of a meeting of the ROF Central Production Committee, 17 October 1949.

17. PRO Air 20/6937: Croyton–Robb, 19 March 1948.

18. Vickers 725: Final Report of the Committee on Reserve Capacity for Armaments Production, 10 May 1948.

19. The reorientation towards an increasingly capital-intensive defence posture slowly evolved out of the military containment doctrine. Military containment was the response to the perception among politicians that the Cold War had escalated to a state of permanent crisis (Schilling, 1962: 8–10; Gaddis, 1982: 90–2). Consequently, many politicians in the United States and Britain called for a substantial increase in defence outlays in the late 1940s. As an integral part of this strategy the United States committed itself to frontline defence and the stationing of troops in Europe and the Far East. The economic implications of massive rearmament led to increased reliance on highly sophisticated weapons systems and the threat of massive retaliation (Gaddis, 1982: 133–6 and 145–52). European countries started to adopt capital-intensive defence postures in the late 1950s (Geyer, 1984: 200–17). In Britain the publication of the 1957 Defence White Paper (Ministry of Defence, 1957) marked the end of the transition towards a capital-intensive strategy.

20. Peck and Scherer (1962: 57–60) have argued convincingly that there can be no truly competitive market for weapons. In the British case the desire of the supply department to maintain the semblance of competition between weapons manufacturers reflected a risk aversion strategy. By awarding several development contracts for a weapons project (e.g. jet fighters, V-bombers), weapon procurement agencies tried to ensure that at least one system would be available in the event of war; compare also Peck and Scherer (1962: 488–92). In other words, the objective was to ensure technical competition between defence contractors rather than the existence of a competitive market; see PRO CAB 131/9: DO (50) 47, 'Size and shape of the aircraft industry: need for planning to preserve war potential', 28 June 1950.

21. This conjecture draws on the theoretical work of Schumpeter who argued that monopolistic competition could be justified on the grounds that larger firms innovate more rapidly than smaller firms. The profit accrued due to the

competitive advantage gained through technical advance should be seen as positive rather than negative as it leads to continued growth of the economy (Kamien and Schwartz, 1982: 7–13 and 22–48). Empirical studies do not necessarily support these hypotheses. Indeed, most studies found that quite the reverse was true for most large firms (Kamien and Schwartz, 1982: 49–104). Some analysts have argued that this is particularly true for the defence sector as it tends to be far more concentrated than the rest of the economy (Kaldor, 1983: 65–72; Kennedy 1983: 155–61). Given the high degree of technical uncertainty and considerable amount of time needed to develop a new weapons system, the high degree of concentration within the defence industry can be regarded as almost inevitable (Kennedy, 1983: 164–9). Indeed, Galbraith has argued that the willingness of the government to underwrite large scale research projects is an intrinsic characteristic of the new industrial state (Galbraith, 1974: 336). In this light the supply departments' industrial policy must be seen as delaying the move towards a higher degree of concentration among defence contractors. By the mid-1950s critics urged the government to encourage such a concentration of research, development and production, particularly in the aircraft industry (Devons, 1958: 62–5). The contention here is that if the government had encouraged mergers in the defence sector earlier, this would have been beneficial in two ways. First, the need to subsidise smaller inefficient firms would have been greatly reduced. Secondly, through the concentration of design teams and production facilities as well as available financial resources on fewer development projects more contracts might have been completed; compare also Harlow (1967: 10–4).

22. PRO T 247/71: 'Sir W. Eady's note on the cost of defence in relation to the budget and our foreign exchange reserves', Keynes–Bridges, 23 March 1945. PRO T 225/653: Keynes–Gilbert, 3 January 1944.

23. PRO T 171/392: note by Trend of a meeting of Dalton on details of the budget with Bridges, Hopkins, Eady, and Gilbert, 30 September 1947.

24. PRO T 229/704: Hitchman–Plowden, 22 October 1948; see also: Gilbert–Brook, 24 July 1948; Plowden–Brittain, 19 August 1948; Helmore–Graswell, 20 August 1948.

25. PRO CAB 131/5: DO 17(48)1, minutes of a meeting of the Defence Committee, 23 August 1948. At that time Robert Hall reassured the government that the economic effects of rearmament would be limited to a small deterioration in the balance of payments; PRO CAB 21/2104: 'Economic impact of increased defence expenditure', Hall–Richett, 8 September 1948; 'Defence Programme', Johnston–Attlee, 8 September 1948.

26. See for example PRO CAB 21/2104: note by Plowden on a conversation with Finletter and Bliss, 29 September 1948.

27. PRO T 229/850: Spicer–Pitblado, 29 December 1950.

28. PRO T 229/372: Strath–Jay, 11 September 1950.

29. PRO CAB 130/65: GEN 344: Production of Jet Aircraft; minutes of an ad-hoc meeting of ministers in the PM's room at the House of Commons, 23 November 1950.

30. PRO Air 20/6937: Croyton–Robb, 19 March 1948.

31. Ministry of Labour, *Ministry of Labour Gazette,* various issues; total employment rose from 44,500 (1951) to 72,900 (1954); Business Statistics Office (1978: 31). Also compare Tables 8.4 and 8.5. When the increased defence programme was

drawn up, experts did not expect that rearmament would lead to a significant increase in the labour force of defence contractors. At the same time they voiced concern about the economic implications of the increased manpower levels of the Armed Forces; PRO T 229/372: 'Labour problems of additional defence production programmes', minutes of a meeting held in Strath's room, 14 August 1950; minutes of a meeting held in the Financial Secretary's room to discuss labour problems likely to arise out of expanded defence production programmes, 17 August 1950.

32. Throughout 1951 there were signs that raw material shortages impeded the defence programme. When the Churchill government revised the defence programme, ministers decided that priority should be given to the production of a small number of weapons systems (e.g. jet fighters, tanks). The super-priority scheme allowed contractors and subcontractors first priority in the purchase of steel and other basic materials. On the super-priority scheme, see PRO CAB 128/24: Cabinet Conclusions 30 (52), 13 March 1952. See also Vickers J99: Sandys–Micklem, 26 March 1952.

33. PRO CAB 134/880: Economic Steering Committee, ES(53) 5, minutes, 17 July 53. See also PRO T 229/851: 'Scope of super-priority', Jenkins–Turnbull, 16 February 1953. For the original cabinet decision see PRO CAB 128/24: Cabinet Conclusions 30 (52), 13 March 1952. The Minister of Supply submitted two reports to the Cabinet which describe the procedure of the scheme in general terms. They are less than helpful; see PRO CAB 129/52, Cabinet Paper (52) 120, 15 April 1952; and PRO CAB 129/52, Cabinet Paper (52) 187, 10 June 1952. After the report in June the Ministry ignored the original request of the Cabinet.

34. PRO CAB 131/8: minutes of the Defence Committee, DO 3 (50) 4, 31 January 1950. PRO T 225/369: DO (50) 47: 'Size and shape of the aircraft industry', Humphrey-Davies–Cripps, 4 July 1950.

35. PRO CAB 130/65: GEN 344: Production of jet aircraft: minutes of an ad-hoc meeting of ministers in the PM's room at the House of Commons, 23 November 1950.

36. PRO T 229/850: Spicer–Plowden, 13 January 1951.

37. In a minute in 1944 Keynes warned that this might be the consequence of the supply department's industrial policy towards the aircraft industry; see PRO T 225/653: Keynes–Gilbert, 3 January 1944.

38. PRO T 229/850: Preliminary report, Combat Vehicle Task Force, 12 October 1950; Turnbull–Spicer, 20 October 1950; Spicer–Turnbull, 26 October 1950; Hutchinson–Wheeler, 31 October 1950; Spicer–Pitblado and Turnbull, 7 November 1950.

39. PRO T 229/850: Spicer–Pitblado, 5 January 1951.

40. PRO T 229/850: Jones–Pitblado, 5 January 1951; 'Increase of capacity for production of tanks', Spicer–Plowden, 13 January 1951; Plowden–Armstrong, 15 January 1951.

41. PRO T 229/850: Shinwell–Gaitskell, 18 January 1951; Compton–Plowden, 18 January 1951; Gaitskell–Shinwell, 19 January 1951.

42. PRO T 229/850: Alexander–Cherwell, 18 January 1952; Shaw–Jenkins, 25 July 1952; Jenkins–Shilitto, 25 July 1952; memorandum D(52)42 by Sandys, 25 October 1952. PRO T 229/851: Macpherson–Shaw, 9 February 1953. Vickers J99: Muirhead–Dumphie, 1 July 1952.

43. PRO T 229/851: 'Scope of super-priority', Jenkins–Turnbull, 16 February 1953.
44. Vickers J99: Dumphie–Muirhead, 22 July 1952; Muirhead–Dumphie, 24 July 1952. The ROF Leeds and Dalmuir started to reduce working hours in 1953; see PRO WO 185/162: minutes of a meeting of the ROF Central Production Committee, 18 May 1953.
45. PRO T 229/850: Jones–Pitblado, 5 January 1951.
46. PRO T 229/850: 'EPC(51)26: Tank production: Leyland agency factory', paper by Bretherton, 19 March 1951; EPC(51)26, note by Jenkins, 20 March 1951. PRO T 229/372: Shawcross–Gaitskell, 8 May 1951.
47. PRO T 229/373: 'Labour situation in the Coventry area in relation to the defence programme', draft paper, 9 November 1951.
48. PRO WO 185/162: minutes of a meeting of the ROF Central Production Committee, 30 April 1951, 30 July 1951, 29 October 1951.
49. PRO T 229/850: Jones–Pitblado, 5 January 1951.
50. Vickers J99: memorandum 'Centurion tank production', 10 January 1951; Muirhead–Micklem, 31 January 1951; Crawford–Micklem, 21 February 1951. PRO WO 185/162: minutes of a meeting of the Central Production Committee, 30 October 1950. PRO T 229/850: Spicer–Butler, 30 January 1952.
51. Modern Record Centre MSS 226/ST/1/5/1: Standard Motor Co. Ltd., minutes of the executive directors' meeting, 5 February 1951, 10 January 1952, 14 March 1952. (I am grateful to Tim Whisler for letting me use his notes.)
52. The important role of strategic planning, information and knowledge within a war economy is stressed by Peter Howlett (1989). Peck and Scherer (1962: 500–1) argue that the uncertainty intrinsic to the weapons acquisition process may lead to the overcommitment of resources.
53. The defence planners' assessment of the likelihood of global war may seem unduly pessimistic with hindsight. Post-war leaders as well as the general public felt strongly that they should not appease the Soviet Union. These sentiments might be best described as a reaction to the catastrophic consequences of Appeasement (Mass-Observation, 1947: 21–2; Watt, 1984: 54–9; Loth, 1989: 130–1).
54. PRO T 160/1407/F.18876: 'Post-war expenditure', Gilbert–Bridges, 7 November 1942; assumed that three years after the end of the war £550 million (in 1942 prices) would be spent on defence. In 1948 prices this would have been almost £850 million (my calculation; this estimate makes some allowance for the loss of economies of scale in the production of new equipment). Actual expenditure was £770 million.
55. PRO T 160/1407/F.18876: 'Post-war expenditure', Gilbert–Bridges, 7 November 1942; expected that £220 million (in 1942 prices) or £369 (in 1948 prices, my calculation) would be spent on new equipment. The 1948 Defence White Paper set aside £188 million for expenditure on production and research. This heading includes the acquisition of new weapons.
56. Vickers 652: Report on capital expenditure 1947/8, Committee on Capital Expenditure and Commitments, 19 June 1947.
57. My calculations based on Table 8.1, Central Statistical Office (1958) and the ratio of defence equipment expenditure (official NATO figures, communication by B. Bros, SAS(87)151, 7 December 1987).
58. Ministry of Labour, *Ministry of Labour Gazette*, various issues. For example, the

report on the labour situation in Coventry emphasized the high proportion of overtime work at Courtaulds in Coventry; PRO T 229/373: 'Labour situation in the Coventry area in relation to the defence programme', draft paper, 9 November 1951.

Bibliography

Archives

PRO: Public Record Office, Kew

Air	Air Ministry
CAB	Cabinet Office
T	Treasury
WO	War Office

Cambridge University Library

Vickers Vickers-Armstrong Ltd. Collection

MRC: Modern Record Centre, University of Warwick

MSS 226 Standard Motor Co. Ltd.

Books, articles, official publications

Becker, J. and Knipping, F. (1986), *Power in Europe? Great Britain, France, Italy and Germany in a postwar world, 1945–1950*, Berlin, Walter de Gruyter.
Blackaby, F. (1978), *De-industrialisation*, London, Heinemann.
Breheny, M. (1988), *Defence Expenditure and Regional Development*, London, Mansell.
Burn, D. (1958), *The Structure of British Industry: A symposium*, volume 2, Cambridge, Cambridge University Press.
Business Statistics Office (1978), *Historical Record of the Census of Production, 1907 to 1970*, London, HMSO.
Cabinet Office (1951), *Defence Programme: Statement made by the Prime Minister in the House of Commons on Monday, 29th January, 1951*, (Cmd. 8140).
Cairncross, A. (1985), *Years of Recovery: British economic policy, 1945–51*, London, Methuen.
Central Statistical Office (1958), *National Income and Expenditure 1958*, London, HMSO.

Chan, S. (1985), 'The impact of defence spending on economic performance: a survey of evidence and problems', *Orbis* 29: 403–34.

Chick, M.J. (1986), 'Economic planning, managerial decision-making and the role of fixed capital investment in the economic recovery of the United Kingdom, 1945–55', unpublished Ph.D. thesis, University of London.

Deighton, A. (1990), *Britain and the First Cold War*, Basingstoke, Macmillan.

Devons, E. (1958), 'The Aircraft Industry', in Burn (1958: 45–92).

Dockrill, M. (1988), *British Defence Policy since 1945*, Oxford, Basil Blackwell.

Dow, J.C.R. (1965), *Management of the British Economy, 1945–1960*, Cambridge, Cambridge University Press.

Freeman, C. (1978), 'Technical innovation and British trade performance', in Blackaby (1978: 56–73).

Gaddis, J.L. (1982), *Strategies of Containment: a critical appraisal of postwar American national security policy*, Oxford, Oxford University Press.

Galbraith, J.K. (1974), *The New Industrial State*, 2nd edn., Harmondsworth, Penguin.

Geiger, T. and Ross, D.M. (1991), 'Banks, institutional constraints and the limits of central banking: monetary policy in Britain and West Germany, 1950–52', *Business History*, forthcoming.

Geyer, M. (1984), *Deutsche Rüstungspolitik, 1860–1980*, Frankfurt/Main, Suhrkamp.

Gorst, A. (1990), 'British military planning for post-war defence 1943–1945', in Deighton (1990: 91–108).

Harrison, M. (1988), 'Resource Mobilisation for World War II: the USA, UK, USSR and Germany, 1938–1945', *Economic History Review* 2nd ser., 41: 171–92.

Harlow, C.J.E. (1967), *The European Armaments Base: A survey; Part 2: National procurement policies*, London, Institute for Strategic Studies.

Henderson, P.D. (1962), 'Government and industry', in Worswick and Ady (1962: 326–77).

Hitch, C.J. and McKean, R.M. (1960), *Economics of Defence in the Nuclear Age*, Cambridge, Mass., Harvard University Press.

House of Commons (1948), *Seventh Report from the Select Committee on Estimates: Use of Royal Ordnance Factories and Royal Naval Establishments in connection with the production and export drive*, London, HMSO.

Howlett, W.P. (1989), 'Towards a model of the central decision-making process in a war economy', Discussion Paper in Economics 89/7, Department of Economics, University of Stirling.

Kaldor, M. (1980), 'Technical change in the defence industry', in Pavitt (1980: 100–21).

Kaldor, M. (1983), *The Baroque Arsenal*, London, Sphere.

Kamien, M.I. and Schwartz, N.L. (1982), *Market Structure and Innovation*, Cambridge, Cambridge University Press.

Kennedy, G. (1983), *Defense Economics*, London, Duckworth.

Kennedy, P.M. (1985), *Realities behind Diplomacy: Background influences on British external policy*, rev. edn., London, Fontana.

Keynes, J.M. (1936), *General Theory of Employment, Interest, and Money*, Collected Writings of John Maynard Keynes, vol. 7 (1974), Basingstoke, Macmillan.

Kolodziej, E.A. and Morgan, P.M. (1989), *Security and Arms Control. Volume 1: A guide to national policymaking*, New York, Greenwood Press.

Kornai, J. (1982), *Growth, Shortage and Efficiency: A macrodynamic model of the Socialist economy*, Oxford, Basil Blackwell.

Loth, W. (1989), *Die Teilung der Welt, 1941–1955*, 7th rev. edn, Munich, Deutscher Taschenbuch Verlag.

Lovering, J. (1988), 'Defence expenditure and the regions: the case of Bristol', in Breheny (1988: 122–37).

Mass-Observation (1947), *Peace and the People*, London, Longman.

Milward, A.S. (1984), *The Reconstruction of Western Europe, 1945–1951*, London, Methuen.

Ministry of Aviation (1965), *Report of the Committee of Inquiry into the Aircraft Industry*, (Cmnd. 2853).

Ministry of Defence (1946), *Statement relating to Defence 1946*, (Cmd. 6743).

Ministry of Defence (1947), *Statement relating to Defence 1947* (Cmd 7042).

Ministry of Defence (1957), *Defence: Outline of Future Policy* (Cmnd. 124).

Ministry of Labour, *Ministry of Labour Gazette*, London, HMSO.

Mitchell, J. (1963), *Crisis in Britain 1951*, London, Secker and Warburg.

Organization for European Economic Co-operation (1957), *Statistics of National Product and Expenditure, 1938 and 1947 to 1955*, Paris, Organization for European Economic Co-operation.

Ovendale, R. (1984), *The Foreign Policy of the British Labour Governments 1945–1951*, Leicester, Leicester University Press.

Pavitt, K. (1980), *Technical Innovation and British Economic Performance*, Basingstoke, Macmillan.

Peck, M.J. and Scherer, F.M. (1962), *The Weapons Acquisition Process: An economic analysis*, Boston, Graduate School of Business Administration, Harvard University.

Peden, G. (1986), 'Economic aspects of British perceptions of power on the eve of the Cold War', in Becker and Knipping (1986: 237–61).

Pollard, S. (1969), *The Development of the British Economy, 1914–1967*, 2nd edn, London, Edward Arnold.

Reppy, J. (1989), 'On the economics of national security', in Kolodziej and Morgan (1989: 73–95).

Roberts, F. (1984), 'Bevin as Foreign Secretary', in Ovendale (1984: 21–42).

Schilling, W.R. (1962), 'The politics of national defence: fiscal 1950', in Schilling, Hammond and Snyder (1962: 1–266).

Schilling, W.R., Hammond, P.Y. and Snyder, G.H. (1962), *Strategy, Politics and Defense Budgets*, New York, Columbia University Press.

Singleton, J. (1986), 'Lancashire's last stand: Declining employment in the British cotton industry, 1950–1970', *Economic History Review*, 2nd ser., 39: 92–107.

Tomlinson, J. (1989), 'Labour's management of the national economy, 1945–51: survey and speculations', *Economy and Society* 18: 1–24.

Watt, D.C. (1984), 'Britain, the United States and the opening of the Cold War', in Ovendale (1984: 43–60).

Who's Who (1952), London, Adam and Charles Black.

Willet, S. (1988), 'The impact of defence procurement on the electronics sector: a London case study', in Breheny (1988: 140–72).

Worswick, G.D.N. and Ady, P.H. (1962), *The British Economy in the Nineteen-Fifties*, Oxford, Oxford University Press.

9 The ambiguities of British colonial development policy, 1938–48[1]

L.J. Butler

Within the expression 'colonial development', central to the official historiography of British decolonization, lies a fundamental ambiguity: development for whom? This ambiguity is reflected in the distinct interpretations of the term current at different times. One interpretation understood colonial development to mean the development of colonial territories for the benefit of their populations, through economic growth geared to local needs, the extension of ameliorative social provision, the improvement of nutritional standards and the application of internationally-recognized labour conventions. In the inter-war period, this definition came to appeal to the metropolitan humanitarian lobby, to liberal and socialist critics of colonial rule, and, increasingly, to the Colonial Office in London, a process which exposed in the framework of British colonial rule fundamental organizational constraints inhibiting major policy initiatives by a reform-minded bureaucracy.[2]

The second broad definition of development, originating with imperial visionaries such as Joseph Chamberlain, and kept alive between the wars by acolytes such as Leopold Amery, saw the colonial territories as 'undeveloped estates', which Britain had a right and a duty to bring into productivity and into the world trading system. At the heart of this view was the belief that the British and colonial economies were complementary to one another, bound in a relationship in which Britain supplied manufactures in return for colonial raw materials (Constantine, 1984: 228; Meredith, 1975: 495).

This dichotomy of interpretations, although convenient, was artificial. In practice, the distinction between the two was blurred, and advocates of one interpretation could reinforce their arguments by appealing to elements of the other. For instance, calls for improved colonial conditions during the 1930s sometimes came from British manufacturers, concerned at the threat allegedly posed to their export interests by cheap colonial labour in the Far East. Similarly, metropolitan desires for increased productivity in the Colonial Empire were sometimes expressed in calls for improved health and dietary

119

standards (Drummond, 1974: 440; Meredith, 1975: 496). On the other hand, the majority of those who adopted the 'welfarist' stance on development also accepted uncritically the free-trading precept of comparative advantage, and therefore shared the belief in a complementary economic relationship between Britain and the colonies (Fieldhouse, 1984: 101–2).

The relative importance attached to these two images of colonial development ebbed and flowed with the fortunes of the British economy. The second, overtly exploitative strand, encouraged by rising unemployment in Britain in the 1920s, produced the Colonial Development Act of 1929, openly intended to promote colonial development projects which would create demand for British exports (Abbott, 1970: 73–89; Meredith, 1975: 486–7). In the late 1930s, because of Britain's need to justify its colonial rule before international opinion, given accumulating evidence of the extent of colonial poverty, the welfarist strand came into the ascendant, leading to the 1940 Colonial Development and Welfare Act, which promised grant aid for colonial economic and social development (Constantine, 1984: 227–66; Morgan, 1980: vol. 1, 80–8). The Act illustrates the conversion of the Colonial Office, for both pragmatic and humanitarian reasons, to an essentially welfare-centred development strategy after a long period of drift between the world wars. Prior to the late 1930s, colonial 'policy' existed only in the most general sense, revolving around the maintenance of law and order in the colonial territories. The role of the Colonial Office was largely reactive, its ability to manœuvre stifled by the negative orthodoxy of colonial 'trusteeship', which obstructed interventionist policies. However, the changing international climate demanded a constructive response, and when presenting its case for additional funds to Cabinet early in 1940, the Colonial Office argued that in any post-war settlement, Britain's continuing role as a colonial power would depend on its ability to demonstrate a commitment to improved colonial living standards, a commitment which for the Colonial Office became the dominant and central theme in its policy.[3]

The new colonial development policy was, however, stillborn. Progress with development was halted in wartime as supplies of finance, materials and personnel were effectively suspended. As welfarism retreated, an un-precedented era of exploitation began with attempts to extract the maximum possible contribution to the Allied war effort from colonial resources, including a massive expansion in the development of Africa's strategic mineral reserves (Cowen and Westcott, 1986: 40–61; Westcott, 1983; Lee and Petter, 1982: 73–114; Dumett, 1985). Moreover, wartime conditions led to major, and embarrassing, policy reversals, notably with the reimposition of forced labour in order to maintain mineral supplies from Africa.[4] Nevertheless, the commitment to colonial development remained the cornerstone in Britain's wartime justification of her status as a colonial power, and the propaganda value of development rhetoric was deployed to the full, especially to placate American anti-colonial sentiment (Lee and Petter, 1982:

129–43; Louis, 1977: 121–286; Thorne, 1978: 209–10; Smythe, 1985).

The importance of the development ethos for the Colonial Office grew after 1943, when the Office began to address the problems involved in post-war reconstruction. Development became the unifying theme for the Office's entire range of activities, underpinning its subsequent expansion, and providing officials with a new role and sense of collective purpose, thus replacing the 'drift' of the inter-war years. Development policy injected a new cohesion and coherence into the Office and its work (Lee, 1977; Lee and Petter, 1982). The new philosophy demanded and made possible continued restructuring and refinement of the Office's machinery, and officials became increasingly adept at dealing with policy issues thematically, rather than on a fragmented, geographical basis.

Officials became readier to take the initiative in policy formation, instead of simply responding to developments as they arose. An example of this was the Colonial Office's success in securing increased development and welfare funding from the Treasury in 1945 (Morgan, 1980: vol. 1, 198–9; Lee and Petter, 1982: 215–16). Amid growing doubts about the capacity of locally-based administrators to meet the challenges of an active development policy, an emerging younger generation of officials shook off the restraints of traditional thinking. Their creative speculation about future possibilities echoed the excitement inspired by the domestic reconstruction debate in Britain. The resulting discussions in the Colonial Office were grounded firmly in a colony-centred understanding of development, and were not obviously dictated by an overriding concern for Britain's economic interests.

A major spur to the Colonial Office's deliberations on reconstruction was the watershed policy statement made in July 1943 by the Colonial Secretary, Oliver Stanley. Seeking to assuage American suspicions of Britain's Imperial ambitions, Stanley declared that the ultimate goal of colonial rule was self-government, and committed Britain meanwhile to the economic and social development of the colonies.[5] Whereas in the late 1930s colonial development had been an end in itself, a patching-up exercise born of metropolitan embarrassment, from 1943 development became the officially acknowledged precursor to political advance in the colonies, a view held not only within the Colonial Office, but also by informed commentators ranging from the Establishment's own colonial expert, Lord Hailey, to erstwhile critics of the Colonial Office such as the Fabian Colonial Bureau.[6] However, the primacy given to economic and social development reflected the absence of a settled agenda for *political* development. Although the Colonial Office had come to accept by 1943 that existing political structures in the colonies and the essential framework for collaboration between colonial rulers and local élites no longer met modern requirements, no agreement had yet emerged on what should replace them (Pearce, 1982: 17–69; Lee and Petter, 1982: 164–99; Flint, 1983; Porter and Stockwell, 1987: 32–8).

The need for economic and social improvements tapped into an unconscious, yet still pervasive, vein of paternalism in the Colonial Office's thinking. Officials believed that true self-government would remain impossible while colonies were dependent on external aid to maintain even rudimentary social services, and the essentially long-term character of economic and social development postponed the need for a decision on the shape of future political development, a situation reinforced by the Colonial Office's inherently gradualist approach to development.[7]

During this 'reconstruction' phase, the Colonial Office sought to take a long-term view of development, extending beyond immediate palliative measures of the kind which had characterized the narrowly 'welfarist' discussions of the late 1930s. Officials' predictions about post-war conditions were informed strongly by painful experiences after 1918, when a brief boom in commodity prices had been followed by a long period of barely relieved depression.[8] A major theme in the Office's discussions was therefore a concern to achieve long-term commodity price stability, and avoid the violent market fluctuations which colonial producers had experienced between the wars. This made officials determined to continue wartime arrangements for the state marketing of colonial agricultural produce (Meredith, 1986). Encouraged by an apparent liberalization in Whitehall's traditionally cool attitude, officials also showed a growing interest in the benefits of promoting colonial economic diversification through a measure of industrial development.[9] Nevertheless, the key to improved colonial living standards was still assumed to be more efficient agriculture, but officials now explored the scope for making colonial economies less dependent on a narrow range of primary exports.[10] By 1945 the Colonial Office felt confident enough in the thawing of the views of traditional critics of colonial industrialization like the Board of Trade to issue guidelines to colonial governments on appropriate steps to encourage the growth of local manufacturing.[11]

Between 1943 and 1946, the Colonial Office's discussions centred on the problem of finding the capital and entrepreneurship necessary for development. Officials realized that increases in Colonial Development and Welfare funding were insufficient to meet the task ahead, pointing to a continuing, prominent role for expatriate private capital.[12] A key obstacle, especially in West Africa, usually at the centre of these discussions, was the growing hostility of local populations to the activities of expatriate firms such as the United Africa Company.[13] To prevent this hostility stifling progress with development, officials in London made broad-ranging and imaginative attempts to redefine the role of the colonial state, and to widen the parameters of acceptable state intervention in the colonial economies. This in turn fuelled official interest in the role of publicly-owned development corporations to provide the capital, expertise and momentum necessary for development.[14] Under state auspices, the development corporation would, theoretically, be free from the taint of exploitation often attached to private enterprise, and create opportunities for the involvement of local populations in the development process, a factor considered essential to the success of the whole strategy.[15] This demonstrated the Colonial Office's growing appreciation of the political dimension to economic development, and its attempts to anticipate the reactions of politically articulate sections of colonial opinion. Until 1946, the Colonial Office was generally able to retain the initiative in the more specific areas of policy-making. There was relatively little interference from the rest of Whitehall, and the colonial governments made only a muted and spasmodic contribution to the policy debate, confirming London's misgivings about their capacity to assume a dynamic role in development.[16]

The unprecedented exploitation of colonial economic resources by Britain during the war was justified with the promise that with the return of normality, the work of colonial development could be resumed. For example, the colonies were assured that the currency reserves which they had accumulated in London from Britain's bulk purchase of their exports would become available for development purposes.[17] However, the post-war years failed to satisfy the expectations thus raised. Instead of the emphasis in development policy reverting to a welfarist, colony-centred approach, a brief, largely stagnant interlude immediately after 1945 was followed by a fresh phase of attempted exploitation, concentrated particularly in the period 1947–8, in which the Labour government sought to ease Britain's problems of financial recovery by drawing on colonial resources. In the process, the development policies evolved by the Colonial Office during the war came under increasing threat.

As David Fieldhouse has commented, nearly everything done by the Labour government in the sphere of colonial development is open to the charge that principle was subordinated to pragmatism, and that the Labour Party's previous policy statements were flouted (Fieldhouse, 1984: 84). The problem here is that, in many respects, particularly regarding economic development, Labour's colonial policies in 1945 were poorly defined. Compared to major domestic issues such as public ownership and welfare reform, colonial questions remained a minority interest within the Party, a situation which gave an undue prominence to the views of the small number of activists, concentrated in the Fabian Colonial Bureau, who closely followed developments in the Colonial Empire (Goldsworthy, 1971; Gupta, 1975).

Labour's most recent policy statement on the colonies had been produced in 1943 by Arthur Creech Jones, close associate of Ernest Bevin and the Party's principal spokesman on colonial issues, nicknamed 'MP for the Kikuyu' in the 1930s, and appointed Colonial Secretary by Attlee in 1946 (Pearce, 1982: 90–131). On economic development, this statement called for the nationalization of natural resources, the preservation of communal landownership, and equal economic rights for the colonial peoples. A distrust of European capital operating in the colonies, for example, the large trading houses such as the United Africa Company, led Labour's enthusiasts to look to the colonial state, and not private enterprise, as the agent of modernization, especially since the Colonial Development and Welfare Act of 1940 seemed to make economic investment by the state practicable for the first time.[18] This optimism, curiously naïve in retrospect, was reinforced when the provision was expanded under the subsequent Colonial Development and Welfare Act of 1945. Broadly, Labour's development policy comprised a mixture of negativism, directed at expatriate capital, and paternalism, resulting from the neo-Fabians' virtually exclusive control of the development agenda within the Party.

From 1947 Attlee's government faced a contradiction between its continuing rhetoric, which emphasized welfarist, colony-centred development, and the reality of attempts at economic exploitation. For the first 18 months of the government's life, there is little evidence to suggest that Attlee and his Cabinet were exploring possible colonial solutions to Britain's obvious financial problems. Bevin's initial hopes that multilateral trade was the key to an expansion of Britain's export revenue, shared by the majority of the Cabinet, were crushed by the failure of the convertibility operation in August 1947, aggravated by the crippling fuel shortage of the previous winter, the rapid depletion of the American loan negotiated in 1945, the slow growth of exports and mounting concern about the level of food imports from the dollar area. It was in these circumstances that ministers turned their attention to the assistance the Colonial Empire might provide in achieving recovery (Gupta, 1983: 105–6; Cairncross, 1985: 20–1; Hyam, 1988: 149).

Attlee's Cabinet succumbed, like no other before it, to the legendary attraction of the colonies, and especially Africa, as an 'El Dorado', possessing vast untapped wealth which offered an escape route from Britain's problems. In this climate, a reversion to an earlier, exploitative definition of colonial development seemed not only possible but dangerously probable. For more than two years after the crisis of 1947, the Cabinet equated colonial development with the rapid maximization of colonial commodity production. Bevin was the principal advocate of this strategy, although his views appear to have been shared by Attlee, and later by Cripps.[19] Bevin developed a near obsessive faith in the potential of Africa, particularly its mineral wealth. He aimed to free Britain from its financial dependence on the United States, whose continued assistance he felt could not be assumed, and he was pessimistic about the prospects of recovery based on Britain's former export trade in manufactures, given the increasing trend, stimulated by the war, towards overseas industrialization.[20] A similar motive for promoting colonial development was implicit in Herbert Morrison's Cabinet paper, *Planning for Expansion*, drafted in May 1947, which claimed that Britain's recovery was being 'strangled' by shortages of raw materials, food and fuel, and that unless an 'ample flow' of commodities could be achieved, economic planning would be nullified and crises would recur.[21]

Such attitudes, nascent and largely uncoordinated in the first half of 1947, were brought sharply into focus by the balance of payments crisis in August.

Immediately, efforts were made to incorporate the colonies in the strategy to achieve recovery. The colonies were asked to continue building up their currency reserves in London, to strengthen the position of the sterling area as a whole.[22] They were asked not only to limit their dollar expenditure, but also to curb imports from the sterling area, thereby releasing goods for export to dollar markets, and they were told to increase their production of goods which Britain currently bought with dollars, or of goods which could be sold for dollars.[23] From the British government's point of view, an increase in commodity exports was the *major* contribution which the colonies could make to recovery. The hollow justification for these exhortations was that the crisis was an unprecedented opportunity for the colonies to develop their production and trade, thereby bringing advantages to themselves and to Britain.[24]

The emphasis on maximizing the colonial output of raw materials became the dominant theme in development policy in the period 1947–8. However, this bias conflicted with the Colonial Office's desire to encourage gradual economic diversification in the colonies. The Office's wartime efforts to produce a coherent policy on colonial industrialization were threatened in the post-war period by the weight of opinion in Whitehall which regarded this kind of development as at best an irrelevance under current conditions, or at worst, as inherently damaging to British interests. Yet the Colonial Office could not ignore the growing enthusiasm for industrial development, especially in the African colonies, where industrialization was increasingly seen by expanding local political élites as the key to future economic growth and a symbol of economic 'maturity'.[25] If the Colonial Office were seen to be obstructing development on these lines, political capital for emerging nationalist (or 'proto-nationalist') leaders might be created.

The Cabinet's development strategy was reinforced by the serious shortage of necessary capital goods in the colonial territories. Starved of imports during the war, the colonies now found that their needs took third place after those of dollar markets and British domestic reconstruction. In August 1947 the colonies were instructed to limit their imports, especially those from hard currency sources, to 'minimum essentials' and soon after the stringent wartime system of colonial import controls was reimposed.[26] Furthermore, Whitehall was slow to establish the administrative machinery needed to discover what goods the colonies required for development. As pressure grew after summer 1947 for the integration of colonial development with domestic economic planning, the Colonial Office seized the opportunity to propose an interdepartmental body to examine the allocation of supplies to the colonies.[27] However, whereas the Colonial Office saw this as a means of securing increased supplies, other departments wanted to cut back colonial imports still further. Above all, the Colonial Office was seeking a means of educating its Whitehall colleagues in the unappreciated difficulties attaching to colonial development.[28]

Only in January 1948 was an attempt made to discover the colonies' forseeable needs of basic capital imports such as steel and cement.[29] The interdepartmental Colonial Development Working Party concluded that the major impediment to development was the shortage of imports into the colonies.[30] The Working Party concluded also that the priority in the near future should be to restore and improve *existing* capital equipment such as railways, and to avoid the dangerous attraction of large new development schemes which, while firing the imagination, might take a long time to become productive.[31] In effect, this was a call to patch up colonial infrastructures which had been severely stretched during the war, and which, more importantly, were geared almost entirely to the production and export of colonial raw materials. It was, therefore, an implicit call for a bias in development towards tangible benefits for Britain. It was not until summer 1948 that Whitehall recognized the principle that the colonies should receive the same treatment in the allocation of British exports as countries with which Britain had bilateral trading agreements. Although the Colonial Office saw this as a major breakthrough, it realized that constant pressure would have to be maintained to give this principle substance.[32]

Just as the post-war years witnessed a sharp reduction in Britain's capacity to meet the colonies' material needs, so too the period saw the Colonial Empire being effectively starved of development finance. Although unprecedented amounts of grant aid had been promised under the 1945 Colonial Development and Welfare Act, the supply of investment capital shrank. Colonies were discouraged from borrowing on the London money markets on the grounds that domestic reconstruction took precedence over colonial needs (Morgan, 1980: vol. 1, 46–52). Creech Jones raised this problem with the Treasury, because of his concern that restricting the colonies' borrowing rights might be seen as exploitative. The Colonial Development Working Party subsequently advocated development loans of up to £60 million over the following three to four years. This was admitted to be a small figure, but loans were seen as only one of the available sources of funding.[33]

Even the vaunted Colonial Development and Welfare funding proved to be a disappointment. The total allocation of £120 million for development seemed impressive at first sight, but when distributed among a colonial population of over sixty million, and over a period of ten years, its true significance was modest. Even these sums were not fully expended. By 1951 only about £40 million had actually been spent, approximately one-sixth of the net colonial contribution to sterling in loans by colonial governments to London and the sterling balances amassed by the state marketing boards which purchased colonial produce under monopolistic conditions, generally on terms advantageous to the British consumer.[34]

At the height of post-crisis enthusiasm for colonial development, officials in London discussed borrowing dollars to achieve a faster rate of progress, for example by enabling colonies to buy American agricultural machinery.

Informal contacts with American officials revealed a growing interest among private US investors in African opportunities.[35] The Colonial Office responded publicly that foreign private investment in the colonies was acceptable if it complemented existing development plans and observed local welfare and labour regulations. Privately, however, the Office was unenthusiastic. Officials were uneasy about foreign control over individual development projects, the local political ramifications of foreign investment, and the repatriation of profits made in the colonies.[36] Similarly, the Colonial Office was cool towards investment by the United States government or by the International Bank for Reconstruction and Development. IBRD loans were considered to be too expensive for most colonies, but more important was official concern that the loans might have 'strings', for example giving the Bank the right to observe how its money was spent. Borrowing directly from the US government might, it was feared, result in a reduction in Britain's allocation of Marshall Aid.[37] The Colonial Development Working Party eventually concluded that the whole subject of attracting private US capital was problematic. Moreover, IBRD loans could be used only for purchases outside Britain and the colonies, and since the kind of goods which it was difficult to obtain in Britain were equally scarce in the United States, there seemed to be no advantage in borrowing dollars for this purpose.[38]

   The colonial development strategy pursued by the British government after 1947 exposed tensions within Whitehall and the conflicting interests of different government departments. Clearly, much of the new emphasis in development was at odds with the broad strategy evolved by the Colonial Office during the war. Moreover, the Office faced problems in having its voice and views heard. The department lacked political weight in Whitehall, demonstrated in Attlee's successive choices of Colonial Secretary, and was poorly placed to confront a Treasury that was fast regaining control of economic policy after the temporary eclipse of its influence during the war (Lee, 1980: 102–3; Cairncross, 1985: 50–6). This was not a new problem. The Colonial Office had become accustomed to being effectively ignored by the central policy-making machinery. In several key instances during the war, for example when the Committee on Post-War Commercial Policy was formed, the Office was not invited to participate.[39] In part, this reflected the continuing tendency among politicians and bureaucrats to assume an identity of interests between Britain and the colonies, an assumption they dared not apply to the Dominions or, increasingly, to India: in short, what was good for Britain was good for the colonies. This had been frustrating enough for the Colonial Office in the past, for example, during the 'reconstruction' period, when attempts had to be made to map out colonial economic policy with no clear guidelines concerning the future nature of imperial tariff arrangements. After 1947, with the metropolitan government showing an increasing interest in colonial development, its integration into the wider economic recovery programme and the record of the Colonial Office, the inferior status of the

Office within Whitehall and its inability to secure predominant influence in the shaping of colonial policy became ever more apparent, putting under strain the Office's theoretical dual role as the representative of British interests in the colonies, and of colonial interests in Britain. The Office found it difficult to retain the initiative in development policy when confronted with the interest and influence of other departments, especially the Treasury. As calls grew after 1947 for colonial development to be more closely integrated into Britain's own economic planning, the spectre of centralized control of development from London emerged, a prospect wholly unacceptable to the Colonial Office, which was caught between exhorting the colonial governments to greater activity and reserving for itself such metropolitan control over development as might prove necessary.

It became equally apparent after 1947 that behind the bland uniformity of imperial rhetoric lay important differences among Whitehall departments in their expectations of colonial development. The Treasury remained adamant that strict import control by the colonies was essential to maintain the colonial currency reserves held in London as a support for sterling (Morgan, 1980: vol. 1, 53–63). The Board of Trade, however, expressed concern that continuing import controls would deprive some British exporters of valuable colonial markets.[40] In this instance, the Board was representing interests such as the Lancashire cotton industry, which renewed the campaign it had waged between the wars to preserve its market share in relatively prosperous colonial regions such as West Africa.[41]

Official discussions after 1947 also revealed fundamental disagreement about the proper economic relationship between Britain and the Colonial Empire. In 1948 the Central Economic Planning Staff, with the Treasury's approval, drafted guidelines on colonial investment priorities. The Colonial Office described the suggested priorities as 'almost incredible', since they did not consider colonial needs but only the tapping of colonial resources for Britain's benefit.[42] For instance, the CEPS implied that proposals for colonial industrialization should be assessed in the light of their possible repercussions on British exporting interests. The Treasury had already argued that colonial labour should be deployed on immediately productive schemes, and that as little effort as possible should be deflected from the production of food and raw materials which could either earn or save dollars.[43] To the Colonial Office, 'deplorable' attitudes such as these fully bore out accusations that colonial development was a pretext for exploitation of the colonies by Britain.[44]

During 1948 the CEPS even proposed curbs on colonial welfare expenditure, on the grounds that social development could proceed only at a rate warranted by the level of local economic development, otherwise the colonies might incur expenditure commitments beyond their means and require financial assistance from Britain, which would delay their progress towards self-government.[45] This was, in effect, an attempt to return to the discredited pre-war doctrine of colonial financial self-sufficiency, an orthodoxy which had in theory been abandoned with the 1940 Colonial Development and Welfare Act. On this occasion the Colonial Office managed to convince its colleagues in Whitehall that if serious political problems in the colonies were to be avoided, future development would have to balance economic and social requirements. Even this concession was mitigated, however, by a continuing stress on deriving the maximum contribution from colonial resources to resolving the sterling area's balance of payments problems, an objective which, officials acknowledged, required a particular bias in development.[46]

Ironically, the very enthusiasm for colonial development evident in official circles after 1947 posed problems for the Colonial Office, Unrealistic expectations, grounded chiefly in British ignorance of colonial conditions, were encouraged. Yet development fever was pervasive and infectious. Writing after his African tour late in 1947, the Chief of the Imperial General Staff, Field Marshal Montgomery, displayed a comprehensive insensitivity to the political, economic and social realities of post-war Africa. He saw 'immense possibilities' in the development of the continent, and 'almost unlimited quantities' of vital raw materials, which could be tapped to maintain British living standards.[47] Montgomery, voicing a criticism of the Colonial Office and its methods which became increasingly common in Britain during 1947–8, attacked what he felt was the current uncoordinated approach to development, and called for a dynamic 'grand design', with the ruthless elimination of obstacles, human or otherwise.[48]

The report of the Select Committee on Estimates, published in June 1948, made a similar, if more moderately phrased criticism of progress with colonial development. The Committee found particular fault with the Colonial Office's development machinery, calling for much greater co-ordination and the centralized planning of development by London.[49] Again, the notion of imposing on the colonies development schemes formulated in Britain was totally at odds with the philosophy of development nurtured within the Colonial Office since the late 1930s. It took time for the Office to persuade other departments that the approach to development advocated by Montgomery and the Select Committee was quite impracticable and potentially dangerous. What the Colonial Office's critics were prone to overlook was the *political* dimension to development. The Colonial Office had consistently argued that development should be planned by *local* agencies, with London providing resources and guidance where necessary.[50] This principle was enshrined in the 1940 Colonial Development and Welfare Act, even though during the period of reconstruction planning, the Colonial Office became frustrated and alarmed at the apparent inability of colonial governments to absorb the new importance attached to *planned* development.[51] Moreover, given the British government's public commitment to progressive devolution in the colonies and the need to win the co-operation of the colonial populations in development, it was impossible, politically, to impose development plans arbitrarily from London. Only towards the end of 1948 did ministers grasp the message that development was a complex process which required delicate handling. Henceforth, discussions in Whitehall on what was achievable in colonial development became noticeably more sober than they had been 18 months earlier. A new sense of realism supplanted the reckless optimism of mid-1947.[52]

Symbolizing the new twist given to development policy after 1947 was the creation and subsequent role of the Colonial Development Corporation (CDC). The Corporation, created in 1948, was an expression of briefly fashionable attempts at dynamic, technocratic solutions to the problem of achieving rapid and efficient colonial development, and was also an example of a widespread faith in public enterprise. Not initially successful, the CDC provided ammunition for critics both of British colonial policy and of increased state economic intervention.

The idea of promoting desirable development through state action was not confined to circles within the Labour movement, though it was in line with calls by the Labour Party and the Fabian Colonial Bureau for a more interventionist role for the colonial state.[53] As has been suggested, the notion of state-sponsored development had been examined during the war by the Colonial Office, with important contributions to the debate being made by the Nigerian government.[54] The Colonial Office's interest in publicly-operated development corporations arose from two preoccupations. First, British corporate investment had shown only a selective interest in the colonies before 1939, concentrating on mining and plantation agriculture. Second, and more important in the Colonial Office's view, was the growing hostility of colonial opinion, especially among politically articulate groups, towards the operations of expatriate private enterprise, a sentiment increasingly shared by administrators in London and Africa.[55] By the end of the war, the Office had concluded that African hostility to the firms was paralysing development, and that only direct state intervention could introduce the necessary momentum.[56] Furthermore, the Colonial Office saw the public corporation as the ideal vehicle for local involvement, essential to the success of development. The Office envisaged a development corporation supported by local subsidiaries in individual colonies, to bring capital and expertise to a wide range of development schemes in agriculture and industry (Cowen, 1984). The idea was swiftly approved by the Cabinet in March 1947.[57] This decision was probably accelerated by the imminent exhaustion of the American loan and a growing conviction that Britain derived little immediate benefit from Colonial Development and Welfare expenditure.[58]

The new CDC, with borrowing powers of up to £100 million, was given an explicit brief to undertake development likely to ease Britain's balance of payments problems, earning dollars through exports to the United States, or saving dollars through the production of raw materials which Britain could import.[59] Initially, the Corporation's activities would be directed towards short-term projects requiring a minimum investment of capital goods.[60]

For the Colonial Office, the early record of the CDC was disillusioning. The Corporation, intended to be commercial and self-supporting, was given a wide measure of operational independence. However, a rift soon developed between the Office and the CDC, whose chairman, Lord Trefgarne, was determined to preserve his freedom of action and took as scriptural the injunction to bind the Corporation's activities to strictly commercial principles.[61] Advocates of this commercial role claimed that the immediate development needs of the colonies themselves had been met through successive Colonial Development and Welfare Acts. The Colonial Office even had to resist Treasury attempts to use part of the Development and Welfare Vote to finance the CDC.[62]

Ironically, the CDC, designed as a vehicle for development acceptable to colonial opinion, soon became a target for colonial criticism, to the dismay of the Colonial Office. The Corporation soon came to be regarded as a mechanism for exploitation, not development, and its creation did nothing to allay intense colonial suspicion of anything which could be interpreted as exploitation by external capital, whether its source was private or public investment. Fundamentally, the CDC's commercial character precluded it from undertaking urgently required, though not immediately profitable, development. The influential pan-Africanist, George Padmore, described the Corporation as 'a system of State Capitalism, operated on behalf of the Labour Government by salaried executives working for a semi-official Corporation rather than for shareholders. This constitutes a new form of Economic Imperialism'.[63] Distancing itself from the new Corporation's activities, the Colonial Office revived its earlier enthusiasm for individual, colony-based corporations, less susceptible to accusations of exploitation.[64]

Some Cabinet ministers understood the scope for charges that Britain was exploiting the Colonial Empire. Bevin was especially conscious of the potential international consequences of an apparently exploitative colonial policy, and was anxious to avoid criticism in the United Nations, notably from the Soviet Union.[65] Consequently, great stress was placed on the mutual benefits which the CDC's operations would bring to Britain and the colonies, although it was acknowledged that the entire question would have to be handled carefully when plans for the CDC were made public.[66] The Overseas Resources Development Act (1948), which created the CDC, also established an Overseas Food Corporation, entrusted with the later notorious East African Groundnuts Scheme, and directly responsible to the Ministry of Food for food-producing projects. The Colonial Office, concerned about colonial reactions to a body whose undisguised purpose was to benefit the British consumer, successfully established the principle that the OFC should operate in colonies only with the express permission of the Colonial Secretary.[67] Similarly when, early in 1948, ministers expressed general support for the rapid development of African resources to reinforce Britain's political and economic position, the Cabinet Secretary, Sir Norman Brook, reminded Attlee of the difficulty of defending such a policy, which could easily be interpreted as 'imperialism', adding that it was especially important for a Labour government not to alienate its supporters and 'enlightened' public opinion.[68]

Partly as a result of the growing awareness within the government of the risks it was running in appearing to be exploiting the colonies, a fresh emphasis was increasingly placed on the mutual benefits which Britain and the colonies could derive from the latter's development.[69] For example, the bias in development towards schemes for quick, dollar-earning production acquired a new justification at the hands of the Treasury and the CEPS. This involved the argument that a 'temporary' bias in development was necessary to restore Britain's balance of payments position, so that ultimately Britain would return to a condition which would enable it to devote more resources to colonial development.[70]

How, then, did the government's supporters reconcile themselves to the course of colonial development policy after 1947? It was not always an easy process, requiring considerable back-tracking and nimble footwork. There is some evidence of soul-searching, as when Rita Hinden, Secretary of the Fabian Colonial Bureau, wrote in 1949 that Britain had no intention of promoting colonial development at the expense of its own living standards and admitted Britain's self-interest in the existing development plans (Gupta, 1975: 324). On balance, however, supporters such as the FCB struggled to present the goverment's strategy in positive terms.[71] The belief remained that development under state auspices would not be exploitative, would not siphon off profits from the colonies, would enter into a partnership with local populations, and would ultimately lead to enterprises being transferred to local management. These views mirrored exactly the Colonial Office's motives in supporting public enterprise.[72]

Therefore, the role of the Colonial Development Corporation, particularly the bias in its mandate towards dollar-earning agriculture, was potentially embarrassing for the government's supporters. Since the 1930s critics of colonial rule, who later included the FCB, had warned of the dangers of colonial economies being overdependent on primary export production, given the volatility of commodity markets.[73] Yet after 1947 the British government was apparently encouraging the colonies to concentrate on primary exports. This called for some intellectual gymnastics by the FCB. After 1947 they began to argue that economic specialization was not inherently dangerous to the colonies, and even that concentration on export agriculture offered the greatest opportunities for the colonies. Having argued for the previous seven years that diversification into processing and manufacturing was essential to the colonies, the Bureau now suggested that industrialization should not be confused with increased colonial productivity.[74]

Like the Colonial Office, Labour's few specialists on colonial affairs held the view that political development towards colonial self-government must be grounded in secure economic and social foundations. No time-scale was attached to this preparatory period, but the common assumption until the end of the 1940s was that colonial rule might continue for generations to come. In the post-war years Labour's enthusiasts for colonial development hoped, as did some leading figures in the Colonial Office, that the colonies could be guided not only towards democracy but also towards *social* democracy. This gradualist vision, tinged with an unconscious paternalism, enabled most of Labour's supporters to acquiesce in the development policies implemented after 1947.

To conclude, British colonial development policy did not follow a one-directional evolution after the later 1930s. For the Colonial Office, the broad goals of policy remained relatively consistent, but circumstances demanded important shifts in emphasis in policy implementation. For the most part, the Colonial Office had to react to externally dictated obligations and restrictions, including the force of international opinion and the requirements of other government departments. Yet between 1943 and 1946 the Office assumed a clearly pro-active role. Enjoying the brief experience of some freedom of manœuvre in policy formation, the Office attempted to establish coherent long-term policy goals while trying to anticipate the aspirations of an emerging class of articulate colonial élites before these were translated into unmanageable demands.

In practice, however, the new and intoxicating experience of development planning impaired the judgement of officials, and they miscalculated wildly the time-span available to them. When the time came to put into effect the fruits of 'reconstruction' planning, the Colonial Office discovered not only an increasing divergence between its thinking and the ideas of the rest of government, but also that it had failed to keep abreast of rapidly developing colonial aspirations. Finally, development policy was always open to two interpretations: the first, adopted and institutionalized by the Colonial Office, stressed the importance of relating development to colonial needs; the second, apparent in the attitudes of departments such as the Treasury and the Board of Trade, saw colonial development as a means of safeguarding and promoting British interests. On balance, the inferior status and relative isolation of the Colonial Office within Whitehall prevented it from defending its policy goals and resisting the tendency to substitute development with exploitation.

Notes

1. I am grateful to Dr Helen Mercer of the University of Leeds and to Prof Andrew Porter of King's College, London for their comments on an earlier version of this chapter.
2. The following are prominent among the growing literature on this subject:

Morgan (1980); Constantine (1984); Meredith (1975); Porter and Stockwell (1987); Johnson (1977); Lee and Petter (1982).

3. Public Record Office, Kew (PRO) CAB 67/4/WP(G)(40)44: memorandum by Secretary of State for the Colonies, 'Statement of policy on colonial development and welfare and colonial research', 3 February 1940.

4. Sir John Shuckburgh, 'Colonial civil history of the war Volume I', unpublished manuscript (University of London, Institute of Commonwealth Studies Library), 29f; see also Hargreaves, 1988: 49–53.

5. *Parliamentary Debates (Commons)*, 391, cols. 66–8, 13 July 1943.

6. Lord Hailey (1943a); 27f.; Lord Hailey (1943b): 24–5; see also Lord Hailey, *Native Administration and Political Development in British Tropical Africa* (originally produced 1940–2, reprinted with introduction by A.H.M. Kirk-Greene, Neuden 1979), 62; for the thinking of the Fabian Colonial Bureau see esp. Hinden (1945) and Fieldhouse (1982) esp. 485f.

7. This problem had been identified at a relatively early stage in the debate on development policy; see minute by Sir John Campbell (Financial Adviser, Colonial Office), 12 June 1939, quoted in J.H. Bowden, 'Development and control in British colonial policy, with reference to Nigeria and the Gold Coast, 1935–48', unpublished Ph.D. thesis, University of Birmingham, 1980, 69; PRO CO 859/40/6: minute by Caine, 30 March 1940; CO 96/781/31475/1944, Papers on Colonial Affairs No. 3 (C.M. No. 3): 'The planning of social and economic development in the Colonial Empire', April 1944; Cmd. 6713 *Colonial Development and Welfare. Despatch dated 12th November, 1945 from the Secretary of State for the Colonies to Colonial Governments*.

8. PRO CO 852/503/9, CPP 65: paper by G.L.M. Clauson for Colonial Office Committee on Post-War Problems, 'Colonial economic problems in the reconstruction period', 31 March 1941.

9. PRO CO 852/480/1: minute by Dawe to Gater, 5 May 1943, and minute by Stanley, 6 May 1943; CO 852/409/13: memorandum by Board of Trade, 'U.K. participation in Empire secondary industries', July 1943; CO 852/554/7: note by Treasury, 'Overseas investment in the next few years', January 1944; CO 990/1, CEAC(44)15: memorandum by Colonial Office, 'The development of secondary industry in the Colonial Empire', (n.d., but early 1944).

10. See, e.g., PRO CO 852/482/2, letter from Stanley to Swinton (Resident Minister, West Africa), 5 June 1943; *Parliamentary Debates (Commons)*, 391, cols. 66–8, 13 July 1943; CO 990/1, CEAC(44)15: memorandum by Colonial Office, 'The development of secondary industry in the Colonial Empire', (n.d.); CO 990/17, CEAC(Ind)(44)5: memorandum by Caine, 'Possible scope for industrialisation in the Colonies', 25 April 1944; CO 852/578/5, CEAC(44)32: 'The development of manufacturing industries', 29 August 1944. Towards the end of the 'reconstruction' planning phase, there is evidence of the Colonial Office's continuing belief in the benefits of diversification through industrialization. As the Colonial Secretary, Hall, informed Governor Richards of Nigeria on 12 April 1945: 'there is no doubt in my mind that industrial development in itself offers one of the most promising means we can have of raising the general level of prosperity of the people in a country like Nigeria' (PRO CO 852/574/10).

11. PRO CO 852/578/6: circular despatch, 'The development of manufacturing industries', 27 February 1945.

12. See, e.g., *Parliamentary Debates (Commons)*, 391, cols. 66–8, 13 July 1943; PRO CO 554/132/33718/1/1943: memorandum for West African Governments, 'Post-war planning for West Africa' (n.d.); CO 990/2, CEAC(43)5: 'Social and economic planning in the Colonial Empire', 25 November 1943; CO 852/588 Pt 1: 'The planning of social and economic development in the Colonial Empire', April 1944.

13. PRO CO 583/263/30560/1943: note of meeting in the Colonial Office on Nigerian development, 22 June 1943; CO 852/482/2: draft memorandum by Carstairs, 21 November 1943; ibid., minutes by Cohen, 31 December 1943, and O.G.R. Williams, 4 January 1944; CO 852/578/8: draft note by Cohen, 'Development corporations in West Africa', August 1944.

14. Ibid.; see also Cowen, 1984: 63–75.

15. PRO CO 852/482/2: draft memorandum by Carstairs, 21 November 1943; ibid., minute by O.G.R. Williams, 27 November 1943.

16. See esp. PRO CO 852/588/2: memorandum by Caine to Gater, 16 August 1943; CO 583/271/30572/1944: minutes by Cohen, 21 January 1944, and Caine, 28 January 1944; CAB 104/257: Swinton to Stanley, 14 June 1944.

17. Cmd. 6299 *Certain Aspects of Colonial Policy in War-Time*, 5 June 1941; PRO CO 852/588 Pt 1: 'The planning of social and economic development in the Colonial Empire', April 1944; Westcott, 1983: 4, 7, 8.

18. Labour Party (1943), *The Colonies. The Labour Party's Post-War Policy for the African and Pacific Colonies*, London.

19. PRO CO 537/3047: Bevin to Attlee, 13 September 1947; ibid., Bevin to Attlee, 16 September 1947; see also Hyam, 1988: 149; CO 847/36/2/24: speech by Cripps to African Governors' Conference, 12 November 1947.

20. PRO CAB 130/19: GEN. 179/5th meeting, 28 July 1947; ibid., GEN. 179/14th meeting, 20 August 1947; CO 537/3047: Bevin to Attlee, 16 September 1947; see also Gupta, 1983: 106.

21. PRO CAB 124/1079: memorandum by Lord President of the Council, 'Planning for expansion', 31 May 1947 (final version CP(47)169).

22. Hinds, 1987: 151–5; PRO CO 852/870/2: circular telegram from Creech Jones on UK balance of payments position, 6 August 1947.

23. Ibid.

24. PRO CO 852/870/2: circular telegram from Creech Jones on UK balance of payments position, 6 August 1947.

25. See, e.g. PRO CO 537/3226: report by Rees-Williams, 'West African Tour—1948', 27 September 1948.

26. PRO T.236/688: circular telegram no. 98 from Creech Jones, 'Import licensing policy', 5 September 1947.

27. PRO CO 852/871/1: minute by Caine to Creech Jones, 10 November 1947; ibid., minute by Rees-Williams, 11 November 1947; ibid., Creech Jones to Cripps, 22 November 1947; ibid., minute by Caine to Clauson, Eastwood, Davies and Melville, 24 November 1947; CO 852/831/1: minute by T.W. Davies to Clauson and Caine, 11 November 1947.

28. Ibid.

29. PRO T 229/220: minute by Strath to Plowden, 22 January 1948; CO 852/875/1: telegram from Caine to Beresford-Stooke (Nigeria), 24 January 1948; CO 852/871/1: circular telegram from Creech Jones, 27 January 1948.

30. PRO CO 852/868/3, CEDC(48)2: Colonial Development Working Party draft interim report, 12 April 1948.
31. Ibid.
32. PRO CO 852/889/3: telegram from Poynton to Rees-Williams, 18 August 1948; ibid., Poynton to Rees-Williams, 20 August 1948.
33. Morgan, 1980: vol. 1, 46–52; PRO CAB 134/65: 'Report of the Colonial Development Working Party' (revised), 11 October 1948.
34. Fieldhouse, D.K., review of Morgan (1980) in *English Historical Review* (April 1982): 386–94.
35. PRO CO 852/875/1: Trefgarne to Colonial Office, 12 January 1948; PRO, CDWP(48)5, 12 January 1948; CO 852/877/1: letter from Roger Makins (FO) to Caine, 15 August 1947.
36. PRO CO 852/875/1, CDWP(48)20: memorandum by Colonial Office, 'Investment of foreign capital in the Colonies', 9 March 1948.
37. PRO CO 999/4, CEDC(47)6: note on colonial borrowing from IBRD following meeting of CEDC, 10 Feburary 1947; CO 852/877/1: Caine to Roger Makins, 18 August 1947; ibid., minute by Thomas, 18 September 1947; ibid., minute by Caine to Rees-Williams, 6 November 1947; CO 852/857/1, CDWP(48)20: memorandum by Colonial Office, 'Investment of foreign capital in the colonies', 9 March 1948.
38. PRO CAB 134/65: 'Report of the Colonial Development Working Party' (revised), 11 October 1948.
39. The Office was, however, invited to submit its comments on the Committee's draft report. See PRO CAB 117/68, 'Report of the Committee on post-war commercial policy', 6 January 1943. The Colonial Secretary subsequently complained to the Chancellor of the Exchequer, Sir John Anderson, that the Colonial Office had once more been excluded from official discussions on future commercial policy; see PRO CAB 123/221: Stanley to Anderson, 26 January 1943.
40. PRO CO 537/3095, CD(47)7: Dollar Drain Committee. Colonial Empire. Progress Report by the Treasury, 10 December 1947.
41. Buxton and Aldcroft, 1979: 43–4; Hopkins, 1973: 265; PRO BT 175/5 CB 7330a: Cotton Board (1948) 17th meeting, 14 December 1948; ibid., CB 7420a: Cotton Board (1948) 21st meeting, 4 February 1949.
42. PRO CO 852/876/1: letter from A.T.K. Grant to Croome (CEPS), 9 August 1947; ibid., minute by Newsam to K.E. Robinson (comments on CEPS' draft memorandum, 'Principles for the guidance of colonial investment'), 9 August 1948.
43. PRO T 236/696, letter from Rowe-Dutton to Caine, 5 February 1948.
44. PRO CO 852/876/1: minute by Newsam to K.E. Robinson, 9 August 1948; ibid., minute by Robinson to Gorell Barnes, 9 August 1948; ibid., minute by Gorell Barnes to Robinson, 10 August 1948; ibid., note of meeting held in CEPS on 'Principles of colonial investment', 11 August 1948.
45. PRO CO 852/875/3, CDWP(48)50: 'Principles for the guidance of colonial investment', 14 September 1948.
46. PRO CO 852/876/1: note of meeting in CEPS on 'Principles of colonial investment', 11 August 1948; CO 852/875/3, CDWP(48)50: 'Principles for the guidance of colonial investment', 14 September 1948; CAB 134/65: 'Report of the Colonial Development Working Party' (revised), 11 October 1948. The Colonial

Office's qualified success in moderating the CEPS' demands was probably due in no small measure to the recent startling experience of disturbances in the Gold Coast, hitherto regarded as a 'model' colony, which had shaken metropolitan complacency about the indefinite time available to London's architects of devolution; added to the chastening effects of the Accra riots was mounting evidence, confirmed by first-hand ministerial reports, of growing African demands for progress in economic development. On the Accra riots, see Hargreaves, 1988: 114–15, 125, 140; Pearce, 1982: 188–9, 194–5; *Report of the Commission of Enquiry into Disturbances in the Gold Coast, 1948* (Col. No. 231 of 1948); PRO CO 537/3226: 'West African Tour—1948', report by Rees-Williams, 27 September 1948.

47. PRO T 220/17: memorandum, 'Tour in Africa in November–December 1947 by Field Marshal the Viscount Montgomery of Alamein', 19 December 1947.

48. Ibid.; for the Colonial Office's reactions see ibid., letter from Watson (CO) to Fogarty (Treasury), 6 January 1948; and CAB 130/31, GEN.210 1st meeting, 9 January 1948.

49. House of Commons 181, *Fifth Report from the Select Committee on Estimates Session 1947–48. Colonial Development. 30 June 1948.*

50. Cmd.6175 *Statement of Policy on Colonial Development and Welfare*, February 1940; *Parliamentary Debates (Commons)*; Cmd.6713 *Colonial Development and Welfare. Despatch dated 12th November, 1945 from the Secretary of State for the Colonies to Colonial Governments.*

51. See esp. PRO CO 852/588/2; memorandum by Caine, 12 August 1943; CO 583/271/30572/1944, minute by Cohen, 27 January 1944; ibid., minute by Caine, 28 January 1944.

52. PRO CO 852/878/1, Economic Planning Board (EPB(48) 13th meeting, 21 October 1948; CAB 134/216, Economic Policy Committee EPC(48) 35th meeting, 9 November 1948; Gupta, 1983: 108.

53. See, e.g., Hinden (1945), esp. Introduction by Creech Jones, 12–16; Hinden (1941), *Plan for Africa*, London, 207–8, 216.

54. PRO CO 852/578/8, note of meeting in Colonial Office, 24 October 1944; CO 583/271/30572/1944, note on 'Nigeria development plan', November 1944.

55. PRO CO 852/482/2, minutes by Cohen, 31 December 1943, and O.G.R. Williams, 4 January 1944; CO 852/578/8; draft note by Cohen, 'Development Corporations in West Africa', August 1944.

56. Ibid.

57. PRO CO 537/2002, Creech Jones to Attlee, 26 March 1947; PREM 8/457, Portal to Attlee, 10 April 1947; CAB 129 CP(47)175, memorandum by Secretary of State for the Colonies, 'The development of colonial resources; CAB 128 CM 53(47)5, 10 June 1947; Gupta, 1983: 106–7.

58. Bodleian Library MS Attlee dep. 48 (Attlee Papers) fos. 116–19, Portal to Attlee, 17 December 1946.

59. PRO CO 537/2002, Creech Jones to Attlee, 26 March 1947.

60. PRO CO 852/875/1, memorandum, 'The Colonial Development Corporation. Method of operation', 5 December 1947.

61. PRO CO 537/3031, minute by Caine to Rees-Williams, 26 June 1948; Cowen, 1984.

62. PRO CO 537/2002, note of informal discussion at Treasury, 14 May 1947.

63. Quoted in *Empire*, November 1948.
64. PRO CO 537/3033, minute by Cohen, 9 August 1948; ibid., minute by Gorell Barnes, 9 August 1948; ibid., minute by Gorell Barnes to Lloyd, 12 August 1948.
65. PRO PREM 8/456, Bevin to Attlee, 4 October 1947.
66. PRO CO 999/1, CEDC 13th minutes, 10 March 1947.
67. PRO PREM 8/456, memorandum by Ivor Thomas to Attlee, 'Definition of functions of Colonial Development Corporation and Overseas Food Corporation', 1 October 1947.
68. PRO CAB 21/1690, minute by Norman Brook to Attlee, 14 January 1948.
69. PRO CO 852/870/2, letter from Lloyd to Colonial Governors, 26 July 1948, enclosing memorandum, 'The Colonial Empire and the economic crisis'.
70. PRO CAB 134/65, 'Report of the Colonial Development Working Party' (revised), 11 October 1948.
71. E.g. Hinden, R. (1949), *Common Sense and Colonial Development*, London, Fabian Colonial Bureau; the Bureau's journal, *Empire*, played a leading part in the projection of policy in these years, e.g. in articles such as 'Critical times', vol. 10, no. 4, October 1947.
72. E.g. 'Opening up the colonies', *Empire*, vol. 10, no. 1, July 1947; and 'Development crusade', *Empire*, vol. 10, no. 6, December 1947.
73. E.G. Hinden, 1941: 50–1.
74. *Empire*, vol. 10, no. 1, July 1947.

References

Abbott, G.C. (1970), 'British colonial aid policy during the nineteen thirties', *Canadian Journal of History*, 5.

Abbott, G.C. (1973), 'A re-examination of the 1929 Colonial Development Act', *Economic History Review*, 24.

Brett, E.A. (1973), *Colonialism and Underdevelopment in East Africa: The politics of economic change, 1919–1939*, London, Heinemann.

Buxton, N.K. and Aldcroft, D.H. (eds) (1979), *British Industry between the Wars*, London, Scolar Press.

Cairncross, A. (1985), *Years of Recovery: British economic policy 1945–51*, London, Methuen.

Constantine, S. (1984), *The Making of British Colonial Development Policy 1914–1940*, London, Frank Cass.

Cowen, M. (1984), 'Early years of the Colonial Development Corporation: British state enterprise overseas during late colonialism', *African Affairs*, 83.

Cowen, M. and Westcott, N.J. (1986), 'British imperial economic policy during the war', in D. Killingray and R. Rathbone (eds), *Africa and the Second World War*, London, Macmillan.

Drummond, I.M. (1974), *Imperial Economic Policy, 1917–1939*, London, George Allen and Unwin.

Dumett, R. (1985), 'Africa's strategic minerals during the Second World War', *Journal of African History*, 26.

Ehrlich, C.C. (1973), 'Building and caretaking: economic policy in British Tropical Africa, 1890–1960', *Economic History Review*, 26.

Fieldhouse, D.K. (1982), 'Decolonization, development and dependence: a survey of changing attitudes', in P. Gifford and W. Roger Louis (eds), *The Transfer of Power in Africa, Decolonization 1940–1960*, New Haven, Yale University Press.

Fieldhouse, D.K. (1984), 'The Labour governments and the Empire–Commonwealth, 1945–51', in R. Ovendale (ed.), *The Foreign Policy of the British Labour Governments, 1945–1951*, Leicester, Leicester University Press.

Flint, J. (1983), 'Planned decolonization and its failure in British Africa', *African Affairs*, 82.

Frankel, S.H. (1938), *Capital Investment in Africa*, Oxford, Oxford University Press.

Goldsworthy, D. (1971), *Colonial Issues in British Politics, 1945–1961. From 'colonial development' to 'wind of change'*, London, Oxford University Press.

Gupta, P.S. (1975), *Imperialism and the British Labour Movement, 1914–1964*, London, Macmillan.

Gupta, P.S. (1983), 'Imperialism and the Labour government of 1945–51', in J.M. Winter (ed.), *The Working Class in Modern British History*, London, Cambridge University Press.

Hailey, Lord (1938), *An African Survey*, Oxford, Oxford University Press.

Hailey, Lord (1943a), *Britain and her Dependencies*, London, Longman.

Hailey, Lord (1943b), *The Future of Colonial Peoples*, Oxford, Oxford University Press.

Hargreaves, J.D. (1988), *Decolonization in Africa*, Harlow, Longman.

Hinden, R. (ed.) (1945), *Fabian Colonial Essays*, London, George Allen and Unwin.

Hinden, R. (1941), *Plan for Africa*, London, The Fabian Colonial Bureau.

Hinds, A.E. (1987), 'Sterling and Imperial Policy, 1945–1951', *Journal of Imperial and Commonwealth History*, 15.

Hopkins, A.G. (1973), *An Economic History of West Africa*, London, Longman.

Hyam, R. (1988), 'Africa and the Labour government, 1945–1951', *Journal of Imperial and Commonwealth History*, 16, 3.

Johnson, H. (1977), 'The West Indies and the conversion of the British official classes to the development idea', *Journal of Commonwealth and Comparative Politics*, 15.

Lee, J.M. (1980), *The Churchill Coalition 1940–1945*, London, Batsford.

Lee, J.M. (1977), ' "Forward thinking" and war: the Colonial Office during the 1940s', *Journal of Imperial and Commonwealth History*, 6.

Lee, J.M. and Petter, M. (1982), *The Colonial Office, War, and Development Policy: Organisation and the planning of a metropolitan initiative, 1939–1945*, London, Temple Smith.

Louis, W. Roger (1977), *Imperialism at Bay: The United States and the decolonization of the British Empire*, London, Oxford University Press.

Macmillan, W.M. (1938), *Africa Emergent*, Harmondsworth, Penguin Books.

Meredith, D. (1975), 'The British Government and colonial economic policy 1919–1939', *Economic History Review*, 28.

Meredith, D. (1986), 'State controlled marketing and economic "development"', *Economic History Review*, 39.

Morgan, D.J. (1980), *The Official History of Colonial Development*, vols 1 and 2, London, Macmillan.

Munro, J. Forbes (1984), *Britain in Tropical Africa 1880–1960: Economic relationships and impact*, London, Macmillan.

Pearce, R.D. (1982), *The Turning Point in Africa: British colonial policy 1938–1948*, London, Frank Cass.

Porter, A.N. and Stockwell, A.J. (1987), *British Imperial Policy and Decolonisation 1938–51*, London, Macmillan.

Rampersad, D.G.M., 'Colonial economic development and social welfare: the case of the British West Indian colonies, 1929–47', unpublished Oxford D.Phil. thesis, 1979.

Smythe, R. (1985), 'Britain's African colonies and British propaganda during World War II', *Journal of Imperial and Commonwealth History*, 15.

Thorne, C. (1978), *Allies of a Kind: the United States, Britain and the war against Japan*, London, Hamish Hamilton.

Westcott, N.J. (1983), 'Sterling and Empire: The British Imperial Economy, 1939–1951', unpublished seminar paper, University of London, Institute of Commonwealth Studies.

10 Kenya: Decolonization through counterinsurgency

Frank Furedi

> It is certain that gaining the fullest possible information on African political activity, particularly among the Kikuyu, is now and will be an intelligence task of equal if not greater importance than keeping track of the terrorists.
> (Lieutenant General Sir Gerald Lathbury, 26 January 1956)[1]

As the shooting-war phase of the Kenya Emergency was drawing to a close, the British Commander-in-Chief, General Lathbury, rightly expressed the view that the line between military and political considerations could not be drawn with any degree of exactitude. His immediate predecessor in Kenya, General Sir George Erskine, would have agreed. In January 1954, at the height of the anti-Mau Mau campaign, Erskine warned that any 'military plan adopted must NOT be such as to prejudice any long term political policy aimed at effecting a permanent solution to the political aspects of the Kikuyu problem in particular and African nationalism in general'.[2] Like all of Britain's post-Second World War colonial emergencies, that of Kenya was designed to establish a political framework for the management of nationalist resistance. Counterinsurgency was developed to complement a wider strategy of political decolonization (Furedi, 1989a).

By 1956, at least in Kenya, counterinsurgency warfare was relatively sophisticated and developed. After four years of the Emergency, the civil and military leaders were now primarily concerned with winning the support of a section of African public opinion.[3] Military tactics were clearly focused and selectively applied. The Special Forces had as their main task the elimination of the key Mau Mau leaders.[4] Also, the Nairobi administration was carefully setting about the task of establishing the political framework for the process of controlled decolonization.

The advantage of hindsight can create the impression that the gradual termination of the British Empire proceeded along the lines of a carefully constructed plan. Such impressions are highly misleading for as the events of Kenya showed, this period is more one of unexpected events leading to actions

141

with unintended consequences. In the case of Kenya, pre-emptive policies and counterinsurgency tactics were belated responses designed to provide a breathing-space for a beleaguered colonial administration. In reality the declaration of the State of Emergency in October 1952 was instrumental in transforming anti-colonial protest into an armed revolt. In effect the colonial government in Nairobi lost control over the situation. It took about a year and a half for the British military to regain the situation and although the Mau Mau ceased to be a military threat by the end of 1954, its ability to survive and carry on the revolt represented a major problem for Britain.

Anti-colonial nationalism had an unpleasant habit of arriving un-announced. By the time Whitehall was aware of the danger represented by the newly emergent anti-colonial forces, the situation was no longer susceptible to conventional imperial solutions. The explosive outburst of nationalism in Burma came as a shock to the British government. By 1948, unexpected struggles were breaking out throughout the Empire and Malaya was on the brink of a twelve-year-long Emergency.

The issue facing London was that of control. Consequently the Colonial Office had a tendency to relate to local political problems from the perspective of law and order. Popular anti-colonial movements were difficult to manage through the procedure of piecemeal constitutional devolution. Such movements tended to be defined as subversive and the appropriate response to them was to be found in the sphere of policing. Whitehall's failure to anticipate the outbreak of anti-colonial agitation was itself interpreted as proof that it was the work of subversive conspirators. The failure to recognize the warning signs was understood in London as a consequence of poor intelligence and inefficient policing.

It was in this vein, that Colonel Nicol Gray, former Inspector-General of the Palestine Police and soon to be dispatched to Malaya, reacted to unforeseen events in the Gold Coast and South East Asia. In July 1948 he informed General Sir Leslie Hollis of the Cabinet Defence Committee that as far as he was aware, no one at Whitehall was directing the problem of colonial policing.[5] Hollis promptly wrote to the Minister of Defence to express his concern and argued for the review and overhaul of the Colonial Police Service. According to Hollis, 'the fire has been allowed to get out of hand due to the absence of an efficient firebrigade.'[6]

Hollis' proposals won the endorsement of the Cabinet, and the Secretary of State for the Colonies was requested to organize a review of the Colonial Police.[7] The restructuring of the Police and of intelligence-gathering which followed was paralleled by a co-ordinated effort to sensitize colonial administrators to the threat of subversion. The aim of Whitehall was to prevent major disorder through pre-emptive measures. For the Colonial Office, the orientation of the High Commissioner of Malaya, Henry Gurney, provided the model approach towards the problem of anti-colonial resistance. In January 1949 Gurney was requested to summarize the lessons of the experience of the Malayan Emergency for the guidance of other colonial governors.

Gurney's dispatch outlined a general framework for the conduct of an internal colonial war. At the first sign of unrest the government had to mobilize all its powers against its opponents, argued Gurney.[8] The failure of the British authorities to contain the insurgency in Palestine was used by Gurney as a negative example of what happens when Emergency regulations are implemented one by one in a makeshift fashion. He concluded that if 'all these powers had been taken and exercised immediately at the beginning' in Palestine, 'perhaps the outcome might have been different'.[9] The immediate implementation of a comprehensive range of special powers to prevent the growth of resistance was the foundation of Gurney's formula for dealing with anti-colonial resistance.

The second element of Gurney's strategy called for the militarization of policing and the preparation of the forces of the state to deal with the outbreak of disorder. For Gurney the police were the ultimate guarantor of colonial rule. He was of the opinion that the military lacked the expertise and the local knowledge to deal with anti-colonial resistance. In contrast the police could conduct an 'underground war' if it was 'built up well in advance with long and thorough training'.[10] Such an emphasis on the police implied the extension of their functions to what in contemporary language is known as a special counterinsurgency force. This orientation was fully endorsed in London since efficient policing could help reduce the demands on Britain's already overextended resources.[11] The third important strand of Gurney's outline was the subordination of the military to civil power. Gurney was insistent that 'the withdrawal of the civil power and the substitution of military control represent the first victory for the terrorist.'[12] According to him, a military-dominated government would endow the resistance with legitimacy. Elsewhere Gurney conceded that the 'effective taking of the initiative against terrorists amounts to nothing short of war'. However, it was important for the authority of the colonial regime that an internal war should be seen as a law and order problem created by subversives. Through the pretence of normalcy and civil rule, Gurney sought to criminalize anti-colonial resistance. This is a tradition that has endured to this day. It also helps explain why Britain's colonial wars have tended to be characterized by the more neutral term of an 'emergency'.

Gurney's dispatch was widely distributed and provided guidance for colonial administrators throughout the Empire. Governor Arden Clarke of the Gold Coast noted that when confronted with the threat of a general strike in January 1950, he was 'greatly helped' by Gurney's dispatch. He added that it was of 'the greatest value in establishing early control of the situation to bring in emergency powers before disturbances occurred'.[13] However, 'establishing early control of the situation' was not always possible to achieve. The reorganization of the police and the investment of resources in intelligence-gathering were not sufficient in themselves to counter political unrest. A pre-emptive strike could target nationalist politicians but not a mass movement. Moreover, as the experience of Kenya showed, the declaration of emergency itself could drive militant nationalists towards the option of an armed revolt.

The political objectives of the Kenya Emergency

The colonial regime in Nairobi was obsessed with the question of security, policing, intelligence-gathering and emergency powers from the late 1940s onwards. The Nairobi administration self-consciously sought to learn from the experience of the Gold Coast and Malaya to pre-empt mass unrest. The Colonial Office was reasonably satisfied with security in Kenya and widely advocated its system of population registration as a model for other colonies.[14] The Kenya experience shows that there are no security techniques for preventing the emergence of mass resistance. Indeed it seems that many of the repressive measures taken prior to the Declaration of Emergency directly contributed to the radicalization of anti-colonial protest. There were of course other important factors that inspired anti-colonial resistance, but the catalyst that transformed political agitation into an armed revolt was the Declaration of Emergency in October 1952 (Furedi, 1989b).

Evidence suggests that the detention policy practised by the Nairobi administration was designed to eliminate the African intellectual politician. Baring made a sharp distinction between the 'activists' and the 'intellectual' or semi-educated type. The latter would be held indefinitely, according to Baring.[15] As late as June 1958, Baring was still determined to hold the 'politicals'.[16] The targeting of this group indicates that the goal of taking out the politician took precedence over the detection of the so-called terrorist.

The main political objective of the British regime in Kenya was to isolate the radical wing of the nationalist movement, destroy it and build up a party of moderate African politicans. Back in October 1952, the more conservative African politicians were on the defensive and increasingly on the margins of the nationalist movement. In European settler-dominated Kenya there was little room for absorbing African nationalist demands and anti-colonial agitation acquired an increasingly militant complexion. By the summer of 1952, the radical plebian elements of the nationalist movement dominated African politics (Furedi, 1989b). The newly appointed Governor, Evelyn Baring, had as his priority the elimination of the radical leadership as a prelude to the construction of a moderate African alternative. Baring and the Colonial Office conceived of the Emergency as a short policing operation. A major memorandum by Phillip Rogers of the Colonial Office which had the support of his superiors concluded that 'quite unlike the position in Malaya, Mau Mau can be dealt with, or kept under control, fairly readily now that

Government has shown that it is prepared to be tough.'[17] Rogers also reviewed the perspective which was to inform Whitehall's strategy during the subsequent eleven years:

> Our major problem with African discontent as I see it is to isolate the extremists and in effect split the Africans . . . . I think it is most important that further efforts should be made to find further African leaders who can be built up as political leaders.[18]

The objective of 'splitting the Africans' required that Mau Mau should remain restricted to within the Kikuyu community.[19] Radical nationalism had to be prevented from gaining a nation-wide following. During the very early phase of the Emergency, Baring was more concerned to prevent Mau Mau winning cross-community support than in defeating it militarily. In reality political and military tactics overlapped. Military repression enforced a physical quarantine around the Kikuyu regions. The political isolation of Mau Mau required the elaboration of a multidimensional framework of containment.

From the outset, Mau Mau's claim to represent the aspiration of nationalism had to be discredited. A carefully constructed image of Mau Mau was built up. It portrayed Mau Mau as an expression of primitive tribal atavism. At the same time radical nationalism was equated with criminal subversion. For this reason it was necessary to portray a colonial war as an emergency against an upsurge of tribal terrorism. Even the attempt by the Nairobi-based War Council to have the Emergency declared as an 'operational theatre' was resisted in London.[20]

Today, partly as a result of the successful propaganda campaign which criminalized Mau Mau, the nationalist motivation of this movement is called into question by a significant section of the specialist literature (Lonsdale, 1986). However, at the time, those in charge of the British civil and military power in Kenya, and those who supervised the Emergency at the Colonial and War Offices were in no doubt that their enemy was the force of militant African nationalism.[21] Many of their interpretations contained a strong irrational strand which insisted that Mau Mau was a bestial manifestation of primitive tribalism. Such emotional reactions, however, were never allowed to cloud the judgement when it came to operational and practical matters. Thus a 'Brief for the Commander in Chief', written in June 1953 by the senior Intelligence Adviser, stated that the 'Mau Mau insurrection, despite its outwardly primitive character, derives from political, racial and economic motives and is symptomatic of developing African political consciousness.'[22]

By the middle of the Emergency, the standard interpretation of Mau Mau among key civil and military officials was that it was a form of extreme nationalism. C.M. Johnston, the Provincial Commissioner of Central Province, the area most affected by the revolt, compared Kenyatta to Nkrumah and pointed out that the objectives of Mau Mau were the return of land expropriated by European settlers and political independence. Johnston argued that these objectives as such were neither 'subversive or unreasonable'; it was the violent methods used for achieving them that constituted the problem.[23]

Most of the serious appraisals made by the British military and civil leaders measured their success at least in part by the degree to which Mau Mau failed to realize its objective of winning a nation-wide following. One brief written for Michael Blundell, the leading European settler politician on the War Council, directly linked the decline of Mau Mau during the summer of 1954 to the failure of 'its attempt to achieve tribal–intertribal unity on a grand scale to the Government'.[24] Intelligence briefs produced for the Chief of Staff also emphasized the importance that the Mau Mau leadership attached to transforming itself from a Kikuyu to a nation-wide African movement. One such brief stated that the strategic aim of the Mount Kenya Council of Mau Mau was to win support from the Kamba community and of the Aberdare Council to win influence among the Masai.[25]

The capacity of Mau Mau to gain support on a cross-communal basis was never underestimated and explains why the colonial administration went to great lengths to prevent contact between Kikuyu and other African peoples in Kenya. British officials were sensitive to the danger that African communities other than the Kikuyu might be drawn towards Mau Mau, especially if it appeared to be winning. The first major military assessment of the revolt warned that the 'fighting tribes', that is those African communities from which the local military and police forces were drawn, 'must be insulated from Kikuyu agitators'.[26]

In fact, in circumstances where Mau Mau activists had direct access to Africans from non-Kikuyu communities, they were able temporarily to win significant support. Mau Mau activists in Nairobi succeeded in establishing cells amongst the Kamba, Masai and the Munyalla communities during the summer of 1953. Mau Mau was particularly successful amongst African railway workers. Special Branch was shocked by its discovery of Mau Mau cells composed of railway employees from the Munyalla, Msamia, Bunyore and Maragoli communities. Special Branch was concerned that if the Mau Mau could win support from these communities, it also had the potential to infiltrate the Luo people, the second largest African ethnic group in Kenya. 'The situation would be extremely grave as a united Kikuyu–Luo front would be formidable,' reported the Special Branch.[27] It is not surprising that the physical isolation of the Kikuyu from the rest of the African population became top priority for the Kenya government.

Despite placing the Kikuyu regions under a military quarantine, Mau Mau did succeed in providing a focus for the growth of African nationalism throughout Kenya. In May 1954 the Director of Intelligence complained that among the people of Nyanza, there is 'a tendency to regard the Emergency not as a Kikuyu struggle but as a fight for African freedom'.[28] More than a year later, the Minister of Defence conceded that in Nyanza 'public opinion is generally sympathetic towards the aims of Mau Mau'.[29]

From the outset of the military campaign against Mau Mau, London placed a major emphasis on discrediting its claim to represent the aspiration of African nationalism. Destroying the nationalist claims of the Mau Mau was perceived by London as critical for the winning of the war. At the outset of the Emergency, the Colonial Office was appalled by the lack of attention that Nairobi paid to the organization of propaganda.[30] One of the first criticisms that the War Office made of the Nairobi administration was the slowness with which Governor Baring undertook the task of a co-ordinated propaganda campaign.[31] Every conceivable resource was mobilized in an international propaganda campaign against Mau Mau. Even pulp fiction like Ruark's, *Something of Value* had a role to play in this project. One Foreign Office diplomat noted that this novel 'on the whole has done the British name more good than harm, by exposing the purely criminal nature of the Mau Mau conspiracy and exploding its claim to the distinction of a social and economic origin'.[32] It was precisely because those in charge of the Emergency were aware of the movement's nationalist appeal that even third-rate pulp fiction had a place in the propaganda war.

The loss of control

The response of the Mau Mau to the Declaration of the Emergency went way beyond the expectations of the Colonial regime. A relatively small police operation designed to detain the leadership of Mau Mau unleashed a serious guerrilla war which in the end took nearly four years to bring under control. In the end it took a combined force of over 42,000 including 13,288 British troops to defeat Mau Mau.[33] Instead of gaining control by following Gurney's procedures, the Nairobi government lost it. It took four to five months before the government finally realised that over 95 per cent of the Kikuyu people supported the aims of Mau Mau and that a significant section of the other African communities were also sympathetic to its goals. The capital city, Nairobi, threatened to provide a stable base of cross-community support for the resistance movement. The government's loss of control was most evident in Nairobi—until April 1954 the Mau Mau exercised day-to-day control over the African locations.

The reaction of the government and of the European settler community to the escalation of resistance was poorly thought-out and panicky. Indiscriminate repression created the impression that war had been declared on the Kikuyu people as a whole, and as stories of government atrocities began to circulate, the option of armed revolt gained new adherents. As the resistance gained momentum, the European settlers expelled thousands of Kikuyu resident labourers, known as squatters, from their farms. Many of these exsquatters were embittered by their experience of repatriation into the Kikuyu Reserves and headed straight into the forest to join units of the Mau Mau. According to military intelligence it was largely this group of refugees which provided the core of the Mau Mau forest fighters.[34] Paradoxically, it was the uncontrolled reactions of government and of European settlers that helped boost the number of recruits for Mau Mau.

By the spring of 1953, there were between 10,000 and 12,000 Mau Mau fighters in the forest. This militant wing of Mau Mau was supported by a passive wing, which was organized through committees in the localities of the Kikuyu-Embu and Meru districts, in Nairobi and amongst resident labourers on European farms. According to the Director of Operations, Major-General Robert Hinde, Mau Mau leaders displayed 'good initiative' and the 'gangs were well disciplined'.[35] Mau Mau's military revolt was initiated in January 1953 and throughout the rest of the year the guerrillas retained the initiative. According to one British military assessment, Mau Mau as a force was most effective during the period October 1953 to April 1954.[36] The turning-point from a military point of view was in April 1954, when Operation Anvil launched by British-led forces removed around 30,000 Kikuyu from Nairobi and destroyed the logistics and communications system of Mau Mau.

After Anvil Mau Mau lost its offensive capacity and by September 1954 it ceased to represent a serious military challenge. However, despite its military decline Mau Mau constituted a major problem by virtue of its continued existence. As long as Mau Mau survived, the government could not launch any serious political initiative. Nor could it claim to have defeated the enemy. Success and failure could not be measured in conventional military terms.

From late 1954 onwards British strategists faced the dilemma of how to deal with an enemy that would not recognize defeat. Intelligence reports confirmed that the perception among supporters of Mau Mau and other Africans was that the resistance movement was winning or at least that it was not defeated. It was the failure to defeat Mau Mau within a credible time that must explain the extraordinary emphasis that Nairobi placed on repression during the post-Anvil period. An illustration of this hard line is the case of eight women sentenced to death in May 1955 for being present at an oath ceremony. The objective of the exercise was to discourage other women from supporting the Mau Mau. Nevertheless, as late as the autumn of 1955, the ability of Mau Mau to survive called into question the claims of the government that it was winning the war.[37] Therefore the Mau Mau did not just have to be crushed militarily—the very idea of militant struggle and its goals had to be discredited. That was why during the last phase of the Emergency, the Nairobi government was actively engaged in a campaign to destroy the 'memory of Mau Mau'.[38] The political isolation of militant nationalism had to complement its military defeat.

The quest for control

The colonial intelligence and security services had anticipated that the Emergency would provoke a short burst of violent protest, which could be quickly defeated by the authorities. Instead, militant nationalists were organizing an underground movement without any major public protests. Mau Mau rapidly grew into a formidable force and after three or four months of preparation was able to strike at selected targets. Hinde observed:

> anticipating an explosive Kikuyu reaction [to the Emergency] the forces of law and order were deployed for that occasion in positions and for tasks which were primarily defensive, and it can be said that from that moment the Government lost the initiative.[39]

The government's ability to win control was undermined by its one-dimensional emphasis on repression. Repression excluded any plausible political options, it weakened the position of African collaborators since in the circumstances the tactics advocated by militant nationalists appeared credible.

On his arrival in Kenya, just prior to the Declaration of Emergency, Baring was not hostile to the project of political reform. However, when it became evident that in Mau Mau he faced a formidable foe, his instinct drew him towards a repressive perspective. With a suggestion of panic, Baring wrote to the Secretary of State for the Colonies, Oliver Lyttelton, in November 1952 that the 'Kikuyu have arms and will use them'.[40] He provided a list of sanctions necessary to contain the situation. Stiffer sentences and corporal punishment were proposed and swiftly implemented. A punitive tax on all Kikuyu was introduced. New identity cards were issued. Finally Baring demanded that the size of Special Branch be doubled and that a Director of Operations of at least the rank of a Major-General be appointed.[41] During the next four months Baring went further and asked for the introduction of summary justice and the death penalty for those convicted of administering the Mau Mau oath.[42]

Although in the end he won the endorsement of Whitehall for his proposals, senior figures in the Colonial Office were disturbed by the intensity of the repression practised by the Baring Administration. It was suggested that Baring was going much further than the Government of Malaya and that the scale of communal punishment went 'beyond reasonable bounds'.[43] Even General Sir Gerald Templer, Britain's hard man in Malaya was taken aback by Baring's proposal to get rid of the right of those convicted of Mau Mau offences to an appeal.[44] In January 1953 Major General Hinde was dispatched to Kenya to assume the role of Director of Operations and to reorganize the flagging campaign against Mau Mau. Baring and Hinde made a very uninspiring combination. They lacked a strategic perspective and tended to react to events with new forms of repression. Hinde continually under-estimated the challenge posed by Mau Mau. In March 1953 he concluded that the hard-core Mau Mau fighters numbered only a hundred and he assumed that the resistance could be stamped out within six months.[45]

During the early months of 1953 the Colonial Office was faced with a flood of demands for raising the stakes in the fight against Mau Mau. Baring requested new rules of engagement so that troops could shoot anyone in the prohibited areas without issuing a warning. He also demanded more troops and greater firepower. By early March 1953 Whitehall was clearly concerned with Baring's growing list of demands. Lyttelton gently rebuked Baring: 'it does seem to me that we are in serious danger of losing the game, however much military success we may have against Mau Mau.'[46]

The restraining influence of the Colonial Office terminated in April 1953, in the aftermath of a number of spectacular Mau Mau operations. From this point onwards, Whitehall itself took the initiative in reorganizing the campaign against Mau Mau. It is worth noting that it was not the Colonial Office but the War Office that sought to take matters in hand. General Sir John Harding, Chief of the Imperial General Staff, was in correspondence with Michael Blundell, a leading European settler politician in Kenya. Blundell's unflattering condemnation of the indecisiveness of the Baring administration and of the ineffectiveness of Hinde led Harding to dispatch General Nicholson to provide a firsthand account of the situation in Kenya.[47] Nicholson's report on the progress of the war fully confirmed the War Office's worst fears.

Nicholson reported that Baring was 'most indecisive'. He wrote that Hinde had 'not succeeded in establishing himself as Commander in the field'. He proposed that Hinde 'be replaced with the minimum of delay' and suggested that the situation demanded a 'military governor'. On the conduct of the war against Mau Mau, Nicholson was far from optimistic about the possibility of a quick victory. His analysis pointed to a long engagement and he noted that it was 'better to plan for the worst case than to hope for the best'.[48] The War Office moved fast on Nicholson's proposals. Within a few weeks a decision was made to separate Nairobi from the Middle East Command, and General George Erskine was appointed Commander-in-Chief of the East African Command. On 7 June 1953 he arrived in Nairobi to take up his command.

When Erskine arrived in Kenya, the Government had still not gone on the offensive against Mau Mau. During the first six months of the Emergency, British forces were deployed defensively in the Kikuyu Reserves and the European-settled areas. This prevented the Mau Mau from gaining 'complete control' over the Kikuyu regions but that was all. The first serious probes against Mau Mau guerrillas in the forest began on 10 May 1953. However, it was only after Erskine's arrival that British forces went on the offensive. Operation Buttercup, launched on 24 June 1953, sought to make contact with Mau Mau in the forest around Fort Hall. A few weeks later Erskine initiated

Operation Coronation in South Nyeri around the Eastern slopes of the Aberdares.[49]

The experience of these two operations provided Erskine with a realistic assessment of the challenge posed by Mau Mau. Crown forces were not able to make contact with the guerrillas in the forest. The casualties they inflicted were mainly on Kikuyu civilians residing in the reserves. The failure to make contact against an elusive enemy led Erskine to conclude that he faced a 'war of attrition and a long drawn out affair'.[50] Erskine was shocked to discover the depth of support for the Mau Mau and reported that some of the locations in the district of Fort Hall 'were almost Mau Mau Republics'. Operation Coronation convinced him that Mau Mau units 'are determined, well organised, well protected and in hideouts deep in the forest and difficult to reach' and their 'supporters in the reserves are numerous'.[51] Erskine's observations were confirmed during the next two months. In October 1953 he reported that 'Mau Mau is far wider spread and deeper rooted than was thought possible even 6 months ago'. He added that practically every Kikuyu, even those 'who have now thrown in their lot with Government, still have some sympathy with Mau Mau if not with Mau Mau method'. Finally, he observed that the Embu, Meru and Kikuyu–Masai half-castes were 'seriously infected' and that the 'Kamba needed watching'.[52]

By October 1953 Erskine had concluded that Mau Mau could not be defeated through conventional military means. By all accounts the British troops were ill-suited for the anti-Mau Mau campaign. They had little experience of jungle warfare and their forest tactics left a lot to be desired. As late as July 1955 the staff officers reiterated the need to improve the 'forest skills' of the soldiers.[53] According to the Secretary of the Emergency Committee, the army had little grasp of local conditions and was unsophisticated. He wrote of one senior officer dealing with the Emergency for six months who 'asked the other day what a "squatter" was'.[54]

Erskine had succeeded in developing a coherent perspective on the war by the end of August. He was in a position to formulate two important objectives necessary for regaining the initiative. The first objective was to destroy Mau Mau's influence in Nairobi. Nairobi provided the ideal location for the Mau Mau to influence non-Kikuyu Africans and for providing the guerrillas with military and other supplies. A plan for psychological warfare set in motion in August 1953 had as its principal aim the prevention of the Mau Mau gaining influence among non-Kikuyu Africans. A propaganda working party established in September was charged with this campaign.[55] Erskine's second objective was to isolate the forest fighters from their supporters in the Reserves. It took until January 1954 for Erskine and his staff to work out a strategic plan for the conduct of the war. The plan consisted of two phases. In February and March 1954 the British forces would concentrate on consolidating their hold over the Reserves, and in April they would move on Nairobi to expel the Kikuyu population from this city. Erskine informed the

War Office, 'we will want a detention of a capacity of nothing less than 100,000 to hold the expelled population.[56]

The realization of Erskine's plan required an improvement in the quality of operational intelligence. From August 1953 onwards the British military promoted the policy of seeking surrenders from individual Mau Mau fighters. Most of the hard intelligence available to British forces was obtained from surrendered Mau Mau fighters. The captured Mau Mau leader, General China proved to be an invaluable source of information. In March 1954 Operation Wedgewood was initiated: its aim was to use China to induce groups of Mau Mau fighters to surrender to gain intelligence.[57] Although Wedgewood did not result in any spectacular surrenders, enough information was obtained from the operation to arrest 1,200 members of the passive wing in the middle of April.[58]

Improvement in intelligence gathering was paralleled by the restructuring of the co-ordination of the military and civil initiatives in the war. In March 1954 a three-man War Council was established for co-ordinating all aspects of the campaign against Mau Mau. The stage was now set for a major drive against the Kikuyu population of Nairobi. Operation Anvil, launched in April 1954, led to the mass expulsion of Kikuyu from Nairobi. By breaking up the Mau Mau organization in the capital, the guerrillas' system of communications was destroyed. It represented the first significant stage in the isolation of Mau Mau. According to Erskine, 'ANVIL had proved the turning point in the Emergency.'[59] After more than 16 months of the Emergency, the colonial administration was ready to take the initiative.

Winning the initiative

Sir Arthur Young, one of Britain's most astute colonial policemen, with direct experience of counterinsurgency in Palestine, the Gold Coast and Malaya, arrived in Nairobi to take up his post as Commissioner of Police in the middle of Operation Anvil. A few months later he wrote to a senior official at the Home Office in London that the military would make only a limited contribution to the resolution of the political problems posed by the Kenya Emergency. He noted that

the part the Police can play in Kenya is not so influential as that which was possible in Malaya, since the problem in Kenya is almost exclusively a political one

and added that

most authorities in Kenya now accept my view that the best which the Police and Military together can hope for is that they may prevent the situation getting worse and to hold the present emergency until political reforms and development can take place.[60]

Operation Anvil stabilized the situation from the British point of view and created the foundation for the initiation of a series of political policies designed to defeat Mau Mau. In March 1954 Lyttelton's proposals for a constitutional advance were announced, indicating that Whitehall was determined to take the political initiative. These proposals were followed up in October, when the recently appointed Colonial Secretary, Lennox Boyd, announced that the Coutts Commission would conduct an inquiry into the mechanics of introducing African elections for the Legislative Council. These broad constitutional initiatives of course required political and military progress on the ground.

Operation Anvil helped not only to destroy the Mau Mau's infrastructure but also to isolate Kikuyu activists from having access to other African communities. Now the goal of Baring and Erskine was to isolate Mau Mau further from their passive wing and at the same time to strengthen the position of loyalist collaborators in the Kikuyu community. At the same time Baring was keen to nurture the evolution of a moderate nationalist leadership with which Britain could do business after the Emergency was over.

The expulsion of Kikuyu from Nairobi facilitated the task of fostering the growth of a new group of moderate African politicians. Government officials presented the expulsion of the Kikuyu as an opportunity for the advancement of other African communities in Nairobi. Anti-Kikuyu sentiments were encouraged and ambitious African politicans were advised to think in tribal and regional terms. As one official in Whitehall reported, the policy adopted was 'the encouragement of local and tribal identities with the objective of impeding the resumption of national control by the Kikuyu'.[61] Non-Kikuyu African trade union officials and politicians were actively if discreetly assisted by the Nairobi administration.

Within the Kikuyu regions, the government set about reinforcing the position of its loyalist allies. Kikuyu collaborators were assisted through a package of measures designed to consolidate a base of support for the government. Loyalists were rewarded with land, economic benefits and were given special concessions such as free schooling for their children.[62] Loyalist chiefs and members of the Kikuyu Home Guard were protected by the government from facing prosecution for the atrocities they committed on a number of occasions.[63] Baring and his field administrators were insistent that nothing should be done to undermine the morale of the Kikuyu collaborators.[64]

In the military sphere the most pressing task was to neutralize civilian support for the guerrillas. According to Erskine's successor as Commander-in-Chief, Lieutenant-General Sir Gerald Lathbury, 'the outstanding problem of the Emergency' was to break the links which the Mau Mau had with the civilian population.[65] Lathbury explicitly recognized that the resolution of this problem required special measures.

Even from the point of view of narrow military concerns, conventional warfare proved singularly inappropriate to the task at hand. The military gains made by British troops through the post-Anvil follow-up operations were relatively modest. It can be argued that the unselective character of military tactics, particularly of the mass detention of around 100,000 Kikuyu people, actually sustained the resolve of Mau Mau to carry on the struggle. Colonel Young, for one, was shocked by what he called the 'horror' of the 'so-called Screening Camps', the widespread practice of torture and the routine use of capital punishment for relatively trivial offences.[66]

The British General Staff was continually frustrated by the failure of its forces to engage the Mau Mau in combat. Well entrenched in the forests, the guerrillas proved to be an elusive target. Baring reported in July 1954 that British troops were experiencing difficulty in catching small groups of Mau Mau.[67] Erskine sought to remedy the situation by closing the net around the forest and concentrating large deployments of troops against selected Mau Mau units. War Council Directive Number 2 of September 1954 envisaged a series of major operations in January and February 1955 with the objective of re-establishing civil power in the administration of the Kikuyu Reserves by the summer of 1955.[68] Typically Erskine recognized that success would depend on isolating Mau Mau from their supporters and sources of supplies in the Reserves rather than through spectacular military victories.

The contribution of major military operations to the implementation of War Council Directive Number 2 is worth noting before considering the role of non-conventional tactics. Operations Hammer and First Flute directed at Mau Mau forces in the Aberdare and Mount Kenya forests respectively during the first quarter of 1955, inflicted a major blow against the organization of the guerrillas. Although Mau Mau became disorganized, nevertheless it managed to disperse and re-form into smaller units. The main gains made by British forces were due to the tactic of cutting Mau Mau off from its supplies, by which means Erskine was able to force the guerrillas to the fringes of the forest, where a large number of casualties could be inflicted on them.

As military operations, Hammer and First Flute were not an unqualified success. The operations were resource intensive and far from effective in tracking down Mau Mau. Military intelligence was aware by February 1955 that troop movements alerted the guerrillas and the noise gave Mau Mau plenty of time to slip away.[69] Halfway through First Flute, a brigadier warned, '[our] kills are falling off' and 'we have got to get many more kills'. He concluded that 'we must hit them a hard knock. Up to now we have not done this.'[70] During the course of these operations it also became painfully obvious that the level of training and motivation of British troops was inadequate for the job at hand. Senior officers were exhorted to improve the performance of their men in the forest. In July 1955 Lathbury was 'most anxious' to see an improvement in 'the standard of forest tactics'. He lectured his officers on the realities of the situation and stated that 'Commanders should understand that until the forest terrorists were killed the Emergency would continue.'[71]

The forest operations between 1 January and 10 August 1955 led to the elimination of 700 Mau Mau fighters. However, an examination of the statistics shows that most of those who died were not killed in the forest but in the Reserves, where, according to Lathbury, the 'killing rate was high'.[72] With the passing of time the tactic of forest sweeps became less and less effective. Mau Mau quickly learned from the experience of Hammer and understood that large military sweeps were designed to force them to the fringes of the forest. Their reaction was to hide and stay in the forest. Lathbury therefore concluded that 'the mounting of large scale operations involving heavy concentration of forces was unlikely to be profitable.'[73]

The potentially wasteful deployment of large-scale operations was appreciated by the British military commanders from the beginning of the Emergency. The experience of Malaya directly influenced British military planning and both Erskine and Lathbury were in principle committed to the economic use of military resources. Counterinsurgency tactics—in the spheres of intelligence-gathering, psychological warfare and covert operations—were seen as 'essential to the economic use of the Security Forces'.[74] As we shall argue, it was these tactics—villagization, psychological warfare, intelligence-gathering and other forms of covert operations—which altered the balance irreversibly in favour of the British authorities. Although the tactics were in practice interlinked, it is possible to isolate the main strands in order to clarify the role of counterinsurgency in the Mau Mau war.

Villagization

The defeat of Mau Mau required that the war should be fought against the Kikuyu people as a whole. According to the analysis of the Kenya Intelligence Committee, 'Mau Mau's greatest tactical weakness is that it obtains its administrative support from areas accessible to the Security Forces. It will be hurt most easily and to the greatest degree by denying it these sources.'[75] This weakness was to be exploited to the full by Erskine and Lathbury. To separate the Kikuyu civilian population from the guerrillas, British authorities imposed a comprehensive system of penalties on them. Those suspected of supporting Mau Mau could be detained under Governor's Orders. Communal fines, seizure and forfeiture of livestock and other possessions could be imposed. Curfews were in operation and everyday movement and transport were restricted. There was also a range of economic sanctions. Trading activities required special permits. Coffee factories, markets, shops and schools could be closed to punish areas where Mau Mau-related incidents occurred. Convicted Mau Mau activists had their land forfeited.[76]

In contrast to these sanctions, Kikuyu loyalists were encouraged by a number of incentives to stay firm. Administrative penalties were relaxed in areas where co-operation was forthcoming. Loyalist villages were assisted with funds for amenities and were provided with special allocations of sugar, medical supplies and vitamins for children. Permits for trading and for shops were made available for loyalists.[77]

Despite the draconian measures introduced against the Kikuyu population, support for Mau Mau remained widespread well into 1955. According to the assessment of the War Council in November 1954, the 'will to resist of both active and passive wings did not seem likely to break under the pressure of the operations, which had been undertaken so far'.[78] Consequently the offensive against the civilian population was stepped up and more coercive measures were introduced, particularly against female supporters of Mau Mau.[79] However, the most important policy adopted during the November 1954 deliberations of the War Council was to promote the villagization programme on a systematic basis.

Traditionally, the Kikuyu people lived on homesteads and firmly resisted suggestions to move into villages. The restructuring of Kikuyu society into villages implied such a major revolution in life-style that District Officers were loath to face the consequences of such a dramatic measure. Early in the Emergency, Hinde requested the Chief Native Commissioner to carry out a feasibility study of villagization. In June 1953 the Member for African Affairs reported that all the District Officers who were canvassed for their views indicated that Kikuyu prejudices made a programme of villagization impracticable. This sentiment was strongly criticized by the Commissioner of Police who countered by stating that the security of the Reserves could not be enforced without establishing villages. Nevertheless, while everyone in civil and military administration recognized that from a security point of view villagization was ideal, there was some hesitation about irrevocably alienating the entire Kikuyu population through such a deeply provocative measure.[80]

Continued frustration with containing Mau Mau gradually began to shift the argument in favour of villagization. In February 1954 Baring issued a directive instructing District Officers to do their best to push ahead with villagization. He qualified his instructions by stating that it was not a blanket order, but he stressed that he would 'require good reasons against its adoption' especially in areas close to the forests. The Nairobi civil administration envisaged that two types of villages would be set up. The first type were 'voluntary villages', established essentially for protecting Kikuyu loyalists from the retribution of the Mau Mau. These villages were provided with social amenities and economic assistance. The second type of villages were created by the Administration as a punishment—these were seen as 'punitive' villages designed to provide greater military control of a recalcitrant population.[81]

From April 1954 villagization was promoted more aggressively, particularly to punish areas which demonstrated consistent support for Mau Mau. However, many District Officers and other officials continued to be confused by the purpose of villagization: 'was it punitive or was it a measure designed to assist economic development', 'were they to be temporary or permanent' were some of the questions asked. Such confusion meant tht the villagization programme lacked coherence. In the Kiambu District, for example, there were virtually no villages established as late as November 1954. This casual attitude towards elaborating a coherent formula towards villagization was finally tackled in November 1954. The war had continued for more than two years, and despite the success of Anvil, the Mau Mau showed no signs of abandoning the field. The ruthless pursuit of villagization became the centrepiece of the new campaign of sanctions directed against the Kikuyu population in November 1954. Villagization now had to be 'pushed ahead as fast as conditions permit'. The programme was linked to a series of intensified control measures designed to break the passive wing of Mau Mau.[82]

During the next six months villagization was stepped up and for the first time led with a single-minded efficiency. In effect villagization became the cornerstone of British military strategy. Erskine argued that the success of his military operations depended on forcing Mau Mau into the forests and preventing them from fleeing into the Reserves. He stated that this required 'tightening administrative control by increased villagisation and the creation of conditions which will enable drastic sanctions to be applied to those sections of the African population which actively support the terrorist cause'. It is worth noting that the punitive emphasis of villagization was to be slightly modified after General Lathbury assumed the command of the Crown forces in May 1955. A new directive issued by the War Council proposed to complete the concentration of all Kikuyu, Embu and Meru into villages by the end of August 1955 through 'employing a judicious mixture of punishment for co-operating with the enemy and rewards for loyal service'. This carrot-and-stick approach to villagization was made possible by a series of defeats inflicted on Mau Mau during the course of the implementation of War Council Directive Number 2. During the period between November 1954 and June 1955 the programme of concentrating Kikuyu into villages proved decisive in forcing Mau Mau onto the defensive. Villagization and the escalation of administrative controls gradually eroded civilian support for Mau Mau. By early 1955 the passive wing was neutralized and the population showed clear symptoms of war weariness.[83]

The role of intelligence

From the outset of the Emergency, the Nairobi administration were aware that they possessed little intelligence regarding the structure of Mau Mau. The military suffered from an absence of operational intelligence and as a result many of their initiatives were hit-and-miss affairs. A framework for the gathering and analysing of information was established with the setting up of the Kenya Intelligence Committee in February 1953. This committee co-ordinated all intelligence operations and was the apex of a system of provincial and district intelligence committees. Important innovations were also achieved through the creation of District Military Officers, who worked closely with the Special Branch and had at their disposal groups of Field Intelligence Assistants (FIAs). The Kenya Regiment, composed mainly of local European personnel, provided sergeants to work as FIAs. Their task was to gather intelligence on Mau Mau and to penetrate its passive wing. By the end of 1953 the FIAs were beginning to provide information on Mau Mau.[84] According to Clayton, by September 1953 the British authorities could identify the leading Mau Mau personalities, and the captured Mau Mau leader, General China, provided comprehensive information on the guerrilla operation in the Mount Kenya forest area. Archival sources confirm Clayton's arguments, though they indicate that intelligence on forces under the leadership of Dedan Kimathi in the Aberdares Forest was still very poor.[85] Moreover, the Mau Mau possessed a surprisingly effective counterintelligence capacity. In July 1953 the Mau Mau succeeded in eliminating several agents planted within its ranks by the British. The American Consul-General commented that 'there is no evidence that the security forces have yet been able to come to grips with the current leadership of Mau Mau, whose intelligence operations would appear to be very effective.'[86] It was the information gained through Operation Anvil that gave the British military access to a steady flow of intelligence.

The development on intelligence expertise was closely linked to gaining access to guerrillas. Soon it became evident that surrendered or captured Mau Mau fighters were the best source of intelligence. It was for this reason that Erskine and his successor Lathbury regularly sought to organize campaigns of surrenders through offering amnesty. The policy of amnesty was closely modelled on the Malayan example, and as early as June 1953 the Colony Emergency Committee was actively considering the implementation of the so-called Malayan procedures. The interrogation of General China provided the basis for Operation Wedgewood, an initiative oriented towards achieving a mass surrender of Mau Mau fighters. Operation Wedgewood was formally launched on 13 April 1954. It provided the British military with a tremendous amount of intelligence, particularly on the passive wing. Two Mau Mau leaders, General Tanganyika and Kaleba took part in the surrender discussion through which Special Branch picked up fresh information on the resistance movement. A large group of Mau Mau who had assembled to surrender were frightened off at the very last moment by an unexpected battle nearby and Wedgewood collapsed. However, in terms of intelligence gathering Wedgewood was a major success. In the succeeding months hundreds of passive wing activists were picked up and detained. Most important of all, the British security service had managed to penetrate the passive wing of Mau Mau. The military could now engage in a covert operation to exploit signs of cleavage between the active and passive wings of Mau Mau.[87]

Through Wedgewood, Special Branch had penetrated the passive wing in Nyeri District. Two months after the termination of Operation Wedgewood, information obtained from South Nyeri indicated that there was renewed interest in surrender negotiations among certain Mau Mau units. Most of the senior civil administrators argued against any new amnesty initiative lest it be perceived as a sign of weakness on the part of the authorities. Erskine on the other hand was keen on another surrender campaign on the grounds that it could shorten the war and at the very least provide fresh intelligence.[88] After months of deliberation it was decided that it was possible to sell a new surrender initiative by linking offers of amnesty to loyalist Kikuyu Home Guard convicted for atrocities with similar offers to Mau Mau.[89] This way Baring hoped to deflect the charges made by hard-line European settlers that the government was appeasing Mau Mau.

Operation Chui, the new surrender campaign, was initiated on 18 January 1955. These surrender talks were to prove even more fruitful than Wedgewood. The British negotiators were able to deepen the bitter rivalry between the two main Mau Mau leaders, Stanley Mathenge and Dedan Kimathi. During the negotiations the British developed a working relationship with Mathenge via intermediaries in an unspoken common effort to isolate Kimathi. Although Operation Chui failed to induce large-scale surrenders, British intelligence was able to increase its penetration of the Mau Mau passive wing. It was only a matter of time before captured Mau Mau fighters would be exploited not only for intelligence but also for operational purposes.

Psychological warfare

The British military, and in particular General Erskine, placed an extraordinary emphasis on psychological warfare. Leading figures from the Colonial Office and in the Nairobi government were initially sceptical about its effectiveness. Harold Evans, the head of the Colonial Office's Information Department, during his visit to Nairobi noted with contempt that 'they are back to this old idea that if you can get something called a "psychological warfare expert" you solve all your difficulties.'[90] In Kenya psychological warfare came to mean a total propaganda war. As Lathbury explained: 'psychological warfare is not merely a propagation of facts. It involves special interpretation of facts, the dissemination of rumours, the use of guile and to some extent, trickery.'[91]

In Kenya psychological warfare was organized through the African Information 'Working Party'. In addition special *ad hoc* committees were established to co-ordinate propaganda warfare with specific military operations. A Special Propaganda Committee was established in 1955 and met monthly to consider non-operational psychological warfare, and in July responsibility for propaganda was vested in the Chief Secretary. Lathbury was unhappy with the lack of overall co-ordination and insisted that a special committee be established for the co-ordination of psychological warfare. This was agreed by the War Council, and in October 1955 the Psychological Warfare Staff was established. Chaired by Norman Harris, the committee included Ian Henderson and Lt. Col. N.C. Stockwell.[92]

The initial hesitations about the relevance of psychological warfare soon gave way to wholehearted commitment. Soon it was perceived as the solution for defeating Mau Mau. Leading security officers regularly provided ideas about black propaganda and for tricks to confuse the Mau Mau. In this vein, Ian Henderson of the Special Branch proposed using Kikuyu rituals to curse the forest and circulating compromising photographs to lower the morale of Mau Mau. Much of this energy devoted to black propaganda was wasted on working out impractical schemes. But the more considered propaganda initiatives were to prove of some use to the anti-Mau Mau campaign.

The African Information 'Working' Party carefully monitored developments in Kikuyu society and developed selective propaganda for its target audience. It first of all banned all international news on the radio to create a sense of isolation amongst the Kikuyu. With the non-Kikuyu African population the emphasis of the propaganda was to discredit the nationalist claims of the Mau Mau. Within the Kikuyu community, propaganda did not attack the aims of the Mau Mau but rather the terrorist methods it used. Special propaganda was directed at Kikuyu women, loyalists, waiverers and the hard-core Mau Mau supporters. Until November 1954, the main message of the propaganda campaign against the Kikuyu population was that the Mau Mau could not win. Propaganda experts conceded that there was no point in attacking the policies of the Mau Mau since these were supported by the majority of the Kikuyu. As the fortunes of the Mau Mau declined the focus of propaganda changed from suggesting that it could not win to arguing that its aims were also wrong.[93]

Reports showed that the propaganda initiatives made only a marginal impact on the Kikuyu population. At the same time it appears that it did make an important contribution to the isolation of the Mau Mau from the non Kikuyu African communities. By highlighting the drastic penalties imposed on the Kikuyu civilian popultion, the Nairobi Administration was able to provide an object lesson to other Africans, the militant struggle did not pay. With the defeat of Mau Mau the tasks of propaganda became easier. The very experience of military defeat could be used to score propaganda points about the need to play the game according to the rules of the colonial authorities. In a sense this experience showed that propaganda had to express real experience if it was to be successful.

Psychological warfare was also deployed in conjunction with military operations. For example during Operation Wedgewood and Chui, a *Surrender Propaganda Committee* was established, which met daily to exploit the situation. This Committee used the threat of land forfeiture to pressurise the Mau Mau fighters to surrender. It also had at its disposal an impressive range of resources from sky-shouting airplanes to broadcast vans. Although this committee did not materially alter the rate of surrenders it appeared to make an impact on the morale of the civilian population.[94]

Psychological warfare really came into its own once it was evident that Mau Mau's days were numbered. From October 1955 onwards the Psychological Warfare Staff began to make modest gains in realising its goal of inducing surrenders and splitting the resistance. The job of discrediting Mau Mau was facilitated by the experience of defeat.[95] It was precisely at this juncture that the task of propaganda warfare became critical. With the end of the shooting war, the very experience of Mau Mau had to be destroyed as a credible alternative for the future. Psychological warfare now had to 'counteract extremist political propaganda' and to'eradicate the 'memory of Mau Mau'.[96] This job was pursued with some vigour until the very day that formal decolonization was completed.

Special Forces

Discussions of counterinsurgency in Kenya tend to glorify that role of covert operations, Special Forces and countergangs. In reality the contribution of the Special Forces to the British war effort only became significant once the Mau Mau had lost the initiative. The precondition for the emergence of an effective counterinsurgency force was the availability of ex-Mau Mau collaborators who were captured or who had surrendered.

During the first half of 1954 the FIAs attached to the First Company of the Kenya Regiment in conjunction with Special Branch developed important skills in infiltrating Mau Mau through the use of ex-guerrilla fighters. In October 1954 the Kenya Regiment was restructured to allow for the recruiting of new Field Intelligence Officers (FIOs). By this time there were two special schools for training FIOs and Kikuyu agents in the skill of impersonating Mau Mau fighters. The so-called pseudo or countergangs emerged as a new resource for the British military.[97]

The much-sensationalized countergangs and Special Forces came into their own after Erskine's departure. By this time the main military phase of the war was over and the outstanding issues were clearly political. In any case large-scale military operations had proved counterproductive and small groups of Special Forces were needed for the hunt and search campaign against the remnants of the Mau Mau force. In May 1955 the War Council authorized the raising of five Special Force Teams, each consisting of ten ex-Mau Mau fighters commanded by specially trained European officers. As Lathbury later recalled, these teams under the control of the Commissioner of Police 'formed the basis of an organisation which was subsequently to become the most effective weapon against the terrorists'.[98]

The specific objective of the Special Forces was the elimination of leading Mau Mau fighters. Britain's military campaign had become more selective in one sense, though the kill rate remained remarkably high. During the first seven months of 1956 around 1,230 Kikuyu were killed.[99] Intensive repression was still seen as essential for creating the foundation for a political solution.

The shifting emphasis towards covert operations from June 1955 onwards reflected the new priorities of the British administration. Except for eliminating a handful of Mau Mau leaders hiding in the forest, there was little for the military to do. In early 1956 General Lathbury was mainly preoccupied with developing a political strategy for dealing with the resurgence of African nationalism in the post-Emergency era. The shooting war had become a massive covert operation designed to ensure a smooth transition to 'normal' political life. Lathbury noted in June 1956 that the 'elimination of the remaining terrorists is already almost entirely dependent on intelligence and the action of ex-terrorists directed by the intelligence organisation.' Lathbury was realistic enough to realize that the war had not solved the underlying political conflict. His assessment was that 'the general attitude of the majority of at any rate the Kikuyu tribe has not basically changed'. And he warned:

> It is certain that gaining the fullest possible information on African political activity, particularly among the Kikuyu, is now and will be an intelligence task of equal if not greater importance than keeping track of the terrorists. As the terrorist problem diminishes, it will become the principal task of intelligence.[100]

The covert and administrative control of African political activity became the final episode of the Emergency.

Politics in command

The relaxation of the military efforts in early 1956 did not mean that the Emergency was over; the question of control still preoccupied senior administrators. R. Catling, the Commissioner of Police, made a distinction between the 'shooting war' stage of the emergency and the

> beginning of a new phase of abnormal conditions in Kenya which, although less violent than those which beset the country since October 1952, are unlikely to be simple to control and more likely to place a heavy burden of responsibility upon the Police.

Catling's prediction was based on the analysis that the aspirations which led to growth of radical nationalism before the Emergency had not lost their force. He noted that 'intelligence shows that while the African population generally has come to realise that Mau Mau methods have failed' it has 'deviated little from Mau Mau objectives'.[101] According to Catling, intensive police vigilance was required for the restoration of African political life.

Although security considerations remained at the forefront of the thinking of the Nairobi administration, Baring was now most concerned about establishing a framework for controlling decolonization. The debate on constitutional reform and the formation of African party politics is not the subject of this chapter. It should, however, be noted that the tactics pursued through the shooting war phase of the Emergency shaped the subsequent development of African politics.

Throughout 1956 and 1957 Whitehall and the Nairobi administration were preparing the ground for the resumption of African political life. Militant activists were carefully watched and when they appeared to pose problems they were promptly detained. Moderate African politicians and trade unionists were strongly supported and encouraged to involve themselves in tribal and district politics. Baring was particularly concerned to exclude Kikuyu politicians from political life until a group of creditable moderate politicians from other African communities had emerged. The intent of the Baring administration was to split African nationalists so that government action could be used to isolate the militants and to strengthen the moderates. Encouraging tribal politics became the obvious tactic for the pursuit of this strategy.

The military phase of the Emergency leading to the confinement of the Mau Mau to the Kikuyu regions created the condition for the political phase of curbing the appeal of nationalism with a profound parochial identity.

There were no clear-cut victors in the Mau Mau war. The Mau Mau was first militarily defeated and then politically neutralized. Indeed radical nationalism in Kenya never regained its strength to this day. However, the Mau Mau revolt had gone on too long for the Colonial administration to be triumphant. There could be no return to pre-Emergency days. Radical nationalism could only be contained if Britain showed that it was prepared to hand over power to a new group of African collaborators. Somewhere along the way the aim of counterinsurgency changed from restoring the authority of the colonial state to preparing the way for the process of controlled decolonization.

Notes

PRO refers to documents found in the Public Records Office, Kew, Surrey, United Kingdom.

RHL refers to items found in the Rhodes House Library, Oxford, United Kingdom.

NARA refers to the documents found in the National Archives, Washington DC, USA.

1. PRO: WO276/4: 'Appreciation by Commander in Chief from 1 April 1956 to end of the year', 26 January 1956.

2. PRO: WO216/863, 'Appreciation on Future Military Policy in Kenya 1954' by General G. Erskine, 27 January 1954.
3. See the discussion in PRO: CO822/1303, January 1954.
4. PRO: WO276/529, 'War Council Directive No. 9, Emergency Policy', 27 March 1956.
5. PRO: DEFE 11/32, 'General Sir L. Hollis to Minister of Defence', 5 July 1948.
6. Ibid.
7. PRO: DEFE 11/32, 'Meeting of Cabinet', 13 July 1948.
8. 'The rather ruthless character of terrorism, the ineffectiveness of any defence against it and the suddenness with which it may be launched demand that the Government . . . should be ready to take the initiative with its full-scale measures at the very outset' (PRO: DEFE 11/33, 'Gurney to Secretary of State', 30 May 1949).
9. Ibid.
10. Ibid.
11. Ibid.
12. PRO: DEFE 11/33, 'Gurney . . .', 30 May 1949.
13. PRO: CO 537/5812, 'General Strike, January 1950, Gold Coast', by Sir C. Arden Clarke.
14. PRO: CO 986/283, Secretary of State Circular 332152, 4 April 1952. This circular noted that 'Kenya Registration of Persons Ordinance appears to be the most comprehensive and has been followed by several other Colonial Governments'.
15. NARA: RG59 754 R.00, 'Dorsz to Department of State', 15 August 1957.
16. PRO: CO 822/1242, 'Baring to Lennox Boyd', 24 June 1958.
17. PRO: CO 822/440, 'Memorandum' by P. Rogers to Gorell Burnes, 24 October 1952.
18. Ibid.
19. NARA: RG59 745 R.00, 'M.J. Tibbets to Department of State', 29 January 1953.
20. The War Council hoped that if Kenya was declared an operational theatre it would be possible to issue campaign medals.
21. In particular military appreciations were clear on this point and avoided the irrational language with which many colonial administrations described the Mau Mau.
22. RHL: Papers of Major-General Sir Robert Hinde, File 12, 'Brief for C in C Intelligence Appreciation' by the Intelligence Adviser, 6 June 1953.
23. Ibid., File 1, 'The civil problem of the Mau Mau and some thoughts on its possible solution', by C.M. Johnston, January 1954.
24. RHL: Papers of Sir Michael Blundell (PMB), Box 43/2, 'Brief for Mr Michael Blundell MLC, WAR/C/365', circa December 1954.
25. PRO: WO276/232, 'Brief for Chief of Staff on operations against Mau Mau from 20 March to 27 June 1954'.
26. RHL: PMB, Box 34/3, 'Appreciation of the situation by Major General W.R.N. Hinde', 5 March 1953.
27. Ibid., Box 38/3, 'Subversive activities, East African railways and harbours administration', by V. Espie, 27 April 1954.
28. Ibid., Box 38/2, 'Security situation in Nyanza. Appreciation by the Director of Intelligence and Security', 17 May 1954.
29. Ibid., Box 46/3, 'Security of Nyanza. memorandum by the Minister of Defence', 15 July 1955.

30. PRO: CO1027/40, see unsigned 'minute 23 October 1952'.
31. RHL: Papers of Major-General Sir Robert Hinde, 'Major General R.A. Hall, Chief of Staff, C.H, MELL to Hinde', 18 March 1953.
32. PRO: FO371/113462, J. Russell, New York to British Ambassador in Washington, 1 June 1955.
33. See PRO: CO822/441, 'Baring to Secretary of State' 13 October 1953 for a breakdown of the composition of the Crown forces.
34. RHL: *Papers of Major General Sir Robert Hinde*, File 12, 'Brief for Commander in Chief', 6 June 1953.
35. Ibid.
36. RHL: RMB, Box 43/2, brief for Mr Michael Blundell MLC, WAR/C/365, November 1954.
37. RHL: PMB, Box 46, memo by the Minister of Defence, 25 May 1955. For a discussion of the problem posed by the Mau Mau's ability to continue to survive, see PRO: CO822/776.
38. PRO: WO276/114, note by Secretary of the Emergency Joint Staff, 8 September 1956.
39. 'Brief for the Commander in Chief', 6 June 1953, op. cit.
40. PRO: CO822/439, Baring to Secretary of State, 28 November 1952.
41. Ibid.
42. Ibid., 29 November 1952.
43. Ibid., minute by N.D. Watson to P. Rogers, 2 December 1952.
44. In February 1953 Baring requested Templer for information on the procedures adopted in Malaya, which allowed courts to convict terrorists without giving them the right of appeal. See PRO: CO822/467, Baring to Templer, 10 February 1953. Templer replied that the right of appeal had not been abolished in Malaya.
45. Appreciation of the situation, by Major General W.R.N. Hinde, 5 March 1953, op. cit.
46. See PRO: CO822/440, Lyttelton to Baring, 5 March 1953.
47. See correspondence in PRO: WO216/851.
48. PRO: WO216/852, Report on the Commander in Chief, Middle East Land Forces, visit to Kenya, 11–16 May 1953, by General Sir A. Nicholson.
49. See PRO: CO822/441, Baring to Colonial Office, 13 October 1953, WO276/409, Appreciation of Operation Buttercup, 10 July 1953; and CO922/693, Erskine to CIGS, 23 July 1953.
50. PRO: CO822/692, Baring to Secretary of State, 9 June 1953.
51. PRO: CO822/693, Erskine to CIGS, 23 July 1953.
52. PRO: WO216/861, The situation in Kenya, General G. Erskine, 3 October 1953.
53. PRO: WO276/197, minutes of the Chief of Staff's Conference for Brigade Commanders at Thika, 10 July 1955.
54. PRO: CO822/697, Moreton to Hall, 14 August 1953.
55. PRO: WO216/857, Erskine to CIGS, 12 August 1953.
56. PRO: WO216/863, Appreciation on future military policy in Kenya 1954, by G. Erskine, 27 January 1954. The War office was taken aback by Erskine's request. Field Marshall Sir John Harding, Chief of the Imperial General Staff, remarked that 'it is even more drastic than anything that has ever been attempted in Malaya', in ibid., Harding to Secretary of State, 2 February 1954.
57. PRO: WO276/7, brief for Chief of Staff on operations against Mau Mau,

20 March–27 June 1954.

58. Ibid., 'Operation Overdraft' 11–15 April 1954. The intelligence gained during Wedgewood is detailed in WO276/90, 'War Council Directive', no. 1, 23 April 1954.

59. PRO: WO276/511, The Kenya Emergency, June 1953–May 1955, by Erskine.

60 .RHL: Sir A.E. Young Papers, MSS Brit. Emp. S486, Box 2, File 6/1, Young to Sir Frank Newson, 25 August 1954.

61. PRO: CO822/799, I.W.A.C. Mathieson to Gorell Barnes, 21 September 1956.

62. See PRO CO822/799, Baring to Secretary of State, 28 July 1956.

63. See Young Papers, op. cit., and the discussion of Home Guard crimes in PRO: WO216/879.

64. See Baring's letters on this subject in PRO: WO216/879.

65. PRO: WO276/517, The Kenya Emergency May 1955–November 1956, by Lt.-Gen. Sir C.W. Lathbury.

66. Young Papers, op. cit., Narrative Kenya, 1967, and Young to Baring, 22 November 1954.

67. PRO: CO822/799, Baring to Lyttelton, 28 July 1954.

68. PRO: WO276/90, War Council Directive, no. 2, 16 September 1954.

69. PRO: WO276/279, Circular, by Brigadier Commanding HQ 70 (EA) Inf. BDE, 12 February 1955.

70. PRO: WO276/193, Circular, by Brigadier Commanding, 70 (EA) Infantry Battalion, 14 March 1955.

71. PRO: WO276/197, minutes of the Chief of Staff's Conference for Brigade Commanders at Thika, 10 July 1955.

72. Ibid., Minutes of the Operational Conference for Brigade Commanders held at GHQ, 10 August 1955.

73. PRO: WO276/517, The Kenya Emergency, May 1955–November 1956, by Lt.-Gen. Sir Gerald W. Lathbury.

74. RHL: PMB, Box 42/3, Field Intelligence Assistants, memorandum by the Emergency Joint Staff, 22 September 1956.

75. Ibid., Box 41/1, 'Mau Mau Strategy and Tactics', note by the Chairman of the Kenya Intelligence Committee, 6 August 1954.

76. For a list of these penalties, see ibid., Box 38/3, 'Emergency Administration Policy', 17 April 1954.

77. Ibid.

78. Ibid., Box 52/2, 'War Council—Sixty-first Meeting', November 1954.

79. See 'Female Mau Mau terrorists', note by the Secretary of the War council, 5 Noember 1954, ibid., Box 43.

80. See Hinde Papers, 'Hinde to Commander in Chief', 7 January 1954; and RHL: PMB, Box 36/1, '13th Meeting of the Colony Emergency Committee', 23 June 1953.

81. See RHL: PMB, Box 38/2, 'Emergency Nationalist Plan', 30 March 1954; and Box 38/3, 'The Governor's Directive no. 1 1954', February 1954.

82. See PRO: WO276/172, 'Post Phase II operations', 15 October 1955; RHL: PMB, 43/3 'Intensification of operations against Mau Mau', memo by Member for African Affairs, 22 November 1954.

83. See RHL: PMB, Box 43/3, 'Baring to Secretary of State', 21 February 1955; PRO: WO216/879, 'Forecast of the security force operations in 1955' by

R. Erskine, 9 December 1954; and PRO: WO276/90, 'War Council Directive Number 5', 22 June 1955.

84. See RHL: PMB, Box 42/3 'Field Intelligence Assistants', memorandum by the EJS, 22 September 1954; and Box 44/1, 'Kenya Intelligence Committee Appreciation', memorandum by the KIC, 31 December 1954.

85. A. Clayton, *Counter-insurgency in Kenya: A study of military operations against Mau Mau*, Nairobi, 1976, p. 34; and PRO: WO276/526 'GHQ East Africa. Operation Instruction no. 9', 30 October 1953.

86. NARA: RG59 745R.00/7-2453, ' E.J. Dorsz to Department of State', 24 July 1953.

87. RHL: PMB, Box 36/1, '29th Meeting of the Colony Emergency Committee', 18 June 1953; and PRO: CO827/774, 'Short history of the Wedgewood operation' by the Chief of Staff, 13 April 1954, and 'Acting Governor to the Secretary of State', 23 March 1954 and 11 April 1954.

88. RHL: PMB, Box 52/2, 'War Council: 23rd Meeting', 15 June 1954, 'War Council: 24th Meeting', 18 June 1954, and 'War Council: 61st Meeting', November 1954.

89. PRO: CO822/775, 'Baring to Secretary of State', 9 January 1955.

90. PRO: CO1027/40, 'H. Evans to C. Carstairs', 11 August 1953.

91. RHL: PMB, Box 48/2, 'Propaganda and Psychological Warfare', note by the Commander in Chief, 28 September 1955.

92. The activities of the African Information 'Working Party' are discussed in PRO CO1027/46 and CO1027/55. Lathbury's complaint is recorded in his 'Propaganda and psychological warfare', 28 September 1955, op. cit. and the establishment of the Psychological Warfare Staff is discussed in PRO, WO276/90: 'War Council Directive Number 8', 25 October 1955.

93. See the discussion on propaganda in PRO: CO1027/41, CO1027/55 and RHL: PMB, Box 43/2, 'Anti Mau Mau Propaganda', memorandum by the Acting Chief Secretary, 11 November 1954.

94. For the activities of the Surrender Propaganda Committee, see PRO: CO822/776.

95. See PRO: WO276/529, 'War Council Directive Number 9', 27 March 1956.

96. PRO: WO276/114, 'Note by Secretary of the Emergency Joint Staff', 8 September 1956.

97. See PRO: WO276/529 'GHQ Operation Instruction no. 36: pseudo gangs', 17 February 1956; and WO276/192, 'Major General Heyman to HQ49', 21 October 1954.

98. PRO: WO276/517, op. cit.

99. PRO: WO216/892, 'Lathbury to CIGS', 28 June 1956.

100. See 'Appreciation of possible future Mau Mau intentions', 16 January 1956; and 'Appreciation by Commander in Chief from 1 April 1956 till end of year' in PRO: WO276/4.

101. PRO: WO276/114 'R.C. Catling to the Secretary of Defence', circa July 1956.

Bibliography

Clayton, A. (1976), *Counter-insurgency in Kenya: A study of military operations against Mau Mau*, Nairobi, Transafrica.

Furedi, F. (1989a), 'Britain's colonial emergencies and the invisible Nationalists', *Journal of Historical Sociology*, vol. 2, no. 3, September 1989.

Furedi, F. (1989b), *The Mau Mau Revolt in Perspective*, London, James Currey.

Lonsdale, J. (1986), 'Explanations of Mau Mau revolt', in T. Lodge (ed.), *Resistance and Ideology in Settler Societies*, Johannesburg, Raven.

11 The Labour government's policy and publicity over Palestine 1945–7

C.J. Morris

Kenneth Morgan has argued that the 'disaster and tragedy' of the Labour government's involvement in Palestine can largely be explained by Foreign Secretary Ernest Bevin's mishandling of public relations: 'Bevin's faults in Palestine were essentially, defects of style and presentation rather than of substance. Never was his crudeness in dealing with the press and the machinery of public relations shown to worse effect' (Morgan, 1989: 158). Conversely, Peter Partner, the official historian of the BBC's Arabic Service, has written that projection was hampered because

> official policy had been overtaken by events to a disastrous degree, and that when the whole Middle East was in the melting pot.... The information services which were supposed to interpret government policy had to wait until there was one.
>
> (Partner, 1988: 86)

Both Morgan and Partner base their arguments on mistaken assumptions about the potential and role of propaganda in furthering foreign policy objectives and about the public relations efforts undertaken by the government and Information Services concerning Palestine. Using Bevin's public relations record concerning Palestine as a scapegoat, Morgan ascribes greater power to propaganda than it can ever achieve independently of policy. As Ivone Kirkpatrick recognized, 'Propaganda is never effective unless it is linked with policy.'[1] Similarly, the 1954 Drogheda Report on the Overseas Information Services found that:

> Propaganda is no substitute for policy: nor should it be regarded as a substitute for military strength, economic efficiency or financial stability. Propaganda may disguise weakness, but the assertion of strength will deceive nobody unless the strength is there.
>
> (Taylor, 1989: 9)

Even Bevin identified propaganda as part of the diplomat's armoury: 'In the international field we have, particularly at the present juncture the most delicate tasks and publicity must march so closely with policy that the Foreign Secretary cannot delegate control of information policy and its execution.'[2] When the government considered the future of the Information Services after the Second World War, Bevin sought to transfer the foreign responsibilities of the Ministry of Information back to the Foreign Office: 'It is important, if we are not to speak in foreign countries with two voices, that the functions of representation and publicity should be more closely related, and this can best be done by integration of the services.[3]

The resulting organization of publicity machinery was a compromise. Although the Foreign Office was unable to secure total control of overseas publicity, the Central Office of Information functioned as a co-ordinating advisory service department for other ministries while the individual departments had primacy in policy matters and also retained their own information staff. The study of propaganda inevitably leads to the study of British policy-making. However, Partner is wrong in suggesting that there was no Palestine 'policy'; it was never haphazard, undefined or even reactive. Instead, the government was seeking to achieve the impossible by persuading opposing parties of the justice of British plans for Palestine's future.

Palestine had wide international implications and could not be approached as a simple counterinsurgency problem. It had complications for Britain's global prestige and reputation, for Britain's position in the Middle East and for Britain's relationship with the United States. It was hoped that Britain's post-war economic difficulties would be short-lived and that Britain would soon recover her position as a leading economic power. In the meantime, the United States and the Soviet Union must be shown that Britain could not be written off as a secondary power (Adamthwaite, 1985: 223–35).

The foundation of Britain's claim to world power status was the very existence of her Empire. Noel Sabine, head of the Colonial Office Information Department, defined in October 1944 the theme of national projection: 'The future of Great Britain depends on its future as an Empire and Commonwealth and not as a small island in the North Sea with a population of 46 million people.'[4] Where Britain withdrew, the Soviet Union could fill the vacuum and Britain's influence would be displaced permanently.

Britain viewed the Middle East as an area to be defended as a British sphere of influence, a principle which was to be applied as much against the United States as against the Soviet Union. While American involvement in confronting Soviet ambitions in Persia was welcomed, it was on British terms and following Britain's lead. Britain would not obstruct the development of American economic interests in the Middle East, but resolutely defended her political predominance; the American influence in Persia 'while encouraged, must be regarded as perhaps rather a special case'.[5]

Protection of Britain's political, economic and strategic interests in the

Middle East depended on Arab goodwill towards Britain. Britain promoted the Arab League as an association of pro-British Arab states. The association would be reinforced, not by British occupation but by treaties of alliance with Egypt, Iraq and Transjordan. Bevin advocated 'schemes of economic development which would benefit the common people'.[6] Kirkpatrick felt that publicity towards the Middle East should emphasize that it was 'to Britain that the Middle Eastern countries should look for guidance and support'.[7]

Bevin acknowledged:

> Our presence in the Mediterranean serves a purpose other than a military purpose which is vital to our position as a Great Power.[8]

Withdrawal from the Middle East

> would be disastrous to our position there, in the neighbouring countries, in Europe and the world.... Even if we do not believe that the Russians have plans for world domination, I am certain that they will not be able to resist advancing into any vacuum we may leave.
>
> (Bullock, 1985: 351)

However, British economic weakness meant Britain was unable to give substance to their rhetoric, and it severely limited the ability to achieve their requirements by coercion. Increasingly Britain would have to depend on its ability to persuade reluctant Arab states of the compatibility of British and Arab interests. The Arab League did not meet British expectations and was not a testament to Anglo-Arab friendship. Arab leaders were able to use their support of Palestinian Arab aspirations for domestic ends. In challenging British aims in Palestine, Arab leaders mitigated popular opinion who perceived that their interests were being sacrificed in order to serve Britain.

At the same time Britain had to acknowledge that it was dependent, at least in the short term, upon economic aid from the United States, first through the 1946 Anglo-American Loan Agreement and then through the Marshall Plan. Therefore, President Harry Truman's interest in Palestine meant that Britain had to accept the reality of American involvement, if not interference, which strained relations at a critical point in the post-war loan negotiations.

Compared with American and Arab opinion, public opinion in Britain was less important for policy-makers and publicists. It was a general Parliamentary Convention that, in foreign policy, the government would receive bi-partisan support. Richard Crossman concluded:

> No British election would ever be decided on the merits of the Government's handling of Palestine. The British press at this time showed no interest in the Jewish problem, and in the little space which it gave to it, no very violent partisanship. The British people would be ready to accept any solution which seemed reasonable and averted the risk of bloodshed.
>
> (Crossman, 1946: 59)

On the whole the British public was ignorant and disinterested in Palestine and the issues involved. While terrorist activities by the Jews in Palestine raised public awareness, public opinion was never a consistent pressure on the government comparable with Arab or American opinion. Few could understand concepts like Zionism, and a disturbing undercurrent of anti-Semitism was apparent. In a Mass Observation poll of July 1946 asking, 'How do you feel about the Jews in this country?', 45 per cent classed themselves into the category of 'Nothing against them/Pro-Jews' but 33 per cent classed themselves as 'Definitely anti'.[9]

The Labour Party had endorsed a pro-Zionist policy in its 1944 conference resolution of the International Post-war Settlement. Independence for Palestine would rapidly be followed by a transfer of populations in which Arabs would be 'encouraged to move out', as the Jews moved in, thus creating a Jewish state. The policy, however, was produced by a dedicated minority within the movement, including Harold Laski, George Dallas, chairman of the International Subcommittee of the NEC, and the policy's author, Hugh Dalton, rather than as the result of a balanced debate, and the Arab case fell by default. Moreover it was largely a humanitarian response.[10] It did not address the practical and political consequences of the transfer of populations it advocated. The Labour Party was not 'emotionally pro-Jew, but only rationally anti-anti Semitic', which was 'a very different thing' (Crossman, 1946: 61).

Between 1945 and 1947 the British government tried to implement a long-term policy over Palestine which would preserve British political, economic and strategic interests in the Middle East while influencing the day-to-day discussions over the future of the Mandate. For this policy to succeed, the Foreign and Colonial Offices had to integrate it with a comprehensive propaganda effort which would control the information received at home and abroad about Palestine. Domestic opinion in Britain had to be convinced not to oppose the government's efforts, but the main targets of British propaganda were audiences abroad. British policy in Palestine had to reconcile the differing objectives and opinions of three constituencies: Arab, Jewish and American. Optimally, propaganda sought to persuade each constituency to consider compromise rather than holding rigidly to its goals. Failing that, propaganda tried to maintain Anglo-Arab and Anglo-American friendship, limiting the potential damage Palestine could have on these relationships.

Palestine entered the post-war political agenda with the publication in June 1945 of a report commissioned by President Truman of the conditions of displaced persons in European camps, particularly the Jews. Throughout the summer Truman lobbied the British government for the immediate admission of 100,000 Jews, the figure left in the camps, to Palestine.[11] This associated two problems in public perception which the British government wished to separate: the problems facing European Jewry and the future of Palestine.

Even if the new government accepted the principles of the International Post-War Settlement, no definite plans for its implementation existed. Bevin summoned all British representatives in the Middle East to London in September to discuss Palestine policy and review general policy in the Middle East, indicating that Palestine would be dealt with in a regional context.[12] Prime Minister Clement Attlee resurrected the idea of a wartime Cabinet Committee on Palestine, at the first test it was judged that the Labour Party's existing policy on Palestine was impractical. To maintain Arab friendship, Britain could not contemplate large-scale Jewish immigration into Palestine. Instead it stood by the 1939 White Paper, which restricted Jewish immigration to 75,000, a figure due to expire by the end of November 1945. To reconcile Jewish and Arab opinion, a government statement would avoid the 'provocative' effect of the phrase 'adhering to the White Paper policy' and speak instead of 'continuing' or 'extending' it. Britain would ask the Arab states to accept immigration at a rate of 1,500 a month beyond the prescribed quota until a long-term policy was devised. In spite of American pressure, the policy announcement would be delayed until after the annual pilgrimage to Mecca in mid-November and until military reinforcements, to deal with violent outbursts in reaction to the announcement, had reached Palestine, which the Chiefs of Staff assessed would arrive by 24 October.[13]

In the event, no statement was made. On 4 October Bevin proposed the establishment of an Anglo-American Committee of Inquiry to investigate the problems of displaced persons in Europe.[14] The Foreign Office was sceptical, feeling the inquiry would be interpreted by Arab and world opinion as Britain yielding to 'American pressure,' and it tried to ensure that Arab criticism would target the Americans and not Britain. The American Chargé d'Affaires in Syria reported to the State Department that the United States was a scapegoat for Arab resentment because of the 'sensational treatment accorded by British-controlled press and radio in Near East'.[15]

Bevin gambled that if a rapid settlement, consistent with British requirements, was concluded, Arab opposition would be negligible. Furthermore, with negotiations beginning on the US Loan to Britain, American support for Britain's Middle Eastern plans would be a diplomatic success. Strengthening Britain's political ties through economic agreements with Arab states also depended on American finance. Thus, Britain could not afford to appear pro-Arab, and she would have at least to pay lip service to American Zionist opinion.

When details of the establishment of the Committee of Inquiry were leaked to the *New York Times* at the end of October,[16] the government was pressed by Parliament for a statement. The story was repeated in the British press, and Francis Williams, the first Public Relations Officer at No. 10, extracted a promise from British journalists that they would not imply that British delay in announcing a new policy on Palestine was due to elections in New York.[17] To sell the Committee of Inquiry to the Arabs, already suspicious of Zionist influence on American policy, British representatives in the Middle East would publicize its beneficial aspects. It would be useful, it was argued, for the US government to see the issue from a different perspective other than that of the purely Zionist.[18]

Lord Halifax, the British Ambassador to Washington, warned that the price of American participation in the inquiry was concessions to the Americans over the terms of reference, although the mention of Palestine as a specific solution would inflame Arab opinion:

1. To examine political, economic, and social conditions in Palestine as they bear upon the problem of Jewish immigration and settlement therein and the well-being of the peoples now living therein.
2. To examine the position of the Jews in those countries of Europe where they have been the victims of Nazi and Fascist persecution, and the practical measures taken or contemplated to be taken in those countries to enable them to live free from discrimination and oppression and to make estimates of the extent to which emigration to Palestine or other countries outside Europe may be necessary.[19]

The State Department's Loy Henderson told Halifax that the US government had no objection to the way in which the terms of reference were presented to mitigate adverse Arab reaction to the idea that Palestine would be asked to bear the whole responsibility for the problem of European Jewry.[20]

The Eastern Department of the Foreign Office, drafting the statement announcing the Committee of Inquiry, tried to stem Arab criticism. While Palestine would contribute to the Jewish displaced persons problem, it would 'not by itself provide sufficient opportunity for grappling with the whole problem'. An appeal was made against the Jews resorting to violence to force a solution, as it would only prejudice their case. The statement ended by emphasizing that 'it would need a united effort by the powers to relieve the miseries of these suffering peoples.'[21]

To ensure a good reception for the statement, Risdale, Head of the Foreign Office News Department, suggested that Bevin should hold separate off-the-record press conferences with British and American journalists. Halifax would hold a similar press conference in Washington. George Hall, Colonial Secretary, would meet the Empire Press for fear of offending them if they were 'in this way excluded from the "family"'. A 'background paper' giving a 'factual summary of the course of events since the Balfour Declaration', was prepared by the Foreign Office Research Department for the British press. It could be used by the British Information Services in the United States, but not distributed to the American press because 'any such document coming from a British official source is apparently found to be misrepresented.'[22] To help favourable reception of the new policy announcement, the Cabinet decided that Chuter Ede, the Home Secretary, would announce on the same day that

Britain would accept a limited number of refugees from Nazi oppression.[23]

Bevin, however, undermined the publicity when he departed from his brief in the House of Commons and in his comments to American journalists. In the Commons he rashly stated that he was determined to solve the Jewish displaced persons problem: 'I will stake my political future on solving this problem but not in the limited sphere presented to me now.' In spite of the qualification, attention was focused on the man, not the policy. Asked by American journalists about the possibility of future Jewish immigration into Palestine, he argued that the Jews were not accepting the certificates available and were using the immigration issue as a political lever. He undermined his own argument for a multilateral approach to the Jewish displaced persons problem by criticising other countries: 'All nations are frightened of a racial development within their settlement and the Jews present a very vexed problem indeed.'[24]

Making further concessions to the Americans, Britain agreed that the Committee would report within 120 days,[25] and that the Inquiry's deliberations would begin in the United States. Beeley, Bevin's special adviser on Palestine, suggested telling the Arabs that the Inquiry, an Anglo-American body, would have to sit in the United States. Going to Washington first and then to London would be convenient, as London would be the point of departure for Europe. Another advantage, but not to be used in publicity, was that 'it was preferable that the Committee's sojourn in Washington should take place at an early stage rather than later when it will be preparing its report.'[26]

The Foreign Office attempted to ensure that the contents of the report would be acceptable to Arab opinion, and it secretly encouraged Arab states to invite the Committee of Inquiry to visit their capitals. If nothing else, Arab opinion would be impressed that the Committee of Inquiry was neutral, which would increase the chances of the final report being accepted and store up Arab goodwill for the future.[27] The Eastern Department arranged for an RAF transport plane to ferry the Committee of Inquiry around the Middle East.[28]

Meanwhile the government publicly assumed a neutral posture to obtain the support of American and world opinion. Nothing was to be said or done which implied that Britain was hindering the work of the Committee of Inquiry. No retaliation followed an attack by a Jewish terrorist organization on a Jerusalem police station on 27 December, which killed ten Britons. The Cabinet disagreed with the demand of the High Commissioner, General Sir Alan Cunningham, for a widespread arms search: 'It would throw power into the hands of the extremists, would produce a strong reaction in the United States, and, above all, would make it impossible for the Anglo-American Commission to carry out its work in Palestine.'[29]

Just as Bevin's outbursts undermined British policy, the statements of others outside the policy-making process produced new problems for publicity. Lieutenant-General Sir Frederick Morgan, an organizer of the

United Nations Relief and Rehabilitation Administration in Germany, described Jewish illegal immigration to Palestine as the 'second exodus . . . a well-organised positive plan to get out of Europe' (Bethell, 1980: 220). The Zionist propaganda machine portrayed this as a further example of the anti-semitism of the British government, and Bevin told the Cabinet that Morgan's comments had caused a storm of protest in the United States. Risdale of the Foreign Office News Department recommended that during a press conference Bevin was due to have with American journalists, he should emphasize Morgan's war record. Bevin could also divert attention from the Morgan case by giving 'a broad outline of our policy responsibilities' on the Jewish issue, feeling that it was 'timely to rub this in'. The London Press Service also distributed, world-wide, a leader from *The Daily Telegraph* which commended Morgan's war record.[30]

The Committee of Inquiry presented its report to the two governments on 20 April 1946. Although the report recommended the establishment of Palestine as an independent bi-national state, rejecting the creation of a Jewish state, it advocated the immediate admittance of the 100,000 Jews without linking this to the wholesale disarmament of illegal Jewish organizations.[31] A Committee under Cabinet Secretary Norman Brook informed the Cabinet that the report was unenforceable and would 'spell the beginning of a long period of unrest in the whole Arab world. The anti-British feeling which would be stimulated would make much more difficult the satisfactory negotiation of revised treaties with Egypt and Iraq.' The report could only be enforced if Britain received financial, political and military 'support' from the United States, and if illegal Jewish organizations were disarmed.[32]

Beeley proposed that the government's persuasion efforts should target the American military, since the military provided more effective counterweight against American public opinion than did the State Department. The Joint Planning Staff endorsed the communication of the *in camera* military evidence heard by the Committee of Inquiry of the US Chiefs of Staff.[33]

The Cabinet agreed that Britain and the United States would issue simultaneous statements after the publication of the report. The report itself was to be published as soon as possible to avoid accusations of delay and to commit the US government before they got 'cold feet'.[34] The High Commissioner advised that both the report and the government's attitude towards it should be published at the same time to ease the task of the security forces in Palestine, who would then have to deal with only one period of heightened tension instead of two.[35]

On 22 April a large part of the report, including maps, was printed in the *New York Times* after a White House leak to journalist Sidney Gruson. The State Department wanted to hasten publication of the report but the Foreign Office stalled them by arguing that technical difficulties made it impossible to meet the demands for copies of the report until 1 May.[36]

Halifax reported that the Zionists in the United States were still largely in the dark,[37] but all British representatives in the Middle East predicted an 'unfavourable' Arab reaction to the report, thus destroying any Arab goodwill towards Britain. Ronald Campbell in Cairo asserted that the report, if enforced, would have a disastrous effect on Britain's Middle Eastern position, highly undesirable at the time of the renegotiation of the 1936 Anglo-Egyptian Treaty. It would 'antagonise the Arabs without conciliating the Jews'.[38]

The Cabinet decided to pursue an Anglo-American policy, while acknowledging that even if the US government offered financial and military support to implement the report, Britain would be perceived as 'sacrificing Arab interests' on the altar of Anglo-American co-operation. Colonial Secretary George Hall would see Lobby correspondents before the statement was made in the Commons and indicate that the US government should not offer advice on Palestine without taking a share of the responsibility. Attlee would inform Opposition Leader Winston Churchill of the government 'line' to avoid the embarrassment of a full debate.[39]

Within hours of the Cabinet decision Halifax cabled London that Truman was about to issue a unilateral statement on Palestine, saying he was happy that his suggestion concerning the 100,000 Jewish refugees had been 'unanimously endorsed' by the report. Truman completely ignored the other nine recommendations. He offered no condemnation of Jewish terrorism, the *quid pro quo* for British acceptance of the 100,000 Jews, and no promise of American aid in implementing the report.[40]

Truman undercut the British attempt to seize the initiative over Palestine and put the publicity services on the defensive. An announcement which merely stated that Britain was consulting the US government over future policy was now inadequate. Bevin said furiously that 'the United States must be put right up against it.'[41] An amended statement would stress the practical difficulties of absorbing large numbers of Jews into Palestine without disarming the illegal organizations and would question the extent to which Britain could rely on American co-operation in implementing the report. Realizing that US support was necessary, however, the statement could not blame the United States in the event of a failure to implement the report. Instead the Jews would be blamed for the troubles in Palestine.[42]

To forestall opposition criticism, the government announced continued consultations with the Americans, and the statement was 'well-received' in the House of Commons. In a·press conference following the announcement, journalists focused on the question of future American support for implementing the report.[43]

Arab reaction to the report was extreme, however. The United States was judged to have blackmailed Britain by threatening to withhold approval of the Loan Agreement.[44] Britain's Middle Eastern representatives stressed that no final decision on the future of Palestine would be taken before the Arab states had been consulted,[45] and Beeley arranged for a Foreign Office statement to give the desired assurance.[46]

Arab opinion, still not placated, continued to claim that Britain was motivated by economic considerations and the American Loan. Gordon Merriam, Head of Near Eastern Affairs at the State Department, felt that the British had made the Americans into the scapegoat for their difficulties with the Arabs. He felt the anti-American outbursts were not spontaneous, and claimed that British representatives in Syria and Saudi Arabia were spreading the story

> to the effect that the British members of the Anglo-American Committee of Inquiry had yielded to the pressure of their American colleagues (and specifically the ultimatum that non-compliance would prejudice passage of the British loan) before acquiescing in proposals favourable to further Jewish immigration into Palestine.[47]

In spite of Truman's statement, Britain continued to press for an American commitment to Palestine, and the US government agreed to consult the British government through the mechanism of a committee of officials, which would be followed by a conference of all interested parties.[48] Bevin was encouraged, as it seemed the US government were 'willing to remove this question from the realm of propaganda and to study its practical implications on a business-like footing'.[49]

Out of the reach of his Foreign Office advisers, however, Bevin vented his irritation with the US government. Speaking at the Labour Party Conference in Bournemouth in June, he commented:

> There has been the agitation in the United States, and particularly in New York, for 100,000 Jews to be put into Palestine. I hope I will not be misunderstood in America if I say that this was proposed with the purest of motives—they do not want too many Jews in New York.[50]

The Zionist propaganda machine in the United States used Bevin's outburst to great advantage, suggesting that the American Loan to Britain should be refused until the Foreign Secretary had retracted his comments. Lord Inverchapel, the new British ambassador to Washington, remarked that the speech had 'not only hit the nail on the head but driven it in woundingly deep'. On Inverchapel's advice, Bevin issued a statement welcoming Truman's establishment of a 24-man Committee on Palestine, due to arrive in London in July.[51]

Inverchapel managed to have published in the *New York Times* an almost-complete version of the Bournemouth speech which dealt with the Anglo-American alliance and suspicions about the motives of Soviet foreign policy,[52] and Bevin wrote to two influential Senators, Wagner and Mead, to set his comment about the 100,000 Jewish refugees in the context of the full speech.[53]

On 20 June the Cabinet decided, in response to the kidnapping of five British officers, to take the initiative against Jewish terrorists.[54] On 29 June thousands of Jews were detained and Jewish Agency buildings were searched for evidence of links between the Agency and terrorist organizations. A vital part of the initiative, code-named *Operation Agatha*, was its projection. The Colonial Office press section would be responsible for general enquiries and guidance for the London Press Service. The Foreign Office News Department, responsible for enquiries concerning the United States, would tell enquirers that the US government had been informed but not consulted and indicate that the Anglo-American talks were continuing. The Colonial Office would defend the action as a response to Jewish 'terrorist' activity, using the Committee of Inquiry's condemnation of terrorism as justification.[55]

Despite the preparations, the operation was a propaganda disaster. Failing to separate Jewish extremists from the moderates, it did nothing to break-up the illegal organizations (Bethell, 1980: 248–53). Truman, who was not informed of the operation in advance, said the next day that he regretted the occurrence and hoped the Jewish leaders detained during the operation would be released.[56] Arabs saw the operation as too litte, too late, and not nearly as thorough as action taken against Palestinian Arabs in 1936.[57]

British hopes for American support now rested on the talks between the American Committee of Officials, headed by Henry Grady, and the British team, headed by Norman Brook. It was agreed that no statements would be made, except those jointly agreed by the delegations.[58] In the meantime, Britain decided to make no statements on Palestine, 'to remove the Palestine issue from the headlines'. Hall's suggestion of publicity for the cessation of military searches in Palestine, together with a warning that renewed terrorism would be opposed with the utmost rigour, was rejected because official statements only produced 'counter-statements receiving much greater publicity'. Likewise Bevin's idea for a statement to help the passage of the Loan Agreement through Congress was rejected by the Cabinet because the motivations were transparent.[59]

On 25 July the Cabinet decided that if the US government supported the proposal for a single state with provincial autonomy for the Arabs and Jews, Britain would compromise over the issue of the 100,000 Jewish refugees. Grady accordingly recommended that the United States support provincial autonomy.[60]

Before Truman's reaction to the plan was received, the King David Hotel in Jerusalem, housing the Secretariat of the Palestine Government and Military Headquarters, was bombed by Jewish terrorists, killing 91 people. Attlee opposed reprisals:

The right course was to press on and to seek an early agreement with the United States Government on a long-term policy. If such an agreement could be reached, we should announce our joint policy and try to rally the support of world opinion in favour of its adoption.[61]

He would also 'appeal to the more moderate elements among the Jewish population to stamp out the dissident organisations'. In the Commons, Attlee did not go even as far as this, merely repeating that the government was discussing a settlement for Palestine with the Americans and would not 'be diverted by acts of violence from their search for a just and final solution of this problem'.[62]

Meanwhile, Britain sought public condemnation by the Americans of terrorism. Truman's subsequent statement condemned the 'wanton slaying of human beings', but its value as a check on Jewish extremism was nullified when the President, seizing the opportunity to appeal to Zionist opinion in the United States again supported the 100,000 Jews.[63]

Any sympathy for Britain in the aftermath of the King David Hotel bombing was dissipated when the General-Officer-Commanding in Palestine, General Sir Evelyn Barker, issued a non-fraternization order. He told troops to punish the Jews in the 'way the race dislikes—by striking at their pockets'. Abba Eban, a future Israeli Foreign Minister, was working at the British Middle Eastern Centre for Arab Studies in Jerusalem, and saw the order posted on the notice-board. He passed its contents to Jon Kimche, a journalist, and it was published around the world 'where it reverberated with full force' (Eban, 1977: 62–3).

Government publicity was to say that the terms used by Barker were inadvisable, but the Chief of the Imperial General Staff, Montgomery, refused to act against the General. Privately, Montgomery advised Barker that in future it would be advisable to use the spoken and not the written word.[64]

In the United States the incident was portrayed as an indication of the anti-Semitic nature of the British government. Inverchapel wanted to issue a counterstatement to the effect that the British government was not anti-Semitic, but F.B.A. Rundall of the North American Department, a future British ambassador to Israel, minuted:

> To my mind our replies to U.S. criticism on Palestine has been far too much on the lines of 'No, you cads, we're not.' We shall never convince nor appease the Zionists, but we may well convince the general public by keeping them fully informed—in advance where possible—of what we are doing and why we are doing it.[65]

Truman dealt another blow to the British by refusing to join them in support for the provincial autonomy plan drafted by the Brook–Grady Committee. Assistant Secretary of State Dean Acheson forestalled a Presidential statement disavowing the Grady mission, but Truman privately favoured a new Jewish Agency plan advocating the establishment of a Jewish state in an adequate area of Palestine.[66]

With the prospect of Truman's support shattered, the Palestine policy needed a new impetus. An army intelligence summary on British attitudes to Palestine found that as the majority of the population were 'growingly anti-semitic', there was 'little doubt' that the British people would 'support any strong and reasonable action in Palestine'. Therefore, the Palestine Conference of all interested parties, due to open in London in September, would receive a high public profile.[67]

Only the Arab states had agreed to attend the Conference, a fact which privately and at lower levels in the Foreign and Colonial Offices, passed unlamented. A meeting on 26 August concluded that no concessions would be made to obtain Palestinian Arab and Jewish Agency attendance:

> There is little hope of a solution which will receive the open support of either the Palestinian Arabs or the Jewish Agency. Any solution must necessarily be a compromise and the leaders on either side would probably lose their positions if they retreated from their official demands. There is thus small prospect of getting the leaders committed even if they were permitted to attend and the argument based on the importance of associating them with the solution loses much of its force.[68]

If the conference failed to negotiate a solution, the Foreign Office could refer Palestine to the General Assembly of the United Nations. Since the likelihood of a General Assembly vote in favour of a Jewish State was remote, the United Nations 'would mobilise a majority against the extreme pretensions of Zionism and would manifest sympathy for the Palestinian Arabs as representing a small nation'. Furthermore, it might ask the British to stay in Palestine under a new Trusteeship agreement on the basis of the Brook–Grady plan, with eventual independence for a unitary state.[69] It was essential that the agreement should be achieved by negotiation.

Bevin however, still pursued the aim of American involvement in Palestine, either through their unqualified support or their mediation with the Jews. Therefore it was necessary for the Jews to attend the conference. The government was prepared to go as far as possible to arrange Jewish attendance without giving the Arabs the impression that Britain was negotiating separately with the Jews, and the Jewish Agency representative, Nahum Goldmann, told the government that the Agency would attend if the Arabs demonstrated a willingness to discuss partition.[70] Five days before the opening of the conference Weizmann wrote to the government, explaining that the Jewish Agency could not attend unless the basis of discussion was a Jewish State in an adequate area of Palestine.[71]

The correspondence between the government and the Jewish Agency over the conference was to be published on 7 September. According to Bevin, this would 'place the blame for refusing to attend the Conference squarely on the shoulders of the Jewish Agency' and show the world that the Jews had refused to attend except on their own terms, for their leadership was 'sacrificing the prospects for peace in Palestine for the sake of their own ambitions'.[72] If the United States saw that the Jews were being awkward, they would have to support Britain's attempts to find agreement with the Arab states. Brook arranged for 'private and informal' contact with the US Embassy in London for the duration of the conference. To keep the contacts secret, the Foreign Office News Department told inquirers that 'H.M.G. are still maintaining close contact with the U.S.G. regarding Palestine and has [sic] done during recent months'.[73]

Privately the British government was quite prepared to accept partition in principle, as it had received strong indications that both Transjordan and Egypt would support the solution.[74] The British government had two problems, however. First, Arab leaders were bound by the Bludan Conference decision of 8–12 June, which supported the Palestinian Arabs. Publicly they would refuse to consider partition, using the 1939 White Paper as an 'Arab Bible'. Britain could not afford to be perceived as sponsoring a partition solution as it would result at least in a breakdown of the conference.[75] Second, in practice, partition meant different things to each party. Britain's concept included the Negev Desert in the Arab area to link the Arab world and serve British defence requirements, but the Jews saw the Negev as part of their state.[76]

Publicly the British government advocated the provincial autonomy plan as the first item on the conference agenda while emphasizing to both sides that Britain would consider amendments or new plans. In his opening speech to the conference on 10 September, Attlee stressed to the Arab delegates that 'Arab freedom was the result of our victories in the 1914–18 war', and that Iraq and Transjordan owed their independence to Britain.[77] He spoke of the 'natural partnership' between Britain and the Arab World, at one over all issues except that of Palestine.[78]

To promote British–Arab agreement, equal publicity had been arranged for the Arab reply to Attlee, but the strategy backfired when Syria's Faris el-Khouri, on behalf of the Arabs, stated: 'The impossible has been asked of Palestine, for she alone has been required to be an instrument in the realisation of the dreams and ambitions of political Zionism.'[79] The rejection of provincial autonomy by the Arabs made the private indications of willingness to compromise all the more frustrating. The Lebanese felt the Arabs might be willing to accept 30,000 to 40,000 Jewish immigrants, and Iraqi Prime Minister Nuri es-Sa'id thought a federal solution might be acceptable,[80] but publicly the Arab delegations maintained that provincial autonomy would increase Jewish demands for territory, and rejected Bevin's stipulation that substantial Jewish immigration would have to be part of any solution.[81] Under the Arab plan for an independent state, the Jews would live as a permanent minority with guaranteed rights and no further immigration.[82]

A subcommittee under the chairmanship of Norman Brook came close to a solution. A compromise was agreed over Jewish participation in the government of the state and a treaty of alliance fulfilling Britain's strategic requirements. The stumbling block was immigration, as the Arabs refused to see Jewish motivations as anything other than purely political.[83] No further progress could be made and the conference was therefore adjourned on 2 October. The press release merely announced that Arab delegates were to attend the UN meeting in New York. No mention was made of the deadlock in negotiations or the nature of the Arab proposals.[84]

Behind the scenes of the conference the government continued discussions with the Jewish Agency. The government was even prepared to issue a statement that following talks, the Jewish Agency would participate in the conference 'to join in the discussions with HMG and to present their views as to the solution of the Palestine problem'.[85] However, the Inner Zionist Council, because of HMG's ban on the attendance of detained leaders such as Ben-Gurion and Moshe Shertok, insisted that the Agency continue its efforts to obtain 'preliminary conditions' enabling future attendance.[86] On 1 October Bevin told a Jewish Agency delegation led by Weizmann that he would not force the Arabs to accept partition at the 'point of bayonets', and that Britain would release detained Jews only as part of a general settlement on law and order.[87]

Although Britain informed Truman of the progress made in the talks with the Jewish Agency and the possibility of a 'truce' in Palestine, the State Department advice was that a statement might do more harm than good, Truman reaffirmed his support for Zionist aims in a speech on 4 October, the eve of Yom Kippur. To influence voters in the forthcoming Congressional elections, Truman stated that the Jews were disheartened at the prospects of another winter in European camps. He regretted the adjournment of the Palestine Conference, restated his support for the 100,000 Jewish refugees, and, for the first time, declared that the Jewish Agency's proposal for the creation of a Jewish state in an adequate area of Palestine was a solution which would 'command the support of public opinion in the United States'.[88]

The British government was incensed, claiming that the President's statement had undermined their negotiating position with the Jewish Agency,[89] but, reluctant to criticize Truman directly, the Foreign Office News Department advised the press to 'emphasise Zionist responsibility for the delay in concluding the conference', and insisted that no new decision on Jewish immigration could be reached 'in advance of a general decision on the future of Palestine'.[90]

Following the adjournment of the Palestine Conference and Truman's Yom Kippur statement, there was little optimism that a settlement could be reached by negotiation. Weizmann now said immigration was the 'crucial problem'.[91] Moreover, with the appointment of Colonial Secretary Arthur Creech-Jones, partition had a firm supporter within the Cabinet. Creech-Jones believed the Jews willing to compromise on the details of partition and suggested they join the Palestine Conference after making a public statement dissociating themselves from terrorist violence.[92] Arab opinion, however, labelled partition as the Zionist solution, and the Foreign Office assessed that 'The Government of Iraq and Syria (and possibly other Arab states) would be compelled to swim with the tide of public opinion or risk being swept out of office.'[93]

Bevin, in the United States, attending the Council of Foreign Ministers, continued to urge American involvement in Palestine to influence the Zionist negotiating position. A Foreign Office Research Department paper prepared for US Secretary of State Byrnes outlined the possible solutions and concluded, 'the deduction which the ordinary reader would draw is that the objections to partition are very serious and that a scheme of provincial autonomy is perhaps the best option.' Targeting persuasive efforts at Byrnes was ineffective, however. By the end of 1946 Byrnes was out of favour with Truman and soon to be replaced by General George Marshall.[94]

The demise of moderate Zionist opinion and possible compromise with Britain was illustrated by Weizmann's loss of the Presidency of the World Zionist Congress on 16 December. The Colonial Office's policy of supporting the moderate opinion was bankrupt. Montgomery told the Defence Committee that unless a political solution was soon achieved, 'strong military action' would be necessary.[95]

Yet British objectives precluded the abandonment of Palestine to the Jews. On 13 January 1947 Bevin and the military were authorized to devise a defence strategy in which Britain's Middle Eastern position was vital to the imperial defence, a concept which Attlee had resisted since the summer (Smith and Zametica, 1985). The implication was that it would be better to 'throw in [H.M.G's] hand' over Palestine than to enforce a solution which antagonised the Arabs. The Foreign Office hoped that the London Conference still offered an opportunity for 'one last vigorous effort to arrive at a generally satisfactory settlement'.[96]

Creech-Jones argued in Cabinet before the conference reopened on 27 January that British public opinion would support partition as would the United States and the Labour Party. The Foreign Office felt British public opinion would support HMG over 'any firm policy'.[97] Bevin had no objection to partition in principle but insisted that its implementation would present insuperable difficulties. He queried whether British opinion would support such a policy if force against the Arabs were required to implement it. If a last chance at negotiation failed, 'the question would have to be brought in some form before the UN', and Britain would not dictate what form the solution should take. The Cabinet agreed but ruled out a solution imposed against the will of the communities in Palestine, i.e., the Arabs.[98]

When the London Conference reconvened, the Arabs rejected the British compromise plan of provincial autonomy because it would increase Jewish immigration. On 4 February the Palestinian Arabs declared they were prepared to go to war to prevent the plan's implementation.[99] Beeley told the representative of the Arab News Agency that if the Arab rejection of provincial autonomy was reported in the Arab press, it would be 'more difficult for the Arabs to continue negotiation'. Instead, Beeley 'induced' the representative to say that 'Arab States were at present considering whether to continue negotiations.'[100]

Before the final session of the Conference, Creech-Jones told the House of Commons that British women and children would be evacuated from Palestine so the government and the armed forces were not hampered 'in their task of maintaining law and order'.[101] The Foreign Office told the British Embassy to emphasize that the decision for evacuation was taken 'in order that there should be no impediment to any action which the government might think necessary to enforce the laws'. Above all, it had no connection with the developments at the London Conference.[102] After Beeley consulted with Lewis Jones of the US Embassy in London, General Marshall issued a 'helpful' statement that he did not believe Britain was intending strong action in Palestine, and that the US government was being kept fully informed of developments and hoped the London Conference would produce a peaceful settlement.[103]

Bevin and Creech-Jones reported to Cabinet on 7 February, however, that there was 'no prospect' of a solution broadly acceptable to the Arabs and Jews. The Conference would be presented with an alternative solution of local autonomy under British trusteeship. After five years, independence would be introduced with safeguards for the Jewish minority. Immigration would continue at 4,000 a month for the next two years. Although this might be unacceptable to the two communities in Palestine, it was a solution Britain 'could conscientiously recommend and defend to public opinion in the United Nations'. Explaining his reversal over partition, Creech-Jones noted its enforcement would create 'conditions of rebellion and disorder in Palestine which might last for a considerable time and would introduce a substantial military commitment for us'.[104]

The plan was rejected by Ben-Gurion, the new Zionist leader, who called for a return to the pre-1939 Mandate, and by the Arabs, who labelled the plan 'another guise for partition.'[105] Accordingly, on 14 February Bevin and Creech-Jones recommended immediate referral to the United Nations. Hopefully the announcement of referral would have 'a restraining influence on both peoples', as neither community would want to 'prejudice' its case 'in the eyes of the General Assembly'.[106]

Bevin was even optimistic that the announcement might bring the Arabs and Jews back to the conference table and to 'a more reasonable frame of mind'.[107] Meanwhile, Britain should maintain the *status quo* in Palestine. If immigration was relaxed, an Arab state might present Palestine to the UN Security Council and the danger that Britain might 'estrange the Arabs without placating the Jews'.[108]

The announcement of referral concentrated on HMG's difficulties in facing an 'irreconcilable conflict of principles' in Palestine. The Foreign Office advised Bevin not to reveal the decision to maintain the *status quo* because of the Jewish outcry this would produce. Still attempting to project an American share of the responsibility for Palestine, Attlee ordered that the statement imply that Britain and America had developed the same plan for a settlement. It was not 'our own proposals' which would be 'described' to the United Nations, but 'the proposals of the Anglo-American Committee and the various proposals which we ourselves have put forward'.[109]

Arab and British public opinion welcomed the announcement of 18 February in the House of Commons. Kirkbride reported from Amman that the Transjordan government and public thought the decision was 'right', in spite of criticism that the delay in a settlement would 'enable the Jews to continue to immigrate and acquire land in Palestine'.[110] A Gallup poll of March 1947 indicated that only 12 per cent of the British public disapproved of referral and 65 per cent approved (Gallup, 1976: 153). The US government, however, foresaw problems with American public opinion and realized, to their dismay, that its unwillingness to support fully a British plan meant they would probably have to bear the 'responsibility of leadership' in the United Nations and 'furnish the chief economic support' for any agreed plan.[111]

Britain was not cutting her losses in Palestine by referring it to the United Nations. As Creech-Jones declared in the House of Commons on 28 February, 'We are not going to the UN to surrender the Mandate.' The Foreign Office saw referral as a tactical retreat, hoping that the United Nations would support Britain's plan. As long as Britain was perceived as a 'neutral' in the United Nations and avoided the odium of being associated with an anti-Arab solution, Anglo-Arab friendship and Britain's Middle Eastern position could be maintained.[112]

The Labour government did not fail in its objectives because its policy was projected wrongly or because it ignored 'public opinion' over the Palestine issue. Ultimately, it could not convince the two most crucial opinions, Arab and American, to support British plans. Because Arab and American goals could not be reconciled, the attempts of the Colonial and Foreign Offices to control information received by the various audiences were utopian. The Foreign Office could never dictate the interpretation of information, nor could they control news agencies abroad. Whitehall could not control statements made by British officials outside the policy-making process. It could not dictate to Truman. At times, it could not even control Bevin's deviations from carefully prepared briefs.

However, the results of the propaganda efforts over Palestine were not universally negative. At home, although the government faced criticism from a small section of the Labour Party that it had failed to fulfil pre-election pledges, this never developed into a back-bench revolt. British public opinion, which had little sympathy with the aims of political Zionism, never turned against the government over Palestine. Army morale suffered but there was no complete collapse of discipline.

The potentially harmful influence of American public opinion was contained although Britain's efforts to persuade the American government to refrain from a pro-Zionist policy were unsuccessful. The British managed to isolate Palestine from the general development of Anglo-American relations and, specifically, secure the all important Loan Agreement. More importantly, although Britain was unsuccessful in its appeal to the Zionists to moderate their aims, this was not disastrous for the long-term aims of British policy in the Middle East. In refusing to impose partition and in consulting the Arab states, Britain avoided the responsibility in Arab eyes for the creation of a Zionist state. Arguably, Britain maintained her dominant position in the Arab World until 1956. In real terms, no matter what the residual image of inglorious failure over Palestine, Anglo-Arab friendship and the Anglo-American relationship emerged from the end of the Mandate relatively unscathed.

Notes

1. PRO, FO371/56885/N6092/5169/38, Memorandum by Kirkpatrick, 15 May 1946.
2. PRO, FO800/480/MIS/471/52.
3. PRO, CAB129/2, CP(45)168, 13 September 1945. Bevin was sceptical and occasionally abusive when referring to Morrison's 'mishandling of information services', (Pimlott, 1986: 374).
4. PRO, CO875/20/8, memorandum by Sabine, 4 October 1944.
5. PRO, FO371/58685/N7816/5169/38, meeting of the Russia Committee, 11 June 1946; FO371/58685/N5169/5169/38, meeting of the Russia Committee, 2 April 1946.
6. PRO, CAB129/1, CP(45)130, 28 August 1945.
7. PRO, FO371/56887/N15609/5160/38, Kirkpatrick memorandum, 11 October 1946.
8. CAB131/2, DO(46)40, 13 March 1946.
9. The Tom Harrison Mass Observation Archive, Mass Observation Survey (2515), Report on Attitudes to Palestine and the Jews, September 1947. Mass Observation Survey (2411), Report on Anti-Semitism and Free Speech (2324), July 1946.
10. *Labour Party Conference Report 1944*, p. 9.
11. Cf. L. Dinnerstein, 'America, Britain and the Anglo-American Committee of Inquiry and the Displaced Persons, 1945–6', *Diplomatic History*, 4: 3(1980); FO934/5, vol. 5, Palestine Question, '54.
12. PRO, CAB129/2, CP(45)130, 28 August 1945; CAB128/1, CM(45)26, 30 August 1945.
13. PRO, FO371/45379/E6953/15/31, P(M)1st Meeting, Cabinet Committee on Palestine, 6 September 1945; CAB129/2, CP(45)156, 8 September 1945; CAB128/1, CM(45)30, 11 September 1945; CAB129/2, CP(45)196, 28 September 1945; CAB128/1, CM(45)40, 4 October 1945.
14. PRO, CAB128/1, CM(45)40, 4 October 1946.

15. PRO, FO371/45380/E7479/15/31, Foreign Office minute, October 1945; F[oreign] R[elations] U[nited] S[tates] 1945, vol. VIII, p. 749.
16. PRO, FO800/498/PRS/45/7, Washington to FO, Cable 7300, 1 November 1945.
17. PRO, FO800/498/PRS/45/13, Attlee to Bevin, 5 November 1945.
18. PRO, FO371/45382/E8055/15/31, FO to Cairo, Cable 1648, 20 October 1945.
19. PRO, FO371/45383/E8539/15/31, Washington to FO, Cable 7445, 7 November 1945.
20. Ibid.
21. PRO, FO371/45382/E8144/15/31, FO to Washington, Cable 10755, 26 October 1945.
22. PRO, FO371/45383/E8450/15/31; FO371/45383/E8593/15/31.
23. PRO, CAB128/2, CM(45)52, 13 November 1945.
24. *Hansard*, 13 November 1945; PRO, FO371/45384/E8742/15/31, Bevin's interview with American correspondents, 13 November 1945.
25. FRUS 1945, vol. VIII, p. 827.
26. FO371/45389/E9828/15/31, FO to Cairo, Cable 1971, 20 December 1945.
27. PRO, FO371/52509/E1185/4/31, minute by Wikeley, 9 February 1946; FO371/52510/E1462/4/31, Morgan and Wikeley minutes, 19 February 1946.
28. PRO, FO371/52511/E1725/4/31.
29. PRO, CAB128/5, CM(46)1, 1 January 1946.
30. PRO, CAB128/5, CM(46)3, 8 January 1946; FO800/498/PRS/46/2, Risdale to Bevin 8 January 1946; FO930/509/FP29, Gore to Dudley, 6 January 1946.
31. A summary of the recommendations of the Anglo-American Committee of Inquiry can be found in CAB129/11, CP(46)258, 8 July 1946.
32. PRO, CAB129/9, CP(46)173, 27 April 1946.
33. PRO, FO371/52514/E3057/4/31, Beeley to Baxter, 25 March 1946. CO537/1755, Joint Planning Staff report, 14 April 1946; Truman noted in his memoirs that 'the Joint Chiefs of Staff were also of the opinion that carrying out the findings of the report by force would prejudice British and US interest in the Middle East' (Truman, 1956, p. 159.)
34. PRO, FO371/52516/E3630/4/31, Washington to FO, Cable 2574, 22 April 1946; FO371/52514/E3057/4/31, Morgan minute, 5 April 1946.
35. PRO, FO371/52513/E2721/4/31, Palestine to CO, Cable 484, 23 March 1946.
36. PRO, FO371/52516/E3662/4/31, Washington to FO, Cable 2608, 23 April 1946; FO371/52516/E3666/4/31, FO to Washington, Cable 3745, 22 April 1946.
37. PRO, FO371/52517/E3850/4/31, Washington to FO, Cable 2712, 27 April 1946.
38. PRO, FO371/52517/E3757/4/31, Wikeley minute, 26 April 1946; FO371/52516/E3664/4/31, Bevin to FO, Cable 365, 23 April 1946; FO371/52517/E3757/4/31, Cairo to FO, Cable 734, 25 April 1946.
39. PRO, CAB128/5, CM(46)173, 27 April 1946.
40. PRO, FO371/52519/E3915/4/31, Washington to FO, Cable 2742, 30 April 1946.
41. PRO, FO371/52519/E3921/4/31, Bevin to Attlee, Cable 26, 1 May 1946.
42. *Hansard*, vol. 422, cols 195–7, 1 May 1946.
43. *Hansard*, vol. 422, cols 197–9, 1 May 1946; PRO, FO371/52519/E3956/4/31, FO to Cairo, Cable 888, 8 May 1946; FO371/52519/E3921/4/31, FO to Paris, Cable 44, 1 May 1946.
44. PRO, FO371/52520/E4034/4/31, Beirut to FO, Cable 394, 3 May 1946.
45. PRO, FO371/52523/E4358/4/31, Baghdad to FO, Cable 390, 10 May 1946.

46. PRO, FO371/52523/E4358/4/31, FO to Paris, Cable 247, 14 May 1946.
47. PRO, FO371/52526/E4922/4/31, Beirut to FO, Cable 472, 27 May 1946; FO371/52527/E5043/4/31, Beirut to FO, Cable 482, 31 May 1946; FO371/52527/E5227/4/31, Cairo to FO, Cable 212, 4 June 1946; FRUS 1946, vol. VII, pp. 620–2, 7 June 1946.
48. PRO, CAB128/5, CM(46)50, 29 May 1946.
49. Ibid.
50. PRO, FO371/52529/E5546/4/31, Transcript of Bevin's speech at Bournemouth, 12 June 1946.
51. PRO, FO371/52529/E5444/4/31, Washington to FO, Cable 3900, 13 June 1946.
52. PRO, FO371/52529/E5472/4/31, Washington to FO, Cable 3946, 14 June 1946.
53. PRO, FO371/52530/E5700/4/31 FO to Washington, Cable 6072, 20 June 1946.
54. PRO, CAB128/5, CM(46)60, 20 June 1946.
55. For details of the operation see PRO, WO275/27 and 29. PRO, FO371/52531/E5804/4/31, Martin (CO) to Beeley (FO), 23 June 1946; PRO, FO371/52531/E5804/4/31, CO 'Notes for guidance', undated.
56. FRUS 1946, vol. VII, p. 642, 2 July 1946.
57. PRO, FO371/52536/E6335/4/31, Bevin to FO, Cable 625, 6 July 1946; FO371/52539/E6606/4/31, Cairo to FO, Cable 1224, 11 July 1946; FO371/52539/E6607/4/31, Baghdad to FO, Cable 545, 12 July 1946.
58. PRO, FO371/52542/E6918/4/31, Washington to FO, Cable 4649, 20 July 1946.
59. PRO, FO371/52538/E6560/4/31, CO to Palestine, unnumbered, 10 July 1946; FO371/52538/E6569/4/31, Washington to FO, Cable 4506, 12 July 1946; CAB128/6, CM(46)66, 8 July 1946. The Loan was passed on 13 July by 219 to 155 votes, after leading Jewish Congressmen had argued that Palestine should not affect Anglo-American friendship.
60. See FRUS 1946, vol. VII, pp. 644–67; PRO, CAB129/11, CP(46)295. Plan approved by Cabinet on 25 July, CAB128/6, CM(46)73.
61. PRO, CAB128/6, CM(46)72, 23 July 1946.
62. Ibid.; *Hansard*, vol. 425, cols 1877–9, 23 July 1946.
63. PRO, FO371/52543/E6965/4/31, FO to Washington, Cable 7244, 22 July 1946; FRUS 1946, vol. VII, p. 651.
64. PRO, CAB128/6, CM(46)75, 30 July 1946; WO216/194, CIGS to CinCMELF, 3 August 1946.
65. PRO, FO371/52548/E7474/4/31, Washington to FO, Cable 4933, 3 August 1946; Ibid Rundall Minute, 10 August 1946.
66. PRO, FO371/52546/E7316/4/31, Washington to FO, Cable 4853, 30 July 1946; FRUS 1946, vol. VII, p. 682.
67. PRO, WO261/562, Fortnightly Intelligence Summary for 22 June to 4 August 1946, Part II, 'Attitude in England to the Palestine problem'; FO800/485/PA/46/77, Attlee to Bevin, 28 August 1946.
68. PRO, PREM8/627/Part 4, 'Note on the question of the admission to the Palestine Conference of Arab and Jewish leaders detained or liable to detention', meeting between Colonial Office and Foreign Office Officials, 26 August 1946.
69. PRO, FO371/52550/E7589/4/31; FO371/52551/E7720/4/31. Bevin voiced support for partition as early as July 1946. He foresaw a plan in which 'the major part of the Arab province would be attached to Transjordan and the Arab portion of Galilee to the Lebanon', CAB128/6, CM(46)67, 11 July 1946. See also

Glubb Pasha's memorandum, 'Partition of Palestine,' FO371/52547/E7371/4/31, 17 July 1946.

70. PREM8/627/Part 4, Parish to FO, Cable 607, 30 August 1946.
71. PRO, FO371/52642/E8914/8035/31, FO to Paris, Cable 1339, 5 September 1946.
72. PRO, FO371/52642/E8915/8035/31, Paris to FO, Cable 696, 5 September 1946.
73. PRO, FO371/52643/E9025/8035/31, Norman Brook to Hamilton, 2 September 1946 and subsequent minutes.
74. PRO, FO371/52553/E8106/4/31; FO371/52551/E7868/4/31 (see further, Shlaim, 1988, 73–87).
75. PRO, FO371/52556/E8885/4/31, Amman to FO, Cable 39, 27 August 1946; FO371/52530/E5657/4/31, Beirut to FO, Cable 559, 18 June 1946; FO371/52553/E8221/4/31, Jedda to FO, 19 August 1946.
76. PRO, PREM8/627/Part 4, CO to Palestine, unnumbered, 2 September 1946.
77. PRO, FO371/52643/E9119/8035/31, Henniker to Beeley, 8 September 1946.
78. PRO, FO371/52643/E9121/8035/31, Attlee's Speech, 10 September 1946.
79. PRO, FO371/52643/E9122/8035/31, transcript of the second meeting of the Palestine Conference, 11 September 1946.
80. PRO, FO371/52558/E9220/4/31, record of Furlonge's meeting with the Lebanese Prime Minister, 14 September 1946; FO371/52558/E915/4/31, Istanbul to FO, Cable 71, 15 September 1946.
81. See PRO, FO371/52643–5.
82. PRO, FO371/52644/E9391/8035/31, Transcript of the sixth meeting, 20 September 1946.
83. Ibid.; FO371/52644–5.
84. PRO, FO371/52644/E9394/8035/31, CO to Palestine, Cable 1870, 2 October 1946.
85. PRO, PREM8/627/Part 5, Bevin–Hall–Goldman meeting, 14 September 1946.
86. PRO, FO371/52645/E9692/8035/31, Palestine to CO, Cable 1567, 25 September 1946.
87. PRO, FO371/52560/E10030/4/31, transcript of meeting, 1 October 1946; FO371/52560/E9948/4/31, CO to Palestine, Cable 1863, 1 October 1946.
88. FRUS, 1946, vol. VII, pp. 700–1.
89. PRO, PREM8/627/Part 5, Attlee to Truman, 4 October 1946.
90. PRO, FO371/52561/E10164/4/31, FO to Washington, Cable 9560, 4 October 1946.
91. PRO, FO371/52653/E10911/4/31, Beeley to Dixon, 13 November 1946; PREM8/627/Part 5, CO to Palestine, Cable 1932, 10 October 1946.
92. PRO, CAB128/6, CM(46)91, 25 October 1946.
93. PRO, FO371/52562/E10668/4/31, Howe memorandum on Clayton and partition, 23 October 1946.
94. PRO, FO371/52646/E11259/8035/31, New York to FO, Cable 1685, 15 November 1946; FO371/52646/E11893/8035/31, New York to FO, Cable 2273, 4 December 1946.
95. PRO, CAB131/3, DO(46)145, 19 December 1946.
96. PRO, FO371/61761/E74/46/31, FO minute for Attlee, 23 December 1946.
97. PRO, CAB129/16, CP(47)32, 16 January 1947; FO371/61858/E877/115/31, Howe to Bevin, 21 January 1947.

98. PRO, CAB128/11, CM(47)11, 22 January 1947.
99. PRO, FO371/61747/E1121/2/31, transcript of 10th meeting, 4 February 1947.
100. PRO, FO371/61748/E1358/11/31, Henniker minute, 8 February 1947.
101. *Hansard*, vol. 432, col. 1778, 6 February 1947.
102. PRO, FO371/61765/E1210/46/31, Washington to FO, Cable 786, 6 February 1947; FO to Washington, Cable 1204, 8 February 1947.
103. PRO, FO371/61748/E1358/11/31, Henniker minute, 8 February 1947; FO371/61765/E1256/65/31, Washington to FO, Cable 832, 8 February 1947.
104. PRO, CAB129/17, CP(47)49, 6 February 1947; CAB128/9, CM(47)18, 7 February 1947.
105. PRO, FO371/61874/E1328/2/31, DO to Ottawa, Cable 146, 14 February 1947; FO371/61874/E328/2/31, Arab states to HMG, 10 February 1947.
106. PRO, CAB129/17, CP(47)59, 13 February 1947.
107. PRO, CAB128/9, CM(47)22, 14 February 1947.
108. PRO, PREM8/627/Part 6, Brook to Attlee, 14 February 1947.
109. PRO, FO371/61749/E1581/49/31, draft statement for the House of Commons, 15 February 1947.
110. PRO, FO371/61767/E1560/46/31, Amman to FO, Cable 51, 19 February 1946.
111. FRUS, 1947, vol. 5, p. 1049.
112. *Hansard*, vol. 443, col. 2007, 25 February, 1947.

References

Adamthwaite, A. (1985), 'Britain and the world, 1945–9: the view from the Foreign Office', *International Affairs*, 61: 2, 1985.

Bethell, N. (1980), *Palestine Triangle*. London, Futura.

Bullock, A. (1985), *Ernest Bevin Foreign Secretary*. Oxford, Oxford University Press.

Crossman, R.H.S. (1946), *Palestine Mission*. London, Hamilton.

Dinnerstein, L. (1980), 'America, Britain and the Anglo-American Committee of Inquiry and the Displaced Persons, 1945–6', *Diplomatic History*, 4: 3, 1980.

Eban, A. (1977), *An Autobiography*. New York, Random House.

Gallup, G. (1976), *The Gallup International Public Opinion Polls: Great Britain, 1937–1975*, vol. I, *1937–1964*. New York, Random House.

Morgan, K. O. (1989), *Labour People, Leaders and Lieutenants: Hardie to Kinnock*. Oxford, Oxford University Press.

Partner, P. (1988), *Arab Voices*. London, BBC Publications.

Pimlott, B. (1986), *The Political Diaries of Hugh Dalton, 1918–40 and 1945–60*. London, Cape.

Shlaim, A. (1988), *Collusion Across the Jordan*. Oxford, Clarendon Press.

Smith, R. and Zametica, J. (1985), 'The Cold Warrior: Clement Attlee reconsidered, 1945–47', *International Affairs*, 1985.

Taylor, P.M. (1989), 'The projection of Britain abroad, 1945–51', in M. Dockrill and J.W. Young (eds), *British Foreign Policy, 1945–56*. London, Macmillan.

Truman, H. (1956), *Years of Trial and Hope, 1945–53*. London, Hodder and Stoughton.

United States Department of State, *Foreign Relations of the United States*. Washington, Government Printing Office, various dates.

12 Unquiet in death: the post-war survival of the 'Special Operations Executive', 1945-51

Richard Aldrich

Introduction

Research into the history of the last years of the Special Operations Executive (SOE), Britain's wartime sabotage organization, can be a frustrating process for all but the official historian. The surviving records of SOE are closed to public inspection and are unlikely to be released in the foreseeable future.[1] Consequently, a logical starting-point for any inquiry into the post-war fate of this organization might be a survey of the writings of official historians. This survey will not detain us long.

Curiously, official accounts of SOE's wartime activities do not pass much beyond 1944. For example, while Professor Hinsley's official account of the impact of intelligence on British wartime operations examines SOE's contributions to intelligence during 1943 and 1944 in detail, SOE is barely mentioned in the context of 1945 (Hinsley *et al.*, 1981 and 1988). The same is true of Charles Cruickshank's account of SOE in the Far East, where one might expect extensive coverage of the last days of SOE in the context of a conflict stretching into August 1945 (Cruickshank, 1983). Only in Professor Foot's work on France do we find any reference to the end of SOE. A single sentence records that Ernest Bevin 'himself signed SOE's death warrant on lines laid down by Eden in 1945' while a chronological table, indicates that SOE was 'disbanded' in January 1946 (Foot, 1966: 443).[2]

The contention of this chapter is that such official references to 'death warrants' and the 'disbandment' of SOE in the winter of 1945/6 are inappropriate and in some senses misleading.[3] On the contrary, many components of SOE marched out of the Second World War into the Cold War without breaking step. Furthermore, SOE's survival facilitated strong continuities between British special operations in wartime and in the post-war period that can be traced in terms of distinct operational doctrines, experience and personnel. Therefore, far from suffering abrupt termination, SOE enjoyed an active and influential afterlife in the years 1945–51 that is of significance for our wider understanding of the development of the post-war British intelligence community.[4]

However, before proceeding with a detailed discussion of the fate of SOE, it is worth pausing briefly to consider the general importance of intelligence and clandestine activities in relation to the formulation and execution of British high policy. Certainly few would now dispute the significance of intelligence in the Second World War, particularly given the demonstrable impact of Ultra upon the grand strategy of the Allied powers (Hinsley *et al.*, 1981 and 1988; Lewin, 1978; Bennett, 1979 and 1989). But special operations in the post-war period are not quite the same thing. One might be forgiven for questioning the wider historical significance of, for example, a few men in woolly hats leaping in and out of a rubber boat on the coast of Albania in 1949. Some respected historians, notably Herbert Butterfield, have developed *a priori* arguments suggesting that any area that governments are anxious to close to public inspection must necessarily be significant, otherwise it would not be closed (Butterfield, 1951: 186).[5] Furthermore, they advance the proposition that if such an area is investigated successfully, considerable light will be thrown upon policy. However, practical experience demonstrates that such generalizations are far wide of the mark. So often collections of closed papers, when finally released, prove to be remarkable only for the extreme dullness of their contents. Worse than this, *a priori* assumptions about the closure of papers can serve to encourage historians in a misplaced search for conspiracies that may have no counterpart in historical reality.

Rather than attempting to substantiate such general arguments regarding the more secret aspects of policy, it seems more useful to advance five specific points concerning the nature of British special operations in the post-war period.

First, it is sometimes suggested that clandestine activities, including covert propaganda, loomed large within the early Cold War because they were peculiarly suited to a Cold War conflict that involved the pursuit of objectives 'by all means short of war'.[6] Undoubtedly, this argument, often deployed to explain the post-war growth of intelligence communities, has much force. This interpretation has also served, however, to obscure the equal significance of organizational and doctrinal momentum bequeathed by the Second World War. Most clandestine services operating in the late 1940s were not new organizations and indeed British, and even American, clandestine services shrank rather than expanded between 1945 and 1947.[7] The well-known dictum of the British Chiefs of Staff (COS) during this period that in the event of war Britain would have to fight with what she had, applied as much to SOE as anything else.[8] Therefore, special operations formed part of Britain's post-war overseas policy partly because, as in the parallel case of clandestine propaganda, by 1945 a large body of expertise was available in this area. In this sense British post-war activities were very much shaped by the previous conflict.

Second, bureaucratic continuity had a significant impact upon the particular sort of operations that were attempted. Because some components of SOE came under the control of the Secret Intelligence Service (SIS) in January 1946, British post-war special operations, for good reason, often employed experienced SOE personnel in familiar areas with well-tried wartime techniques and objectives, typically in south-east Europe. Some of this activity made use of contacts established during SOE's previous operations in these countries.[9]

Third, bureaucratic continuity also helped to preserve a temperamental dislike on the part of the wartime Foreign Office for special operations. This antipathy had owed much to SOE's tendency to develop its own independent foreign policy in some regions. The continuity of this diplomatic aversion to SOE and all its works contributed much to the national style of Britain's post-war clandestine community. British diplomats remained hesitant and uncomfortable when presented with the option of covert activities in the late 1940s. This persistent disquiet assists in explaining why Britain cannot be said to have a particularly activist tradition when compared with parallel intelligence communities in the United States, France or the Soviet Union.

Fourth, in the context of both the Cold War and the end of Empire, SOE's legacy consisted of problems for British overseas policy as much as solutions. As early as December 1944 British troops in Greece joined battle with partisans that had been armed or trained by SOE. Thereafter British troops would meet similar difficulties in Burma, Indochina, Malaya and elsewhere. These insurgents, although one of SOE's most important post-war legacies, cannot be considered within the scope of this chapter. Nevertheless, the dividing line between SOE and their all too persistent protégés was not always a clear one. In 1948 senior British ex-SOE officers cut loose from British authority altogether, transferring their allegiance to local insurgents in direct opposition to mainstream British policy. Meanwhile, in both Palestine and Malaya, SOE officers were called in to redress the balance by launching their own special operations in a counterinsurgency context. In this sense SOE contributed strongly to a rather neglected tradition of post-war special operations in British colonial territories. They achieved this by being both part of the problem and part of the solution.

Finally, in the light of new evidence advanced by historians working on Soviet policy in Eastern Europe, it might be suggested that our picture of some of the better-known British post-war special operations in Eastern Europe stands in need of substantial revision. In rehearsing the familiar caricature of 'unprofessional' and badly penetrated British operations in Albania and elsewhere, somewhat sensationalized accounts have tended to overlook the volatile Soviet over-reaction to both British and American special operations which resulted in considerable turmoil in Eastern Europe.[10] The remainder of the chapter will discuss the arguments outlined above in relation to the limited documentation presently open to public inspection in Britain and elsewhere.

Whitehall and the post-war future of SOE, 1945–6

It now seems to be firmly established that well before the end of the Second World War in Europe the British COS and their subordinates were busily engaged with planning for three different sorts of conflict. The COS were preparing for the war against Germany and Japan. Other planners were considering post-war strategic requirements against the possible threat of the Soviet Union. Yet others were preparing for a bitter post-war conflict with the Treasury on the question of defence spending (Lewis, 1988; Rothwell, 1982: 114–23; Kitchen, 1986:198–204; Baylis, 1983). By late 1944 the COS had requested the views of many different bodies on the future of SOE in relation to these three different forms of forward planning. Meanwhile, the question of SOE's immediate future and of its relations with SIS were delegated in 1945 to an *ad hoc* committee under Victor Cavendish-Bentinck, Chairman of the Joint Intelligence Committee.[11]

Cavendish-Bentinck's inquiry was conducted with some regard to Whitehall politics. There was little consideration of the military requirements generated by the last year of the war, or of the possible value of SOE in the context of some future Soviet threat. The latter may have been partly due to SOE's own wartime relations with the Soviet Union, which had often been rather better than those established by some of the Service ministries. For example, the diary of Sir Alexander Cadogan, wartime Permanent Under-Secretary at the Foreign Office, along with other sources, record Foreign Office approval for a number of joint SOE–NKVD operations into occupied Western Europe.[12] During 1944, the COS urged SOE not to demand reciprocity for facilitating NKVD liaison missions in south-east Europe. Meanwhile SOE allowed the NKVD to veto its plans to subvert Soviet citizens belonging to Vlasov's Liberation Army and other German-controlled organizations.[13] There were certainly difficulties later in the war over Czechoslovakia, Hungary and Poland, but even in Poland, the COS and SOE were anxious to co-operate closely with the NKVD. Therefore SOE's wartime legacy contained some strong elements of Anglo-Soviet co-operation.[14]

The discussions held by Cavendish-Bentinck's *ad hock* committee reflected the determination of SIS, the COS and especially the Foreign Office to establish the sort of firm control and co-ordination over special operations that had hitherto been noticeably absent. SOE's tendency to play a 'semi-lone hand' and to develop its 'own foreign policy' during the war had resulted in a great deal of administrative friction both in Whitehall and at the headquarters level of the major operational theatres of war.[15] Consequently, in 1945, Cavendish-Bentinck found no shortage of prominent personalities eager to offer frank testimony on how special operations should be restructured and controlled in the post-war period. Foreign Office disdain for clandestine activities was typified by Esler Dening, the Senior Foreign Office representative in south-east Asia. In May 1945 he informed Cavendish-Bentinck that relations between SOE and SIS 'have reached the point where one rather despairs of their working together at all', adding that if the Supreme Commander in South East Asia, Admiral Lord Louis Mountbatten, had not imposed a special arbitrating committee upon them both, 'they would not do so'. Dening confessed that he did not know what the answer to these difficulties was but felt it lay in reform at the centre in London, rather than in the Far East. Maverick political operations by both SOE and SIS, which had not been co-ordinated with the Foreign Office at any level, had caused Dening much anxiety in the latter stages of the war. Consequently he added that 'reforms will be much appreciated by all of us who for our sins are in frequent contact with these organisations'.[16]

Intelligence chiefs in the same region joined Foreign Office officials in advocating the end of SOE as a separate organization, albeit from a more partisan perspective. In May 1945 Mountbatten's Director of Intelligence in South East Asia Command, Brigadier Penney, wrote to the Secretary of the COS Committee in London confirming Dening's view that a multiplicity of clandestine organizations had resulted in 'too much back-biting on all sides'. But Penney also expressed anxiety that special operations 'with its promise of action' tended to appeal to high-level commanders and thus triumphed over the 'less spectacular but none the less necessary claims of intelligence proper'. Elaborating on this point he expressed the deepest regret that Military Intelligence and SIS had lost their joint responsibility for special operations in 1940. Instead, small components had been taken from these two bodies to form a nucleus that then become SOE, a separate and independent establishment responsible to the Ministry of Economic Warfare under Hugh Dalton. 'Inevitably,' Penney lamented, 'SOE came into being in *other* than a Service Ministry, where imagination was welcomed and allowed to have full play, and where resources were readily obtainable. It is hoped that this will never occur again.'[17]

In the Middle East, where the SOE wartime experience had been far from happy, the same dissatisfaction was evinced at a high level (Smith, 1983: 81). On 13 March 1945 John Slessor, Deputy Commander of the Allied Air Forces in the Mediterranean, confessed that 'the intelligence set-up in Cairo is a mess'. There were, he insisted, 'far too many different agencies and organisations, all with direct access to the great, too often crossing each others wires and cutting each others throats'. Slessor was aware that after the war, Whitehall would 'have time to sit back and consider their post war organisation' and so decided to advance his own firm prescription:

> Of course, the real answer, I am sure to all this is a drastic reorganisation at the top of all our Secret and Underground Services SIS, SOE, 'A' Force [deception], and PWE [propaganda], all as inter-related branches of one service under a single head who would be an associate member of the Chiefs of Staff Committee.[18]

The view from Europe was equally hostile to the prospect of SOE's survival as an independent establishment, for wartime bureaucratic difficulties in this area had also been intense. Relations between SOE, SIS and other clandestine organizations had been marked by competition for scarce air transport and mutual accusations of enemy penetration. By February 1944 Churchill was moved to complain of 'the warfare between S.O.E. and S.I.S. which is a lamentable, but perhaps inevitable, feature of our affairs'. This turbulence resulted in attempts to place SOE directly under the authority of the Foreign Office or the COS.[19] Therefore in 1945, while detailed prescriptions offered by individuals differed, the general recommendations reflected a strong diplomatic and military consensus. The universal recommendation was for much closer control of special operations, ideally through the amalgamation of SOE and numerous other clandestine bodies.

It was not in the nature of SOE to be amalgamated or abolished without resistance. The Director of SOE, Sir Colin Gubbins, and his Deputy, Harry Sporborg, were painfully aware that SOE had made few allies in Whitehall in the course of the war and so pressed the COS for SOE to be assessed on military as well as administrative criteria. Consequently, with encouragement from Gubbins, the COS set up a separate 'SOE Evaluation Committee' in May 1945 whose purpose 'was to obtain from the [Regional] Commanders in Chief an unbiased opinion of the SOE organisation'.[20] The papers solicited from Regional Commanders were voluminous and therefore their analysis lies beyond the scope of this chapter. However, it should be noted that while some of these reports spoke highly of the military value of SOE, they echoed parallel submissions to Cavendish-Bentinck's Committee in calling for closer co-ordination and control at every level.[21] Together, the two committees and their inquiries offer a representative overview of high-level opinion amongst many of those that had dealt with SOE during the war. Nevertheless, it should be noted that they did not represent all the thinking devoted to post-war special operations at this time. Typically, the War Office was about to begin its own investigation into special operations and their relation to SIS activities, while at a higher level, Sir Findlater Stewart chaired a committee tasked with revising Whitehall's entire intelligence structure in the context of the forthcoming reforms leading to the amalgamation of the three Service Ministries to form the Ministry of Defence.[22]

In retrospect, it appears that this Byzantine committee structure and its voluminous papers provided no more than background briefs for those who took the formal decisions regarding the future of SOE in London during the winter of 1945–6. The diary of the Chief of the Imperial General Staff, Field Marshal Sir Alan Brooke, reveals that these decisions were taken in mid-January 1946 after much informal discussion at a high level. He recorded:

Our morning COS [meeting] was attended by Caccia of the Foreign Office [the new Chairman of the Joint Intelligence Committee] and by Menzies [the Chief of

SIS] to discuss the future of the Subversive Operations Executive [*sic*]. I had discussed this matter on the previous evening with Sinclair [the Vice Chief] and had decided that by amalgamating the Secret Intelligence Service with SOE, we could provide a combined organisation that would function automatically in Peace and War. I succeeded in getting my plan accepted by all.[23]

As well as revealing the key figures in this decision and the partly informal way in which it was reached, Brooke's diary confirms that SOE was amalgamated with SIS rather than abolished. The meaning of this in terms of the distribution of power between SOE and SIS was illustrated more clearly by the minutes of a COS meeting a few days earlier, which heard 'that the amalgamation of SOE and SIS had taken effect from 15 January and that the Special Operations Branch of the Secret Service was now under the Command of "C" [the Chief of SIS]'.[24] Therefore, at the centre in London, SOE had been disbanded as a separate organization. While a remnant of SOE survived, it now constituted a mere subordinate section of SIS.

Independent SOE stations in Europe and Asia, 1945–7

Although in London SOE no longer survived independently, at the regional level the situation was quite different. Initially, the COS appeared anxious to wind up SOE's regional stations, if only for reasons of manpower economy. However, between 1945 and 1947, as the COS and regional headquarters began to face difficult and often unexpected post-war occupational tasks, it quickly became apparent that some of SOE's large regional components were simply too valuable to dispense with. Contemporaneously, SOE personnel within various regional commands worked actively to prolong their existence. As a result, some regional SOE organizations managed to survive until 1947, independent of and often in parallel with SIS representation. This regional survival was achieved in the face of strong Foreign Office opposition.

In July 1945 British representatives at Eisenhower's Allied Forces Headquarters (AFHQ) in Europe requested permission 'to stop all SOE activities in Austria'. British Troops Austria, the local British military command responsible for this area, argued that all clandestine activities could now be performed by their own military counterintelligence and security units and wished to avoid the possibility of 'duplication and confusion' presented by the continued presence of SOE. This initiative received warm support from the Foreign Office. However, in London SOE's Deputy Director, Harry Sporborg, pleaded for clemency, suggesting that SOE should be permitted to stay 'so that our contacts in Austria which have been built up over the past few years should not be lost'. Sporborg's argument caught the imagination of the COS and they agreed that it was 'unwise, with Europe in her present unsettled state, to lose these valuable SOE contacts'. Therefore, AFHQ was ordered to retain an SOE station in Austria.[25] Notwithstanding this firm directive from the COS, at a local level British Troops Austria were determined to impede the surviving SOE station, ordering them to hand over all information on their Austrian contacts forthwith and to end their own secure communications link with London. SOE were then diverted from their network of Austrian agents to conducting routine interrogations with prisoners in security compounds.[26]

In September 1945 the COS came to hear of SOE's treatment in Austria and were mortified. They recognized that in this routine security work the identity of SOE officers would be 'personally completely compromised'. They also noted that SOE's high-level contacts in Austria 'could only be approached in special ways', for their allegiance had been 'hard to obtain and certainly cannot be transferred at will'. The COS added that if these Austrian contacts were compromised by British Troops Austria, 'not only would their usefulness be destroyed but in many cases their lives would be endangered'. Accordingly, on 24 September 1945 the COS reprimanded British Troops Austria and instructed SOE's remaining 24 personnel in Austria to resume work on their 'long term role'.[27]

The Foreign Office were dismayed by SOE's post-war survival in Austria. In October 1945 Robin Hankey, about to become Head of the Northern Department, warned gravely: 'We have to watch our step in Austria particularly. The Russians are watching us and we must be particularly careful not to allow any activities of the cloak and dagger variety to continue under our auspices'. Hankey stated bluntly that he did not believe there was any work for SOE in Austria to do and that they were 'prolonging their lives unnecessarily'. Moreover, he feared that if they remained, eventually they 'would find work to do' with 'the most dangerous repercussions'. Hankey was particularly troubled by the specific wording of the COS directive to SOE Austria which referred to 'primary operational tasks'. 'I do not know what they mean,' Hankey noted, voicing his suspicion that the COS directive implied much more than merely 'maintaining certain contacts'.[28] Hankey's fears were well grounded. The military file on this matter, to which Hankey was not privy, contains a letter to the Director of Military Intelligence (DMI) detailing a sensitive operation designed to acquire some files which were considered to be 'most valuable'. The letter speaks unambiguously of 'the "lifting" of the material from the Russian Zone'.[29] Despite Hankey's protests it appears SOE were still operating alongside SIS in Austria in early 1946.[30]

Significantly, the survival of SOE in Austria was an example of a wider phenomenon in Western Europe, rather than a mere isolated anomaly. During the same period the Foreign Office were protesting about a similar SOE unit that had survived in Germany under the British Army of the Rhine. This SOE unit had been attached to the Military Intelligence component of Montgomery's 21st Army Group in May 1945. Again the COS would give the Foreign Office no details of what they called SOE's 'extremely useful work', but in October 1945 Robin Hankey voiced his conviction that it was of a 'dangerous political character'.[31]

In the Mediterranean and the Middle East, where active hostilities had long since ceased, the Foreign Office succeeded in abolishing SOE almost entirely. The only voices in favour of SOE were ambassadors who wished to retain single personnel from SOE, or their related clandestine propaganda service, PWE, to continue propaganda work into the post-war period. Typically, in June 1945 Sir Roger Bullard at Teheran stated that 'only one of the present SOE staff will be required—Dr Zaehner, whose chief function is that of bribing the Persian press'.[32] Dr Zaehner therefore remained in Teheran under the cover of press attaché until 1947, returning in 1951 to head the 'Zaehner Mission' as a preliminary to the Anglo-American overthrow of the Mossadegh Government in 1953.[33] Nevertheless, Zaehner was an exception, for Lord Killearn, the Minister Resident in the Middle East, sided with the Foreign Office in resisting the continued presence of even single SOE officers. Expressing a preference for SIS, he argued that SOE were not good at propaganda, and added:

> As regards their other activities, in other words the payment of baksheesh, I'm not myself convinced that we, the Embassy, couldn't do the job adequately well.... I have always disliked SOE playing a semi-lone hand as they have done during this war.... As you know we already have our SS [secret service] arrangements here which work well and adequately.[34]

In London, Orme Sargent echoed Killearn's sentiments. By late 1945, SOE's regional headquarters in Cairo had been closed, although some evidence suggests that SOE remained in the Mediterranean to assist regular British forces against guerrillas in Greece as late as 1948.[35]

The Middle East was the only region where SOE failed to perpetuate its existence on a large scale, for the Foreign Office did not get their way in Asia. Here, with the active support of Mountbatten (a confirmed special operations enthusiast of the boyish sort), SOE contrived to retain literally hundreds of personnel and was still operating in Indonesia and on the Thai–Indochina border in 1947. Mountbatten based his case for retaining SOE upon requirements arising out of the unstable post-war conditions prevailing in Burma, Malaya, Indochina and Indonesia.[36] Reports prepared in March 1946 show clearly that he had succeeded in retaining 549 SOE personnel, about half their wartime strength in Asia.[37] These numbers are startling when it is considered that even at the height of the war, their parallel service, SIS, had only 86 personnel in this region.[38] Consequently, even in 1947, SOE, not SIS, was the predominant British clandestine service in Asia. Its activities were so extensive that they can barely be touched on here. They included attempting to disarm and control guerrillas in Malaya; assisting the French Secret Service against the Vietminh in French Indochina; and conducting curious clandestine currency transactions on behalf of the British Government in China. Above all they provided a comprehensive intelligence screen across an area that was geographically vast and politically volatile.[39] Mountbatten was at pains to disguise the survival of SOE in Asia from inquisitive authorities in London. He changed SOE's regional cover name from the wartime 'Force 136' to 'Para-Military Operations' (PMO) and subordinated it to his own headquarters.[40] Few in London had heard of this new PMO organization and so, overlooked in bureaucratic struggles at the centre, Mountbatten and his successors retained SOE as their own regional intelligence and special operations service.

Consequently, SOE's extensive post-war activities at the regional level offered a sharp contrast to its vestigial survival in London, subordinated to a rival service. The awkward problems of post-war administration in the period 1945-7 ensured the survival of sizeable stations against the wishes of the Foreign Office, thereby facilitating neglected continuities of structure, personnel and doctrine after the Second World War. Yet paradoxically, in remaining active beyond 1945, assorted remnants of SOE sometimes served to confirm the arguments advanced by the Foreign Office in favour of their abolition. Diplomats repeatedly expressed the view that clandestine organizations were temperamentally wayward and inclined to develop ideas that cut across the mainstream British overseas policies of more orthodox departments. This view was confirmed by a number of episodes and can be illustrated by a brief examination of the role of 'renegade' ex-SOE officers operating in Burma during 1948 and 1949.

'A law unto themselves': SOE in Burma, 1948-9

Because surviving SOE stations were usually subordinated within regional command structures in Europe, the Mediterranean and Asia in the immediate post-war period, they often succeeded in escaping the attention of inquisitive and unsympathetic officials in London. There were, however, exceptions to this pattern. In 1948 and 1949 the activities of an élite unit of ex-SOE personnel in Burma had the gravest repercussions for British policy in south Asia. This unit was an entirely renegade SOE station and included two staff officers with the rank of colonel. Their operations, conducted quite independently of any central or regional direction by the British government, served to reinforce the reservations of the Foreign Office concerning clandestine organizations and their intrinsically maverick qualities.

On 4 January 1948 Burma became a newly independent state. At that time and thereafter no British-controlled sections of SOE were operating in that country. However, in common with other states, the government was troubled by guerrilla forces consisting of distinct ethnic groups that had been armed and trained by SOE during the war against Japan. The strongest of these groups were the Karens, occupying much of eastern Burma. Since the declaration of independence a British Military Mission had been in Rangoon to assist the

Burmese Army who were fighting the Karen insurgents. The presence of the mission reflected the generally good state of relations between the Socialist government of Burma and the Attlee government in London.

Barely a month after independence the Burmese Prime Minister informed the British ambassador in Rangoon, Sir James Bowker, that rumours persisted of British SOE officers assisting the Karen rebels against the Burmese government. Bowker assured the Prime Minister that the rumours were 'fantastic'. However, he subsequently learned that the Burmese government had intercepted correspondence between the Karens and a certain Colonel Tulloch, commander of SOE's most successful wartime operations in Burma.[41] At the Foreign Office in London this information caught the eye of Esler Dening, now Assistant Under-Secretary superintending British policy in Asia. Dening's wartime service with Mountbatten in South East Asia Command, where he had had regular dealings with SOE, ensured that he was uniquely qualified to appreciate the awful possibilities offered by this situation. SOE personnel, he believed, were by their very nature a 'law unto themselves' and so it was 'not surprising' that they should turn against British policy.[42] Colonel Tulloch, if he existed, was simply taking SOE's wartime penchant for independent foreign policy-making to its logical conclusion.

Nearly six months later, on 17 August 1948, Dening received a telephone call from the editor of a leading daily newspaper who stated simply that he wished to make an important introduction. That evening, in a bar close to Whitehall, Dening was introduced to Colonel Tulloch. The Colonel advanced the argument that the present government of Burma was unstable and drifting towards communism. With his help the Karens, who leaned to the Right, planned not to secede from Burma but to take over the whole country. The present Burmese Minister of Defence, he maintained, was in the plot along with a variety of interests that he could not name. He had also made an approach to the Americans but had been rebuffed. Dening expressed the strongest possible objections and warned that steps would be taken to put an end to Tulloch's activities.[43] An embarrassed Dening reported this irregular meeting to Ernest Bevin, complaining that the affair had been 'contrived' and 'thrust upon' him.[44] To his dismay he was drawn into a further unorthodox encounter only the next day. Dening minuted: 'Today I have been rung up by Mr Abrahams, Managing Director of the Burmah Oil Company, who has asked me, somewhat mysteriously, to meet him outside the Office to discuss a question connected with the Karens.' The minutes of this meeting, and much of the remaining file are not presently open to public inspection.[45]

By late August 1948 accelerating violence in Burma had persuaded the Foreign Office to warn the Burmese Prime Minister of Tulloch's unorthodox activities.[46] By late 1948 the Karens had captured much of central Burma. They were receiving significant air drops of arms from airbases in India and Thailand and there had been numerous sightings of SOE personnel with the Karens. Meanwhile the British Military Mission were assisting the Burmese government against the Karen rebels by employing aircraft for ground attack and photographic reconnaissance. In doing so they had come upon information of involvement by Americans and Australians with the Karens.[47] As the major city of Moulmein fell to the Karens an anxious Bevin enquired, 'What steps are being taken?' However, Colonel Tulloch had now left Burma for Calcutta where he was arranging further supplies. Bevin's officials replied, 'don't see what we can do to Tulloch in Calcutta'[48]

The Burmese government were more energetic. On 21 September 1948 the Burmese Special Branch arrested a lieutenant-colonel in Rangoon who had served in SOE under Tulloch during the war and recovered documents which revealed him as the link-man in Burma.[49] The Foreign Office wished to avoid a public scandal in South Asia that would link rebel activity against the socialist government of newly independent Burma with the British government and SOE.[50] Such a scandal would badly damage the image that Britain was attempting to project in South Asia, of a liberal power in retreat from empire. It would undermine Britain's attempts to project the message that the dangers for countries in this region lay not in imperialism, but in communism and even non-alignment.[51]

Meanwhile, the Foreign Office turned their attention to Calcutta. Here Colonel Tulloch, under close surveillance by the Indian Special Branch, was operating from a hotel that he left only at night. Reports suggested that he was arranging further arms and finance and that he had organized air transport to deliver further SOE personnel to Burma.[52] Yet the Foreign Office did not dare press the Indian government for his arrest for fear that the episode would explode in the press.[53] After a particularly rigorous police search of his accommodation, Tulloch finally confessed that things in Calcutta were now 'too hot' for him and he agreed to return to Britain in exchange for immunity from prosecution. Subsequently he treated John Shattock and other officials at the British High Commission in Delhi to a partial exposé of his activities, hinting at British commercial support and insisting that his removal would not affect the activities of the renegade SOE station. Tulloch also expressed disgust at Ernest Bevin whom he had previously contrived to meet in London. He claimed that:

> In spite of the 'young nitwits' in the Foreign Office and Bevin's ignorance about South East Asia, he could guarantee to stamp out Moscow's sphere of influence in South East Asia so long as he was provided with the best part of £1 million Sterling.[54]

The impact of SOE's activities upon Britain's position in Burma became clear only in October 1948 as the arrest of the SOE colonel in Rangoon exploded in the Burmese press. The serious newspapers speculated about Churchill's involvement while the popular journals led with headlines such as 'The Expansionist Scheme to re-annex Burma' and even 'Dirty Scheme of the

Bastards'. Worse still, airdrops of arms and sightings of SOE personnel with the Karens continued to be reported as the rebels made advances in 1949. Further British subjects were arrested in 1950.[55] The low point for British policy probably occurred in the spring of 1949 when the Burmese government was close to defeat and held little territory outside Rangoon. A junior Foreign Office official asked bravely 'I wonder what Tulloch is up to now. His friends may soon be the official Government [of Burma].... Do we start to curry favour with him?'. His superior dismissed this idea as 'premature'.[56] Britain suffered further related embarrassments during 1950 for while the Burmese Government remained in control of Rangoon, the Prime Minister dismissed the large British Military Mission, suspecting them also of complicity with the Karen rebels.[57]

Britain's credibility in Burma had been damaged by an 'SOE' episode over which she had no direct control. At a wider level this was symptomatic of various difficulties that confirmed the distaste of senior officials within the Foreign Office for special operations. As early as November 1941 Anthony Eden as Foreign Secretary had written of SOE's activities in Asia: 'I must know about this organisation that makes our ambassador's life a misery and vitiates my policy and they must come under direct Foreign Office control. The present situation is intolerable'.[58] In 1948 and 1949 the same people were causing similar irritation within the Foreign Office and appeared to be reinforcing a long-standing aversion to covert activities.

Two patterns of post-war operations, 1947–51

In the light of Foreign Office opposition to the survival of SOE and its disquiet at various associated post-war activities, it is in some ways surprising that British diplomats gave their assent to any special operations during the late 1940s. The impetus for such activities undertaken by the British government from 1947 can be explained partly by difficulties in the colonial territories and partly by the accelerating pace of the Cold War. These confrontations created new opportunities which tended to be pursued more avidly by the Colonial Office and the COS than by the Foreign Office. Even within the Foreign Office one can detect an initial desire to stay in step with the United States which was expanding its own programme of clandestine activities during the 1940s. Notwithstanding this Anglo-American impetus, diplomatic enthusiasm for special operations after 1947 was short-lived, often because of disagreements between London and Washington over the precise objectives of such activities. Against the background of this continued Foreign Office reticence, it will be suggested that two distinct patterns of British special operations were emerging in the late 1940s: first, subversive operations against the Eastern bloc, and second, counterinsurgency operations in British colonial territories in the Middle East and Asia. Both of these patterns owed much to the wartime legacy of SOE.

During 1948 Britain and the United States achieved a measure of agreement regarding peacetime special operations with *émigré* groups against the Eastern bloc. The target areas appear to have included Albania, Yugoslavia, the Baltic states and the Soviet Ukraine. Popular espionage history has tended to portray these episodes as SIS operations in isolation from mainstream Western policies (Bethell, 1984; Bower, 1989). However, the available evidence indicates that such operations were conducted mostly by the remnants of SOE. Moreover, a number of historians, notably Heuser, have recently demonstrated the important place occupied by these operations within a general programme of vigorous containment or 'roll-back', which included clandestine propaganda and economic warfare, emerging in tandem in Britain and the United States in late 1948 (Heuser, 1989). Any Foreign Office enthusiasm for 'roll-back' tended to emerge in the context of this wider programme, rather than for special operations *per se*. Nevertheless, the idea of destabilizing parts of Eastern Europe had clearly achieved a measure of interdepartmental support by November 1948 when the Russia Committee, under Gladwyn Jebb (himself an ex-SOE official), discussed a paper advocating a policy of offensive rather than defensive containment towards Eastern Europe. This paper, ironically written by Robin Hankey (an ardent opponent of the survival of SOE in 1945 and 1946), mirrored similar ideas developing in the United States. It was agreed to begin operations on a small scale with Albania, which had been isolated by the Tito–Stalin split and where embryonic resistance already existed. The COS were the most enthusiastic and the Chief of the Air Staff, Tedder, contributed the bombastic remark that they should aim at 'the overthrow of the Soviet regime in five years time'.[59]

Any enthusiasm for special operations on the part of the Foreign Office was uncharacteristic and short-lived. Ernest Bevin and other Foreign Office officials were soon to be found objecting to activity in Albania and Yugoslavia, for fear of provoking Soviet intervention. This is indicated by the record of a conversation between Schuman, Acheson and Bevin on the subject of Albania in mid-September 1949:

> The present differences between the US and the UK revolve around the question of whether we should attempt to make more trouble for the Albanian regime at this time. The US is inclined to answer in the affirmative, though admitting that the situation must be handled with the greatest care to avoid having the Greeks precipitate a crisis or the USSR intervene. The British are inclined to feel there is no substitute for the present Hoxha government and that the Free Albanian Committee is not a hopeful prospect.[60]

Britain had displayed a similar lack of enthusiasm when confronted with CIA attempts to undermine Tito during 1948. Charles Bateman, the superintending Under-Secretary denounced this as 'inconceivably stupid', while Orme Sargent, the Permanent Under-Secretary spoke of 'idiotic American behaviour'. Bevin joined American diplomats in Belgrade in pressing Washington for an end to the operation.[61]

SOE's wartime legacy of disputes with their parallel American service, the Office of Strategic Services (OSS), over the Balkans was recalled by further Anglo-American disagreements during September 1948. With regard to Albania, Bevin's reticence regarding future operations clearly owed much to the question of who would succeed Hoxha. He was openly sceptical of the CIA-funded Free Albania Committee, and at another meeting with Acheson he asked, 'Are there any Kings around that could be put in?...a person we could handle was needed'. Bevin knew full well that the available kings were more amenable to British than to American influence.[62]

The limited scale of operations that Britain did undertake against Albania during 1949, and the unpleasant fate of those involved, are best known in the context of their suggested betrayal by Kim Philby, the SIS liaison officer in Washington.[63] The Albanian operations were indeed overseen by the SIS Special Operations Branch, the surviving remnant of SOE in London. However, in reality, SIS lacked the resources to undertake these operations and so re-engaged ex-SOE personnel with Albanian experience, including David Smiley. Dr Zaehner also participated, having completed his work at the Teheran Embassy in 1947.[64] Consequently this became a copybook SOE activity in most of its operational details.

No discussion of British post-war special operations would be complete without brief reference to activities elsewhere in Europe. According to secondary sources Britain also conducted operations into the Baltic and the Ukraine (Simpson, 1988: 173–5; Bower, 1989). These latter operations are important in two respects. First, it appears that they owed less to SOE. Second, while they did not achieve their intended objectives, they appear to have had considerable impact in Eastern Europe. Vojtech Mastny in particular has argued that in November 1949 the Cominform began to issue urgent calls for vigilance against enemy agents, at a time when all internal political opposition had been liquidated and there was no sign of the spread of Titoism. Near-hysteria gripped Eastern Europe and alleged Western agents were uncovered by the hundreds. At their show trials they confessed to elaborate plots. In a curious way British and American efforts had perhaps scored an unintended success. Knowledge of Western efforts seems to have driven Stalin to purge numerous innocent East European protégés on imaginary charges of subversion. In this sense Stalin may have inflicted far more damage in Eastern Europe than the CIA or the SIS Special Operations Branch could have conceivably hoped to do (Mastny 1988: 27–9).

Yet these British special operations against communism in Eastern Europe during the late 1940s represent only the better-known pattern of SOE's post-war legacy. During this period remnants of SOE conducted some of their most successful operations in the counterinsurgency context in Palestine and

Malaya.[65] Here, in colonial territories, they were relatively free from the ambivalent attitudes of the Foreign Office, the complexities of Anglo-American liaison and the problems of Soviet penetration. In Palestine in 1947 special operations were the response of security forces that were cracking under pressure from three sophisticated insurgent organizations: the Haganah, the Irgun and the Lechi (Charters, 1989: 123, 150-3; Charters, 1979).[66] In February 1947 the new Assistant Inspector-General of Police, Colonel Bernard Fergusson, reviewed the situation and then made recommendations to the Palestine Secretary in London. He argued that the increasing frequency of large-scale terrorist operations necessitated special measures for which normal resources and organization were inadequate. He continued:

> There is in the Army a small number of officers who have both technical and psychological knowledge of terrorism, having themselves engaged in similar operations on what may be termed the terrorist side in countries occupied by the enemy in the late war.[67]

Two special operations units were subsequently formed, one under an ex-SOE officer, Alistair McGregor, and the other under an ex-SAS officer. Reports vary widely about their effectiveness (Charters, 1979: 59-61).

SOE played a more significant role during the early stages of the Emergency in Malaya in 1948. Here the Commander-in-Chief Far East Land Forces, General Ritchie, raised six special operations units to meet an urgent requirement for highly trained teams able to operate deep into the jungle for prolonged periods.[68] In 1949 he wrote: 'There was fortunately no lack of material to hand ... a number of ex-Force 136 [SOE] officers with intimate knowledge of both the country and the enemy were available and performed duties of the utmost value.' This was hardly surprising for SOE were fighting the Malayan Communist Party (MCP), an enemy that they had themselves trained for operations against the Japanese between 1942 and 1945. In early 1949 Ritchie attempted to disband these revived SOE units with the idea that their personnel could be used to spread expertise gained in these operations to other formations.[69] But by 1951 the Director of Operations in Malaya had found it essential to revive such units for action against high ranking members of the MCP.

Conclusion

The quantity of open archival material relating to British post-war special operations is limited. Nevertheless, it seems sufficient to demonstrate that SOE survived in various forms well beyond January 1946 and to sketch out some of its influential post-war legacy. In the period 1945-51 special operations were not conducted by a new organization growing in response to an accelerating Cold War. Instead, the complex occupational problems in Europe, the Mediterranean and Asia ensured the survival of old SOE machinery, despite the pressures of post-war financial stringency. Consequently, the component of SOE in London absorbed by SIS in January 1946 represented only one facet of SOE's post-war survival.

The survival of SOE can also be identified in terms of continuities that stretched well beyond those of personnel and operational procedure. The bureaucratic restructuring of SOE in London and its subordination to SIS did not erase the prevailing dislike on the part of the Foreign Office for special operations. Moreover, although the subject lies beyond the scope of this short chapter, jurisdictional disputes between SOE and its wartime American counterpart OSS, appear to have been pursued with the CIA after 1947.[70] Meanwhile, some of SOE's post-war activity in both Europe and Asia underlined the contention of the diplomats that, by their very nature, such organizations were difficult to control and often cut across the mainstream policies of more orthodox departments.

The hesitant attitudes displayed by the Foreign Office towards such operations are particularly interesting. For the Foreign Office to draft a speculative position paper advocating aggressive containment or 'roll-back' was one thing. To find the resolve and resources to implement special operations against a foreign power was quite another. Bevin and the Foreign Office wavered when faced with the challenge of taking widespread action against Albania and Yugoslavia in 1948 and 1949. Meanwhile, these better-known operations in Europe have tended to obscure important developments in colonial territories, where operations were conducted under the general supervision of the Army and the Colonial Police. In this sense, after 1947 two distinct patterns of British special operations appear to have emerged, one under the general direction of SIS and the other under the auspicies of colonial and military authorities in dependent territories.

Peculiarly, these two divergent patterns of operations recall the situation before the formation of SOE. During the early stages of the Second World War, in July 1940, SOE had been created as a new and separate organization. This was done by combining two pre-war bodies: first, Section D, the special operations section of SIS; and second, a parallel organization within the War Office known as Military Intelligence (Research) or MI(R) which had taken an interest in irregular warfare, arising from Army experiences with counterinsurgency in Ireland and elsewhere. By the late 1940s the remnants of SOE had come full circle, finding its reservoir of expertise channelled in two different directions. In this sense SOE contributed to two distinct traditions of British post-war clandestine activity. The first, inherited by the post-war Special Operations Branch of SIS, recalled the pre-war Section D. It was this tradition that led towards British covert action in the Middle East, which characterized SIS in the 1950s. The second post-war development, in the counterinsurgency context, recalled the pre-war thinking of MI(R).[71] Here SOE contributed to what has become a long tradition of successful covert activities in colonial territories where, after all, the majority of Britain's overseas difficulties have arisen since 1945.

Notes

I wish to thank Corpus Christi College, Cambridge and the Harry S. Truman Library, Independence, USA for awards that facilitated the writing of this article. Transcripts from Crown copyright records in the Public Record Office and from India Office Library and Records appear by permission of the Controller, Her Majesty's Stationery Office (HMSO).

1. Throughout this chapter the term 'SOE' is employed in its widest sense to denote surviving components of this wartime organization in any guise, or its personnel. The records from SOE's London headquarters are presently held by the Foreign and Commonwealth Office and are closed to public inspection. Most of the archives maintained by SOE's regional out-stations were destroyed at the end of the war, see for example the request for permission to destroy papers relating to SOE's little-known southern African station at Beira. Permission was granted (Beira to FO No. 20, 26 February 1945, W2934/2934/50, FO371/50430, Public Record Office (hereafter PRO), Kew, Surrey).

2. Professor Foot advances some interesting ideas regarding the impact of SOE on French post-war politics (Foot, 1966: 445). Professor Foot has been more forthcoming in a later, unofficial work noting that Attlee refused to retain SOE, remarking brusquely 'that he had no wish to preside over a British Comintern, and that the network was to end immediately'. Consequently it was 'closed down at 48 hours notice' (Foot, 1984: 245).

3. In contrast American historians have been quick to identify continuities between SOE's wartime American counterpart, OSS, technically abolished on 20 September 1945, and its successor, the CIA, founded in 1947. (See Smith, 1983: 390–420; Troy, 1986: 95–106).

4. The survival of elements of SOE beyond 1945 has received almost no attention. An exception is the illuminating paragraph discussing this matter in Stafford, 1983: 203.

5. Butterfield remarks: 'I must say I do not personally believe that there is a government in Europe which wants the public to know all the truth', and accordingly he advances two maxims: 'First, that governments try to press upon the historian the key to all the drawers but one, and are very anxious to spread the belief that this single one contains no secret of importance; secondly, that if the historian can only find out the thing which government does not want him to know, he will lay his hands upon something that is likely to be significant'. The chapter from which this quotation is drawn, entitled 'Official history: its pitfalls and criteria', contains acute observations on the dangers inherent in scholars

being provided with copies of documents only. These remrks are most pertinent in the context of the current transfer of many public documents to microfilm (1951: 196).

6. The phrase 'by every means short of war' litters the British strategic documentation during this period, particularly in the context of assessments of Soviet policy, see for example, JIC (46) 64 (0) (Final), 'Russia's strategic interests and intentions in the Middle East' (17065), L/WS/1/1050, India Office Library and Records (hereafter IOLR).

7. COS(45) 254th mtg (2), 18 October 1945, CAB79/40, PRO, discussing JIC (45) 263 (Final), 'Manpower requirements for future intelligence organisation', 13 October 1945.

8. The COS noted in January 1949, that Russia was unlikely to embark upon a premeditated war before 1957. If, however, war came unexpectedly, 'we shall have to fight with what we have got', DO(49) 3, 7 January 1949, CAB131/7, PRO.

9. There were undoubtedly exceptions to this. It has been suggested that in the Baltic states British operations were run by SIS officers with long experience of this region who sought to perpetuate German networks in Latvia and elsewhere. On this see Bower, 1989. For an alternative view suggesting that Baltic operations were conducted by remnants of SOE, see Verrier, 1983: 53.

10. For examples of the presentation of these operations as unmitigated failures see Bower, 1989; Bethell, 1984: 193–203.

11. COS(45) 198th mtg (3), 14 August 1945, CAB79/37, PRO. Victor Cavendish-Bentinck had served as Chairman of the JIC since its inception and in the associated position of Head of the Service Liaison Department. He left the post in 1946 amid turmoil in his private life and was replaced by Harold Caccia (Howarth, 1986: 203); Caccia memorandum, 'General review of intelligence concerning Russian military activities in Europe and the Middle East', 15 May 1946, N6092/5169/38, FO371/56885, PRO.

12. Cadogan's diary entry reads '5.00 Meeting with "C" and "CD" [the Directors of SIS and SOE respectively] about dropping Russian agents into France', 24 November 1942, Cadogan MSS, 1/11, Churchill College, Cambridge. The Central Intelligence Agency 1979: 70–1. *Rote Kapelle* was an internal CIA history compiled largely from captured German counterintelligence material.

13. WO/COS circular, 12 January 1944, not foliated, WO193/637A, PRO.

14. COS(44) 68th mtg, 29 February 1944, not foliated, WO193/637A, PRO, COS(44) 165th mtg (0), 20 May 1944, not foliated, WO193/637A, PRO (Foot, 1966: 451).

15. Killearn (Cairo) to Cavendish-Bentinck, 8 June 1945, HF/EP (1154/1/45G), E4569/1630/65, FO371/45272, PRO; memorandum by Myers, 30 October 1943, Box 2, Myers Papers, Liddell Hart Centre for Military Archives, King's College London. This quotation appears by kind permission of the trustees.

16. Dening to Cavendish-Bentinck (JIC) No. 11519, 11 May 1945, fo.1025, WO203/5625, PRO.

17. Penney (SEAC) to Sinclair (DMI), 2 May 1945, 5/21, Penney papers, Liddell Hart Centre for Military Archives, King's College, University of London. Quotation appears by kind permission of the trustees. Pre-war responsibility for British special operations was divided between British Military Intelligence and SIS (see Foot, 1981; Andrew, 1985: 471–7).

18. Slessor (AFHQ) to Grigg, 13 March 1945, AIR23/874, PRO.
19. Churchill to Ismay, 10 February 1944, D41/4, CAB120/827, PRO. See also DO(44) 2nd mtg (Final), CAB69/6, PRO discussing JIC (43) 500 and JIC (43) 517; "C" to Jebb (SOE) C/5966, 10 March 1941, CAB120/827, PRO. The fact that the above Cabinet Defence Committee minutes had, quite exceptionally, undergone more than one draft underlines the volatile nature of these discussions. (See also Stafford, 1988: 137–43; and Hinsley, Vol. III i, 462–3.)
20. COS (45) 304, 'Evaluation of lessons learned during the war' memorandum by Gubbins (SOE), 2 May 1945, not foliated, AIR20/7958, PRO; COS (45) 123rd mtg, 10 May 1945, not foliated, AIR20/7958, PRO.
21. COS(45) 106, 'Value of SOE operations', memorandum by SHAEF, 18 July 1945, not foliated, AIR20/7958, PRO; COS(45) 665 (0), 'Value of SOE operations', memorandum by SACMED, 18 November 1945, not foliated, AIR20/7958, PRO; AMP to Tedder (CAS), 20 November 1945, ibid.
22. 'Control of special units and organisations', T1/1/1054, not dated [presumed July 1946], not foliated, WO106/6024, PRO; Stafford, 1983: 203.
23. Entry for 23 January 1946, Alanbrooke diary, Liddell Hart Centre for Military Archives, King's College, University of London. Quotation appears by kind permission of the trustees.
24. COS(46) 9th mtg (6), 17 January 1946, (17003), L/WS/1/970, IOLR.
25. Note of COS(45) 461 (0), 'Future of SOE activity in the British Zone of Austria', 16 July 1945. WO193/673A, PRO; Sporborg (SOE) to COS HNS.2052, 8 September 1945, in COS(45) 572, 'Future of SOE activity in the British Zone of Austria', 10 September 1945, C6072/72/G3, FO371/46604, PRO.
26. BTA Directive No. 1031, 'Future employment in Austria', annexed to COS(45) 577 (0), 'Future of SOE activity in the British Zone of Austria', 18 September 1945, C6129/72/G3, ibid. This may have been an SIS 'ramp', given that SIS had representatives within the security organizations in Austria during 1945; on this see, Mack (Allied Commission for Austria) to Oliver, 3 May 1945, C2226/141/G3, FO371/46609, PRO, reproduced in Thomas, 1986: 565.
27. Cabinet Offices to BTA No. 5811, 21 September 1945, WO193/637A, PRO.
28. Hankey minute, 1 October 1945, C6129/72/G3, FO371/46604, PRO; Hankey minute, 28 October 1945, C7716/72/G3, FO371/46604, PRO.
29. The Chiefs of Staff were reluctant to set such a precedent unless the DMI considered the files to be not only 'most valuable' but also 'essential', ACIGS (O) to DMI, 2 October 1945, WO193/637A, PRO.
30. Mack noted that while SOE were slowly being supplanted by SIS, eight SOE officers remained. Meanwhile Edward Renton, the head of the SOE station in Austria had returned to London to discuss SOE's long-term future: Mack to Troutbeck, 13 December 1945, C9727/72/G3, FO371/46604, PRO; Caccia minute, 21 December 1945, ibid.
31. The post-war SOE unit in Germany was given the designation ME 42. Hankey believed that General McCreery, C.-in-C. BAOR, had come under 'much pressure from Mr Sporborg' of SOE. He resolved to try and restrain such activities by making representations to Sir William Strang, McCreery's Foreign Office adviser, COS(45) 577 (0), 'Future of SOE activity in the British Zone of Austria', 18 September 1945, C6129/72/G3, FO371/46604, PRO; Hankey minute, 28 October 1945, C7716/72/G3, FO371/46604, PRO. See also statement by

Keswick (provisional) minutes of the FO-SOE Committee, 41st mtg, 23 May 1945, C2608/23/G18, FO371/46728, PRO.

32. These replies prompted a debate amongst the Eastern department on the utility of covert subventions to local newspapers. Young noted: 'My own view has always been that though it may produce good results for a time its ultimate result is only to increase the anti-British tone, and consequent bribability of the newspapers concerned'; minute by Young summarizing replies of Middle Eastern ambassadors, 16 June 1945, E4569/1630/65, FO371/45272, PRO. See also Cavendish-Bentinck minute, 12 June 1945, E4569/1630/65, FO371/45272, PRO.

33. Minute by Berthoud, 15 June 1951, FO371/91548/EP1531/674, PRO, discussed in Louis, 1984: 659–60. See also Woodhouse, 1982: 111.

34. Killearn (Cairo) to Cavendish-Bentinck, 8 June 1945, HF/EP (1154/1/45G), E4569/1630/65, FO371/45272, PRO. For a detailed review of the post-war British intelligence organization as it emerged in this region, see JIC(48) 60 (Revised Final), 'Review of intelligence organisation in the Middle East', 12 November 1948, fo. 21, (17065), L/WS/1/1051, IOLR.

35. Sargent minute, 10 June 1945, E3881/1630/65, FO371/45272, PRO. The PRO hand-list for WO106 lists several files dealing with SOE in Greece, 1945–8, but they are presently closed to public inspection.

36. Mountbatten to COS (SEACOS 570), 10 December 1945, F11146/9752/61, FO371/46423, PRO. On SOE and OSS in post-war Asia see Aldrich, 1988: 41–55.

37. Memorandum by Seymour, 'ALFPMO Digest 15 November 1945–31 March 1946', not foliated, WO203/2331, PRO.

38. JIC(45) 17, 'Allocation of personnel with knowledge of Far Eastern Languages', 14 January 1945, WO220/52, PRO.

39. COS to Mountbatten (COSSEA 418), 23 November 1945, fo. 28, WO203/1735, PRO; 'Liquidation of Force 136 [SOE]' enclosed in Lavensdall (SOE) to HSD SACSEA, 16 October 1945, WO203/4288, PRO; Report by Cowper and Mirehouse, January 1947, F211/21/40, FO371/63882, PRO.

40. SAC(45) 179, 'Transfer of control of Force 136 [SOE]', 26 October 1945, fo. 14, WO203/1735, PRO: SACSEA to WO, 9 February 1946, WO203/4943, PRO.

41. Bowker to Dening, Personal, 28 February 1948, F4171/1087/79, FO371/69509, PRO.

42. Dening to Bowker, 16 March 1948, F4171/1087/79, FO371/69509, PRO. It should be noted that British officers had been arrested in Burma in connection with the theft of large numbers of automatic weapons on behalf of rebel forces as early as the summer of 1947; see, for example, CIGS (Montgomery) to SoS for War, Pepper 174, 4 August 1947, BLM181/28, Montgomery papers, Imperial War Museum, London.

43. Dening minute to Bevin, 18 August 1948, F10053/1087/79, FO371/69509, PRO. See also FO to Bowker No. 696, 20 August 1948, fo. 1, L/P&S/12/1378, IOLR.

44. Dening to Bowker, 17 September 1948, F13277/1087/79, FO371/69509, PRO.

45. Dening minute to Bevin, 18 August 1948, F10053/1087/79, FO371/69509, PRO. The minutes of the meeting with Burmah Oil appear to be withheld at either F10053/1087/79 or F10646/1087/79, FO371/69509, PRO.

46. Dening minute to Bevin, 18 August 1948, F10053/1087/79, FO371/69509, PRO. See also FO to Bowker No. 696, 20 August 1948, fol. 1, L/P&S/12/1378, IOLR.

47. Bowker to FO No. 837, 4 September 1948, F12243/1087/79, FO371/69509, PRO;

Glass minute, 5 October 1948, not foliated, (13048), FO643/113, PRO; Harrison minute, 13 October 1948, fo. 73, (3010), FO643/118, PRO.

48. Bevin minute (not dated) upon Bowker to FO No. 866, 12 September 1948, F12608/1087/79, FO371/69509, PRO; Murray minute, 16 September 1948, F12608/1087/79, FO371/69509, PRO.

49. Bowker to FO No. 913, 21 September 1948, fo. 12, L/P&S/12/1378, IOLR; Burma Special Branch search list, Room 50, Strand Hotel, Rangoon, 18 September 1948 and minute by Harrison, 21 September 1948, fo. 11, (3010), FO643/118, PRO.

50. Dening minute to Sargent, F13562/1087/79, FO371/69510, PRO; FO to Rangoon, No. 836, 27 September 1948, fo. 28A, L/P&S/12/1378, IOLR.

51. Bevin minute, 14 October 1948, F14004/1087/79, FO371/69511, PRO. On British attitudes to neutralism and British efforts in the field of propaganda against communism in South Asia see Fletcher, 1982: 99–101.

52. UK High Commission Delhi to CRO No. 3661, 23 September 1948, fo. 23, L/P&S/12/1378, IOLR.

53. Noel-Baker to UK High Commission Delhi No. 2693 (draft), 22 September 1948, fo. 15, L/P&S/12/1378, IOLR; Secretary of State CRO to UK High Commission Delhi (draft), 27 September 1948, fo. 26, L/P&S/12/1378, IOLR.

54. Shattock (Delhi) to CRO, 6 October 1948, enclosing Addison to Bullock, 1 October 1948, fo. 41, L/P&S/12/1378, IOLR.

55. Press summary in Crombie (Rangoon) to FO No. 1135, 22 November 1948, F16376/1087/79, FO371/69513, PRO; *The Progress,* 20 November 1948, and *The Bamakit,* 22 November 1948, in press report at fo. 132, (3010) FO643/118, PRO; Ledwidge minute reporting discussion with MI2, 19 May 1949, F7105/1051/79, FO371/75677, PRO; Bowker to FO No. 196, 31 May 1949, F8598/1051/79, ibid.

56. COS(49) 35th mtg (5), 2 March 1949, not foliated, AIR20/7030, PRO; Joy minute, 31 March 1949 and Ledwidge minute, 3 April 1949, F4642/1051/79, FO371/75677, PRO.

57. Bowker to FO No. 366, 3 May 1950, not foliated, AIR20/7030, PRO.

58. Eden minute, 5 November 1941, F11629/210/40, FO371/28126, PRO.

59. RC(16) 48, 25 November 1948, N/3016/765/38, FO371/71687, PRO. For a perceptive discussion of this meeting, see Heuser, 1989: 76–7.

60. Summary of political conversations held in Washington between Acheson, Bevin and Schuman, 13–15 September 1949, PSF General File (A–Ato) 112, Harry S. Truman Memorial Library, Independence, Missouri.

61. Heuser, 1989: 44–5, quoting minutes by Sargent, Bateman and Roberts, at R2160/10345/92G, FO371/78715, PRO. On French participation in these schemes under the MINOS programme, see Faligot and Krop, 1989: 75–8.

62. Memorandum of a conversation between Acheson, Bevin and a number of officials, 14 September 1948, *Foreign Relations of the United States, The Near East, South Asia and Africa,* vol. VI, 1977: 417–7. Some aspects of the printed record of this meeting are difficult to reconcile with the record of other meetings available at the Truman Library referred to in Note 60.

63. The emphasis upon Philby as the sole focus of co-ordination in relation to these *émigré* operations may be misplaced. Other accounts have stressed the role of other figures. Typically, it has been suggested that the 2nd Earl Jellicoe, an ex-SAS

officer who joined the Diplomatic Service in 1947 and was stationed in Washington, was the British representative on the Special Political Committee that co-ordinated operations against Albania. On this, see Faligot and Krop, 1989: 62, 302, no. 2.

64. Smiley notes that 'only very few SOE people were taken on by M16 (SIS), and many old SOE hands got the impression they regarded us as a lot of bungling amateurs'. Verrier notes that by December 1947 'SIS's Special Operations Branch and Political Action Group had been established for over a year' and describes them as 'revamped SOE units' (Smiley, 1984: 162-8; Verrier, 1983: 51-77).

65. British intelligence was nevertheless always anxious to investigate possible Soviet assistance to insurgent groups within dependent territories. See for example the comments of the Security Service (MI5) on the Soviet Union and the 'Stern Gang', minutes of the Middle East Inter-Departmental meeting, 25 August and 22 September 1948, CO537/5299, PRO. The MI5 officers responsible for these Middle East duties were Major J. Maude, Major D. Scherr and C.T. Young.

66. David Smiley was originally to join this operation in Palestine, Smiley, 162-4. For a British assessment of the insurgent groups see JIC(47) (52) (0) (Final), 'Possible future of Palestine', 9 September 1947, fo. 01(1), (17141), L/WS/1/1162, IOLR.

67. Fergusson to CO, 12 February 1947, (75015/94), CO537/2270, PRO.

68. FARELF to WO No. 13609. 9 August 1948, fo. 1, L/WS/1/1498, IOLR; FARELF to WO No. 13626, 26 August 1948, fo. 2, ibid.

69. 'Report on Operations in Malaya' by General Ritchie, July 1949, pp. 10–12, WO106/5884, PRO.

70. See for example memorandum by representatives of the British Chiefs of Staff, 'Special operations in support of emergency war plans', RHB 1/48, 8 November 1951, discussed in enclosure B to JSPC 808/81, 'Special operations in support of emergency plans', 18 December 1951, CCS 385, (6-4-46) 26 (SO), RG 165, National Archives and Records Administration, Washington DC.

71. On Middle Eastern activities in the 1950s see Gorst and Lucas, 1989: 576–96. On MI(R) and pre-war counter-insurgency, see, Foot, 1981: 167–73.

References

Aldrich, R.J. (1988), 'Imperial rivalry: Anglo-American intelligence in Asia, 1942-7', *Intelligence and National Security*, vol. 3, no. 1. (January 1988), pp. 1–55.

Andrew, C.M. (1985), *Secret Service: The Making of the British Intelligence Community*, London, Heinemann.

Baylis, J. (1983), 'British wartime thinking about a post war West European security group', *Review of International Studies*, vol. 9, no. 4, pp. 273–7.

Bell Smith, T. (1976?), *The Essential CIA*, self-published, no date.

Bennett, R.F. (1979), *Ultra in the West*, London, Hutchinson.

Bennett, R.F. (1989), *Ultra and Mediterranean Strategy*, London, Hutchinson.

Bethell, N. (1984), *The Great Betrayal: The Untold Story of Kim Philby's Biggest Coup*, London, Hodder and Stoughton.

Bower, J. (1989), *The Red Web*, London, Aurum Press.

Butterfield, H. (1951) *History and Human Relations*, London, Collins.

Central Intelligence Agency (1979) *Rote Kapelle: The CIA's History of Soviet Intelligence and Espionage Networks in Western Europe, 1936–1945*, Washington, University Publications of America.

Charters, D.A. (1979) 'Special operations in counterinsurgency: the Farran Case, Palestine, 1947', *Journal of the Royal Institute for Defence Studies*, vol. 124, no. 2 (June 1979).

Charters, D.A. (1989), *The British Army and the Jewish Insurgency in Palestine, 1945–1947*, London, Macmillan.

Cruickshank, C. (1983), *SOE in the Far East*, Oxford, Oxford University Press.

Department of State (1977), *Foreign Relations of the United States: The Near East, South Asia and Africa*, vol. VI, Washington, Government Printing Office.

Faligot, R. and Krop, P. (1989), *Lapiscime: The French Secret Service since 1914*, Oxford, Blackwell.

Fletcher, R. (1982), 'British propaganda since World War II–a case study', *Media, Culture and Society*, vol. 4, pp. 96–109.

Foot, M.R.D. (1966), *SOE In France: An account of the work of the Special Operations Executive, 1940–44*, London, HMSO.

Foot, M.R.D. (1984), *SOE: The Special Operations Executive, 1940–1946*, London, BBC.

Foot, M.R.D. (1981), 'Was SOE Any Good?', *Journal of Contemporary History*, vol. 16, no. 1, pp. 167–82.

Gorst, A. and Lucas, S. (1989), 'The other "collusion": Operation STRAGGLE and Anglo-American intervention in Syria, 1955–6', *Intelligence and National Security*, vol. 4, no. 1 (June 1989), pp. 576–96.

Heuser, B. (1989), *Western 'Containment' Policies in the Cold War: The Yugoslav case, 1948–53* (London, Routledge, 1989), pp. 76–7.

Hinsley, F.H. *et al.* (1979–88), *British Intelligence in the Second World War: Its influence on strategy and operations* (3 vols), HMSO.

Howarth, P. (1986), *Intelligence Chief Extraordinary*, London, Bodley Head.

Kitchen, M. (1986), *Britain and the Soviet Union, 1941–5*, London, Macmillan.

Lewin, R. (1978), *Ultra Goes to War*, London, Hutchinson.

Lewis, J. (1988), *Changing Direction: British military planning for post war strategic defence, 1942–7*, London, Sherwood.

Louis, Wm. R. (1984), *The British Empire in the Middle East, 1945–51: Arab nationalism, the United States and postwar imperialism*, Oxford, Clarendon Press.

Mastny, V. (1988), 'Europe in US–USSR relations: a topical legacy', *Problems of Communism*, vol. XXXVII (January 1988).

Rothwell, V. (1982), *Britain and the Cold War, 1941–7*, London, Cape.

Simpson, C. (1988), *Blowback: American Recruitment of Nazis and its effect on the Cold War*, London, Weidenfeld and Nicolson.

Smiley, D. (1984), Albanian Assignment, London, Chatto and Windus.
Smith, B.H. (1983), *The Shadow Warriors: O.S.S. and the origins of the C.I.A.*, London, André Deutsch.
Stafford, D. (1983), *Britain and European Resistance, 1940–1945*, London, Macmillan.
Thomas, H. (1986), *Armed Truce: The beginnings of the Cold War, 1945–46*, London, Hamish Hamilton.
Troy, T.H. (1986), 'Knifing of the OSS', *International Journal of Intelligence and Counteringelligence*, vol. I, no. 3, pp. 95–106.
Verrier, A. (1983), *Through the Looking Glass: British foreign policy in the age of illusions*, London, Jonathan Cape.
Woodhouse, C.M. (1982), *Something Ventured*, London, Granada.

13 The diplomacy of restraint: the Attlee government and the Korean war

Callum MacDonald

Introduction: the special relationship and the Cold War

In the basement of the Victorious Fatherland Liberation War Museum in Pyongyang, the capital of North Korea, a solitary British bren-gun carrier stands amidst the ranks of captured American equipment, a mute reminder of British participation in a distant Asian war fought under the banner of the United Nations. Britain had no direct strategic or economic interest in Korea and before 1950 the public scarcely knew of its existence. Winston Churchill later complained that he had 'never heard of the bloody place' until he was 74 (Macdonald, 1986: 187). Yet within days of the outbreak of war the government had committed naval forces to the fighting, followed shortly afterwards by two infantry brigades which ultimately served as part of a Commonwealth division. This military contribution, although modest compared with those of the United States and the Republic of Korea, was the second-largest amongst the 16 members of the United Nations which participated in the war, straining British resources.

Britain's involvement sprang directly from the Cold War and the role of the special relationship with the United States in British foreign policy. After 1940 the Anglo-American alliance was regarded as vital to Britain's world role. The aim of Churchill's Coalition government and its Labour successor was to use the United States to bolster Britain's threatened position as a great power. The British nightmare was an American post-war retreat into isolationism, which would leave Britain to face the Soviet Union alone across the ruins of Hitler's Europe. The goal of Ernest Bevin, the powerful Labour Foreign Secretary, was to establish the special relationship as the basic element in American containment of the Soviet Union, an approach which enjoyed broad bi-partisan support. Bevin played a leading role in each step towards the creation of a post-war American containment system, from the Truman Doctrine of 1947, to the emergence of NATO in 1949. So anxious was Bevin to lay the ghost of isolationism that during the Berlin crisis in 1948, he allowed the

218

United States to base strategic bombers in East Anglia without any formal agreement guaranteeing Britain's right to consultation before the airfields were used operationally. Bevin regarded NATO as one of his greatest achievements for it committed the Americans to the security of Western Europe for the first time.

British officials saw the United States as a naïve but well-intentioned giant, in need of guidance by those better versed in world politics. Britain's long experience in this area would compensate for the imbalance of power within the alliance. If the United States provided the brawn, Britain would provide the brains to guide the American colossus. The British thus adopted a patronizing view of the United States which did not always please the Americans. This was reflected when Attlee visited Washington in December 1950 and lectured Truman on nationalism in Asia, emphasizing Britain's experience in India. The British also tended to assume the identity of British and US interests, a conjunction which was not always evident to those on the other side of the Atlantic. If the British regarded the special relationship as a prop for their world position, however, what the Americans wanted out of it 'was support for their hegemony' (Ra, 1984: 315). Britain was rigorously excluded from one area vital to that hegemony, the atomic bomb, despite Anglo-American co-operation in its development during the war. After 1945 Britain lost its veto over the employment of the 'winning weapon' and was denied access to American research as Washington attempted to create a US monopoly. Britain embarked on its own atomic programme but did not test a bomb until October 1952. British control over American employment of atomic weapons was to become an important issue during the Korean war when the world seemed to hover on the brink. In this atmosphere the related issue of US air bases in Britain was also to assume a new urgency.

By 1950 Britain had moved inescapably into the political, economic and military orbit of the United States. In this situation its response to US intervention in Korea was inevitable. As Attlee remarked, 'We'll have to support the Yanks' (Harris, 1982: 459). The Korean war, however, was to emphasize the discrepancies of power within the special relationship and British dependence on the United States in a way which both Attlee and his successor Churchill were to find frustrating. After June 1950 Britain was faced with a new kind of problem. The primary aim was no longer to commit American power but to define the ways in which it was employed, pursuing the diplomacy of restraint within the Atlantic alliance.

British intervention: the reason why

When North Korean forces crossed the 38th Parallel on 25 June 1950, Britain supported American action at the UN and military intervention under the blue banner of the world organization. Unlike Czechoslovakia in 1938, Korea was not defined as 'a far-away country of which we know nothing'. On the contrary Attlee emphasized the British stake in the outcome, warning the public that the 'fire which has been started in distant Korea may burn down your house' (Harris, 1982: 456). The government had little time for the ROK which was regarded as a corrupt police state, peripheral to British concerns. British strategic priorities lay in Europe and the Middle East. In the Far East, south-east Asia, not north–east Asia was the focus of British interests. It was argued, however, that what mattered was not Korea but avoiding the mistakes of the past. In Washington, as in London, there was little doubt that the Soviets had instigated the North Korean attack. Attlee, like Truman, invoked the lessons of the 1930s in favour of a strong stand against totalitarian aggression. Stalin must be discouraged from attempting a similar experiment in more vital areas such as Iran or Yugoslavia, leading perhaps to world war. This appeal to collective security through the United Nations was popular both with the Labour Party and the country at large only five years after the defeat of Hitler.

Principle, however, was reinforced by expediency. Britain would have done little about the North Korean action if the United States had not intervened. It was thought vital to support the Americans in the first clash between the Cold War blocs. The Korean decision was seen as confirmation that Britain was still a great power with a world role, something which would increase British influence within the special relationship. In the following months the government hoped to reap the benefits in terms of increased American support in Europe and financial assistance for British rearmament, a question which was quickly raised by the apparent readiness of the Soviet Union to sponsor armed aggression. Such political considerations lay behind the commitment of a first and then a second British Army brigade to Korea in the summer of 1950 despite the reluctance of the Chiefs of Staff to strip Britain's meagre military reserves. As the ambassador to Washington, Oliver Franks, warned in July, a refusal to send troops would seriously impair the special relationship. The US public and Congress would question the value of alliances and the commitment to NATO if Britain appeared to betray the United States in its hour of need.

The diplomacy of restraint

While supporting the United States in Korea the government was anxious to minimize the risk of global war in which Britain would be first to suffer. The Chiefs of Staff quickly warned Attlee of Britain's vulnerability to Russian retaliation in the event of another world conflict. The Cabinet was anxious to avoid attributing direct responsibility for the North Korean action to Moscow in public, lest this engage Soviet prestige and leave Stalin with no means of backing down. Nor did it want the Americans to convert a 'police action' in Korea into an open-ended crusade against communism. It was not the Soviet

Union, however, but China which became a major issue in Anglo-American relations with the outbreak of the Korean war.

Although Anglo-American co-operation had been close in Europe from the beginning of the Cold War, the two powers had not achieved the same degree of co-ordination in the Far East. Britain was critical of US policy in Asia, particularly as it applied to Communist China. London recognized the Communist regime in January 1950 following Mao's victory in the civil war. This meant abandoning the Guomindang (Kuomintang) regime of Jiang Ji-Shi (Chiang Kai-Shek) which was eking out a precarious existence on the island of Taiwan (Formosa), an existence which the Communists were expected to end by military action in the summer of 1950. The return of Taiwan, formerly a Japanese colony, to China had been pledged by the allies at the Cairo Conference in 1943 and Britain was unwilling to breach this agreement. The Americans, however, refused to follow suit and by the early summer of 1950 were considering some means of denying Taiwan to the Communists. The Truman administration regarded Beijing (Peking) as the tool of Soviet imperialism in Asia, a force to be resisted rather than appeased. As Franks remarked shortly before the Korean crisis, there were the seeds of real trouble in this divergence. The situation was particularly irritating because it was believed that US policy was largely dictated by domestic politics and the attempt by right-wing Republicans to blame the administration for the 'loss of China', a campaign which called for 'Asia first' and gained particular virulence after February 1950 with the involvement of Senator Joseph McCarthy.

British policy towards China and Taiwan was influenced by several factors. Britain was concerned about the Communist triumph in the Chinese civil war and feared a domino effect in south-east Asia, beginning with Indochina where the French were fighting the Vietminh under Ho Chi Minh. It was thought that the fall of Indochina would open the whole region to Communist penetration, undermining the British position in Malaya where a Communist uprising had begun in 1948. The British encouraged the Americans to back the French in Indochina as a barrier against further Communist expansion and welcomed the increase in US aid which followed the outbreak of the Korean war. At the same time Britain hesitated to confront Beijing directly, arguing that with careful diplomacy the Chinese could be prised away from their alliance with Moscow and turned into an instrument of containment. In the long term the Chinese would prove more nationalist than Communist and might quarrel with Moscow over Soviet designs on Manchuria. China should thus have not only a political but also an economic opening to the West. This would not only encourage the emergence of Titoism but would be of direct economic benefit to Britain and preserve the prosperity and security of Hong Kong which was a hostage to China. A second factor was India which was regarded as vital to the unity of the Commonwealth, an organization considered important to Britain's position in the world. Nehru saw the

Chinese revolution as an anti-colonial movement and regarded his country as a bridge between China and the West. Bevin emphasized the importance of Asian opinion and the folly of alienating the new India, an argument which carried little weight with the United States which 'regarded British susceptibility to the opinions of nonaligned India as a complication in the Anglo-American relationship in Asia (Singh, 1990: 220). Lastly there was the unity of the Labour party to consider, for many on the left wished to give Communist China the benefit of the doubt. This was an important consideration for the second Attlee government which had only a small majority in Parliament.

London did not wish to link China with the Korean crisis. If the fighting spread to include China, the Soviet Union might also become involved. At the very least war with China would divert US military power to a peripheral area and leave Europe and the Middle East vulnerable to Soviet pressure. As Attlee emphasized in early July, the situation in Korea must not blind the West to the dangers nearer home. US policy towards China, however, threatened precisely this result. Not only did Washington intervene in Korea under the UN flag, it also unilaterally 'neutralized' Taiwan by deploying the 7th Fleet between the island and the mainland. While this was portrayed as an even-handed action, designed to maintain peace on the flanks of the Korean operation, its practical effect was to preserve the Guomindang and risk a clash between China and the United States. Such an outcome would not only cause grave strategic problems but also divide the Commonwealth and create political difficulties at home. Nehru supported the UN action against aggression in Korea but regarded US intervention in Taiwan as an act of old-fashioned imperialism. According to Bevin, the Americans risked alienating Asia.

In early July Bevin considered an approach to Moscow, proposing a North Korean withdrawal behind the 38th Parallel in return for a general settlement of Far Eastern problems including Taiwan and Beijing's claim to the Chinese seat at the United Nations. Acheson, however, reacted ferociously, arguing that any hint of appeasement would have a serious effect on the Anglo-American alliance. It was an early example of Washington's determination to dominate Western policy in Asia and its impatience with British interference: 'This was the standard formula which the Americans were to use on many occasions . . . and usually effectively, to keep their special ally in line (Ra, 1984: 313). In July the government also deferred to US pressure for restrictions on the export of strategic goods such as oil to China. Taiwan continued to concern Britain throughout the summer of 1950, not least because of the behaviour of General MacArthur, the American commander in the Far East and head of the UN command, who, by visiting the island and publicly emphasizing its strategic importance threatened to link the Korea and Taiwan issues in a dangerous way. It was a precursor of future trouble with the general who sympathized with the Asia-first line of the Republican Right.

In August 1950 Bevin tried to defuse the situation by proposing the creation of a UN commission which would emphasize the continued validity of the Cairo declaration while delaying the return of Taiwan until peace and security had returned to the Pacific. This might reassure India, restrain China and satisfy American arguments against handing the island over to Beijing while the Korean war lasted. Although Acheson stressed that Washington had no intention of sponsoring a Guomindang return to the mainland and promised to consider the idea, the administration had already decided to settle the issue on its own terms by denying permanently the island to the Chinese Communists. While Britain regarded the war in Korea as 'a temporary obstacle to the establishment of the framework for regional peace' outlined at Cairo, for the United States 'the events of June twenty-fifth [1950] had blown up the railroad' (Dingman, 1982: 9).

Crossing the 38th Parallel

In the light of British reluctance to provoke Beijing, it might seem strange that Britain should have supported the decision to cross the 38th Parallel into North Korea in October 1950, drafting the resolution passed by the UN General Assembly on 7 October endorsing reunification. Korea, however, unlike Taiwan, was regarded as a *Soviet* rather than a *Chinese* interest. It was assumed that reunification could take place without alarming the Chinese, who would be reluctant to pull Soviet chestnuts out of the fire and happy to see the eradication of a Soviet satellite on their border. On this issue the politicians were more enthusiastic than the Chiefs of Staff, who were ambiguous about the wisdom of military operations north of the 38th Parallel. Bevin was anxious to emphasize the UN character of reunification in order to reassure Beijing and secure Asian support. He hoped that India would agree to co-sponsor the General Assembly resolution, but he was to be disappointed.

At the end of September the Chinese began relaying a series of warnings through India that China would intervene if US forces entered North Korea. Although Nehru was alarmed, Britain was at first inclined to dismiss the statements as bluff. Only when the Chinese Foreign Minister, Zhou Enlai, summoned the Indian ambassador, K.M. Panikkar, from his bed on 2 October and bluntly stated the Chinese position, did London react. Bevin, returning from New York on the *Queen Mary*, wired Acheson that Chinese intervention would be a great catastrophe and suggested offering Beijing a hearing at the United Nations. The Chiefs of Staff were equally alarmed. In the end, however, Britain did not press for a halt at the Parallel. Bevin was reluctant to risk a controversy with the Americans who were clearly determined to continue or to risk appearing an appeaser at a time when major new US commitments to Europe were under consideration and Britain wanted financial help for the £3,600 million rearmament programme announced on 12 September. According to Bevin it would be risky for political reasons to ask the Americans to postpone their offensive. Britain had exercised a steadying influence on the United States in the previous months but 'influence to be maintained, must continue to be unobtrusive' (Stueck, 1986: 85). The British therefore opted to reassure China about the objectives of the UN advance while urging moderation on the United States. They were clearly uneasy about the belligerent attitude of General MacArthur who did not conceal from British diplomats his determination to unleash a major bombing offensive against China if its troops crossed the Yalu. At the same time, for all their talk about understanding Asian nationalism, the British misjudged the mood of China and the worthlessness of any UN guarantees to the government in Beijing.

Disaster in the north

At first it appeared that the gamble had paid off and that the Chinese had been bluffing. The fall of the North Korean capital, Pyongyang, on 20 October seemed to vindicate Bevin's judgement that there was insufficient evidence for Indian fears that Beijing intended to intervene on a large scale. At the beginning of November, however, Chinese forces appeared on the battlefield, compelled UN troops to withdraw to the Chongchon river and then disappeared. Britain was uncertain about Chinese aims. Chinese intervention might be designed to drive the United Nations from Korea or it might be a defensive move intended to protect the security of the border and the power stations on the Yalu river. There was considerable anxiety about the American reaction since the Republican Right had just made significant gains in the Congressional elections and MacArthur's views on Communist China were well known.

The government was therefore anxious to defuse the situation and Bevin proposed the establishment of a demilitarized zone between the line Hungnam–Chongju and the Yalu. The Chiefs of Staff were appalled by the prospect of fighting China and convinced that MacArthur could not reach the border without bombing Manchuria. A Soviet source in Beijing had warned Panikkar that in this event the Soviet air force would become involved. The problem was that neither the Americans nor the Chinese were interested in the scheme. Although a Polish diplomat at the United Nations implied that China would agree to a buffer zone provided it was coupled with the removal of the 7th Fleet from the Taiwan straits, Beijing made no response to informal British soundings, nor would the Americans accept such a deal. Indeed the United States would not allow Britain to launch a formal diplomatic initiative. The domestic risks of stopping MacArthur were too great, and the administration gambled that he might yet succeed. Britain hesitated to press the issue and risk a major controversy which might affect the European programme and allow the Republicans, strengthened by the results of the Congressional elections in early November, to whip up public opinion against British appeasement.

Until this point Britain had relied on quiet diplomacy to encourage US restraint. When China intervened on a large scale at the end of November to expel the UN command from North Korea, however, and Washington hovered on the brink of a wider war, Anglo-American differences could no longer be submerged. The situation was brought to a head by Truman's remarks on the possible use of the atomic bomb at a press conference on 30 November. Attlee was pushed forward by a strong feeling in the party and the country that the United States was reacting to a hysterical public opinion, whipped up by the Republican Right, and might drag Britain into a major war with China or global conflict with the Soviet Union. MacArthur was an object of particular suspicion. In the aftermath of Chinese intervention, he did not conceal his desire to convert the war into an open-ended crusade against Asian Communism. Many were unhappy not only about the situation in Korea but also about German rearmament, which the United States had proposed in September, and about the cost of the British rearmament programme. They asked whether these moves were necessary or the product of American anti-Communist hysteria. This mood was reflected in the fear of atomic war stimulated by Truman's remarks. Attlee flew to Washington to assert British influence, secure reassurances about the bomb, press for negotiations with China and ensure that the Americans would not be diverted into a major war in the Far East. He also wanted the administration to assert control over its turbulent Far East commander. Attlee, however, faced an acute dilemma. As the Cabinet noted, the ultimate threat to British security came from the Soviet Union and it was difficult to contemplate a breach with the United States in the Far East which might lead to the withdrawal of American support from Europe.

On his return Attlee exaggerated what he had gained in Washington. Truman was prepared to state that the bomb would not be used in an emergency without consulting Britain but this commitment was contrary to the Atomic Energy Act and was watered down in the final comminiqué. The Prime Minister sought a veto over American employment of the bomb until the elections in October 1951 without success. All that finally emerged was a formula on the US air bases in Britain, drawn up in the closing days of the Labour government and confirmed under Churchill, which the Americans believed did not hamper their control over the 'winning weapon'. On China, the administration was quite unwilling to consider the British argument that the Chinese were more nationalist than communist and that some price should be paid for a Korean ceasefire in terms of the UN seat and Taiwan. The British were threatened with the withdrawal of US assistance from Europe if they pressed the issue. According to Acheson, the American people would not understand a policy of resistance in Europe and appeasement in the Far East. As for MacArthur, when the British raised the subject, the Americans treated it as an issue of confidence in American leadership, emphasizing the dangers if similar doubts developed over the appointment of Eisenhower to NATO.

The only real agreement which emerged in Washington was to fight it out in Korea and seek a ceasefire there, rather than evacuate and wage a limited war against China, an idea which had been under consideration in Washington when Chinese intervention threatened the UN command with disaster. It was the stabilization of the front in January 1951, however, rather than Attlee's arguments, which finally proved decisive as evacuation and limited war with China remained under active consideration in Washington for several weeks after his visit. Moreover, the United States, convinced that China was acting on Soviet prompting, believed the crisis indicated increased Soviet readiness for war and stepped up its rearmament programme. Britain was expected to follow suit and both powers pledged in the final communiqué to speed up their preparations. This was to burden an already strained British economy and to create political problems for Attlee in the New Year.

The Attlee visit did not solve the problem in the special relationship which reached its lowest point in January 1951. It was feared in London that whatever the intentions of Truman, MacArthur was retreating in Korea to force an evacuation which would compel the administration to carry the war to China. There were doubts about whether Truman could control MacArthur, given the state of public opinion and a determined Republican assault on the President's policies. Despite the difficulties of negotiating a ceasefire through the United Nations, Britain was reluctant to abandon the process and condemn China as an aggressor, lest this encourage US military action against the mainland. Matters came to a head at the end of January when one group in the Cabinet, which included Bevan, the Minister of Labour, argued in favour of voting against a US resolution condemning China, arguing that Britain must show its independence. Only if Britain stood up for itself would its views receive weight in Washington. This was a repudiation of Bevin's loyal ally approach and reflected frustration with Britain's declining ability to shape events. Others, including the Chancellor of the Exchequer, Gaitskell, argued that such a move would jeopardize US commitments to Europe and financial aid for rearmament by playing into the hands of right-wing Republicans, a line encouraged by Acheson who threatened precisely these consequences if Britain did not fall into line.

On 25 January the Cabinet, in the absence of Bevin who was terminally ill, agreed to vote against the American resolution. It reversed itself the following day, however, and accepted a compromise after Gaitskell had threatened to resign and had mobilized Foreign Office officials against a decision which would have meant voting with the Communist bloc at the United Nations. In effect, Acheson won his point, since the government had backed away from the prospect of confrontation with Washington at a time of intense debate within the United States about the relative importance of Europe over Asia and new US military commitments to NATO. As Pierson Dixon of the Foreign Office remarked on 28 January, a split with the United States

> would mean that we should have to reconsider our policy of opposition to Communism and the USSR and of support for Western defence. Clearly we are not prepared to go to these lengths. If we cannot entirely change American policy, then we must...resign ourselves to the role of counsellor and moderator.... But we should accept the disagreeable conclusion, in the end, that we must allow the United States to take the lead and follow or at least not break with them. It is difficult for us, after centuries of leading others, to resign ourselves to the position of allowing another and a greater power to lead us.
>
> (Dockrill, 1986: 477)

Despite the stabilization of the military situation by the end of January 1951 and the renewed advance of the UN forces, Anglo-American relations remained strained. In February the Americans, alarmed by the build-up of Chinese aircraft beyond the Yalu, proposed giving the Field Commander discretion to bomb airfields in Manchuria in the event of an air attack which endangered the safety of his forces. Britain feared that if MacArthur was allowed to define what constituted a serious attack he might engineer an incident which would cause a major war with China. Not only did Britain dig its heels in over this initiative but it pressed for limits on the UN advance and a new attempt at a ceasefire as UN forces again approached the 38th Parallel. The Americans were unwilling to halt operations unilaterally but were prepared to issue a new call for a ceasefire based on a return to the status quo. This move, however, was torpedoed by MacArthur's famous demand on 24 March that the Chinese either surrender or face a wider war, an action which caused consternation in London when the administration seemed unwilling to discipline the general.

The sacking of MacArthur on 11 April 1951, which roused the fury of the Republican Right and plunged the United States deeper into political crisis, was the prelude to British capitulation to American views on the Far East. Acheson seized the opportunity to bring London finally into line over China, emphasizing that solidarity in Asia would enable the administration to weather the storm over MacArthur and pursue its European priorities. The British could not view with equanimity the possibility of a triumph for the Republican Right and its 'Asia first' policies. In the course of the spring, therefore, it moved towards the US position on China, conceding in the process any pretence of an independent policy. At the same time it pushed through a £4,700 million rearmament programme as a symbol of British commitment to the Atlantic alliance, a particularly important step when Britain was under attack by the Republicans as an appeaser of Communism. Gaitskell's budget, based on these premises, provoked the resignation of

Bevan as Minister of Labour in April 1951, complicated British economic problems and weakened the Labour government, paving the way to the return of the Conservatives in October. Acheson's strategy of using the Republican Right to contain the Labour Left thus paid dividends. By the summer of 1951 little remained of the original British policy on Taiwan and China's UN seat. The British attempt to guide the American colossus in the Far East had ended fruitlessly. Britain had been forced to accommodate to the realities of power and defer to the United States.

Conclusions

The Korean conflict, although described as a limited police action, had global consequences. Within months of the North Korean attack, Washington had proposed the creation of a unified NATO command and German rearmament. It had also embarked upon a massive rearmament programme of its own designed to put the Western bloc in a position to fight and win a global war with Russia by 1954. When China intervened in Korea at the end of 1950, it seemed as if the world would be plunged into a wider war even earlier. Britain was caught up in these events as London attempted to follow Washington's lead. Although Korea was initially a popular cause, the mood rapidly shifted as victory receded and the Treasury attempted to budget for a rearmament programme beyond the country's resources. Economically the effects were disastrous. Recovery was delayed and Britain entered a new balance of payments crisis in 1951. The political consequences were equally dramatic, provoking dissension in the Labour Party, the resignation of Bevan and the weakening of the government.

Korea also produced friction in the Anglo-American alliance. As the country faced the possibility of global atomic war, there were increasing reservations about US policy. American public opinion appeared to be in the grip of the mindless anti-communism symbolized by Senator McCarthy and the feeling grew that Britain must assert itself within the special relationship. Although the immediate crisis passed in the spring of 1951 the fear that the United States might plunge its allies into a wider war persisted until the armistice. In this situation Britain looked longingly towards the exits. Indeed by 1953 Churchill hoped that a Korean ceasefire would lead to broader negotiations between the blocs, reducing international tension and the risk of global war. In pursuing the diplomacy of restraint, Britain came up against the inequalities within the special relationship. The Korean War 'underlined how British power had declined and was continuing to decline (Lowe in Dockrill and Young, 1989: 145). Both Attlee and his successor, Churchill, might demand 'a place on the bridge within reach of the wheel' (*The Economist*, 1952: 218), but they were to be disappointed. Neither was able to regain a veto over the use of the atomic bomb, an issue which became urgent after China intervened, and, despite their best efforts, achieved only an ambiguous formula covering US bases in Britain. There is no evidence that British pressure prevented the Americans from adopting any course which they might otherwise have taken in the Far East. In particular it is a myth that Attlee's visit to Washington saved the world from a wider war. It was the stabilization of the military situation and not Attlee's arguments which kept the Korean war within bounds. British diplomacy was frustrated by the realities of power. It was dangerous to emphasize Anglo-American differences in the Far East because Britain ultimately depended on the United States to contain the Soviet Union and to provide financial assistance for rearmament. It was thus London and not Washington which made compromises for the sake of the special relationship: 'frustration was the price that had to be paid for sustaining the alliance' (Lowe in Cotton and Neary, 1989: 96). Korea exposed British illusions about guiding the American colossus and revealed, well before Suez in 1956, the shift towards US hegemony within the Atlantic alliance.

Bibliography

Dingman, R. (1982) 'Truman, Attlee and the Korean war crisis', *International Studies*, 1982/1, pp. 1–42.

Dockrill, M.L. (1986), 'The Foreign Office, Anglo American relations and the Korean war, June 1950–June 1951', *International Affairs*, p. 477.

The Economist, 2 February 1952.

Harris, K. (1982), *Attlee*, London, Wiedenfeld & Nicholson.

Ra, Jong-yil, (1984), 'Special relationship at war: The Anglo American relationship during the Korean war', *Journal of Strategic Studies*, vol. 7, no. 4, pp. 301–317.

Lowe, P. (1989), 'The Korean war in Anglo-American relations, 1950–1953', in M.L. Dockrill and J.W. Young (eds), *British Foreign Policy 1945–1956*, London, Macmillan.

Lowe, P. (1989), in J. Cotton and I. Neary (eds), *The Korean War in History*, Manchester.

MacDonald, C.A. (1986), *Korea, the war before Vietnam*, London, Macmillan.

Singh, A.I. (1990), 'Britain, India and the Asian Cold War: 1949–1954', in Anne Deighton (ed.), *Britain and the First Cold War*, London, Macmillan.

Stueck, W. (1986), 'The limits of influence: British policy and American expansion of the war in Korea', *Pacific Historical Review*, vol. 55, pp. 65–95.

14 Allied and interdependent: British policy during the Chinese offshore islands crisis of 1958

Tracy Lee Steele

The controversy over the Chinese offshore islands in August 1958 not only posed a threat to the fragile peace of the Cold War world but also to the Anglo-American relationship, newly repaired after Suez. The Washington talks of 1957 produced an agreement between US President Dwight Eisenhower and British Prime Minister Harold Macmillan to co-operate in the Far East, particularly with regard to China. Thus in 1958 Macmillan's first priority was to protect and, when possible, enhance this 'special relationship' by deferring to the judgement of Eisenhower and his Secretary of State, John Foster Dulles, who viewed these islands as a Berlin of the Far East: a place where a show of strength and resolve would make the enemy retreat.

The Chinese offshore islands comprise many small island groups near the coast of the People's Republic of China (PRC/Communist China) but under the control of the Republic of China (ROC/Nationalist China). The two largest of these island groups are Matsu (Mazu), off the Communist port of Foochow (Fuzhou), and Quemoy (Jinmen) near the Communist harbour of Amoy (Xiamen). In 1949, when the Nationalist government evacuated to the Chinese province of Taiwan (Formosa), an island 120 miles from the mainland across the Straits of Taiwan, the Nationalist military maintained control of the islands despite an attempted invasion by the Communists in 1949.

Differences in US and British policy towards the two Chinas arose in January 1950, when Britain recognized the newly established People's Republic, from the principle that recognition simply acknowledged the fact of existence and concern over the continued administration of Hong Kong. Britain recognized the Nationalist authorities as the *de facto* administration of Taiwan and maintained a consul in Tamsui. In theory, British officials in Taiwan dealt only with the provincial authorities and had no relations with the central government.[1]

The United States, on the other hand, recognized the Nationalist authorities as the *de jure* government of all of China, and was represented by an ambassador in Taipei (Taibei) and a large US Military Assistance and Advisory Group (MAAG). The reasons for US policy of non-recognition are generally accepted as the trip of Mao Ze Dong, the Communist Chinese leader, to the Soviet Union soon after liberation, the outbreak of the Korean war and the rise of 'McCarthyism' in the United States.[2] The number of MAAG personnel on Taiwan also indicated that the United States considered the defence of Taiwan and the Pescadores vital to its defence planning of the Pacific.

Despite the seemingly insuperable differences between the United States and Britain over their policy regarding China, they shared the same ultimate objective: to split the Chinese Communists from the Soviet Union.[3] Both countries agreed that Taiwan and the Pescadores deserved protection, if necessary under the auspices of the United Nations, and unofficially understood they were dealing with two Chinas, a concept that both the Nationalist and Communist Chinese vehemently opposed. In 1955 Dulles described the situation in China to then Prime Minister Anthony Eden and Foreign Secretary Macmillan as 'no different than in other countries that were divided'.[4] and compared the Chinese offshore islands to Berlin. Significantly, neither Eden nor Macmillan disagreed with Dulles's premise.[5]

The Chinese offshore islands first gained international attention in 1954, following the creation of the South-East Asian Treaty Organization (SEATO), when shelling on both sides of the Straits of Taiwan escalated to the point of war. The British considered that the islands had no strategic value and urged that they be abandoned.[6] American authorities, including the Joint Chiefs of Staff, were divided over the importance of Matsu and Quemoy. Eisenhower and Dulles never convinced either themselves or Chiang Kai-shek that evacuation was necessary, leaving for the future the decision on intervention on the side of the Nationalists in a battle for the offshore islands.[7]

Two important policy decisions resulted from the 1954–5 episode, the signing of a Mutual Defence Treaty by the United States and the ROC with an Exchange of Notes on 10 December 1954, and more significantly the Formosa Resolution, passed by the US Congress on 24 January 1955. Eisenhower was granted the unprecedented power to engage US forces to defend Taiwan, the Pescadores, and other related territory if the former were deemed to be in jeopardy, without first consulting Congress.[8]

Between 1955 and 1958, US military aid to Taiwan increased dramatically. The number of Nationalist troops on Big Quemoy increased from 50,000 in 1954 to 80,000 in 1957, and in 1957 Matador missiles were stationed in Taiwan under American control. It was evident to American military advisers in Taiwan that the offshore islands, while not strategically important, were now irrevocably linked to the defence of Taiwan and the Pescadores, because of the massive build-up of weapons as well as for psychological and political reasons.

The foundation for Macmillan's policy in 1958 was laid at the Bermuda Conference in March 1957. Macmillan was anxious to abolish the 'China differential' on the embargo list on strategic trade to the Sino-Soviet bloc and determined to inform the United States that Britain would 'go it alone' if progress was not made.[9] At the same time, he desperately needed to repair the damaged Anglo-American relationship.

On 22 March Lloyd and Dulles discussed Chinese representation in the United Nations and the relaxation of East–West trade controls. Confirming his understanding of the conversation to Dulles, Lloyd wrote:

> It would be easier for us to carry our own public with us on this question [of continuing Nationalist Chinese membership in the United Nations] if in the meantime the question of the China differential had been disposed of quickly and without United States opposition.[10]

Dulles concurred. His comment 'Perhaps we shall in practice have to move forward on both fronts in a somewhat synchronized manner'[11] echoed Lloyd's statement at the meeting that while he 'would not wish to give the appearance of striking a bargain', the United States and Britain might 'profitably work on those lines'.[12] Although the British announcement regarding the abolition of the Chinese trade differential in May was fraught with risks, the Bermuda talks and the observations of the British Ambassador Harold Caccia from Washington, indicated that Macmillan and Lloyd could proceed with the confidence that the American response would not be negative and vindictive.

The deal was completed when Macmillan and Lloyd visited Washington in October 1957 and signed a 'declaration of common purpose', in effect a declaration of 'interdependence' with the United States. In return for American agreement on the development of joint policy against Soviet encroachment, pooling of resources for new weapons and co-operation in atomic energy, Macmillan and Lloyd would co-operate with the United States on certain Far Eastern matters. Britain would not seek or support, without prior agreement with the United States, any change in Chinese representation in the United Nations. In return, the United States would regard Hong Kong as a joint defence problem.[13]

Britain had changed its active, and sometimes aggressive, policy to influence and change the American position on China to tacit support for the United States. Knowledge of the decision was limited to high government officials, and Foreign Office officials were either unaware of the agreement or failed to understand the implications for policy. In 1970, before the United States recognized the PRC, Macmillan was requested by the Secretary of the Cabinet to remove the relevant passage for security reasons from Volume IV of his memoirs (Horne, 1989: 56). The China issue was so effectively neutralized by the Washington agreement that when Macmillan and Eisenhower met in the summer of 1958, China was not even discussed. A

Foreign Office dispatch on Anglo-American relations estimated that China would not be a problem in the immediate future.[14]

Later in 1958, however, the sporadic shelling in the Matsu and Quemoy area, dramatically increased, heralding a new crisis. With Selwyn Lloyd and other ministers on vacation, Macmillan and his private secretaries reviewed the policy of 1954-5. Macmillan, despite his concern that nuclear weapons might be used to repel an invasion by the PRC of the offshore islands, gave his relationship with the Americans top priority. In his diary he wrote:

> Our own view is that the Chinese (Communists) have an unanswerable case to the possession of these islands. . . . But if we abandon the Americans—morally I mean, they need no active support—it will be a great blow to the friendship and alliance which I have done so much to rebuild and strengthen.
>
> (Macmillan, 1971: 544)

It was important to both the United States and Britain that they should not appear to be divided, but Macmillan went far beyond the support expected of a trusted ally. His policy sometimes angered and confused Foreign Office and NATO officials, but Macmillan, and, after his return, Lloyd remained steadfast in their support of US policy.

When the State Department asked the British Embassy to restate its policy, it pointedly dismissed the previous British position, declaring that it was now 'scarcely practical politics'[15] to abandon the offshore islands Teddy Youde of the British Embassy warned Peter Dalton, head of the Far Eastern Department, 'that the Americans may find themselves in the position which we hoped they would avoid, of having either to desert the Nationalists or become actively involved'.[16]

When formulating his policy, Macmillan was clearly influenced by his private secretary, Philip de Zulueta. In a background paper for the Cabinet, de Zulueta assessed that Eisenhower's 'great mistake' had been the 'unleashing' or 'deneutralization' of the Nationalist leader Chiang Kai-shek in 1953, when he declared that the 7th Fleet would no longer protect the Mainland from a Nationalist attack, because it left the President open to Nationalist blackmail. De Zulueta suggested that Eisenhower had 'genuinely' tried to escape this situation, albeit without withdrawal from the islands. The British problem was that although the United States had often asked for ideas and help on tactics, the Foreign Office never had any useful suggestions, since neither the Nationalists nor the Communists would compromise.[17] Given the lack of options, Macmillan decided to support American efforts to end the crisis without war.

On 29 August detailed instructions were sent to Viscount Hood in Washington. The guidance acknowledged that the Nationalists for political and psychological reasons probably would not withdraw from the offshore islands, although it was noted that they were acting with restraint during the renewed shelling. Although it was unclear whether Eisenhower would invoke the Formosa Doctrine, the British assumed that he would do so. If hostilities developed and the Americans intervened, the islands might be held if the hostilities were localized. However, the real danger was that they could not be localized, thus, much depended on Communist Chinese determination to invade the islands.

A review of possible action by Britain ruled out an appeal to China. Britain had not gained by the relaxing of the China trade controls and relations with the PRC worsened during the Jordan intervention. The Indians were a possibility, but they had little sympathy with the Nationalist cause and, like Britain, did not have good relations with China. UN arbitration would be rejected by both the Nationalist and Communist Chinese. Britain's only viable option was to approach the Soviets.[18]

Hood concluded from his discussion with Christian Herter, acting American Secretary of State, that the Americans would remain on the defensive and 'do their best to restrain the Nationalists', leaving the ultimate decision on how and when the United States might invoke the Formosa Doctrine until it was absolutely necessary. Herter favoured the British talking to the Soviets 'provided that [they] did not give the impression that [they] had been put up to it by the Americans'.[19] For his part, Herter came away from the discussion with a clear sense of the unpopularity of the issue in Britain and the problems the British government would have in defending military action.[20]

The Foreign Office was divided regarding the Soviet approach. The British ambassador in Moscow reported that the tension in the islands probably suited the Soviets and doubted that they would prevent a Communist Chinese attempt to capture any of the islands if this did not mean world war. The ambassador favoured the approach only if he could unequivocally warn the Soviets that in case of invasion, the Americans would definitely intervene. Con O'Neill, an assistant under-secretary and former British ambassador to Peking, objected that the American position could not be so fully revealed and feared the Chinese might believe that they had successfully split America from her allies. Sir William Hayter, Deputy Under-Secretary of State and British ambassador to Moscow from 1954 to 1957, disagreed and recommended the approach to the Prime Minister.

De Zulueta agreed with O'Neill, minuting 'that it would do more harm than good to try to speak to the Soviets in present circumstances on the suggested lines',[21] but Macmillan left the ultimate decision to Eisenhower. In a letter dated 3 September to Eisenhower, Macmillan was clear that despite his own view that the offshore islands would be abandoned, he would stand by the United States:

> My overriding concern is that our countries should not be divided or appear to be divided. Of course, the Chinese may be bluffing.... All the same, I feel I may have to try to steer public opinion here at very short notice and, if the worst should happen, in critical circumstances.[22]

Macmillan's method of handling public opinion by publicly deprecating any attempt by the PRC to make territorial changes by force and supporting any American initiative to achieve peace evolved into a *de facto* British policy.[23]

Details of the new policy were restricted to a few officials, and several British ambassadors, such as Duncan Wilson in Peking and Gladwyn Jebb in Paris, complained about the lack of information they were receiving. Jebb, chiding Sir Frederick Hoyer Millar, the Permanent Under-Secretary of State, wrote: 'I am only too willing to play the idiot boy on this matter, but I do think I could play this role even better if I knew what our real policy was.'[24] On 17 September Hoyer Millar explained the situation to Jebb, warning him that the information should go no further:

> Ministers are particularly anxious that nothing should come out in public that would suggest any split between the Americans and ourselves on this issue and wish great caution to be exercised even in any private exchanges with the Americans or the representatives of other governments.[25]

Macmillan's policy of not criticizing American policy, either in public or in private, prevented a full exposition of the British views even in NATO deliberations. Sir Frank Roberts, with the UK NATO delegation in Paris bitterly complained about the possible negative consequences:

> I quite realise that we are able to convey our views to the Americans by channels more direct than NATO. But our NATO allies naturally judge our attitude on the basis of the line we take in the Council. There is therefore the danger of misunderstanding, which might be serious if we continue to keep quiet forever on a subject on which we are known to hold views divergent from those of the Americans.

> I am not of course advocating that we should take the lead in opening disagreement with the Americans, but there is, I submit, a half-way house between a policy of silence with its connotations of unwilling satellitism and one of leading the allies against the Americans.

> To sum up, I think that from the NATO point of view, the policy prescribed is ineffective, dishonest, and undignified, and in no way conducive to the maintenance of British influence with our NATO Allies, including the Americans.[26]

Roberts' objections were met in part by the statement of the American delegate to NATO that the United States would value comments from its allies, either in the Council or privately. Following the Foreign Office's guidelines, Roberts defined the main issue as the use of force, on which Britain was in full agreement with the United States.[27] Hoyer Millar reminded Roberts that emphasis should be laid 'on our desire for a reduction of tension, and for progress, if possible, towards some constructive solution, rather than on criticism of the Americans'.[28] Oscar Morland, Assistant Under-Secretary of State, concurred on this line, even though it involved 'a slight further relaxation from the rigid line prescribed by the Prime Minister earlier'.[29]

Others in the Foreign Office were having difficulty meeting Macmillan's policy. On 8 September Macmillan sent Phillip de Zulueta to see Peter Dalton, who had conducted a rather frank conversation with Francis Galbraith, First Secretary of the American Embassy,[30] to ensure that there was no misunderstanding of the Prime Minister's policy. In February 1957 Dalton had failed to comprehend Macmillan's China policy when he told US Embassy officials that Macmillan might inform the United States at the Bermuda conference that it was no longer feasible to continue the moratorium on Chinese representation in the United Nations.[31] This time de Zulueta left Dalton in no doubt of the Prime Minister's policy and its implications. Dalton recorded:

> The Prime Minister's wish was that we should not criticise the Americans or hark back, for example, to the 1955 statements or make too much of the juridical position of the offshore islands or the mistake that had been made in letting the Nationalists put so many of their eggs into the Quemoy basket. The important thing now was to stand by the Americans both in the interests of interdependence and in order not to give comfort and encouragement to our enemies and we should not appear even in private discussion to be sniping at the Americans over the rights and wrongs of the situation.
>
> I said that I had entirely taken the Prime Minister's point. . . . I had thought that I was following too the general line desired when explaining our position to Mr. Galbraith of the American Embassy . . . and in the instructions that I was proposing to send to our Delegation at NATO for the Council debate on the Far East . . . viz: that they should stick in the debate to the official News Department line but that this need not preclude further discussion in private with either the American Delegation or, at their discretion, other delegations if they were specifically approached. With all respect, I thought that it would be very difficult, and not indeed desirable, that, when asked for an exchange of views by the Americans, or members of the Old Commonwealth or reliable members of NATO, we should simply take the line that the Americans were right and we must support them.[32]

Dalton asked for further assurance from the Prime Minister of his intention to maintain an uncompromising policy. De Zulueta discussed this with Macmillan, who agreed that there should be 'certain nuances in our approach in this matter according to the circumstances'.[33]

Other Foreign Office officials took offence at the draft instructions to the British representative at NATO. Dalton felt the avoidance of 'any hint of criticism' of the Americans should be avoided, and Foreign Office officials drafted the more relaxed advice that the British delegation 'should refrain from criticizing' the Americans. Hoyer Millar discussed the matter with Lloyd on 10 September. Lloyd agreed that care should be taken to avoid public criticism, but thought that officials should try to influence American officials privately.[34] No official change in policy was authorized, however.[35]

Macmillan's policy found widespread approval in the US administration, if not at home. Replying to Macmillan's letter to Eisenhower, Dulles expressed the hope that Macmillan could steer British opinion 'so that if the worst should happen we could be together. Anything different would be a great catastrophe for both of us.'[36] Dulles justified American policy with the 'domino theory':

> We continue to believe that the firm position we are taking will in fact deter reckless Communist action. But we also recognize that Krushchev and Mao Tse-tung can be reckless and may miscalculate, and that therefore our position does involve serious risks. But as we said in relation to the Near East situation, it is a case where while acting strongly involves serious risks, these risks seemed less serious than the risks of inaction.[37]

That same day in Newport, Rhode Island, Dulles, after consulting with Eisenhower, made an important statement about the possible use of the Formosa Doctrine. Dulles stressed that there was no evidence that the Chinese Communists planned to attack but hinted that if this happened, the Nationalists could probably defend themselves with US logistical help. Dulles, who had maintained Eisenhower's policy of ambiguity on use of the Formosa Doctrine, stated publicly for the first time that the Administration had 'recognized that the securing and protecting of Quemoy and Matsu have increasingly become related to the defense of Taiwan'.[38]

In a conversation with Hood, Dulles introduced a new proposal for a long-term solution. If the Chinese Communists would accept demilitarization of the islands, Dulles thought the United States could 'persuade Chiang to accept it and withdraw his troops'.[39] Despite the low chance of success, Macmillan immediately adopted the proposal as his own. Macmillan wrote to Dulles that it could prove a 'Munich for the East' if the offshore islands were taken by force, so '[i]n this difficult position ought we to seek some means of solution, or at least a better public posture.'[40] Demilitarization might be a good public posture whether or not it was accepted by the Chinese Communists. Regarding the Soviets, he wrote:

> I can hardly believe that they and the Chinese have agreed to want a war. That would be contrary to the general Russian attitude. But, of course, they may think that they can frighten you out of it by the weakness of your allies. It is that that I am determined to avoid if I can.[41]

Eisenhower and Dulles were heartened by Macmillan's staunch support. Dulles felt, however, that Macmillan's embellishment of the demilitarization idea went 'pretty far', since the main difficulty was restraining the Nationalists.[42] Eisenhower stressed in his reply to Macmillan the unlikelihood of Chiang Kai-shek agreeing to demilitarization. Indeed, if coercive efforts were employed to force him to abandon a 'single foot of his defence perimeter', Chiang would reject it, implying that it 'would end his capacity to retain Formosa in friendly hands'.[43] In conclusion, Eisenhower expressed the hope that the announced willingness of the PRC to resume the Ambassadorial talks would defuse the crisis.

The resumption of talks between the People's Republic of China and the United States in Warsaw provided the chance to take stock and prepare for the next stage of the crisis. O'Neill, representing the views of many in the Foreign Office, strongly urged a return to the policy of 1955, noting:

> It is clear that American policy offers no satisfactory solution. At the worst, it could lead to war. At the best, it can scare the Chinese Communists into leaving the Coastal Islands alone. But such a success can be only temporary. So long as the Nationalists retain the Coastal Islands, the crisis is bound to go on arising from time to time in an acute form.

> My own view is that our policy in 1955 was correct, and that we should act in the same way and whenever this question arises in the future; i.e. we should make it clear to the Americans that we cannot support them over the Coastal Islands and that we consider they should persuade the Chinese Nationalists to withdraw from them.

> We have been reluctant to take this line in recent weeks because the feeling has been strong that we must maintain solidarity with the United States if we possibly can on all issues, even in cases where we believe their policy to be wrong. This is felt to be a kind of obligation on us deriving from the policy of interdependence. It seems to me that such an attitude over this particular question, is somewhat quixotic and not in our best interests, nor indeed in those of the Western world as a whole or the United States itself.

> In taking a less firm line than we did in 1955 we have perhaps been influenced partly by the feeling that our action could not affect developments much one way or the other, and that if America was going to get into a row in any case, which might spread to involve us, we might as well face this prospect in harmony with the Americans rather than in a state of dispute with them. But I think such a feeling under-estimates our power to influence American action in a somewhat marginal case such as this one.[44]

Although Hoyer Millar agreed 'generally' with O'Neill, he did not advocate a return to the policy of 1955 in his minute to Lloyd. However he did feel that more pressure should be applied to the Americans:

> Our anxiety not to appear to be infringing the principles of 'inter-dependence' and

our desire not to upset the Americans more than we can help ought not, I feel, to deter us from doing what we can to dissuade the Americans from pursuing a policy which we feel is bound to create grave difficulties for the Western Governments and put a very serious strain on Anglo-American relations.[45]

He suggested that Macmillan should write to either Eisenhower or Dulles to request they do everything possible to 'find some way out of the present impasse'.

After discussions with Macmillan, Lloyd disregarded much of the Foreign Office advice. Lloyd wrote to Dulles, 'Your troubles are our troubles', and continued in the same vein of Macmillan's correspondence. After briefly mentioning the demilitarization proposal, Lloyd suggested that the ambassadors at the Warsaw talks be replaced by higher-ranking officials.[46]

Lloyd's letter crossed a message from Dulles who was busy trying to dampen British enthusiasm for his own demilitarization proposal. He had warned Hood that he mentioned it 'very much on the spur of the moment, and he had not yet had time to think it through'.[47] Writing to Lloyd, Dulles explained the American dilemma—the difficulty of neutralizing the Nationalists without breaking their will to survive: 'It is easy for those who merely look at a map to come to conclusions about Quemoy and Matsu. But the Far East line is held, not by geography, but by human wills.'[48] Dulles then drew attention to Eisenhower's statement of 11 September that 'there are measures that can be taken to assure that these offshore islands will not be a thorn in the side of peace.' Dulles broadly hinted that certain measures, i.e. some form of demilitarization of the offshore islands could be taken in event of a ceasefire, which, 'while not palatable to the Nationalists, could be made acceptable'.[49]

The United Nations provided another forum for Macmillan, through a sympathetic speech by Lloyd, to support the United States publicly. In a note for Lloyd, Macmillan outlined his policy and authorized a declaration supporting the United States to the Soviet Union if Dulles and Lloyd agreed to an approach to Moscow. Macmillan stressed the American sense of isolation and compared it to Suez:

The American Government are clearly a little hurt with their allies. I hope not with us. They have a feeling that they are being held up as aggressors when they are really the protectors of the free world. This might have very dangerous reactions in the future. The Foreign Secretary can put this right privately with Mr. Dulles and publicly by his speech in the Assembly.

The criticism of the administration inside America has probably increased the nervosity of the administration. They are really going through a kind of Suez, criticized at home and not supported abroad. We must do everything we can to give them a sense of comradeship....

But if the position can be held, there is a good deal to be said for going on just as we did in Berlin. Indeed there is a certain analogy because while it would have been thought provocative to force our way through by land, it was all right to go by air. In the same way, it will apparently be thought an aggression if the Americans attack the Chinese guns on the mainland but I think it would not be thought aggression to continue to convoy even beyond the 3 mile limit.[50]

On 17 September Dulles met Lloyd in New York, the first top-level meeting since the crisis began. Lloyd, for various reasons, did not favour the approach to the Soviets, but Dulles thought the Soviets could be a restraining influence.[51] Further discussions on 19 September were more comprehensive. Dulles reported that the supply situation was better, allowing more time for discussions with the Chinese Communists. Lloyd again proposed raising the level of the talks, since the Communists might be more conciliatory if the agreement were between Chou and Dulles rather than ambassadors, but with the American refusal to recognize the People's Republic of China, Dulles could not accept such terms. Instead, Dulles discussed in detail his plan to eliminate Nationalist 'provocations' by reducing the offshore islands to 'fishing and grazing' ground, while Lloyd agreed to speak to Gromyko.[52]

Reporting to Macmillan, Lloyd expressed great confidence in Dulles's actions and sympathy for the American dilemma. Dulles was 'doing his utmost to avoid a position in which the United States has to embark on hostilities with China' and was 'under no illusion about the virtual isolation of the United States on this issue':

> I am certain that our handling of the Americans so far has been right. If we had tried to lecture them about the rights and wrongs of their policy past and present, the effect would only have been to make them extremely resentful and less liable to take our advice. Indeed I think it would have changed the whole nature of our present relationship.[53]

Macmillan vigorously agreed. He added the caveat that 'difficult decisions' would have to be made if the crisis worsened, but he was confident that the Americans had been handled correctly and added, 'the more isolated they feel, the more important our friendship will be to them now and in the future.'[54]

On 21 September in Newport, Rhode Island, Lloyd had an impromptu meeting with the President. Eisenhower expressed his gratitude to Lloyd for Britain's unwavering support, but remained ambiguous about contingency plans if the Warsaw talks broke down. Lloyd reported that Eisenhower

> knew that he had not got United States public opinion behind him in the way, for example, that he had had it over Lebanon.... A democratic Government could not go to war without the support of the bulk of its people.

> His own personal view was that it was out of the question to use nuclear weapons

for a purely local tactical counter-battery task. If nuclear weapons were to be used, that should be for the "the big thing".... "When you use nuclear weapons you cross a completely different line."[55]

In discussions held with Duncan Sandys, British Minister of Defence, on 22 September, Dulles explained his policy. The situation in the offshore islands was a war of nerves. The United States would lose face if it were perceived to have given way under pressure from the Chinese Communists, but with some form of demilitarization, acceptable to the Nationalist Chinese, 'a *de facto* situation would be created wherein, without any formal agreement, the Chinese Communists would cease their hostile act.'[56] Dulles sought recognition from both Chinas of the principle that as in the case of Berlin, force should not be used to resolve territorial disputes.[57]

On the evening of 23 September, Lloyd met Gromyko to warn him that the Americans were serious. Gromyko took a hard line, stating that it was 'inconceivable that the Soviet Union should bring any kind of pressure to bear on its Chinese ally in this matter', as the 'crisis was exclusively the fault of the Americans'. Gromyko did not answer Lloyd's question about whether Khrushchev had encouraged the Communist Chinese during his visit to Peking. Lloyd reported, 'All I can say is that we had a long and closely argued talk, and that if he had been impressed by what I said he would certainly not have shown it.'[58] Fortunately, the situation in the Straits had eased, making the failure of the approach less important.

Following the announcement by the Communist Chinese that they would extend the ceasefire for two more weeks, Lloyd concluded that with the easing of the shelling, Dulles should persuade Chiang to remove some of his forces from the offshore islands. Lloyd failed to contact Dulles through Caccia before Dulles's press conference that day and the first news from the conference gave the impression that Dulles had taken a completely opposite line. The next day Dulles assured Caccia that his remarks did not signal a change in US policy. Because he was going to Taiwan the following week, he considered it prudent not to give the impression of pressurizing the Nationalists. In his talks with Chiang, he would discuss the level of forces in the offshore islands and seek 'to obtain an overall posture for the Chinese Nationalist Government which would improve its standing in the eyes of the free world and render it more likely to earn the support of the free nations'.[59]

When First Sea Lord, Lord Mountbatten, visited the President on 16 October, Eisenhower explained the package deal encouraging Chiang to withdraw:

The carrot would be that the United States should supply proper amphibious landing equipment to the Generalissimo in view of the fact that it would be militarily unsound to try to use the islands as jumping-off grounds for any leading operation on the China coast. The stick would be the flat statement that from now on the

United States would give the Generalissimo no help over the islands except provision of facilities for the purposes of evacuation. It would also be made plain that the amphibious craft could never be used except as a result of a joint decision by the Americans and Chinese Nationalists, and that on the American side this would only be granted in the event of the Communist regime in China crumbling.[60]

En route to Taiwan, Dulles met Lloyd at the Brize Norton Airfield, England on 19 October. Dulles repeated Eisenhower's proposal and explained that he sought to convince Chiang that it was not in his own best interests to keep large numbers of troops on the islands, to engage in commando raids on the mainland, or enforce a blockade. Dulles, a deeply religious man, said:

After the death of Christ the early Christian Church had expected the Second Coming within a year or two. Chiang Kai-shek in the same sort of way had expected the Chinese Communists to collapse within a year or two. It was now quite obvious that this would not happen and Chiang Kai-shek had got to adjust himself to a different situation.[61]

Lloyd welcomed Dulles's plan, adding that it would help Britain if the United States returned to its previous policy of distinguishing between Formosa and the offshore islands. Dulles warned, however, that he was not going to Taiwan to issue an ultimatum or to force the issue; much would depend on the Communist Chinese and the current state of hostilities.[62]

Inconveniently, Chiang's hand was strengthened on the eve of Dulles's arrival in Formosa when the Communists cancelled the ceasefire, claiming that the United States had violated its conditions. Chiang, insisting that the Communists could not be trusted, was in a better position to reject Dulles's proposals.

The British chargé d'affaires in Tamsui reported that the meeting between Dulles and Chiang had been somewhat "acrimonious". The important achievement of these talks had been Chiang's public renunciation of the use of force in recovering the mainland. The chargé d'affaires baldly reported that 'in return for an ambiguous promise' the United States had 'publicly linked control of the islands with the defence of Formosa'.[63]

Dulles met Caccia within 24 hours of his return to Washington. The Chinese Communists had already announced the peculiar decision to shell the offshore islands on odd-numbered days, allowing the Nationalists to resupply. This confirmed to the Americans and the British that the Chinese Communists intended to continue to use Quemoy as a 'whipping boy', as Dulles described it. Caccia remarked that, 'if it suited the Chinese Communists so well to have Quemoy in pawn', it would be best if the Nationalists withdrew. Dulles was forced to admit that he had not pursued complete demilitarization with the Nationalists, only an agreement to reduce forces on Quemoy and Matsu.[64]

In his letter to Lloyd, Dulles maintained an upbeat assessment of his trip. US intelligence considered the revived shelling before his arrival in Taiwan as simple harassment. Dulles considered that the 'rather fantastic statement' of odd-day shelling confirmed their 'analysis of the Chinese Communist attitude as being essentially political and propaganda rather than military'.[65]

If the position in the offshore islands became untenable due to heavy shelling or inability to resupply, Hood was instructed by Macmillan and Lloyd to suggest evacuation of Quemoy and Matsu, since this would be less humiliating than bargaining with the Chinese.[66] The US Embassy in London estimated that in the case of American intervention without nuclear weapons, Britain would publicly express solidarity with the United States and condemn the People's Republic of China for using force to solve the controversy. However, if nuclear weapons were used, Britain might find themselves in a 'reverse Suez' and exert heavy pressure to take the matter to the United Nations.[67]

In Washington, however, some confusion remained over British policy. Walter Robertson, the Assistant Secretary of State for Far Eastern affairs, in a memorandum dated 24 November to Dulles, summarized recent discussions with Sir Robert Scott, the British Commissioner-General for South-East Asia, de la Mare, a counsellor at the British Embassy in Washington, and Anglo-American intelligence talks. Robertson reported that Sir Robert 'saw no alternative to our present way of handling the issue' of the offshore islands: 'It was clear that your [Dulles's] visit set events in motion which are bringing the United States and the United Kingdom closer together in their attitudes on our China policy.' Sir Robert spoke against US recognition of the People's Republic of China, stating that 'it would be a bad day for the world and the United Nations when they are seated.' De la Mare, who, Robertson stated, 'has been no friend of our China policy', reportedly told an American official 'that there are *now* no significant differences' between Britain and the United States on China policy. The new Dulles policy of promoting Taiwan as a peaceful, 'model China' was paying dividends in terms of international public opinion and goodwill.[68]

Receiving a similar memorandum from Edwin Martin, director of Chinese affairs in the State Department, Galbraith was quick to disagree with the supposition that the Foreign Office's view on the offshore island situation was 'much the same as our own'. Galbraith, accustomed to dealing with the forthright Dalton suggested that the British government had avoided debating the issue in order to avoid disharmony, but 'it would be a mistake to take this reticence for evidence that the British see "eye to eye" with us on the Far East.'[69]

Galbraith altered this view following his discussion of Taiwan and its prospects with Oscar Morland, British Assistant Under-Secretary of State and ambassador-designate to Japan. Morland considered that American and British views did not diverge in regard to the Far East. Galbraith concluded that Morland's view probably represented that of Macmillan, whereas Dalton's was the one more generally held.[70]

Martin picked up the thread of this debate in a return letter on 10 March 1959, long after tensions had subsided. Martin admitted that perhaps the sentiment expressed in the original November memorandum had been too sweeping. State Department officials had been 'struck' by Sir Robert's failure to propose any alternative course of action for handling the crisis. Unhappy though the British were about the situation, there was nothing else they could propose that the United States do under the circumstances. Martin wrote:

> This was heartening to us, both because the critics in this country have accused us of taking a stand on the offshore islands which was not supported by our British allies and because it indicated that the Foreign Office was aware that there was no possibility of making a deal with the Communists regarding the offshore islands.[71]

Since that time, however, Caccia had stated in the tripartite talks that if a line could be drawn down the middle of the Straits, the US and British policies could be aligned, but Britain had no solution to offer.[72] All in all, this was favourable to the United States, which could assume that British criticism was not forthcoming.

In the chapter of his memoirs, titled 'Chinese puzzle', Macmillan waxed poetic about the island crises, likening them to Vesuvius and highlighting the pointless futility of these perplexing exercises:

> After some months of anxiety the volcano which threatened to burst forth with devastating fury gradually ceased its activities and simmered slowly down into its normal condition of an occasional efflux of smoke and a few ashes, in a petulant rather than a destructive mood.
>
> (Macmillan, 1969: 51)

Macmillan knew from the outset that Eisenhower, who himself described the 1958 crisis as a 'Gilbert and Sullivan war' (Eisenhower, 1966: 304), would only require moral support rather than military aid from Great Britain. Undoubtedly, Macmillan proved generous in his support, often overriding the objections of Foreign Office officials. D.R. Thorpe (1989: 305) assesses Lloyd's 'difficult negotiations on such issues as the Formosan straits' as one of his 'notable achievements', a rather fantastic claim when one considers Lloyd's subordinate role to Macmillan and Britain's deference to the United States. However, the rule by which Macmillan and Lloyd measured success would have awarded them full marks: war was avoided without a public or private split with the Americans.

In autumn 1957 Macmillan committed Britain to work closely with the United States in Far Eastern matters, but even without this agreement, he would have been constrained by the lack of policy options for handling the

1958 crisis. In 1954-5, the British were enjoying a 'honeymoon' in their relations with the People's Republic of China, as Eden had established a rapport with Chou and often followed independent leads to possible solutions. Macmillan had no leverage in his dealings with either the People's Republic of China or the Republic of China. Indeed, the cornerstone of his foreign policy was maintenance of a close and friendly relationship with the United States. Jeopardizing the alliance for the dubious honour of scoring points with the Communist Chinese was simply not possible. American officials would have been pleased to entertain any British suggestions and were clearly surprised when none was forthcoming. Circumstances being what they were, however, Macmillan chose to play close confidant, hoping that the Americans would long remember who had been their friend in their time of need.

Notes

1. PRO, FO371/110231 FC1042/1A, FO brief for Geneva conference, 2 April 1954.
2. Ibid.
3. *FRUS, 1952-1954*, vol. III, pp. 710-1, record of discussion between Churchill, Eisenhower, Eden, Dulles, *et al.* at Bermuda, 7 December 1953.
4. USNA, 611.41/7-2255, Dulles conversation with Eden, Macmillan and Phleger, Geneva, 22 July 1955.
5. Ibid.
6. PRO, FO371/110231 FC1042/7, partial record of Cabinet meeting CC(54)60, Item 2, 4 September 1958 (removed from document).
7. For further information on the 1954-5 crisis, see *FRUS*, vol. 14, 1952-4, and *FRUS*, vol. II, 1955-7.
8. *FRUS*, vol. II, 1955-7, pp. 115-19.
9. PRO, FO371/128295 M341/4, Eden minute 7 March 1957: note minutes from Wright, Gore-Booth, Hoyer Millar and initialled by Lord Hood and Selwyn Lloyd.
10. PRO, PREM11/2529, East-West trade, Part V, paper handed to Dulles by Lloyd at Bermuda, 23 March 1957.
11. PRO, PREM11/2529, East-West trade, Part V, Dulles note to Lloyd at Bermuda.
12. PRO, FO371/128300 M3426/43, extract of conversation between Lloyd and Dulles at Bermuda, 22 March 1957.
13. PRO, C.C.(57) 76th Conclusion, minute 2, 25 October 1958.
14. USNA, 611.41/2-758, London Foreign Service dispatch to Washington 7 February 1958.
15. PRO, FO371/133551 FCN1271/25, Youde Washington letter to Dalton, 14 August 1958.
16. Ibid.
17. PRO, FO371/133532 FCN1193/275, de Zulueta minute to Macmillan, 6 September 1958.
18. PRO, PREM11/2300, FO telegram 6176 and 6177 to Washington, 29 August 1958; (held in FO371 at number FCN1193/55).

19. PRO, FO371/133535 FCN1193/326, Dalton minute, 1 September 1958.
20. USNA, 793.00/8-3058, record of conversation between Herter, Hood *et al.*, 30 August 1958.
21. PRO, PREM11/2300, de Zulueta minute, 2 September 1958.
22. PRO, PREM11/2300, FO tel. 6277 to Washington, 3 September 1958.
23. PRO, FO371/133539 FCN1193/437, Hoyer Millar letter to Jebb, Paris, 17 September 1958.
24. PRO, FO371/133539 FCN1193/437, Jebb to Hoyer Millar, 12 September 1958.
25. PRO, FO371/133539 FNC1193/437, Hoyer Millar letter to Jebb 17 September 1958.
26. PRO, FO371/133529 FCN1193/167, Roberts to Dalton, 12 September 1958.
27. PRO, FO371/133531 FCN1193/230, Roberts tel. 295S to FO, 18 September 1958.
28. PRO, FO371/133531 FCN1193/234, Hoyer Millar letter to Roberts, Paris, 23 September 1958.
29. PRO, FO371/133531 FCN1193/234, Morland minute, 23 September 1958.
30. FO371/133528 FCN1193/122, Dalton minute, 8 September 1958.
31. USNA, 61.41/2-2757, Barbour London tel. 4548 to Washington, 27 February 1957.
32. PRO, FO371/133529 FCN1193/173, Dalton minute, 9 September 1958.
33. Ibid.
34. PRO, FO371/133529 FCN1193/173, Hoyer Millar minute, 10 September 1958.
35. Further evidence of the strong pressure regarding the Matsu–Quemoy crisis is revealed in a remark by a CRO official to an American diplomat: 'You can be sure there will be no word of criticism from us.... there are strongest injunctions I have ever known from Whitehall against anyone [meaning officials] saying anything critical of US on this issue' (USNA, 793.00/9-1958, London tel. 1626, 19 September 1958).
36. PRO, PREM11/2300, Dulles to Macmillan, 4 September 1958.
37. PRO, PREM11/2300 Dulles to Macmillan, 4 September 1958.
38. PRO, PREM11/2300, Washington tel. 2433, Dulles statement, 4 September 1958.
39. PRO, PREM11/2300, Hood tel. 2434 to Macmillan, 5 September 1958.
40. PRO, PREM11/2300, Macmillan to Dulles, 5 September 1958.
41. Ibid.
42. USNA, 794A.5/9-758, telephone conversation between Dulles and Parsons, 7 September 1958.
43. PRO, PREM11/2300, Eisenhower to Macmillan, 6 September 1958.
44. PRO, FO371/133529 FCN1193/165, O'Neill minute, 9 September 1958.
45. PRO, FO371/133529 FCN1193/165, Hoyer Millar minute, 9 September 1958.
46. PRO, FO371/133528 FCN1193/155, Lloyd to Dulles, 11 September 1958.
47. PRO, PREM11/2300, Hood tel. 2447 to Macmillan, 6 September 1958.
48. PRO, FO371/133529 FCN1193/156, Dulles to Lloyd, 12 September 1958.
49. Ibid.
50. PRO, PREM11/2300, Prime Minister's note on the Far Eastern situation, 14 September 1958.
51. PRO, FO371/133530 FCN1193/217, Lloyd to Macmillan, 16 September 1958.
52. PRO, FO371/133531 FCN1193/242, Lloyd to Macmillan, 19 September 1958.
53. PRO, FO371/133531 FCN1193/249, Lloyd to Macmillan, 19 September 1958.
54. PRO, FO371/133531 FCN1193/249, Macmillan to Lloyd, 21 September 1958.

55. PRO, FO371/133532 FCN1193/250, New York tel. 1071, Lloyd to Macmillan, 21 September 1958.
56. USNA, 611.41/9-2258, record of conversation between Dulles, Sandys, *et al.*, 22 September 1958.
57. Ibid.
58. PRO, FO371/133532 FCN1193/278 Lloyd to Macmillan, 24 September 1958.
59. PRO, FO371/133541 FCN1193/455, Caccia to FO, 16 October 1958.
60. PRO, FO371/133541 FCN1193/465, Caccia to Lloyd, 17 October 1958.
61. PRO, FO371/133541 FCN1193/477, record of conversation between Lloyd and Dulles at Brize Norton Airfield, England, on 19 October 1958.
62. Ibid.
63. PRO, FO371/133542 FCN1193/499, Veitch to FO, 24 October 1958.
64. PRO, FO371/133543 FCN1193/508, Caccia to Lloyd, 25 October 1958.
65. PRO, FO371/133543 FCN1193/508, Dulles to Lloyd, 25 October 1958.
66. PRO, FO371/133538 FCN1193/406, Dalton minute, 30 September 1958.
67. USNA, 793.00/9-1058, Elbrick memorandum to Dulles, 10 September 1958.
68. USNA, 611.41/11-2458, Robertson memorandum to Dulles, 24 November 1958.
69. USNA, 611.41/1-2959, Galbraith letter to Martin, 12 January 1959.
70. USNA, 611-41/1-1959, Galbraith letter to Martin, 19 January 1959.
71. USNA, 611-41/1-1959, Martin letter to Galbraith, 10 March 1959.
72. Ibid.

Bibliography

Department of State (1979), *Foreign Relations of the United States, 1952–1954*, vol. III, *United Nations Affairs*, Washington, DC, Government Printing Office.
Department of State (1985), *Foreign Relations of the United States, 1952–1954*, vol. XIV, Pt 1, *China and Japan*, Washington, DC, Government Printing Office.
Department of State (1986), *Foreign Relations of the United States, 1955–1957*, vol. II, *China*, Washington, DC, Government Printing Office.
Eisenhower, D.D. (1966), *The White House Years: Waging peace, 1956–61*, London, Billings.
Horne, A. (1989), *Macmillan: 1957–1986*, London, Macmillan.
Macmillan, H. (1969), *Tides of Fortune, 1945–1955*, London, Macmillan.
Macmillan, H. (1971), *Riding the Storm, 1956–1959*, London, Macmillan.
Thorpe, D.R. (1989), *Selwyn Lloyd*, London, Jonathan Cape.

Archival material

Eisenhower Presidential Library, Abilene, Kansas.
PRO: Public Record Office, Kew, England.
USNA: United States National Archives and Records Administration, Washington, DC.

Index